D1327579

The Historical Jesus and the Literary Imagination, 1860–1920

ENGLISH ASSOCIATION STUDIES, 3

JENNIFER STEVENS

The Historical Jesus
and the Literary Imagination,
1860–1920

LIVERPOOL UNIVERSITY PRESS
THE ENGLISH ASSOCIATION

First published in 2010 by
Liverpool University Press
4 Cambridge Street
Liverpool
L69 7ZU

British Library Cataloguing-in-Publication data
A British Library CIP record is available

ISBN 978-1-84631-470-4 cased

Typeset by XL Publishing Services, Tiverton
Printed and bound by the MPG Books Group

Contents

Acknowledgements

First and foremost, I would like to thank Warwick Gould for his expert guidance and unfailing support for this project. I must also acknowledge a special debt to my friend, Pamela Bickley, whose example and encouragement have proved invaluable over the years. Thanks are also due to Alison Clark for her specialist advice and tactful correction, and to Kenneth Wolfe for his unbounded enthusiasm (and extended book loans). I wish to express my gratitude to the English Association for including this study in its Monograph Series and to Liverpool University Press for being the most courteous, efficient, and supportive of publishers. I would also like to thank the staff of both the British Library and the National Library of Ireland for their patience and good humour. My final debt of thanks is to my husband, David, and our children, Patrick and Louisa, for making me tea and making me laugh.

Author's Note

This study deals with a wide range of works and, for the sake of clarity, in-text citation has only been used for those discussed at length. Abbreviations are given in the footnotes after the first citation and from then on in brackets after quotations. For texts that feature more briefly, page references are provided in the footnotes. Quotations from the Bible are taken from the Revised Standard Version.

Translations of French titles and quotations are my own, unless otherwise stated. While I have endeavoured to be as accurate as possible, there are instances where retaining the spirit of the original has taken precedence over the letter.

To avoid stylistic awkwardness, I have used the terms 'Jesus' and 'Christ' interchangeably throughout, while acknowledging the important theological distinction between them.

Introduction

Jesus of Nazareth [...] a symbol of quite perennial, infinite character;
whose significance will ever demand to be anew inquired into,
and anew made manifest.
Thomas Carlyle, *Sartor Resartus*

For centuries now countless visual and literary artists have felt compelled to represent the figure of Jesus 'anew' for their own age. The first decade of the new millennium has already produced numerous re-imaginings of the New Testament narratives from all areas of the creative arts. The Gospels have been recreated by airport novelists such as Dan Brown and Jeffrey Archer, as well as by literary authors such as C. K. Stead and Jim Crace. On stage, the figure of Christ has been portrayed by writers as well established as Edwin Morgan and by absolute newcomers such as Kate Betts, whose play, *On the Third Day*, won first prize in a reality TV show for aspiring dramatists. Film and television have been equally busy bringing Jesus to a wide and varied audience. In the last few years, those with a taste for the controversial and possessed of a strong stomach for violence could take in Mel Gibson's highly successful film *The Passion of the Christ*, while those of a more traditionalist inclination could enjoy the BBC's rather more sedate drama *The Passion*, which ran nightly on British television through Holy Week in 2008. Such examples provide the merest snapshot of the many modern versions of the story of Jesus available to today's readers and audiences, all produced in a period that has seen declining church attendance, waning religious instruction in schools and, as some would have it, the rise of fundamentalist atheism.

For many of today's generation, a reading or viewing of a biblical adaptation is likely to be their first encounter with the Scriptures.

Indeed, they may well be more able to recite the Beatitudes according to Monty Python's Brian, or to outline the creation story as depicted in Robert Crumb's cartoon version of Genesis, than to recall their originals. Nowadays, then, the newly updated version of the Bible is dominant by dint of coming first, just as images of Hamlet contemplating suicide in television adverts or political cartoons are likely to come before any direct encounter their audience might have with the soliloquy on page or stage. The former Poet Laureate and self-confessed unbeliever Andrew Motion has recently expressed grave concerns about the Bible's reversal of fortunes and the consequences for today's English students. How, he wonders, can readers with little or no acquaintance with biblical texts ever hope to understand, let alone appreciate, 'a whole raft of literary work, from John Milton to T. S. Eliot'.[1] It is indeed an important question, especially for university English departments, yet it is also an entirely rhetorical one. There has undoubtedly been a profound shift in the public's relationship with the Scriptures in the last fifty years or so, and no course in Bible studies, delivered in any sector of the education system, is likely to reverse it. While the generations that feature in this study called on literature to supplement, revivify or even replace the all-too-familiar Scriptures, the present one seeks out the Bible to enable it to make sense of canonical works of literature. What was once the master narrative has become for many no more than a work of reference. This was certainly not the case for the writers featured in this study, all of whom had in common a secure knowledge of the Bible, regardless of their own religious convictions and personal perspectives on the Scriptures. For the Victorians and the Edwardians, biblical fiction was an adaptation of an entirely familiar text encountered through the everyday discourse of home, school, church and community. Indeed, D. H. Lawrence's statement, 'I was brought up on the Bible, and seem to have it in my bones', articulates a state of being shared by most writers and readers of his own and earlier generations.[2]

Why biblical fiction should continue to flourish at a time when the source text itself is so little known is thanks in part to the strength of its foundations. The mid-nineteenth century saw the beginning of what is now a deeply engrained habit of fictionalizing the Scriptures in both Europe and the United States. In the sixty or so years covered by this study, the story of Jesus would be told in a variety of radical, often highly inventive, modes of imaginative writing, providing templates for later New Testament novels and drama. However, the significance of these early works has often gone unacknowledged in modern studies of Gospel transformations, with more recent works winning unwarranted praise for originality. Such a state of affairs is hardly surprising, given that so many of the Victorian and Edwardian fictions are out of print and only accessible in research libraries, or in quite expensive reprint editions such as those offered by Kessinger Publishing. Yet the effort of acquiring them is richly repaid. A survey of British biblical fiction that begins as far back as the 1860s, rather than the more usual starting point of the 1930s or 1940s, provides an invaluable insight into the changing attitudes towards Christianity and its texts from the early days of agnosticism. Moreover, it under-lines how from the outset the genre pushed against the boundaries of acceptability, a characteristic that continues to hold true, even in a climate that is, from a Euro-American perspective at least, predomi-nantly secular. The profound changes in moral outlook, especially in respect to sexuality, that emerged from the early 1960s onwards helped bring about the relaxation of censorship and blasphemy laws, affording today's writers of New Testament fictions a freedom undreamt of by their forebears. All the same, it is rare to find them employing a narrative viewpoint, theological theory or structuring agent that has not already been tried out – albeit in a rather more cautious manner – a century or more earlier. Today's Christian conspiracy page-turner, Gospel science fiction, newly discovered evangel or multiple-perspectival novel about the life of Jesus all have their late-nineteenth or early twentieth-century ancestors.

The Victorians and Edwardians produced a wealth of imaginative writing founded on the Gospel narratives, far too plentiful to be adequately covered in one study. Such an embarrassment of riches has necessitated a rigorous, at times quirky, process of selection which has imposed a shape and order on what is, in reality, a highly amorphous topic. There is no question that, had an alternative strategy been applied, a quite different picture of biblical fiction and its significance might have emerged. As it stands, however, the main focus of this book is the historical Jesus as presented in British works of fiction. Such a choice was taken with a mind to supplementing existing works such as Theodore Ziolkowski's *Fictional Transfigurations of Jesus* (1972), which focuses on European and American fiction dealing with what the author describes as the 'kerygmatic Christ of faith' as opposed to the figure of history, and Daniel Pals' *The Victorian 'Lives' of Jesus* (1982), which treats only a semi-fictional mode of representation.[3] The choice of prose fiction over drama and poetry was in most respects a straightforward one. During the period covered in this study, theatre censorship in Britain prevented any biblical play from being staged (in any mainstream public arena at least) and any attempts at New Testament drama tended to be penned with an optimistic sense of futurity: a sub-genre waiting in the wings. By way of contrast, poetry based on the Scriptures was in plentiful supply and enjoyed a wide readership, its very abundance placing it beyond the scope of the present work. This book's focus on the novel and short story is by no means entirely pragmatic, however. As the youngest literary genre, prose fiction held the greatest appeal for those aspiring to modernize and revitalize the Scriptures; it was also best fitted for retelling source narratives that belong essentially to a realistic mode. While there can be no real certainty about how the evangels were conceived and received, it is certain that they have been read for several hundred years now as linear narratives, not far removed from the novel and short-story form. The creative transformation from sacred source to prose fiction was, therefore, a relatively smooth one, and one that offered both a high degree of artistic flexibility and a wide potential readership.

Yet, while settling to focus on the historical Jesus as presented through British fiction might seem to hold the scope of this book firmly in place, there are still points where the topic – rather like a balloon filled with water – is compelled to change shape and character. In some of the studied works, for example, Jesus is usurped by other New Testament personages such as the Magdalene, Judas or St Paul in order to provide the author with an arresting or intriguing perspective on the main hero of the piece. And while the focus on fiction is maintained more or less throughout, there are times when it is perhaps a rather approximate generic term, covering literary modes that defy easy categorization: the oral parable, the dream vision, the biblical play written only to be read. Geographical boundaries are also breached in places to examine the crucial influences of Continental theology and the influence of American and European biblical fictions on their British counterparts. Though neat and precise in their titular brackets, dates, too, take on a somewhat elastic quality at certain points in the book, underscoring the difficulties that inhere in sealing up any body of writing in a specific time period.

Notwithstanding such difficulties of containment, the book seeks to highlight the essential differences between past and present imaginings of the Gospels, by way of looking back at some of the founding models of biblical transformations. Inevitably, given the passage of time, stark contrasts are to be found in intention. While there are still today a substantial number of creative artists for whom the reworking of the Scriptures is a project of great intellectual challenge and, in some cases, of serious spiritual enquiry, they are probably in the minority. For many others the biblical text is merely a convenient cultural reference point, lending itself particularly well to the postmodernist penchant for parody, generic hybridity and the splicing of low and high culture. Unsurprisingly, the situation was quite the reverse in the Victorian era. Though it was possible to find some highly irreverent Bible satires (usually imported from the Continent), composed with no more serious intention than shaking up polite society, the vast majority of authors engaged in writing biblical fiction was very much in earnest. As both the Old and the New Testaments came under increasing pressure from science and radical theology, so the more forward-thinking among the faithful realized that, if the Bible were to continue to hold any sway, it needed to be defamiliarized. Fictionalizing the Gospels offered a means of doing just this, exploiting as it did the gap between the linguistic securities of the Authorized Version and the boldness or elaborations of contemporary re-workings. So, while the text would remain 'in the bones', as Lawrence put it, it would not ossify.

The opening chapter of this study examines how the Bible was read, interpreted and valued in the mid-to-late nineteenth century and explores its often troubled relationship with the fictive. It follows the rapid development of interest in the historical Jesus and how it moved the theological spotlight away from Christ's divinity and onto his humanity, rendering him in the eyes of some creative writers a fitting, even urgent, subject for fiction. As imaginative treatments of both the Old and the New Testaments grew more commonplace, so questions concerning the moral dimensions of fiction came to preoccupy clergy and laity alike. The ongoing debates about the nature of fiction and its relationship to the Bible were highly complex, often contradictory, and, when examined retrospectively, resist straightforward categorization. Nonetheless, some distinct tendencies of thought and attitude emerge quite clearly from them. At one end of the spectrum, staunch fundamentalists argued that *all* fiction was potentially harmful and contrary to the promotion of a healthy Christian life, insisting on the absolute inerrancy of the Bible. 'Fiction' for them was not a semantically unstable term: its meaning was quite securely synonymous with 'falsehood'. At the other end of the spectrum, atheists and freethinkers protested that the Bible was itself an egregious example of fiction, whose sacred status had been upheld by centuries of ecclesiastical dogma and authoritarianism. The *via media* was held by those more liberal theologians and critics who contended that the Bible should be read as any other literary work: neither regarded as an infallible repository of divine revelation and truth, nor positioned *sui generis*. There were, of course, some viewpoints that did not fit neatly into any one of these categories, and there were various points of intersection where two polarized parties shared common ground. Such shades and permutations attest to the complexities of belief and unbelief to be found in Victorian Britain in the second half of the nineteenth century, and serve to remind us of the need for caution when considering a society whose religious preoccupations grow more and more remote, even alien, with each passing decade.

One of the most pressing concerns of the Victorian period was the impact of the Higher Criticism on Christian thought and belief. With this in mind, Chapters 2 and 3 assess the role played by imaginative writing in introducing and promulgating the ideas of modernist theology to the general reading public or, indeed, in refuting them. Chapter 2 examines the enormous popularity of the semi-fictional biographies commonly known as 'Lives of Jesus', which either supported or took up arms against this new critical approach, and which increasingly exploited the fictive mode. Chapter 3 then traces the emerging trend of fully fictional prose works that developed out of the Life of Jesus tradition, some of which paid it homage, with others responding to its perceived inadequacies. During the period covered by this book, the accepted parameters of fictional representations of Christ were pushed against with ever-increasing pressure. By the close of the Victorian era, none but the most fervent evangelical reader was disturbed by the imaginative depictions of Christ's person to be found in the plethora of Lives of Jesus in print, and church congregations were growing more and more accustomed to hearing extracts from religious novels read out – and their virtues extolled – from the pulpit. Creative embellishments of the Gospel stories that would have seemed daring, even profane, by mid-century standards had by now taken on a new orthodoxy, prompting the more avant-garde writers of scriptural fiction to increasingly bold adaptations of their hypotext. By the early years of the twentieth century, the very trajectory of the New Testament narratives would be disordered, as numerous alternative versions of Jesus's life and death were explored through a variety of fictional forms.

The final three chapters concentrate on some of the most venturesome transformations of the Gospels and, most especially, their treatment of the theory that Jesus survived the cross and returned to his everyday life. While somewhat superannuated as a theological position by the late nineteenth century, it was nonetheless a scenario that held great imaginative potential and seemed to chime well with contemporary advances in the fields of archaeology, anatomy and psychology, all of which promised to throw light on the consequences of surviving a crucifixion. Chapter 4 deals with Oscar Wilde's religious imagination and, in particular, his protean oral tales based on the New Testament, several of which engage with speculations about the resurrection in a playful and provocative manner. This is followed in Chapter 5 by a discussion of a range of authors who drew on Wilde's fictional experiments with the Gospels to produce their own imaginative versions of the life (and death) of Jesus, several of which enjoyed considerable success. George Moore's biblical dramas and fictions are also considered by some to derive from Wilde's spoken apologues, yet the final two chapters of the book make a case for their independence. Chapter 6 focuses on the germ of an idea that developed throughout the final twenty years of Moore's life: a meeting between St Paul and Jesus. The final chapter then explores *The Brook Kerith*, the most significant work to emerge from this scenario, and one of the best-selling novels of the First World War years.

The conclusion of this book engages with two enduringly contentious issues: literary value and the relations between literature and theology. In addressing the first, it endeavours to allow for the passage of time and the consequent change in literary taste, giving credit to fiction that, though not always of any intrinsic literary merit, nonetheless contributed to the genre's development and well-being. As concerns the second, it attempts to be even-handed in evaluating both the gains and losses brought about by mixing fiction and theology, and by transforming the shadowy Jesus of historical record into the often compelling, sometimes bathetic, Jesus of the imagination. Ultimately it concurs with Frank Kermode's view that 'Fictions are for finding things out, and they change as the needs of sense-making change.'[4] Regardless of what the fictions featured in this book offered – perhaps still offer – in terms of aesthetic or theological merit, there is no doubt that they helped their readers make sense of some rapid and profound changes in Christian thought, feeling and practice.

Notes

1   Quoted from an interview in the *Guardian* (education news and features), 17 February, 2009, p. 1.
2   D. H. Lawrence, 'The Dragon of the Apocalypse', reprinted in *Selected Literary Criticism*, ed. Anthony Beal (London: Heinemann, 1967), p. 164.
3   Theodore Ziolkowski, *Fictional Transfigurations of Jesus* (Princeton, NJ: Princeton University Press, 1972), p. 10.
4   Frank Kermode, *The Sense of an Ending: Studies in the Theory of Fiction, with a New Epilogue* (Oxford: Oxford University Press, 2000), p. 39.

CHAPTER I

The Victorians and the Bible

Matthew and Mark and Luke and holy John
Evanished all and gone!
Arthur Hugh Clough, *Epi-Strauss-ium*

The Bible: fact and fiction

Up until the middle of the nineteenth century, challenges to the traditional belief in the literal truth of the Bible had not reached far into the public domain. This state of religious innocence, enjoyed by the majority of Christians, is succinctly expressed by the narrator of Samuel Butler's semi-autobiographical novel *The Way of All Flesh*, as he reflects on the beliefs of his godson's clergyman father:

In those days people believed with a simple downrightness which I do not observe among educated men and women now. It had never so much as crossed Theobald's mind to doubt the literal accuracy of any syllable in the Bible. He had never seen any book in which this was disputed, nor met with anyone who doubted it. True, there was just a little scare about geology, but there was nothing in it.[1]

Such complacency was, however, to come under sustained attack throughout the second half of the century. Biblical infallibility could no longer be taken as an indisputable truth by 'educated men and women' when, in 1846, George Eliot's translation of David Friedrich Strauss's seminal work *Das Leben Jesu* (1835) became public enough to make regular appearances in the Classified Advertisements section of *The Times*. The same year saw the founding of T. & T. Clark's *Foreign Theological Library*, its guiding principle being to publish translations of German authors defending the orthodox position; in practice, however, it served only to make more familiar the heterodox ideas its authors sought to kill off. With the publication of *Essays and Reviews* – just one year after Charles Darwin's *Origin of Species* had caused more than 'a little scare' for orthodox Christians – there was no longer any question of the Higher Criticism staying firmly on the other side of the Channel.[2] Resolutely Broad Church in outlook, the volume sought to bring theological scholarship in Britain up to speed with that which had been thriving in Germany for several decades. Though the brief foreword to the work insisted that the essays were 'written in entire independence from each other', the impact of collecting the work of 'the Seven against Christ', as the authors became known, would be felt throughout the century.

By the 1860s, the miraculous elements of the Gospels, Christ's divinity, the relationship between the Old and New Testaments and the authenticity of the Evangelists' testaments had all come under rigorous scrutiny. Unsurprisingly, such a forensic examination and revision of the Scriptures provoked fierce controversy, as what was still a very considerable body of traditional Christians put up a spirited defence of their faith and the sacred texts that underpinned it. The Higher Criticism posed an especially grave threat to the Protestant faith, predicated as it was on the word of the Scriptures and with its distinctive tradition of regular Bible readings. As one Roman Catholic, writing in 1874, points out, 'the [Catholic] Church existed before the New Testament' and could look to its doctrines and dogma to support and protect the faith of its members; Protestants had less to fall back on once the sacred texts were interrogated and found wanting. In a recent discussion of religious fundamentalism, Terry Eagleton contends that 'Meaning which has been written down is unhygienic. It is also promiscuous, ready to lend itself to whoever happens along.'[3] That the text is, as Eagleton describes, inherently vulnerable to infection by outside forces had already been realized by some nineteenth-century Christians who, while asserting the primacy of God's word as set down in the Bible, simultaneously expressed regret that such a collection of documents existed at all. A case in point is the Congregational minister and well-known preacher Joseph Parker, whose *Ecce Deus*, a response to J. R. Seeley's ground-breaking and controversial study of Jesus, *Ecce Homo*, foregrounds the inadequacy of language to encapsulate 'what is deepest in the soul'.[4] Parker states that 'Wisely [...] Christ wrote nothing, for written language is more difficult of interpretation than spoken language [...] The moment that the grammar and the lexicon are called in, strife begins, and logomachy deposes wisdom.'[5] For believers like Parker, then, the records of Christ's life and teachings in the Gospels were a mixed blessing: though central to the development and the perpetuation of the Christian faith, their very textuality rendered them 'unhygienic', laying them open to more and more forensic examination with every new generation of scholars.

Belief in the infallibility of the Scriptures did not only endure in the more extreme regions of fundamentalist dissent. A small but significant body of Anglicans also insisted on the incontestability of the Bible's authority. In December 1891, *The Times* published a letter in its news section under the heading 'The Bible and Modern Criticism', featuring a 'declaration on the truth of Holy Scripture'. Countersigned by 38 Anglicans from various ranks of the clergy, styling themselves 'messengers, watchmen and stewards of the Lord', the declaration read:

> We [...] solemnly profess and declare our unfeigned belief in all the canonical Scriptures of the Old and New Testaments, as handed down to us by the undivided Church in the original languages. We believe that they are inspired by the Holy Ghost; that they are what they profess to be; that they mean what they say; and that they declare incontrovertibly the actual truth in all records, both of past events and of the delivery of predictions to be thereafter fulfilled.[6]

An entirely defensive document, the letter attempts to repair the damage inflicted by at least half a century's remorseless attack on the Bible by 'modern criticism'. Moreover, it demonstrates the extent to which some conservatives wilfully ignored the evidence of translators, theologians and historians in order to maintain belief both in the Scriptures as the direct words of God, and in a typological method of interpreting them. In the four weeks or so that followed the publication of the declaration, *The Times* carried a series of letters in response to it. Although there were a few respondents who applauded the declaration, the majority were vehemently opposed to it. The aforementioned Joseph Parker, though a well-known evangelical and a passionate advocate of Scriptural exposition, took a somewhat Coleridgean stance, accusing the signatories of making the Bible a 'kind of idol'; while the Archdeacon of Manchester, James M. Wilson, regretted their 'theological arrogance', asserting that 'no such theory of inspiration as theirs is recognized by the Church of England'.[7]

Notwithstanding however many column inches of *The Times* the conservative elements of the Anglican clergy managed to occupy, their uncompromising voices were destined to grow increasingly subdued as theology became ever more complex and nuanced and, perhaps as importantly, increasingly available in print. The steady decline and marginalization of the biblical literalist is memorably represented in some of the finest prose fiction of the 1880s and 1890s. Depicting the most extreme end of biblical fundamentalism in the posthumously published *Father and Son*, Edmund Gosse describes how his Plymouth Brethren parents cultivated a rigid and iconoclastic literalness, obliging them to 'read injunctions to the Corinthian converts without any suspicion that what was apposite in dealing with half-breed Achaian colonists of the first century might not exactly apply to respectable English men and women of the nineteenth'.[8] In Hale White's *The Autobiography of Mark Rutherford*, the Dissenting church deacon, Mr Catford, is characterized as 'a plain, honest man, very kind, very ignorant, never reading any book except the Bible';[9] and in Thomas Hardy's *Tess of the D'Urbervilles*, the Reverend Clare, in his strict adherence to biblical infallibility, is deemed 'a clergyman of a type which […] has wellnigh dropped out of contemporary life'.[10] And it was not only liberal-minded authors who regarded such believers as a dying breed. The unimpeachably orthodox clergyman and author Frederic William Farrar roundly defended his best-selling biography of Jesus against the criticism of, in his own words, an 'aged dissenting minister who was positively shocked and horrified at the mere title "The Life of Christ"'.[11]

Holding fast to a belief in the revealed truth of the Scriptures became increasingly difficult as revisionist theology continued to demonstrate that the biblical facts of centuries past were looking more and more like a form of biblical fiction. The first major figure to cast serious doubt on the historical realities of the Bible was David Friedrich Strauss in what would come to be regarded as a cornerstone of the Higher Criticism: *Das Leben Jesu*. The author insisted that the Gospels were dominated by imaginative thought and developed out of a mythopoeic process. According to Strauss, the fictive elements that he uncovered in the New Testament texts stemmed from a particular mode of perception, bounded by its own historical specificity and innocent of any will to deceive. The work opened up a field of enquiry aimed at laying bare the inconsistencies of the four-fold Gospel and separating what might have been an historical event from what was certainly an act of the imagination. As the century moved into its second half, more and more readers of the Bible began to follow Strauss's lead in questioning its authenticity and, consequently, its *sui generis* status. One such, the explorer and author Winwood Reade, writing in his much-quoted history of the world *The Martyrdom of Man*, relegates the New Testament from sacred text to historical biography, putting it on a par with Plutarch's Lives, both texts having in common the 'absurdity of the miracles'.[12] Some Bible commentators refused even to classify it as biography. Writing under the pseudonym 'Sylva', and declaring himself an 'ultra-Unitarian', the author of *Ecce Veritas* (one in a series of responses to John Robert Seeley's *Ecce Homo*) insists that 'most of those who have attempted to write a life of Jesus based on the four evangels, have been compelled honestly to admit the impossibility of any true biographical arrangement'.[13]

Especially extreme in their attack on the Bible's supremacy were the Secularists. The arch-enemies of biblical literalists – though considerably fewer in number – the Secularists promoted the atheist cause as part of a crusade to reform a society that they believed to be repressed and exploited by State and Church alike. If, as it is sometimes averred, there is little nowadays to separate the zeal of the campaigning evangelical groups such as the Christian Voice from that of so-called 'secular fundamentalists' such as Richard Dawkins, so it was in some respects with their Victorian predecessors. Secularists and extreme Protestants were equally fixed on the Bible as a means of promoting their causes, and both groups chose to use the word 'fiction' as a term of opprobrium, albeit in contrasting contexts. For the evangelicals, the Scriptures were truth and 'fiction' was its antonym; for the Secularists, it was the Scriptures that were entirely fictitious and guilty of untruths.

Throughout the final forty years of the nineteenth century, prominent figures in the Secularist movement such as Charles Bradlaugh, Annie Besant, Charles Watts and G. W. Foote strove to expose the fictive nature of both Testaments.[14] Perhaps the most energetic and memorable of these was Bradlaugh, whose profound hatred of the Bible was stridently articulated in lecture halls up and down Britain. In a pamphlet of 1861, writing under the pseudonym 'Iconoclast', he posited that 'Perhaps there was a man who really lived and performed some special actions attracting popular attention, but beyond this

Jesus Christ is a fiction.'[15] And Bradlaugh's close associate, Annie Besant, would underline the unhistorical elements of the life of Christ in works such as *The Myth of the Resurrection*, in which the Passion narratives are treated as 'the hysterical and conflicting babble of an indefinite number of terrified and superstitious women'.[16] As the movement gathered momentum, periodicals such as the *National Reformer*, the *Freethinker*, the *Secular Review* and the *Agnostic Journal* assisted the dissemination of Secularist views of the Bible by printing pamphlets, lectures and debates concerning the Higher Criticism. Particularly prominent in the development of Secularist publishing was Charles Watts, founding in 1885 the *Watts Literary Guide*, which listed and reviewed seminal works, past and present, by liberal authors from Britain and abroad. Additionally, Watts went some way to making these sceptical writings easily available through the Rationalist Press Association, which he helped to launch in the early 1890s.

The Secularist who did most to undermine the veracity of the Bible narratives and to drive home their fictitiousness was G. W. Foote. Founding the *Freethinker* in 1881, Foote used this populist and militantly atheistic journal, and related publications, to overturn any surviving notions of the Gospels as sacrosanct. In *The Bible Handbook*, for example, he declares – tongue firmly in cheek – that the Bible is made up of 'immoralities, indecencies and brutalities' and proceeds to exemplify his contention through some highly impious exegesis of the text.[17] A kind of secular Wyclif of his day, Foote disrupted the familiar cadences of the Authorized Version and replaced them with an earthy vernacular. By transposing the Bible's master narratives into a range of fictional genres, he insisted on their essentially fictitious nature, opening them up for future heterodox treatments. Considering himself a literary man, he used his knowledge of writers such as Blake and Shakespeare, and a range of contemporary novelists, to promote his cause, declaring freethought to be 'an omnipresent active force in the English literature of to-day'.[18] It needs to be said, however, that Foote's animus towards Christianity constantly occluded any sense of literary style or taste, and his iconoclastic treatments of the Scriptures made little or no contribution to the development of radical biblical fiction. Nevertheless, his writings represent a significant assault on a sacred text still revered by orthodox and agnostic alike, while their crassness no doubt underlined the need for more thoughtful and subtle re-imaginings of the Gospels.

The Bible as literature

Allowing the Bible to be preserved in aspic by Protestant fundamentalists or to be torn asunder by the derision of the Secularists were options that held little appeal for a significant number of late Victorians. One such was the women's rights campaigner and Theist Frances Power Cobbe, who feared that 'Underneath this thin ice, over which the controversialists perform their evolutions [...] there lies an abyss – the abyss cold, dark and fathomless – of utter scepticism.'[19] For Cobbe, and many like her, the spread of atheism, spurred on by scientific rationalism, was a deeply disturbing prospect, one that threatened to have a profoundly damaging effect on individual morality and society as a whole. It was certainly too great a threat to be averted by the circular reasoning of the evangelicals or the militant materialism of the Secularists. Consequently, alongside these uncompromising modes of reading the Scriptures, a more accommodating approach developed, encouraging the reading of the text more as literature than letter, in a spirit of intellectual openness. It was an approach that had already been advocated in the early part of the nineteenth century by Samuel Taylor Coleridge, whose theological and literary sophistication prevented him from accepting either what he termed the 'Bibliolatry' of the Low Church or the rationalism of the newly emergent historical criticism.[20] Conversant with German theological thought, and a frequenter of meetings of the British and Foreign Bible Society, Coleridge was well placed to arbitrate between the old and the new theologies, both of which he considered in danger of draining the life blood out of the Scriptures. In *Confessions of an Inquiring Spirit*, posthumously published in 1840, his descriptions of the Bible are unmistakably those of a literary man; he marvels at the text's 'harmonies and symmetrical gradations [...] the intelligencing nerves, and the rudely woven, but soft and springy, cellular substance', qualities that render it a 'breathing organism'.[21] And it was these very qualities that he feared would be lost if the conviction that the Scriptures were 'dictated by Omniscience' were allowed to go unchallenged. For Coleridge, readers of the Bible would only come to fully appreciate 'its superiority to all other books' if they took it up as they would 'any other body of ancient writings'.[22] Relieved from the obligation to accede to the text's infallibility, whoever read it or, indeed, *heard* it, could find 'a correspondent for every movement toward the Better felt in their own hearts'.[23] The Gospel according to

Coleridge was far from an ossified moral code, dictated by an infallible intelligence; rather, it was a vibrant volume in which each individual could find spiritual enlightenment and moral guidance.

As the century progressed and traditional faith waned, Coleridge's vision of the Bible took on more and more appeal for liberal-minded Christians. A prominent advocate of this school of interpretation was the Reverend Benjamin Jowett of Balliol College, Oxford, whose essay 'On the Interpretation of the Scriptures' was a major contribution to the controversial *Essays and Reviews*. Famously, the article attracted much heated debate, not least for its contention that the object of the interpreter is to 'read Scripture like any other book'.[24] It was a statement roundly attacked by one of the day's arch-enemies of liberalism, John William Burgon:

> Here is a Clergyman of the Church of England, and a Lecturer in Divinity, whose difficulty is how he shall convince the world that the Bible is – *like any other book!* Here is the sceptical fellow of a College, conspiring with six others, to produce a volume of which Germany itself […] would already be ashamed![25]

As is frequently the case with controversies, Burgon, like many others at the time and since, chose to emphasize the memorable 'sound bite' captured in italics, and to ignore Jowett's more reverential statement that 'When interpreted like any other book, by the same rules of evidence and the same canons of criticism, the Bible will still remain unlike any other book.'[26]

Reducing Jowett's work to one controversial statement was to by-pass what lay at the heart of the discussion: the desire to recover the original Scriptures from beneath 'the remains of dogmas, systems, controversies […] encrusted upon them'.[27] The essay resonates with images of exfoliation. Bringing a rigorous critical method to bear on the text is likened to the scraping away of sediments to reveal 'a picture which is restored after many ages to its original state' and to the removal of 'films which have gathered over the page'.[28] Such textual excavation involved a radical shift of perspective for the interpreter; he is obliged to 'transfer himself to another age' so as to recover 'the words as they first struck on the ears or flashed before the eyes of those who heard and read them', and in order to appreciate the 'language and […] the feeling of Eastern lands'.[29] But in order to reach this point of illumination, he is first required to carry out a diachronic study of the Bible narratives, a task requiring the painstaking discipline of translation and the evaluation of the accretions of successive generations, each with its own cultural specificity and preoccupations. 'Errors about words, and the attribution to words themselves of an excessive importance' must be corrected, fallacious reasoning must be exposed and challenged, and the previous bending of the book to suit the particular requirements of an age must be straightened out.[30]

Such an ambitious peeling away of the text was, of course, a tall order. Between the closing of the New Testament canon in the fourth century and the beginning of the Victorian era, the books that eventually came together to form the Bible had undergone frequent and extensive rewritings. Sloughing off the Victorian skin before slipping into the skin of first-century figures was as impossible as it was desirable, and uncovering the original words beneath the palimpsest was equally so. But the significance of Jowett's essay resides more in its outlining of the intractable textual difficulties that inhere in scriptural hermeneutics than in its offering of any kind of solution to them. The reader is left with a vivid sense of the Bible's indeterminacy: written at different times and by different authors it is, inevitably, multi-perspectival; placed 'in the hands of persons of all degrees of knowledge and education', it is opened up to countless interpretations.[31] Moreover, the very nature of words, with their tendency towards polysemy and shifts in meaning over time, render the Scriptures vulnerable to manipulation, so that 'the unchangeable word of God [...] is changed by each age and each generation in accordance with its passing fancy'.[32] Yet if Jowett's essay is nothing less than thorough in underlining the protean nature of the sacred text, this is not to say that the author felt entirely at ease with such an idea. While today's postmodernist would accept and even embrace the unfixed nature of the text, the Victorian Jowett keeps faith with the notion of its possessing an ultimate truth and aspires, after the strains of extensive critical scrutiny, to find himself 'alone in company with the author'.[33]

Jowett's writing on biblical interpretation had considerable influence in the later decades of the nineteenth century, not least for its close focus on the language of the Bible and its recommendation of what was essentially a literary-critical interpretive method. In some respects, its imprint can be detected in the religious prose works of Matthew Arnold, whose advocacy of reading the Scriptures as supreme examples of literary writing made a considerable impact on contemporary debates about faith and the Bible in the 1860s and

1870s. A parallel reading of Jowett's and Arnold's discussions of scriptural interpretation reveals a significant number of common ideas, as well as a shared affection for the Bible, the Church and the figure of Christ.[34] Like Jowett, Arnold considers the 'notion that every syllable and letter of the Bible is the direct utterance of the Most High' to be outmoded and highly misleading.[35] He expounds this belief in *Culture and Anarchy* (1869), drawing parallels between Catholic and Protestant temperaments:

> the attitude of mind of Protestantism towards the Bible in no respect differs from the attitude of mind of Catholicism towards the Church. The mental habit of him who imagines that Balaam's ass spoke, in no respect differs from the mental habit of him who imagines that a Madonna of wood or stone winked [...][36]

For both Jowett and Arnold, such rigid views of the text encouraged narrowness of mind, superstition and intolerance, and failed to take account of the nature of language itself. Arnold went on to explore Jowett's contention that the meaning of a word was inherently unstable, in the preface to *Literature and Dogma* (1873). Here he famously insists that the 'language of the Bible is fluid, passing, and literary, not rigid, fixed and scientific', a declaration suggestive of his mistrust of revisionist theology, a mistrust that, in some respects, also aligns him with Jowett.[37] Arnold continued to protest against the Higher Criticism in *God and the Bible* (1875):

> Even while acknowledging the learning, talents, and services of these critics, I insist upon their radical faults; because, as our traditional theology breaks up, German criticism of the Bible is likely to be studied here more and more, and to the untrained reader its vigorous and rigorous theories are, in my opinion, a real danger.[38]

The salient word here is 'untrained'. Arnold's main anxiety is that those who lack the subtlety of intellect to read the German school in an informed and questioning manner may be seduced by the novelty of its theories and end up abandoning the Scriptures altogether. Arnold found the prospect of such a wholesale rejection of the Bible greatly disquieting. Just as Jowett believed strongly that the Bible offered 'a common language to the educated and uneducated, in which the best and highest thoughts of both are expressed',[39] so Arnold believed it was the 'great inspirer', the glue that held society together.[40] And while both men agreed that the language of the Scriptures acted as a common thread through all reaches of society, they followed Coleridge in reserving the sophistications and rigour of biblical criticism for the well-educated minority.

Yet while Arnold followed Jowett in several respects, he departed from him significantly in others, and contemporary readers seemed to have little trouble in distinguishing these differences. The educationist Henry Dunn, for example, took umbrage at Arnold's intellectual elitism:

> no amount of knowledge regarding 'the best that has been known and said in the world,' and no amount of mere intellectual perception, however delicate it may be, will suffice for the right understanding of a book which is, to a great extent, dark to every man who has no spiritual sympathy with it. Hence it is that many a poor peasant, if gifted with what we call good common sense, often exhibits far more *discernment* in reading the Bible than is manifested either by the man of science or by the professional theologian.[41]

Seemingly unaware of – or at least unbothered by – Jowett's opinion that scriptural hermeneutics should be the 'province of few', Dunn holds up the professor's views as the converse of Arnold's.[42] For this commentator at least, Jowett's belief that 'Scripture stands alone as spirit speaking only to spirit' is what separates him most emphatically from Arnoldian aestheticizing, asserting as it does the unique and numinous qualities of the sacred text.[43] It might also have been that readers of Jowett's work were influenced by what Arnold saw as its most admirable quality, namely that it had '*unction*'.[44] Ultimately, the affinities between the two men were superficial. For the poet Arnold, the cultural and devotional virtues of reading the Bible were interdependent; for Jowett, on the other hand, the literary appreciation of the Scriptures was always of secondary importance. Where Jowett feared that German criticism would destroy faith in Christ and his teachings, Arnold's concerns were primarily for the deadening effects it would have on the human mind and its sensitivities to the written word. The clergyman takes the reader back to the text in order to wipe it clean of extra-biblical accretions and reveal its truth; the poet takes the reader back to the text to keep alive Christianity's 'charm for the heart, mind, and imagination of man'.[45] For Arnold, the importance of belief lay not in any 'historicalness of certain supposed facts' but in its 'unconscious poetry'.[46] This religious epistemology offered a way of demythologizing the figure of Jesus without severing links with the much-loved verses of the New Testament. Previously hallowed narratives, such as the Nativity and the Passion, could still be appreciated for their symbolic and poetic qualities, irrespective of their literal truth. G. W. Foote could not have been more wrong in his contention that 'Freethought teachers among the masses of the people [...] only put into homlier [sic] English and publish in a cheaper form the sentiments and ideas which Mr Arnold expresses for the educated classes at a higher price and in a loftier style.'[47] Although Foote is perhaps justified in drawing attention to the issue of social elitism in the discourse of religious controversy, his assertion that Arnold and hard-line freethinkers shared a common goal is characteristically mischievous. Arnold's religious writings were ultimately conservative; the Secularists' entirely destructive. Indeed, Arnold might have been describing the likes of Foote when he criticized the 'hard-headed people' who treat the Bible 'as either an imposture, or a fairy-tale'.[48]

Arnold's mixing of religion and culture led to his being accused of aestheticism by his own generation and those to come. Yet, in foregrounding the literary appeal of the Bible, Arnold was merely making explicit one of its most abiding and powerful features. Human attachment to religious liturgy and Scripture is strong and enduring and, even nowadays, it is not uncommon to find in those who have moved away from the Christian faith a continuing affection for its texts. In the Anglican tradition, the King James Bible might be said to hold pride of place in the canon of post-Reformation works. Commonly spoken of as a masterpiece of English prose, it has retained a foothold in the literary marketplace up to this day. In 1998, for example, Canongate published individual books from the Authorized Version of the Old and New Testaments in its 'Pocket Canon' series. The brief prefatory note to each slim volume ably sums up the enduring appeal and status of the text:

The Authorised King James Version of the Bible, translated between 1603–11, coincided with an extraordinary flowering of English literature. This version, more than any other, and possibly more than any other work in history, has had an influence in shaping the language we speak and write today. Presenting indi-

vidual books from the Bible as separate volumes, as they were originally conceived, encourages the reader to approach them as literary
works in their own right.[49]

By modern standards, then, the Authorized Version is, before all else,
a work of literature, emphasized in the Canongate series by introduc-
tions supplied by literary authors such as A. S. Byatt, David
Grossman, Will Self and A. N. Wilson, as diverse in their religious
beliefs and backgrounds as they are in their styles of writing.

As far as the majority of Victorians were concerned, the King James
Bible was still first and foremost a devotional work, though that is not
to say that its literary qualities went unnoticed. That many orthodox
Christians had a strongly aesthetic appreciation of their sacred text is
nowhere more evident than in the controversies that raged over the
revision of the Authorized Version in the 1870s.[50] One conservative
clergyman wary of relinquishing the King James translation was
Christopher Wordsworth, Bishop of Lincoln, who warned the
revisers to 'Beware lest by altering the text of the authorised version of
the Bible, you shake the faith of many.'[51] Here, the established Church
met Arnold in its appreciation of the attractiveness that inhered in the
sonorous cadences of the King James Bible and of the fearful consequences the loss of such could have on the masses. To disrupt the
rhythms of this seventeenth-century prose, so familiar and reassuring
to many generations past, was to risk disturbing a simple and unques-
tioning faith and, in political terms, the docility of the working classes.
From the Secularist point of view, the appeal of the text was more a
matter of sentimentality than spirit or aesthetics. G. W. Foote
committed himself to undermining the literary supremacy that had
been bestowed upon the King James Bible for so long, insisting that:

> The Authorised Version is indeed a monument of English, but of
> special English. It has always stood aside from the main develop-
> ment of English prose [...] With the single exception of Bunyan's
> masterpiece [...] it is difficult to name a first-class prose competition
> that was greatly indebted to our Authorised Version.[52]

Yet for all this, Secularists were in no doubt that this prose, at once
linguistically strange and familiar, combined with what they considered to be the 'silly sentimentalism of Jesus', made it a powerful means
of preserving the faithful; indeed, the publication of the Revised

Version of the New Testament in 1881 must have been hailed by them as one more nail in the coffin of orthodoxy.[53] For very different reasons, the Revised Version was also warmly welcomed by a number of prominent religious figures, among them F. W. Farrar, then Canon of Westminster, who considered the new text a 'great boon',[54] and the Jewish historian and folklorist Joseph Jacobs, for whom it represented a significant advance on the 'faulty translation' of the Authorized Version.[55] However, there remained a significant number of others, both liberals and traditionalists, who would continue to regard it as an unnecessary and regrettable diminution of a great work.

The Authorized Version's iconic literary status was in some ways compounded by its being frequently yoked with, and compared to, the works of Shakespeare. If the Bible was being increasingly regarded as a work of literature, so literature was gaining the status of a sacred text. The connection between the playwright and the Scriptures had been firmly established by Romantic writers such as Coleridge who, in a note to his infant son Hartley on the occasion of his christening, describes the plays of Shakespeare as 'subordinate only to thy Bible'.[56] It was a link that would be further reinforced by the Victorians. Writing in the early 1840s, Thomas Carlyle portrays Shakespeare as having almost divine status; he is 'a *Prophet*, in his way', and 'there is actually a kind of sacredness in the fact of such a man being sent into this Earth'.[57] Three decades or so later, the Scottish Episcopal Bishop, Charles Wordsworth, nephew of the Romantic poet William Wordsworth, described Shakespeare's writings in a similar vein as 'saturated with Divine Wisdom' and considered it no coincidence that the nation's greatest poet 'and our translators of the Bible lived and flourished at the same time'.[58] As the Authorized Version and the works of Shakespeare became more and more entwined in the hearts and minds of the Victorians, so the orthodox and heterodox alike harnessed the words of the national playwright to uphold their convictions. From the 1860s to the end of the century, extracts uprooted from Shakespeare's drama and poetry were liberally scattered through the pages of devout Lives of Jesus, often with little or no regard for their literary context; while at the other extreme, an article in Foote's *Secular Almanack* placed the playwright 'In the front rank of the Freethinkers', citing Hamlet's dying words – 'The rest is silence' – as proof of their author's profound scepticism.[59] This particular connection between the secular and the sacred has endured well into the present century: the Bible and the complete works of Shakespeare remain the complimentary books given to all castaways on BBC Radio 4's *Desert Island Discs*, for example. It might be argued, however, that while the Bible held on to pride of place well into the twentieth century, in more recent times Shakespeare's predominance in the National Curriculum, among other factors, has pushed it into an inferior position; as Doris Lessing has observed: 'These days, if someone hears "There is a time to be born and a time to die...", they probably think it is Shakespeare, since the Bible [...] is the experience of so few.'[60]

The second half of the nineteenth century saw a number of writers put forward eloquent and convincing arguments for a literary reading of the Scriptures. Nonetheless, it was an approach that continued to be met with considerable disquiet. In the early 1860s, the theologically orthodox writer Isaac Taylor observed that the title of his work *Spirit of the Hebrew Poetry* was 'likely to give alarm to Bible readers of a certain class, who will think that, in bringing the inspired writers under any such treatment as that which these phrases seem to imply, we are forgetting their higher claim'.[61] Taylor's phrase 'Bible readers of a certain class' no doubt refers to the more fundamentalist Dissenting denominations. However, even some relatively moderate Christians remained uneasy with an aesthetic approach to the Scriptures, perhaps heeding the prophet Ezekiel's warning that those who listen to him because he has a 'beautiful voice and plays well on an instrument' (Ezek. 33:32) are unlikely to do the Lord's bidding. One such was William Henry Fremantle, a liberal theologian and acolyte of Jowett. In a published sermon, he argued for combining a literary appreciation of the Bible with a belief in its inspiration:

> The Gospels [...] have a great literary charm in their simplicity, in their freshness and *naiveté*. But who can say that their form is independent of their subject matter? [...] The spirit of Christ is the form as well as the matter, in the grace, in the chasteness, in the reticence [...] in the naturalness and directness of the style.[62]

Fremantle, then, manages to marry inspiration and aesthetics by insisting on the interdependence of form and substance: without the grace of God there would be no 'literary charm'. Other Christians fell back on established historicist approaches to the text as a means of resisting the vogue for reading the Bible as literature. Writing in the first decade of the twentieth century, Bernard Lucas, an active member of the London Missionary Society, explains in the preface of his book *The Fifth Gospel* why he feels moved to champion Pauline writings:

> In the present day, when the Gospels are being more and more regarded as literary compositions [...] it is of supreme importance that we should have some very definite conception of what constitutes a sufficient historical basis for the Christianity which has come down to us.[63]

Yet in 1907, the same year that Lucas's work was published, William Sanday, one of the most influential theologians of his day, insisted that all 'study of the Gospels must really be founded upon close literary analysis'.[64] While too much on the side of orthodoxy to surrender the Gospel texts to a purely literary reading, Sanday's vast experience and knowledge of contemporary theology, both at home and abroad, had no doubt convinced him that the historical method was not in itself sufficient to deal with texts that were essentially literary in nature.

The Bible and fiction

One issue that held an important place in nineteenth-century religious discourse was the escalating popularity of fiction and its potential as a means of religious instruction. While the majority of Anglicans were willing to accept that fiction had a valuable role to play in reaching out to those whose faith was wavering, or in converting those who had yet to find it, exploiting the fictional mode for Christian ends did not meet with the approval of some of the more traditional elements of the clergy. In 1864, *The Christian Advocate and Review* carried an article entitled 'Fiction and Faith', which insisted that the popularity of prose fiction was one of the major contributors to the 'present epidemic of unbelief'.[65] Its opening sentence avers that 'the last new book of sceptical theology runs a race for popularity with the latest sensation novel', a clear allusion to Ernest Renan's *Vie de Jésus*, the first English translation of which had been published that same year.[66] As the author's choice of comparison suggests, Renan's work of modernist theology had more than a touch of literary flair about it; the author presents – and softens – heterodox religious ideas in an alluringly poetic manner, blending together two of the fundamentalists' greatest enemies:

revisionist theology and imaginative prose. For those who were unwilling, or unable, to follow the twists and turns of scholarly argument put forward by the liberal elite, Renan's *Life of Jesus* provided an ideal alternative: one eminently suited to a novel-reading public.

Having sneered at the Gallic enemy, the contributor to the Christian journal continues to argue that reading fiction is a time-wasting and frivolous occupation, leading ineluctably to passivity, indolence and 'a growing feebleness in the grasp of truth'.[67] Fiction is condemned as insidious, manipulative and deceptive. Emotions are vicariously aroused by what is essentially illusory: a narrative 'couched in the form of truth' that promotes the 'habit to be moved and not to act'.[68] The writer reveals a shrinking distaste for any enjoyment that might be gained from reading stories other than those found in the Bible, marking out individuals who engage in the perusal of fiction as weak, decadent and destined for doubt and damnation. Throughout his polemic, he insists on regarding the Bible as literal fact, in stark contradistinction to fiction; where the sacred text is infallible, historically grounded and edifying, imaginative prose is seductive, pleasurable and offers nothing in the way of self-improvement. Like any remorseless exhortation to shun what we desire and to embrace what is good for us, the consequent effect of the article is to draw attention to the attractiveness of the forbidden: namely, the boundless capacity of the novel and short story to create a compelling and satisfying verisimilitude. Fiction emerges as a powerful modern force, while the writer's somewhat splenetic tone emits a sense of hopelessness, of protesting too much.

The contributor to the *Christian Advocate* was by no means alone in voicing his disapproval of fiction. Those who continued to swim against the tide of fiction's popularity may well have seen it as an easier target for attack than theological revisionism which, with its often persuasive evidence for the contradictoriness and instability of the biblical texts, was, like sleeping dogs, better left unnoticed and unprovoked. A few years after the *Christian Advocate*'s anathematizing of all that fiction could provide, the Reverend George William Butler, in a tract entitled '*Is it True?*', proclaimed: 'Entirely different from the principle of the fiction is that of the Bible'.[69] Butler's tract takes its title from a work published in 1838 entitled *The Night of Toil: A familiar account of the labours of the first missionaries in the South Sea Islands*. Its author, Favell Lee Bevan, was a prolific writer of educational tracts for children, much given to delivering dire warnings of the iniquitous effects of fiction. In the Introduction to this account of missionary endeavour, she disassociates herself from imaginative writing in any shape or form:

> No attempt has been made by the slightest exaggeration to heighten the interest of this narrative. It is hoped that its adherence to facts will be a strong recommendation in the eyes of youth, who, while they much prefer narrative to didactic writing, show, by the earnest and oft-repeated inquiry, 'Is it true?' that they value truth above fiction.[70]

In full accordance with Bevan's point of view, Butler asserts that the young need fact and not fiction, deeming the fairy tale an 'unmixed evil', liable to pervert the child's natural taste for the truth.[71] In looking back to a text published three decades earlier, Butler is typical of those clergy who resisted all pressure to move with the times. In the years that separate Bevan's 1830s' missionary tale and Butler's 1860s' invective, the public's perception of the novel had undergone a significant shift. Thanks to the works of authors such as Dickens, George Eliot and Thackeray, prose fiction had shaken off its former reputation as a debased and meretricious form, and had risen in literary status and respectability. Butler, however, goes only so far as conceding that the novels of Dickens and Harriet Beecher-Stowe had helped the cause of the poor and the enslaved, dismissing the vast majority of fiction as a 'snare', and exhorting his readers to 'give heed, first and foremost, to their Bibles; and after their Bibles, to solid studies'.[72] There is no doubt that Butler's anti-fiction pamphlet is extreme for its time; nevertheless, it expresses the views of a small, but adamantine, minority who would continue to deny fiction's right to a place in a morally upright society and to uphold faith in the absolute supremacy of the Bible in the face of any number of hermeneutic systems imported from foreign shores.

Anxieties about the rapid rise in the popularity of fiction were not confined to the more traditional Christian denominations. Some among the educated classes felt sceptical about the quality of a genre produced in such great quantities and consumed by such great numbers. And the enormous volume of fiction published and read was not just a figment of the middle-class imagination. In an article entitled 'On the Admission of Fiction in Free Public Libraries', published in the late 1870s, Peter Cowell, the chief librarian of the Free Public Library in Liverpool, remarked:

Years ago, I observed, in making up the statistics of the Liverpool lending libraries, that the issue of novels was about 75 per cent. of the whole issue. It forms that proportion still. I have not observed much variation from that in other free lending libraries in our country.[73]

A late-twentieth-century article in the *Journal of Librarianship and Information Science* confirms Cowell's estimate of fiction-lending as typical of the whole country, and affirms that 'Throughout the period, fiction remained the overwhelming first choice in lending libraries.'[74] The novel and short story, so popular with so many, were condemned by some as intellectually unchallenging and dangerously seductive, especially for those of an indolent frame of mind. Parallels can be drawn between the anti-fiction discourse of the Victorians and today's discourse surrounding issues of healthy eating and fitness. Writing in the influential *National Review*, William Rathbone Greg draws a distinction between 'wholesome' and 'unwholesome' reading matter, employing the alimentary imagery typical of the time:

> There are peculiarities [...] in works of fiction which must always secure them a vast influence on all classes of societies and all sorts of minds. They are read without effort, and remembered without trouble. We have to chain down our attention to read other books with profit [...] Other books [...] are effective only when digested and assimilated; novels either need no digestion, or rather present their matter to us in an already digested form. Histories, philosophies, political treatises, to a certain extent even first-class poetry, are solid and often tough food, which requires laborious and slow mastication. Novels are like soup or jelly; they may be drunk off at a draught or swallowed whole, certain of being easily and rapidly absorbed into the system.[75]

In an age when self-improvement was considered a cardinal virtue, reading prose fiction was regarded as a wasteful act of self-indulgence, a quick fix not unlike the much maligned 'junk food' of the present century.

Various socioeconomic theories were advanced to account for popular reading habits. Greg ascribed the popularity of novel-reading to the excessive leisure of the moneyed classes, judging its influence on their 'fluctuating or unformed' youth and their 'always impressionable' womenfolk to be particularly pernicious.[76] Thirty years later, in a review of one of the century's best-selling religious novels, Mrs Humphry Ward's *Robert Elsmere* (1888), William Gladstone suggests that the 'increasing seriousness and strain of [our] present life' is largely responsible for the 'large preference [...] exhibited in local public libraries, for works of fiction'.[77] It is a form of reasoning that places fiction within the context of a rapidly evolving industrial society, with its increased leisure time and, even more significantly, its expanding rates of literacy. It also betrays a strong mistrust of imaginative writing. By fulfilling the need for light relief, for a change from the 'seriousness and strain' of quotidian existence, fiction becomes associated with what is trivial and undemanding, rendered all the more disturbing by its ready availability in public libraries. Free lending meant that the influence of fiction could move beyond the bourgeois world of reading so penetratingly observed in Flaubert's *Madame Bovary* to permeate the most economically deprived sectors of the community, generally regarded as the most susceptible to undesirable influences and the most in need of improvement through edifying works of non-fiction. As Peter Cowell insisted, in his report on fiction-reading in the late 1870s, 'Free libraries were primarily intended to carry on the education of our schools and to enable the poorer classes to develop any latent talent or ability they might possess.'[78] For all the theories that circulated about fiction's effect on the moral and educational welfare of society, they did little to impede its growth. In his *Autobiography* of 1883, Anthony Trollope commented on how 'Novels are read right and left, above stairs and below, in town houses and in country parsonages, by young countesses and by farmers' daughters, by old lawyers and by young students.'[79] Viewed from Trollope's perspective, the novel emerges as a democratizing agent, and it was no doubt this aspect of the genre that proved threatening to the more traditional elements of society.

Yet if some regarded the novel's ubiquity as running counter to the improvement of the 'poorer classes', others saw it as holding great educative potential. If Cowell and many like him considered prose fiction to 'unfit the mind for close and attentive reading and study', others considered it the most direct and efficient means of engaging and informing the popular mind.[80] An early exponent of fiction's instructive potential was the eminent Scottish judge, Lord Charles Neaves. In a lecture delivered in 1869, he argued that teaching through fiction was 'lawful and laudable [...] proved by the fact that it is freely resorted to in Scripture. Our Saviour's parables are unrivalled compositions.'[81] It was a view that was fiercely resisted by some evangelicals. In a tract published the same year as Neaves's lecture, George William Butler gives what could stand as a direct response to the Scotsman's ideas:

> It is common for those who promote fictions to justify themselves by appealing to the Bible, and especially to the example of the Lord Jesus Himself. 'Are not the parables fictions, every one of them?' it is asked; 'and is not the novel, or story-book, a legitimate extension of the same principle?' Certainly not [...] In the parable a spiritual truth is told in symbolical language; but in the fiction there is no spiritual event or doctrine in view.[82]

By and large, though, the image of Christ as the supreme storyteller came to provide one of the most persuasive arguments for the virtues of fiction. If Jesus could use fictional methods to instruct, so the argument went, the novel was a perfectly legitimate means of education in an increasingly complex and text-dependent age. A developing acceptance of fiction as a suitable medium for a devout Christian reader is evident from the publications catalogues produced by the high-church Society for Promoting Christian Knowledge. In the 1874 catalogue, the section headed 'Stories and Tales' takes up a meagre seven pages, with 65 pages devoted to tracts, sermons and meditations. In contrast, the 1890 edition includes a section of just 24 pages headed 'Tracts', and another of over 50 pages entitled simply 'Books'. Under this broad category, non-fiction and fiction works are listed together alphabetically, so that *Martyrs and Saints of the first Twelve Centuries* rubs shoulders with the edifying *Mary and Willy: A Tale for Easter Sunday*.[83]

In the second half of the nineteenth century, then, imaginative writing was becoming one of the most important means of reaching the faithful. George William Butler's complaint that 'Religious story-books [...] are as plentiful as flowers in summer' and that the 'two great Tract Societies have admitted such a vast amount of fiction into their lists of books' proves one of the few exceptions to Richard Altick's rule that 'the disapproval of fiction never extended to narratives specially written to convey some useful moral or religious lesson'.[84] What might be considered the normative Christian view of fiction is well captured in a conduct book for young men by

Cunningham Geikie, author of one of the most popular English Lives of Jesus:

> Not to read Fiction now-a-days would be to make a vow of ignorance, and count reading heretical. Imaginative literature never had so wide or so beneficent a reign. It is multiplying readers immensely, and supplying them with an infinite variety of healthful food. The greatest trouble is, lest the appetite should grow tyrannical, and refuse anything in other forms. Novels have their true place, after all, only as a relaxation.[85]

Yet try as clergyman like Geikie might to keep prose fiction in its rightful place, its force was destined to break through barriers once held inviolable and, as the next two chapters reveal, Christianity and its texts would never again be free from its 'tyrannical' influence.

Notes

1 Samuel Butler, *The Way of All Flesh* (London: Grant Richards, 1903), p. 52.
2 In *Studies of a Biographer*, 4 vols (London: Duckworth, 1898–1902), Leslie Stephen suggests that 'The controversy raised by *Essays and Reviews* even distracted men for a time from the far more important issues raised by the publication of Darwin's *Origin of Species*' (II, p. 129).
3 Terry Eagleton, *After Theory* (London: Allen Lane, 2003), p. 203.
4 Joseph Parker, *Ecce Deus* (Edinburgh: T. & T. Clark, 1867), p. 74.
5 Parker, *Ecce Deus*, p. 74.
6 *The Times*, 18 December 1891, p. 5.
7 *The Times*, 25 December 1891, p. 5; 22 December 1891, p. 8.
8 Edmund Gosse, *Father and Son: a study of two temperaments* (London: William Heinemann, 1907), p. 75.
9 Hale White, *The Autobiography of Mark Rutherford*, ed. Reuben Shapcott (London: Trübner, 1881), p. 35.
10 Thomas Hardy, *Tess of the D'Urbervilles* (London: Macmillan, 1912), p. 202.
11 Frederic W. Farrar, 'A Few Words on the Life of Christ', *Macmillan's Magazine*, 31 (March 1875), pp. 463–71 (p. 468).
12 Winwood Reade, *The Martyrdom of Man* (London: Trübner, 1872), p. 524.
13 Sylva [pseud.], *Ecce Veritas: An Ultra-Unitarian Review of the Life and Character of Jesus* (London: Trübner, 1874), p. viii.
14 For a detailed account of the Secularist movement, see Edward Royle, *Radicals, Secularists and Republicans: popular freethought in Britain, 1866–1915* (Manchester: Manchester University Press, 1980).
15 Iconoclast [Charles Bradlaugh], *Who was Jesus Christ?* (London, 1861), p. 8.

16 Annie Besant, *The Myth of the Resurrection* (London: Freethought Publishing Company, 1884), p. 141.

17 *The Bible Handbook*, ed. G. W. Foote and W. P. Ball (London: Progressive Publishing Company, 1888), p. ii.

18 G. W. Foote, 'Freethought in Current Literature', reprinted from the *Freethinker* in *Arrows of Freethought* (London: H. A. Kemp, 1882), p. 31.

19 Frances Power Cobbe, *Broken Lights: An Inquiry into the Present Condition & Future Prospects of Religious Faith* (London: Trübner, 1864), p. 5.

20 Coleridge defines the views of those whose arguments are 'grounded on the position, that the Bible throughout was dictated by Omniscience, and therefore in all its parts infallibly true and obligatory' as 'Bibliolatry'. See *Confessions of an Inquiring Spirit* (London: George Bell and Sons, 1884), pp. 318, 333.

21 Coleridge, *Confessions*, p. 305.

22 Coleridge, *Confessions*, p. 331.

23 Coleridge, *Confessions*, p. 324.

24 *Essays and Reviews*, ed. J. Parker (London: John W. Parker and Son, 1860), p. 338.

25 John William Burgon, *Inspiration and Interpretation: Seven Sermons Preached before the University of Oxford* (Oxford and London: J. H. and Jas. Parker, 1861), pp. ccix–ccx.

26 *Essays and Reviews*, p. 375. Reviewing the theologian's work retrospectively almost three decades after its original publication, the freethinking critic Mirabeau Brown foregrounds the phrase about reading the Bible as any other work, averring that though 'The maxim is simple [...] its consequences will be portentous'. See *Watts Literary Guide*, 43 (15 May 1889), p. 2.

27 *Essays and Reviews*, p. 339.

28 *Essays and Reviews*, pp. 375, 391.

29 *Essays and Reviews*, pp. 338, 367.

30 *Essays and Reviews*, p. 344.

31 *Essays and Reviews*, p. 379.

32 *Essays and Reviews*, p. 372.

33 *Essays and Reviews*, p. 384.

34 Mrs Humphry Ward, in her autobiographical work, *A Writer's Recollections* (London: W. Collins Sons, 1918), comments on how her uncle, Matthew Arnold, 'Like Mr. Jowett [...] would have liked to see the Church slowly reformed and "modernised" from within' (p. 235). Arnold discusses his generally approving views of Jowett's contribution to *Essays and Reviews* in his essay 'The Bishop and the Philosopher'. See *The Complete Prose Works of Matthew Arnold*, ed. R. H. Super, 11 vols (Ann Arbor: University of Michigan Press, 1960–77), III, pp. 53–54.

35 Matthew Arnold, 'Dr. Stanley's Lectures on the Jewish Church', in *Complete Prose Works*, III, p. 79.

36 Matthew Arnold, *Culture and Anarchy*, in *Complete Prose Works*, V, p. 173.

37 Matthew Arnold, *Literature and Dogma*, in *Complete Prose Works*, VI, p. 152.

38 Matthew Arnold, *God and the Bible*, in *Complete Prose Works*, VII, p. 375.

39 *Essays and Reviews*, p. 405.

40 Arnold, *Literature and Dogma*, in *Complete Prose Works*, VI, p. 363.

41 Henry Dunn, *Facts, Not Fairy Tales. Brief Notes on Mr Matthew Arnold's "Literature and Dogma"* (London: Simpkin, Marshall, 1873), p. 25.

42 *Essays and Reviews*, p. 405.

43 Dunn, *Facts, Not Fairy Tales*, p. 25.

44 Arnold, 'The Bishop and the Philosopher', in *Complete Prose Works*, III, p. 54.

45 Arnold, *God and the Bible*, in *Complete Prose Works*, VII, p. 377.

46 Matthew Arnold, 'On Poetry', in *Complete Prose Works*, IX, p. 63.

47 G. W. Foote, 'Freethought in Current Literature', in *Arrows of Freethought*, p. 29.

48 Arnold, *Literature and Dogma*, in *Complete Prose Works*, VI, p. 363.

49 The editorial note appears on p. v of each of the 'Pocket Canon' volumes (London: Canongate Books, 1998).

50 For a detailed discussion of the decade-long process of revising the King James Bible, see Owen Chadwick, *The Victorian Church, Part Two, 1860–1901* (London: SCM Press, 1987), pp. 44–50.

51 Quoted in Chadwick, *The Victorian Church*, p. 44.

52 George William Foote, *The Book of God in the Light of the Higher Criticism, with special reference to Dean Farrar's New Apology* (London: R. Forder, 1899), p. 76.

53 'The Irreligion of Shakespeare', in *The Secular Almanack*, ed. G. W. Foote (London: The Freethought Publishing Company, 1900), p. 15.

54 Farrar added this approbatory comment on the Revised Version in a footnote to the original preface to his *Life of Christ*, printed in the revised text (London: Cassell, 1893), p. xiii.

55 *The Book of Job with designs by Granville Fell and an introduction by Joseph Jacobs* (London: J. M. Dent, 1896), p. ix.

56 Quoted from a note published in *Shakespeare: The Sonnets – A Casebook*, ed. Peter Jones (Basingstoke: Macmillan, 1977), p. 41.

57 Thomas Carlyle, *On Heroes, Hero-worship and the Heroic in History* (London: James Fraser, 1841), pp. 179, 181.

58 Charles Wordsworth, *Shakespeare's Knowledge and Use of the Bible* (London: Smith, Elder, 1864), pp. 2, 6.

59 'The Irreligion of Shakespeare', p. 15.

60 Doris Lessing, writing in the Introduction to *Ecclesiastes* (London: Canongate, 1998), p. vii.

61 Isaac Taylor, *Spirit of the Hebrew Poetry* (London: Bell and Daldy, 1861), p. 24.

62 W. H. Fremantle, *The Gospel of the Secular Life* (London: Cassell, Petter, Galpin, 1882), p. 102.

63 Bernard Lucas, *The Fifth Gospel: being the Pauline Interpretation of the Christ* (London: Macmillan, 1907), p. 203.

64 William Sanday, *The Life of Christ in Recent Research* (Oxford: Clarendon Press, 1907), p. 155.

65 *The Christian Advocate and Review*, 43 (September 1864), pp. 385–91 (p. 385).

66 *The Christian Advocate and Review*, p. 385. The first English translation of Ernest Renan's *Vie de Jésus* (Paris: Michel Lévy, 1863) was the *Life of Jesus*, trans. unknown (London: Trübner, 1864).

67 *The Christian Advocate and Review*, p. 389.

68 *The Christian Advocate and Review*, p. 387.

69 George William Butler, '*Is it True?': A protest against the employment of fiction as a channel of Christian influence* (London: William Macintosh, 1869), p. 7.

70 Favell Lee Bevan, *The Night of Toil; or A familiar account of the labours of the first*

missionaries in the South Sea Islands (London: J. Hatchard and Son, 1838), p. vi.

71 Butler, *'Is it True?'*, p. 5.

72 Butler, *'Is it True?'*, p. 28.

73 Peter Cowell, 'On the Admission of Fiction in Free Public Libraries', in *Transactions and Proceedings of the Conference of Librarians*, ed. Edward B. Nicholson and Henry R. Tedder (London: Chiswick Press, 1878), p. 61.

74 Paul Sturges and Alison Barr, '"The fiction nuisance" in nineteenth-century British public libraries', *Journal of Librarianship and Information Science*, 24 (March 1992), pp. 23–32 (p. 24).

75 William Rathbone Greg, 'False Morality of Lady Novelists', *National Review*, 8 (January 1859), pp. 144–67 (p. 146).

76 Greg, 'False Morality of Lady Novelists', p. 145.

77 W. E. Gladstone, '*Robert Elsmere* and the Battle of Belief', *Nineteenth Century*, 23 (May 1888), pp. 766–88 (p. 766).

78 Cowell, 'On the Admission of Fiction in Free Public Libraries', p. 66.

79 Anthony Trollope, *An Autobiography by Anthony Trollope* (New York: John W. Lovell, 1883), p. 159.

80 Cowell, 'On the Admission of Fiction in Free Public Libraries', p. 60.

81 Charles Neaves, *On Fiction as a Means of Popular Teaching* (Edinburgh and London: William Blackwood, 1869), p. 12.

82 Butler, *'Is it True?'*, pp. 7–8.

83 See Catalogue 'C' of the *Society for Promoting Christian Knowledge: Catalogues of Publications* (London and Brighton: The Church of England, 1890), p. 29.

84 Butler, *'Is it True?'*, pp. 3, 21. See also Richard D. Altick, *The English Common Reader: A Social History of the Mass Reading Public 1800–1900* (Columbus, OH: Ohio State University Press, 1998), p. 121.

85 Cunningham Geikie, *Entering on Life* (London, New York and Bombay: Longmans, Green, 1896 [1882]), p. 226.

CHAPTER 2

Nineteenth-Century Lives of Jesus

> [I]f all the Bibles and Testaments were destroyed tomorrow,
> they could almost be reconstructed from the literature that has
> grown up around the life of Christ.
> Samuel Ayres, *Jesus Christ Our Lord*

From the late 1830s to the end of the nineteenth century, scholarly preoccupation with the historicity of the Gospels generated a form of biblical literature generically classified as 'Lives of Jesus'.[1] In *The Quest of the Historical Jesus* (1906), the first comprehensive survey of over a century of critical enquiry into the life and teachings of Christ, Albert Schweitzer states that 'Not all the Lives of Jesus could be cited. It would take a whole book simply to list them', a claim not to be dismissed as mere hyperbole.[2] More recent studies in the field estimate that 60,000 or so such works were published in Europe and the USA in the mid-to-late nineteenth century.[3] Reaching the peak of its popularity in the early 1870s, the genre was undeniably jaded by the century's end, the varieties of different angles on the Gospel narratives being all but exhausted. The American author Elizabeth Stuart Phelps, anxious to signal the novelty of her own late contribution to the Lives tradition, *The Story of Jesus Christ* (1897), provides a succinct account of the forerunners she is attempting to leave behind:

> This book is not theology or criticism, nor is it biography. It is neither history, controversy, nor a sermon [...] It is not a study of Jewish life or Oriental customs. It is not a handbook of Palestinian travel, nor a map of Galilean and Judean geography. It is not a creed; it speaks for no sect, it pleads for no doctrine.[4]

Though this catalogue of negations refers most directly to American Lives, it equally well categorizes British ones. Some of these took the form of published sermons; some presented the conservative counter-argument to the Higher Criticism; others situated their picture of Jesus in his 'authentic' geographical, cultural and religious contexts; and most aligned themselves firmly with a doctrinal position, most usually orthodox. For the most part undistinguished in style and unre-markable in content, these British Lives were characterized by pious, often sententious, prefaces, highly sentimental depictions of the Gospel narratives, and a doughty determination to beat off Conti-nental infidelity.

This chapter traces the evolution of this somewhat peculiar literary sub-genre from its radical inauguration abroad to its mainly reac-tionary and conservative closing stages in Britain. Focusing on the relatively few Lives of Jesus that served as blueprints for the super-abundance of imitations, it explores their very considerable impact on contemporary discourse about Christianity, and the impetus they provided for the fictional representations of Christ that emerged from the late 1860s onwards.

Continental infidelities: the influence of D. F. Strauss and Ernest Renan

Many of the Lives of Jesus written in the second half of the nineteenth century were instigated by Strauss's *Leben Jesu*, a ground-breaking study of the Gospel narratives. Mounting as it did a sustained attack on the veracity of the New Testament, the work quickly gained noto-riety, resulting in its author being removed from his post as tutor at the University of Tübingen just a matter of weeks after its publication.[5] It took seven years or so for *Leben Jesu* to reach the British reader. Its first translator explained in the Address that prefaced the four-volume English edition of 1842 that 'The illiberal tone of the public mind [had] prevented its publication being attempted by any *respectable* English publisher, from a fear of persecution.'[6] By 1846, the year of publication of George Eliot's much better known translation of the fourth edition, the softening of the blasphemy laws such that only works that were deemed to 'scoff' at the Scriptures were liable to pros-ecution ensured that Strauss's *Life* could be more vigorously and openly publicized. Described by Strauss himself as '*accurata et perspicua*' in the Latin preface to the three-volume work, Eliot's trans-lation provided a highly accomplished version of the book and, while it is unlikely that this densely argued and erudite work would have been read from cover to cover by the layman, there is no doubt that its central contentions were widely circulated and energetically debated.

As the century wore on, the public's growing familiarity with Strauss's *Life of Jesus* is evidenced in the way that both author and title appear more and more frequently in the domain of prose fiction. By the 1880s it had, in the words of the eponymous hero of Eliza Lynn Linton's *The Autobiography of Christopher Kirkland* (1885), 'long been known to the English reading public, thanks to the fine translation by Marian Evans' and, indeed, it could be found resting on the bookshelves of fictional characters in novels such as W. H. Mallock's *A Romance of the Nineteenth Century* (1881) and Edna Lyall's *Donovan* (1882), a sure signifier of religious scepticism either confirmed or approaching.[7] And in Mrs Humphry Ward's *Robert Elsmere*, the extensive library of Squire Wendover, biblical scholar and confirmed sceptic, boasts 'most of the early editions of the "Leben Jesu", with some corrections from Strauss's own hand'.[8] In other novels, such as George Gissing's *Workers in the Dawn* (1880), Strauss's work is actually taken off the shelf to play a crucial role in the life of one of its central characters. In this bleak depiction of urban working-class poverty, a chance encounter with an English translation of the *Life of Jesus* brings about a radical transformation in the heroine, Helen, expressed in language closely akin to that of religious revelation:

> Helen [...] sat at her reading-desk, bending over the pages of him whose eyes saw with surpassing clearness through the mists of time and prejudice, whose spirit comes forth, like a ray of sunshine in winter, to greet those toiling painfully upwards to the temple of Truth.[9]

Once emancipated from the Christian beliefs of her years as a clergyman's daughter, Helen wastes no time in organizing a study visit to the University of Tübingen, home of the Higher Criticism, where a close reading of Darwin's *Origin of Species* completes her education in sceptical thinking.

Novelists tended to portray their imagined readers of Strauss embracing the work as liberating and revelatory, drawing scant attention to its density of detail, or the considerable time and effort required to read it in its entirety. Separated into three chronological parts, each one divided into chapters and further into sub-chapters, Strauss's penetrating analysis of the Gospels is anything but a quick, easy read. Moving methodically through the New Testament sources, the author endeavours to distinguish between the recording of what might have been actual events and what might have been constructed solely by the religious imagination. He rejects the supernaturalist approach to the Scriptures as contrary to contemporary understanding and knowledge of the world, at the same time holding up the often convoluted and far-fetched theories of the rationalists to intellectual ridicule. Influenced by the idealist philosophy of Hegel, he breaks down the stalemate that had persisted between these two opposing schools of thought, and expounds his own interpretive strategy based on the belief that the Gospels grew out of a mythopoeic process. What rationalists such as Reimarus had condemned as lies and forgeries, Strauss regarded as the consequence of a mode of thought peculiar to a bygone age when perceptions of 'truth' differed radically from those of the nineteenth century. In order to grasp the essential differences between the minds of the disciples and those of modern men, Strauss insisted, the religious historian must resist anachronistic thinking and 'transplant himself in imagination upon the theatre of action, and strive to the utmost to contemplate the events by the light of the age in which they occurred'.[10]

Strauss's heterodox reading of the Scriptures left an immeasurably deep scar on the hearts of the faithful. Almost three decades after the publication of Eliot's translation of the *Life of Jesus*, a writer for the highly orthodox *Christian Observer*, though reviewing one of Strauss's least controversial titles, *The Life and Times of Ulrich von Hutten*, still feels moved to denounce the earlier work in the most intemperate of terms as 'blasphemous hallucinations, mischievous, revolting'.[11] That the *Life* should cast so long a shadow over conservative Christians is perhaps unremarkable, given that it had adumbrated the agenda for future decades of theological tussles; the miraculous elements of the New Testament narratives, the identity and intentions of their authors and the historical value of the Fourth Gospel were all areas laid open for argument. Moreover, Strauss's insistence that 'the line of distinction between history and fiction [...] was not drawn so clearly as with us' was a perplexing notion for the many orthodox readers who regarded fact and fiction as binary opposites, and who associated the term 'fiction' with fakery and lies.[12] Strauss notes how, as far as traditional Christians are concerned, the

Bible is strictly true, while 'the histories related by the heathens of their deities, and by the Mussulman of his prophet, are so many fictions'.[13] Fiction for the traditional Christian, then, is associated with error, false belief and the unconverted. Strauss's reading of the Scriptures blurred such a rigid demarcation of truth and lies; for him, the very development of the Christian faith was embedded in a complex evolutionary process whereby the real and the fictive were interwoven. Strauss explains the process thus:

> In general the whole Messianic era was expected to be full of signs and wonders [...] These merely figurative expressions, soon came to be understood literally [...] and thus the idea of the Messiah was continually filled up with new details, even before the appearance of Jesus. Thus many of the legends respecting him had not to be newly invented; they already existed in the popular hope of the Messiah, having been mostly derived with various modifications from the Old Testament, and had merely to be transferred to Jesus, and accommodated to his character and doctrines.[14]

Viewed from Strauss's diachronic perspective, Christ's contemporaries are seen to have had linguistic difficulties with the pronouncements of their elders, just as nineteenth-century Christians sometimes struggled to understand the religious imagination and idiom of the disciples. In addition to this unintentional fiction, created by the superimposing of the past on the present, Strauss identified an entirely aesthetic fiction that developed once myths were established and became 'the subject of free poetry or any other literary composition'.[15] Akin to literary fiction, this poetic embellishment of the dominant religious ideas was contrived to strengthen belief, though still, according to Strauss, 'without evil design', being in accordance with the will of a community.[16]

The implications of Strauss's work for the theology of its time and their potential impact on faith were forcefully expressed by a critic writing in the *Westminster and Foreign Quarterly Review*:

> It is the pride of Strauss, that he *un-creates*. At his spell, the warmth of every faith, the accumulated glow of old ages, that alone renders the Present habitable, suddenly becomes latent: the facts, the scenes, the truths that re-absorb it, run down in liquefaction, pass off in vapour, and restore the world to a nebular condition.[17]

Here, the arresting notion of 'un-creation' and the images of deliquescence convey a hauntingly desolate picture of a post-Straussian world, in which civilization reverts to original chaos. Reviews such as this one made it clear that Strauss's work had struck too fierce a blow against traditional Christianity for it to remain solely within the community of scholars, and one of its consequences was, somewhat paradoxically, a revitalization of the traditional Church. Looking back from a distance of forty years, F. W. Farrar defines the *Life of Jesus* as the *'reductio ad horribile* of current scepticism' and recalls, approvingly, the rallying of the faithful against its insidious influence, so that 'pulpits rang once more with vital truth and manly eloquence'.[18] Uplifted and strengthened by the newfound energy of the clergy, individuals could continue to nourish their faith with any one of a plethora of orthodox Lives of Jesus published to counter and reject the apostasy of Strauss. If Continental criticism had reduced Jesus to an idea, a figment – albeit a highly significant one – of the religious imagination, the biographical works that succeeded it attempted to reinstate a sense of historical reality. The authors of these Lives transformed the relatively slender Gospel stories into hefty volumes, supplementing New Testament stories with extra-biblical material and psychological conjecture, and rewriting them in a prose style frequently verging on the pleonastic. If Strauss's trenchant analysis threatened irrevocably to undermine the verity of the Gospels, Lives of Jesus offered a means of rehabilitating or even replacing them.

In the preface to *A New Life of Jesus*, published in 1864, Strauss avers that 'We must address the people since theologians refuse to listen.'[19] While ostensibly directed at the professional theologian, it is also a covert undermining of the achievement of Ernest Renan's *Vie de Jésus*, published just a year earlier.[20] Having gone through ten editions of 5,000 copies each in its first year and having been translated into eleven European languages by the end of 1864, Renan's study of Christ could be said to have already accomplished the task of conveying current thinking on the Gospels to the non-specialist.[21] Though Strauss claims to have 'joyfully hailed the work of Renan on its appearance', he goes on to damn it with faint praise: 'I accept it respectfully, and though by no means tempted by its example to alter my own plan, I may say that all I wish is to have written a book as suitable for Germany as Renan's is for France.'[22] It is evident here that for Strauss, as for the majority of theologians of his time, studies in the historical Jesus were inseparable from the national characteristics of both authors and readers. Such a deterministic mode of thinking was also to be found in the periodical press. The *Edinburgh Review* regarded the *Life* as proof of the unbridgeable gap between the French and English temperaments: 'The French mind, in particular, is so easily dazzled by brilliancy, and so readily captivated by dramatic finish and vivid portraiture [...] Englishmen have not so much faith in the laws of dramatic unity, or in the irrefragibility of logic.'[23] And forty years on, reflecting on a century or so of Christological research, Schweitzer was forthright in his assertion of the superiority of the German temperament in matters theological and the relative weakness of the French, which he considered to be writ large in Renan's *Life*.[24] It was an argument with which Renan himself had already engaged in an essay entitled 'The Critical Historians of Jesus', published in *Studies of Religious History* (1857). In this he asserts somewhat bullishly:

> We can affirm that if France, better endowed than Germany with the sentiment of practical life, and less subject to substitute in history the action of ideas for the play of passion and individual character, had undertaken to write the life of Christ in a scientific manner, she would have employed a more strict method, and that, in avoiding to transfer the problem, as Strauss has done, into the domain of abstract speculation, she would have approached nearer to the truth.[25]

This was, of course, no empty boast: Renan would put his theory into practice a few years later in his *Vie de Jésus*, a work whose perceived failings were often put down to the innate characteristics of its Gallic author.

In tones redolent of Wilde's Francophobic Lady Bracknell, a torrent of publications saw the author of *La Vie* roundly denounced for transgressing the *bonnes mœurs* of the Victorian public, as only a Frenchman could; his agnosticism was 'dandified', his depiction of Jesus perfumed, effeminate and far too sensuous. The debate over national temperament, however, went beyond such crude chauvinism; at its heart lay some important issues of methodology, style and intention. Where Strauss's forensic scrutiny of the primary texts was a fitting method for dismantling the once-stable relationship between truth and history, Renan's more impressionistic and imaginative approach was better suited to what was in all respects a gentler, even nostalgic, denial of divinity. In his Introduction to the *Life of Jesus*,

Renan accuses Strauss of concentrating too fully on the theological, thereby rendering the figure of Jesus a mere abstraction. Conscious that 'Many will regret [...] the biographical form' of his study, he takes on the role of biographer regardless, insisting that his subject will only be brought to life with 'some share of divination and conjecture' and by 'combining the texts in such a manner that they shall constitute a logical, probable narrative, harmonious throughout'.[26] Renan's willingness to treat the canonical Gospels as biographical works (an attitude that has found favour with some twenty-first-century biblical scholars), and to reconstruct his own biography from them, did not meet with Strauss's approval.[27] In the first chapter of *The New Life of Jesus*, Strauss states unequivocally that the Christ of the Church is 'no subject for biographical narrative', arguing that the Jesus of dogma and the Jesus of history are irreconcilable, the inevitable result of the biographical method being the demise of theology.[28] Yet whatever Strauss's misgivings about Renan's choice of form might have been, he could not have denied the enormous success that resulted from it.[29] What the work lacked in theological scrupulosity it more than made up for in readability, and its adaptation of the Gospel narratives for a novel-reading public was its *tour de force*. Placed alongside it, Strauss's original *Life of Jesus* must have appeared prohibitively learned and tenebrous to the common reader, conforming to Matthew Arnold's description of the Germanic style as 'blunt-edged, unhandy and infelicitous'.[30]

The response to Renan's *Life of Jesus* was immediate and prolific.[31] Traditional believers were predictably outraged by its denial of miracles and Christ's divinity (one particularly irate female reader repeatedly sending the author an anonymous note to remind him that 'There is a Hell'), and the Catholic Church was swift to place it on the *Index Librorum Prohibito* alongside several of the author's earlier works.[32] While it was welcomed and admired by some of the more liberal-minded readers, freethinkers viewed it as a sentimental dilution of Strauss, and theologians derided it for its lack of scholarly restraint. Leaving aside the religious and moral convictions of its critics, however, there was general agreement that Renan's depiction of Jesus was highly imaginative and executed in a style rather more literary than academic. If some judged Renan's exuberant prose wholly inappropriate for its subject, others regarded it as its greatest quality, establishing the author's reputation as a brilliant stylist.[33] In an address of thanks to Renan, following his delivery of the Hibbert Lectures in

1880, Dr James Martineau praised the lectures for their 'marvellous charm of literary form, in the command of which the French are the first among European nations, and [...] M. Renan among the French'.[34] Even one of Renan's fiercest detractors, the Catholic theologian Marie Joseph Lagrange, had to concede that 'Renan's art stripped exegesis of the heavy garments with which the climate of Germany had smothered it [...] His success was immense, and the sensation still continues.'[35] Indeed, the attraction of Renan's art continued well into the twentieth century. Writing in the 1970s, Edward Said reaffirmed the uniqueness of Renan's *Life of Jesus*:

> The text of *his* book is sober enough, but what it does to the textual forms of the Gospels, their matter and their existence, is highly adventurous, particularly if we take account of the extraordinarily imaginative connection made by Renan between a subject like Jesus, textual records of his life and teaching, and retrospective critical analysis.[36]

While Renan may have declared his preference for the biographical form in his treatment of the Gospels, what Said deems the 'highly adventurous' nature of his work stems largely from its reaching beyond the usual perimeters of biography. As Ben Pimlott remarks in the last of his published essays: 'Most of the world's greatest religions have a biographical element: at the core of Christian teaching are four resonant biographies.'[37] Renan no doubt realized that the biographical mode was not in itself enough to produce an absorbingly fresh version of Christ's life, and manipulated the conventions of contemporary genres such as travel writing, the historical novel and realist fiction to guarantee his work's originality. Countless critics of the *Life* have commented on its kinship with the novel, and there is no doubt that Renan understood how easily what Hans Frei defines as the 'realistic or history-like quality of biblical narratives' could be adapted to appeal to readers more accustomed to prose fiction than history or theology.[38] Yet, while Renan's depiction of setting and character, his manipulation of narrative pace and his literary style invite his *Life* to be read as a work of fiction, its historical foundations – contentious though they were – confound such a straightforward reading. The substantial critical apparatus of the first editions, such as footnotes and appendices, serves to remind readers that they are engaging with a non-fiction text documenting the life of a historical figure.[39]

There are points in the narrative, however, where Renan's adroit fusion of history and fiction threatens to erase the borderline between the two discourses. This is particularly pronounced in his portrayal of the 'missing years' of Christ's life, a textual lacuna that offered great scope for imaginative speculation and one that had already been exploited in numerous apocryphal writings. Take, for example, Renan's description of Jesus's education: 'He learnt to read and to write, doubtless, according to the Eastern method, which consisted in putting in the hands of the child a book, which he repeated in cadence with his little comrades, until he knew it by heart.'[40] Here biographical conjecture, indicated by the parenthetical 'doubtless', is easily cast aside as the sentimental image of the young Jesus chanting merrily with his 'little comrades' takes shape in the reader's mind. Read fleetingly, the second 'he' of the sentence seems to refer to the same substantive as the first 'he', Jesus himself; read more carefully, however, it is clear that it is the typical Eastern child whose cheerful diligence is being evoked. While the grammar of the description acquits Renan of sheer invention, the overall impact owes more to the author's historical imagination than to verifiable 'facts'. And while Renan is assiduous throughout the work in maintaining the technical indicators of the biographical mode, frequently prefacing his comments with phrases such as 'it seems that', 'it must have been' and 'it is probable that', the authorial voice is remarkably protean. Further on in the narrative, for example, he makes an intimate appeal to the reader to consider how 'The last hours of a cherished friend are those we best remember', in order to appreciate the lasting impact of the Last Supper on the disciples.[41] At other times, such as when describing the moments directly following Christ's death on the cross, he shifts his address from the reader to the subject:

Rest now in thy glory, noble initiator. Thy work is completed; thy divinity is established [...] A thousand times more living, a thousand times more loved since thy death than during the days of thy pilgrimage here below, thou wilt become to such a degree the corner-stone of humanity, that to tear thy name from this world would be to shake it to its foundations.[42]

In this emotive apostrophe, Renan offers a redefinition of the concept of Christ's divinity to all who reject the supernatural: Jesus's greatness inheres not in a resurrection but in the enduring impact of his days on earth. Furthermore, the prayer-like rhythms of the prose, aided by the archaic 'thy' and 'thou', seem to emulate the fervent devotion of the faithful, effecting what Mary Robinson aptly termed 'pious unbelief'.[43] Coming at the end of the chapter that depicts Christ's suffering on the cross, it forms the kind of dramatic climax regularly employed by nineteenth-century serial novelists. However, in the opening paragraph of the succeeding chapter, Renan reasserts the voice of the historian, informing the reader matter-of-factly of the Jewish laws concerning crucified corpses, and citing Origen's interpretation of Christ's premature expiry on the cross. Through this diversity of styles Renan's *Life* takes on the heteroglossic quality of prose fiction, the fluctuations of narrative tone resembling the interplay of the diverse social voices provided by the characters in a novel. Employing a range of typifying lexis, the author manages to suggest multiple presences: the scientist, the historian, the worshipper, the *cicerone*. In so doing, he enriches the narrative texture of the writing, greatly enhancing its appeal for the reader.

The voice that seemed to touch contemporary readers of the *Life* most forcefully was that of the traveller. In contrast with the early nineteenth-century Protestant writers who undertook scientific study of the Levant solely to verify scriptural authenticity and prophecy, Renan employs his first-hand knowledge of Palestine to endue his work with an air of antiquarian charm.[44] The 1860s saw a surge of interest in the archaeology and antiquities of the Near East. In 1865 the Palestine Exploration Fund (PEF) was founded in Britain under the patronage of Queen Victoria, with the intention of funding excavations of the Bible lands and of Jerusalem in particular. Surveying a decade or so of its projects, the *London Quarterly Review* pronounced that:

> The 'Land' and the 'Book' are indissolubly associated. The one cannot be fully understood without the other. The land must be seen through the eyes of the book, and the book through the eyes of the land. M. Renan, in a memorable passage, describes the surprise with which he discovered the harmony existing between the gospel narrative and the places to which it refers. He declares that the scenes of our Lord's life are *un cinquième évangile*. [45]

Citing Renan as instrumental in forging a link between landscape and sacred texts confirms the very considerable impact the *Life* had on the

British public, not least because of its use of the phrase '*un cinquième évangile*' [a fifth Gospel], which was common parlance by the late nineteenth century. Being more or less in line with Christian orthodoxy, the aims of the PEF differed fundamentally from those of Renan.[46] Having carried out an extensive itinerary of travel in Palestine in the early 1860s, Renan had plenty of topographical knowledge to contribute to his rewriting of the Gospels, and he used this, for the most part, for aesthetic purposes. The *Life* dispels former nineteenth-century images of Palestine as decaying, desolate and accursed by God by picturing the Bible lands as they might have been in the time of Christ.[47] Taking the reader back to a former age, Renan attempts to show Jesus in his original setting (true to his promise that he would take up some of the historical ground ignored by Strauss), at the same time creating an atmosphere verging on pastoralism:

> The rivulet of Ain-Tabiga makes a little estuary, full of pretty shells. Clouds of aquatic birds hover over the lake. The horizon is dazzling with light. The waters, of an empyrean blue, deeply imbedded amid burning rocks, seem, when viewed from the height of the mountains of Safed, to lie at the bottom of a cup of gold. [48]

Here, syntactical variation, rich imagery and elaborate adjectives paint a reassuring setting in which to envisage the historical Jesus, the appeal of aesthetics replacing that of faith in an age of ever-increasing religious scepticism. And no less atmospheric is his lyrical description of Galilee which, with its shifts from the past simple to the present historic tense, takes the reader on a journey back in time, offering a form of literary escapism to keep the harsher elements of unbelief at bay:

> Galilee [...] was a very green, shady, smiling district, the true home of the Song of Songs, and the songs of the well-beloved. During the two months of March and April the country forms a carpet of flowers of an incomparable variety of colours. The animals are small, and extremely gentle: – delicate and lively turtle-doves, blue-birds so light that they rest on a blade of grass without bending it, crested larks which venture almost under the feet of the traveller, little river tortoises with mild and lively eyes, storks with grave and modest mien, which, laying aside all timidity, allow man to come quite near them, and seem almost to invite his approach.[49]

It was largely this kind of representation of the natural world of Palestine that earned Renan his reputation as a writer more inclined to romanticism than serious theology. One of his most vehement critics, the French Reformed pastor Edmond de Pressensé, took particular exception to Renan's insistence on a spiritual correspondence between Christ and his environment.[50] Pressensé complained that Renan's 'exquisite passages [...] polished like the finest diamond' ascribed 'an exorbitant influence to nature in the development of the soul of Jesus'.[51] Indeed, for the orthodox reader, Renan's urging that the 'birds of heaven, the sea, the mountains, and the games of children, furnished in turn the subject of his instructions'[52] placed Christ too close to the earth and too far away from his heavenly father, rendering him, in the words of John Middleton Murry, little more than a 'village *illuminé*'.[53] Similarly, his suggestion that Christ's soul was enriched and elevated more by the temperate climate of Galilee than by the Almighty placed his subject's sensibilities closer to those of the Romantic poet than the holy man, a characterization that some considered highly irreverent. Nonetheless, Renan's vision of the Palestinian Jesus seemed to stamp itself upon the minds of even his most critical readers. Author of numerous works on Christianity, Frances Power Cobbe, though highly critical of Renan's aestheticism, writes of the impossibility of recovering the person of Christ in a style itself distinctly Renanian:

> Rather do we only look sorrowfully over the waves of time to behold reflected therein some such faint and wavering image as his face may have cast on the Lake of Galilee as he leaned at eventide from the ship of his disciples, over the waters stirred and rippling before the breeze.[54]

Renan, like several of the biographers of Jesus who followed him, brought his subject squarely in line with the spirit of the age. If, as the author states in the preface to the *Édition Populaire*, 'On peut aimer Jeanne d'Arc sans admettre la réalité de ses visions' [One can admire Joan of Arc without accepting the reality of her visions], so his romantic figure of Christ could be admired and loved by those for whom science had long replaced miracle.[55] A Jesus who could be regarded as a product of nature, rather than as a mysterious emanation from the heavens, was welcomed by readers unable to accept the Gospel miracles but reluctant to give up what they saw as the ideal example of human greatness. Renan's portrayal of Christ as the finest human being of all time, a pattern for all to follow, is echoed by agnostics such as John Stuart Mill, who defines him as 'a standard of excellence and a model for imitation', one who could provide a spiritual guide for the unbeliever.[56] Renan's Jesus is a man of 'extraordinary sweetness' and 'infinite charm', kind to women and children and adored by them in return.[57] In some respects this image of Christ proved extremely attractive for nineteenth-century readers, especially those partial to sentimental and idealized images of women and children. Moreover, Renan's speculation about whether Jesus reflected on the 'young maidens who, perhaps, would have consented to love him' during his agony in the Garden of Gethsemane hinted at his potential to become both husband and father, and aligned him more easily with the mid-century normative view of masculinity.[58] Likewise, Renan's description of Christ as 'no longer a Jew' was very much in line with the mid-century view of the Saviour as the instigator of a revolutionary new faith, one who had broken entirely with the Judaic religion.[59]

Renan takes care, though, that his leading character is not unfeasibly good: Jesus is susceptible to adulation, taking pleasure from being hailed as 'son of David'.[60] He is also given to bouts of bad humour and melancholy, leading him 'to commit inexplicable and apparently absurd acts', a changeability that prefigured Albert Schweitzer's vision of Christ as a fervid apocalyptic, and that was frequently criticized by Renan's opponents as inimical to the Christian ideal of an immutable figure of divinity.[61] Renan emphasizes that, like all human beings, Jesus is prone to change, doubt and anxiety, and offers the reader tantalizing glimpses into his putative inner life. He evokes Christ's thoughts in the Garden of Gethsemane through a series of speculations: 'Did he curse the hard destiny which had denied him the joys conceded to all others? Did he regret his too lofty nature, and, victim of his greatness, did he mourn that he had not remained a simple artisan of Nazareth?'[62] Notice here how Renan is careful to maintain the dividing line between fiction and biography, employing authorial questions rather than free indirect discourse. By the following century, however, biographers would start to follow the narrative technique of some contemporary fiction writers to build on Renan's stylistic method, dropping the conjectural syntax and conveying Christ's thoughts as if coming directly from his own mind.[63]

One aspect of Christ's personality that Renan conveys as both constant and indisputable is his way with words. As critics highlighted the author's stylistic felicities, so the author draws attention to the same qualities in his subject. Renan's Jesus has the soul of a poet: he has a sensitive appreciation of the verses of the Old Testament; he enjoys the linguistic energies of wordplay; he inspires an entirely original form of parable, 'charming apologues' articulated in 'beautiful language'.[64] Just as British writers tended to compare the words of Christ to those of Shakespeare, so Renan likens them to those of Molière. Endowing Christ with literary flair is another means by which the heretical contents of the *Life* are softened: Jesus may not be divine, but his eloquence and poetic sensibilities furnish him with a spiritual quality entirely in keeping with the founder of a world religion. It was, perhaps, the coincidence of the literary talents of both author and subject that led some readers of the *Life* to consider it a work closer to autobiography than biography.[65] At the start of the twentieth century, Schweitzer was to make a similar observation in relation to the entire genre of Lives of Jesus: that 'each individual created Jesus in accordance with his own character'.[66] Yet this identification of the writer with his subject fails to recognize the enormous scope and influence of Renan's work. Far from capturing the essence of only one man in Jesus, he succeeds in capturing the mood of the 1860s in all its contradictoriness. In *The Gospels*, Renan claims that 'the life of Jesus will always obtain a great success when the writer has the necessary degree of ability, of boldness, and of *naïveté* to translate the Gospel into the style of his time', and there is no doubt that he more than succeeded in fulfilling his own criteria.[67] His *Life* is, to use Thomas De Quincey's definition, an example of the 'literature of power', in contradistinction to the 'literature of knowledge'.[68] Those readers looking for the latest in theological scholarship would have found little of note in Renan's rewriting of the Gospels; however, those seeking a vision of Jesus that would move, inspire and comfort them in an increasingly materialist century would have found an ideal guide.[69]

Towards a definitive English Life of Jesus: J. R. Seeley and F. W. Farrar

By the mid-1860s, the New Testament studies of Strauss and Renan had left British theology looking outmoded and unfit for the modern age. Fearing the consequences of simply ignoring the Higher Criticism, a number of traditional British Christians called for a more strenuous resistance to its influence, with biographical studies of the historical Jesus being regarded as the best means to this end. In 1864, no doubt prompted by the publication of the English translation of Renan's *Life*, one pseudonymous author wrote to the Archbishop of Canterbury, urging that 'the first-fruits of our native School of Biblical criticism, an English history of the life of our Lord and Saviour Jesus Christ should forthwith be prepared by some thoroughly competent English writer'.[70] Such a Life, the author suggests, would serve as a corrective to the 'absurd fancies' of the likes of Renan and Strauss and would 'without professing to be *authoritative* [...] so commend itself to the reason and feelings of all believers in revelation, as to serve as a standard not only to the members of the Established Church of England, but also to pious and thoughtful Christians of every denomination both in this country and abroad'.[71] Less than a year later, what was to become regarded by some as the definitive English Life of Jesus entered the public arena, though it was far from being the refutation of heresy this particular writer had in mind.

Ecce Homo: A Survey of the Life and Work of Christ was published in 1865.[72] By the end of 1866, the identity of its author had been revealed as John Robert Seeley, then Professor of Latin at University College London.[73] Numerous reviewers compared Seeley's work with Renan's *Life*, asseverating that a British Renan had entered the controversy over the life of Jesus.[74] Yet of the plethora of liberal Lives of Jesus produced in the final forty years of the nineteenth century, Seeley's is in some ways one of the least like Renan's. Certainly it shares some surface similarities. As in Renan's *Life*, Christ's humanity is emphasized throughout, beginning with its bold title, *Ecce Homo* or 'Behold the man!', the words of Pontius Pilate, recorded in John's Gospel (19:5); and in the main body of the work, Seeley expounds his conviction that 'within the whole creation of God nothing more elevated or more attractive has yet been found than he', a human perfection that enables Jesus to inspire 'an enthusiasm of humanity'.[75] Like Renan, Seeley shows an acute awareness of contemporary issues, relating the story of Christ to Victorian debates over issues such as philanthropy, scientific advance and the abolition of slavery. And where Renan compares Jesus to Molière, Seeley chooses to compare him to Britain's equivalent: Shakespeare. Yet Seeley's work differs starkly from Renan's in both its selection of textual material and in its stylistic methods. If Renan wrote with the creative flair of the novelist, then Seeley wrote with the control and clarity of the accomplished lecturer.[76] *Ecce Homo* is structured around a series of sustained discussions of various aspects of Christ's ministry, the second half of the study being separated into a number of meditations on abstract concepts such as morality, mercy and forgiveness. Where Renan creates cliff-hanger endings for his chapters, Seeley supplies chapter summaries, focusing the reader's mind on the salient points of what he describes as his 'investigation' into the life of Christ.[77] Eschewing the traditional methods of the biographer, Seeley selects Gospel incidents to illustrate his ideas rather than presenting them in a linear narrative. New Testament figures such as Mary Magdalene, Judas and Joseph of Arimathea, for all their potential for imaginative development, find no place in Seeley's restrained study. In contrast to Renan's exuberant prose style, Seeley writes in an oddly oblique and often distant manner, defined by one reviewer as 'Power without show of power; a quiet, simply-evolved, unrhetorical form of sentence and paragraph.'[78] Voiced in the third person throughout, *Ecce Homo* has none of the directness of Renan's *Life*; the reader is neither invited to speculate on Christ's state of mind, nor to visualize the Palestinian landscape. Seen through Seeley's vision, Renan's poet-Christ becomes the somewhat less Romantic tutor-figure. The *Edinburgh Review* was typical of its time in accounting for these essential differences between Renan and Seeley in terms of national characteristics: where the Frenchman had approached his subject 'on the side of the Imagination', his English counterpart had produced a work which is 'undramatic' and 'characteristic of [...] the country whence it sprang'.[79] What were deemed English qualities in Seeley's work – austerity, temperance and quiet strength – largely coincided with the Victorian normative view of manliness. Gladstone admired the 'broad and masculine grasp' of *Ecce Homo*, with numerous other reviewers regarding it as a welcome corrective to Renan's feminizing of the Christian narrative.[80]

Hailed by the *Fortnightly Review* as the 'most important religious book that has appeared in England for a quarter of a century',[81] and described by Schweitzer as the 'classical liberal English life of Jesus', *Ecce Homo* was undoubtedly a work of great significance.[82] However, its impact can be attributed more to its omissions and ambivalences than to any more concrete qualities; as the author of the first comprehensive study of Seeley's life and work succinctly puts it 'one misses [...] a decisive yes or no'.[83] After giving the prefatory disclaimer that

'No theological questions whatever are here discussed', the argument that ensues refuses to come down on the side of either religion or science, the author at one point declaring that 'Both are true and both are essential to human happiness.'[84] Seeley assiduously avoids the New Testament debates of his day. He steers clear of discussing whether the Gospel miracles were true or imagined, opting instead to deal 'Provisionally [...] [with] them as real'[85] (a position that the *Westminster Review* judged worthy only of 'the official rhetoric of the less educated bishops'), and, most conspicuously of all, he omits any mention of the Passion, the most vehemently disputed area of the source texts.[86] This theological fence-sitting renders the work unusually open to interpretation, and critical responses did not always align neatly with denominational standpoints. While, for example, the Evangelical J. K. Glazebrook's condemnation of the work as one of the 'infidel publications of the day' was entirely predictable,[87] the praise heaped on the work by Gladstone, a High Churchman, was not.[88] As John Henry Newman so aptly put it in his review of the fifth edition of *Ecce Homo*, the onus is put upon the reader to decide whether Seeley is 'an orthodox believer on his road to liberalism, or a liberal on his road to orthodoxy'.[89] Indeed, *Ecce Homo* generated a formidable number of reviews and monographs by its very indeterminacy.[90] Lacking the scholarly rigour of Strauss and the populist appeal of Renan, and refusing to declare his views on issues as crucial as Christ's divinity, Seeley cannot be easily placed along the continuum of Lives of Jesus. There is no doubt, however, that the stir caused by the work's publication played a crucial role in further animating the quest for the historical Jesus. The title of Seeley's book, which had caused great offence to readers on account of what was then considered to be its pagan origins (Pilate was, after all, a Roman), reverberated in the titles of some of the responses it provoked. Works such as Joseph Parker's *Ecce Deus*, the 'ultra-Unitarian' *Ecce Veritas* and D. Melville Stewart's *Ecce Vir* ensured that the original title was kept in the public consciousness well into the twentieth century.[91]

Though Seeley's study no doubt influenced *what* was written about Jesus and his life, it had less effect on *how* they were presented, and Renan's *Life* remained the dominant stylistic model. While some of the more traditional elements of English society tried hard to ignore Renan's *Life of Jesus* in the vain hope that it might disappear back across the Channel, its imprint on British lives of Christ proved indelible.[92] One of the most intriguing aspects of Renan's influence is the way in which his style was more likely to be emulated by the orthodox writer than by the heterodox; indeed, rationalist writers such as Thomas Scott produced Lives of Jesus that self-consciously resisted the Frenchman's lyricism. Scott's *The English Life of Jesus*, as its title proclaims, is clearly aimed at supplying the nation's demand for its own study of the historical Jesus. Stylistically, it has all the austerity of Strauss and none of the warmth and antiquarian charm of Renan, features that may account for its limited readership and its never posing a serious challenge to Seeley's *Ecce Homo* as the definitive English Life. While it attracted compliments from some of the more liberal-minded clergymen, one of whom admired it for appealing to 'the English sense of truthfulness',[93] its style and method was, as one freethinker put it, too 'business-like' to hold much appeal for the general reader.[94] Where Renan appealed to the emotional empathy of his readers, Scott appealed to their sense of logic. In Scott's Life, the Passion narratives, heavily adorned and emotionally heightened by Renan and his imitators, are dismissed as typological reworkings of the Psalms; and where the French biographer fused the four-fold Gospel into a compelling drama, the English one insisted rather sourly that any 'attempt to harmonize the several contradictory narratives can produce only a ridiculous medley, which may be best compared to attempts to mingle oil and vinegar'.[95] For Scott, the New Testament already contained more than enough fiction – the Fourth Gospel being an egregious example – without writers on the life of Christ adding additional layers to it.[96] There is, indeed, a superciliousness of tone, verging on the puritanical, in Scott's writing that many readers must have found off-putting. His scepticism is expressed with palpable disdain, if not disgust: the early rationalist theory that Jesus might have been revived following his crucifixion is deemed to be 'not merely absurd but revolting' and the poetic qualities that even the most hardened unbeliever appreciated in the Gospel of John are dismissed as sophistic and elitist.[97] The overall impression the reader gains of the author of *The English Life of Jesus* is that of someone intent on reaffirming the unorthodox kernel of Renan's fundamentally Straussian argument, while resolutely refusing to imitate its stylistic flourishes.

There were, however, some biographers of Christ who were more than willing to match Renan's literary exuberance, especially when it was to beat him at his own game. One such was William Hanna, a Free Church of Scotland minister whose six-volume study of Christ was the most expansive British Life of Jesus published. Originating in a series of sermons, Hanna's work was entirely devotional in intention, his structural approach being to 'harmonize the accounts given by the different Evangelists [...] to construct a continuous narrative'.[98] In carrying out such an organization he shows a shrewd appreciation of the Gospels' potential for imaginative retelling. In terms more suited to the theatre than the pulpit, he refers in the preface to 'the motives and feelings of the different actors and spectators' of the New Testament and their place in the story of 'the great Central Character'.[99] His handling of the narrative lives up, in parts, to this promise of drama, particularly in the fifth volume, which is devoted to the Passion. With seemingly unconscious irony, Hanna dedicates much of the seventh chapter of this volume to warning the reader of the dangers of dramatic prose writings in his own highly dramatic prose. Taking Christ's instruction to the daughters of Jerusalem, 'do not weep for me' (Luke 23:28), as his text, Hanna interprets the phrase as warning against excessive emotionalism, in itself a form of 'selfish gratification'.[100] He moves on from this to express the traditional Protestant disapproval of 'indulging to excess the reading of exciting fiction – tales in which the hero of the story passes through terrible trials, endurances, agonies of mind and heart', going on to describe how 'our heart may pulsate all through with pity as we read' and how 'we may wet with tears the page that spreads out some heartrending scene'.[101] Here, Hanna's rousing language only serves to confirm the lure of such a mode of storytelling, and the reader cannot fail to notice the close parallels between his chosen fictional example and the harrowing crucifixion narrative that follows.

Though lacking the flair of Renan, Hanna's retelling of the Passion still manages to evoke the very sensations he advises his readers to resist. He spares no literary device when describing the darkness that, according to the synoptic Gospels, covers the earth as Jesus hangs on the cross:

Did it come slowly on, deepening and deepening till it reached its point of thickest gloom? or was it, as we incline to believe, as instantaneous in its entrance as its exit: at the sixth hour, covering all in a moment with its dark mantle; at the ninth hour, in a moment lifting that mantle off? Was it total or partial: a darkness deep as that of moonless, starless midnight, wrapping the cross so thickly round, that not the man who stood the nearest to it could see aught of the sufferer? Or was it the darkness of a hazy twilight obscuring but not wholly concealing, which left the upraised form of the Redeemer dimly visible through the gloom?[102]

There is certainly plenty here to get the Victorian reader's heart racing as Hanna leads him into the gloom of Golgotha. The posing of direct questions, lent emphasis by grammatical parallelism, activates the imagination, while the personification of the darkness with its 'entrance' and 'exit' lends it a certain self-conscious drama. Yet no sooner is the reader invited to consider just how much of Christ's suffering body an onlooker could make out through the gloom than he is made to feel his own vulgarity and baseness in even desiring to witness such a sight:

> Men gazed rudely on the sight, but the sun refused to look on it, hiding his face for a season. Men would leave the Crucified, exposed in shame and nakedness, to die; but an unseen hand was stretched forth to draw the drapery of darkness around the sufferer, and hide him from vulgar gaze.[103]

Here, Hanna cuts short the reader's imagination with the inept and simple-minded linking of the brutal realities of Roman crucifixion with an entirely supernatural event. Notwithstanding his ability to command the elemental forces of the universe, Hanna's God is Victorian to the core: as much concerned to protect his Son's sexual propriety as he is with expressing displeasure at his slaughter. In moving the spotlight away from the 'upraised form of the Redeemer' to the generic 'sufferer', Hanna employs Renan's grammatical trick of letting the general stand for the specific, a shift that serves to maintain a reverent distance between reader and sacred subject. That is not to say, however, that Hanna is willing to sacrifice the dramatic potential of Christ's final moments:

> A sudden change comes over his spirit. He ceases to think of, to speak with man. His eye closes upon the crowd that stands around. He is alone with the Father. A dark cloud wraps his spirit. He fears as he enters it.[104]

Here, then, the scene is brought back into close focus as the author works hard at stimulating the emotions of the reader through the use of the historic present tense and the accumulation of short, abrupt sentences, stripped of polysyllables. Almost a hundred pages on from this description, and still reluctant to leave the Passion narrative behind, Hanna once again encourages the reader to dwell on the crucifixion scene: 'The burial is over now, and we might depart; but let us linger a little longer, and bestow a parting look on the persons and the place, – the buriers and the burying-ground.'[105] Here, the author's direct address to the reader infuses the writing with a tone of confidentiality – not unlike that exploited by Renan – while his continued use of the present historic tense and his invitation to 'linger' at the death scene seems to once again lure the reader into an unseemly mawkishness.

By the end of the 1860s, works such as Hanna's were in plentiful supply. Indeed, one reviewer, writing in 1872, observed that 'Lives of Jesus multiply with a rapidity that makes hopeless all freshness, and very much worth. They simply repeat one another like sermons.'[106] This sounding of the death knell for the Lives of Jesus genre was, however, somewhat precipitate. Sensing that there was still a strong market for a Life of Jesus with popular appeal, the publishing company Cassell, Petter and Galpin approached Frederic William Farrar with a view to his producing for their readers 'a sketch of the Life of Christ on earth as should enable them to realise it more clearly, and to enter more thoroughly into the details and sequence of the Gospel narratives'.[107] The commission offered a generous payment for the completed work and expenses for an excursion to the Holy Land, the latter detail suggesting that the publishers were keen to replicate the immense success enjoyed by Renan's *Life*, with its sustained focus on Christ's homeland. Choosing Farrar was an astute move. Though by no means a prominent theologian, Farrar's posts as Chaplain to the Queen and headmaster of Marlborough College ensured that his name was familiar to the reading public; moreover, as the author of edifying novels about public school life, he had the credentials to appeal to a more traditional readership.[108] Farrar was doubtless aware of the challenge involved in writing a saleable Life of Jesus at a time when the genre seemed to be reaching its apex and responded to it with great ingenuity. Eager to appeal to the whole spectrum of readers, he made clear in his preface that he was writing both for 'the simple and the unlearned' and the 'professed theologian';[109] and while he insists that his Life is 'unconditionally the work of a believer', he is also keen to stress that it will not prove 'wholly valueless to any honest doubter who reads it in a candid and uncontemptuous spirit'.[110] To carry out his ambitious intentions, Farrar employs diverse methods of interpreting and presenting the Scriptures, calling upon the everyday logic of the rationalist, the linguistic skills of the translator and the literary flair of earlier writers to portray his essentially orthodox vision. At the same time, to demonstrate his knowledge of the Higher Criticism and Jewish Scripture and religious practice, he provides copious footnotes and a list of authorities so long that it prompted one reviewer to point out that, if Farrar had indeed read them all, then 'the duties of the masters of our public schools must be less onerous than has commonly been supposed'.[111]

The Life of Christ enjoyed instant success. The author's son noted in his 1905 biography of his father that:

> Twelve editions, at the rate of one a month, were exhausted in the first year of its publication. Since its first appearance the work has gone through thirty editions in England alone, has been 'pirated' in America, and has been translated into almost every European language, including two independent translations into Russian, and even into Japanese.[112]

Its popularity was no doubt aided by generally laudatory reviews that admired its deft combination of scholarship and piety; approval was even expressed by the Roman Catholic journal, the *Month*, which declared that 'there is more learning about it than about the pretentious flippancy of Rénan [sic]'.[113] It was a comparison that would have afforded Farrar a great deal of satisfaction: Renan was very much Farrar's *bête noire* and would remain so throughout his writing career. In the preface to *The Life of Christ* he warns the reader not to expect 'brilliant combinations of mythic cloud tinged by the sunset imagination of some decadent belief', an obvious jibe at Renan's *Life of Jesus*.[114] Twenty years later, he was still intent on castigating Renan for past crimes, whether denouncing the 'extreme [...] irreverence' of Godefroy Durand's illustrations to the popular edition of 1870,[115] or insisting that the author's work had 'failed to shake a general conviction'.[116]

Yet however contemptuous Farrar might have been of Renan's 'sunset imagination', his own book offers the reader a prose style every bit as vivid and effusive, an irony underscored by a significant number of reviewers. While a small minority of evangelicals took

Farrar to task for using inappropriately colloquial language to narrate the most sacred of lives, the vast majority of criticism was aimed at its flamboyance. The *Athenaeum* was one of the severest critics, judging the rhetoric of *The Life of Christ* 'excessive and artificial, often far-fetched and fanciful', and pitying a reader who, 'dazzled with the gaudy glitter, sighs for repose'.[117] Farrar's son recorded how 'the terms "florid" and "exuberant" have been recorded *ad nauseam*' in response to *The Life of Christ*, and this deriding of the aesthetics of the work seemed to stick in the critical consciousness.[118] Two decades on, in a review of Wilson Barrett's melodramatic Early Christian novel *The Sign of the Cross*, the critic comments that he had 'long feared that someone might arise who would oust the Dean from his proud pre-eminence in classical romance'.[119] Such criticism inevitably recalled that directed towards Renan, and Farrar would doubtless have been stung by the coincidence. In a letter to *Macmillan's Magazine*, written a year after the publication of his *Life*, Farrar defends himself against those reviewers who had accused him of depicting the crucifixion in a gratuitously gruesome manner, insisting that he had no intention 'to add, or to invent, one touch or colour of pain or dreadfulness'.[120] Indeed, throughout *The Life of Christ* Farrar vents his disapproval of all types of sensational writing associated with the Scriptures, accusing the authors of the Apocryphal Gospels of rendering Christ's boyhood 'portentous, terror-striking, unnatural, repulsive' in their over-imaginative writings.[121]

Notwithstanding Farrar's avowed distaste for stylistic over-indulgence, the popularity of *The Life of Christ* was due largely to its author's manipulation of imaginative detail and dramatic language. If anyone deserved the epithet 'the English Renan' it was Farrar, and not only for his literary style. While the orthodox Englishman differed radically from the Frenchman in his essential view of Jesus, he followed him in portraying a man who is sweet-natured, a uniquely gifted storyteller and a lover of nature. Making extensive use of Renan's habit of imaginative conjecture, Farrar's portrait of Christ is filled with the kind of everyday human detail he so admired in the paintings of Holman Hunt, to fill up what he describes in a later work as 'the interspaces of the eloquent silence of the Evangelists'.[122] Drawing on legends passed down through Church tradition, Farrar informs the reader of Jesus's physical appearance and his eating and sleeping habits; his hair 'the colour of wine, is parted in the middle of the forehead, and flows down over the neck' and his skin is 'of a more

Hellenic type than the weather-bronzed and olive-tinted faces of [...] His Apostles'; his diet is plain but healthy, consisting of 'bread of the coarsest quality, fish caught in the lake [...] and sometimes a piece of honeycomb'; and he has 'that blessing of ready sleep'.[123] But however much Farrar's characterization of Jesus might resemble Renan's in certain respects, he was mindful that *his* Christ could not be accused of the effeminacy so frequently identified in the French portrait.[124] In a manner anticipating the muscular Christianity of his friend Thomas Hughes, Farrar interprets Jesus's refusing of an opiate to ease his physical suffering on the cross as a sign of his masculinity, an act of 'sublimest heroism';[125] and where the Fourth Gospel simply reports that 'Jesus wept' (John 11:35) at the death of Lazarus, Farrar qualifies the phrase by adding that his tears were 'silent', the transferred epithet emphasizing the emotional restraint expected of the Victorian male.[126]

As with his methods of characterization, Farrar's editing and selection of his source material suggest the instinct of the popular novelist. Though departing from some of his more evangelical predecessors in admitting in the preface to *The Life of Christ* that a convincing harmony of the Gospels is both impossible and undesirable, he nevertheless follows Renan in selecting and shaping them so as to ensure maximum dramatic impact. Matthew's account of Pontius Pilate is chosen for the intriguing detail of his wife's dream; John's narration of the anointing of Christ's feet with costly ointment is chosen over those of the Synoptists as it features Mary, sister of Lazarus, already a distinctive character in the story, rather than the anonymous women of the other three versions. In other instances, Farrar conflates all four texts: for example, bringing together all the women said to be at the foot of Christ's cross in his re-imagining of the crucifixion scene.[127] In some respects, Farrar regarded his reshaping of the New Testament narratives as a means of making up for the artistic shortcomings of their original authors, mere recorders – as he saw them – of revelation. He explains to the reader that the rude simplicity of the Gospel accounts is in itself proof of their integrity and that men who 'were constantly taking His [Christ's] figurative expressions literally, and His literal expressions metaphorically' could hardly have been expected to produce sophisticated biographies of their Saviour.[128] Indeed, in a letter to *Macmillan's Magazine* he attests that Lives such as his are needed to add life and energy to the spare Gospel accounts of Christ's life 'often narrated without clear notes of time and place'.[129]

While Farrar repeatedly insists that New Testament stories 'transcend[s] all power of human imagination', he has no qualms about embellishing their typically stark outlines.[130] Take, for example, his recounting of the incident of the woman taken in adultery, for the Victorians one of the most revered texts of the Gospels. Told in a spare eight verses most commonly printed in the text of John's Gospel, the story was admired not only for the qualities of love and forgiveness that it illustrates, but also for its aesthetic grace.[131] Oscar Wilde, who gives his own succinct but nonetheless affecting version of the story in *De Profundis*, was among many of his generation who admired the restrained beauty of Christ's verbal challenge to the authorities.[132] In Farrar's own highly emotive reworking of the story, he goes all out to dramatize the scene. Where the King James version records how the woman is 'brought' before Jesus [John 8:3], Farrar describes how she is 'dragged' before him; where the original text leaves the reader to judge the behaviour of the scribes and the Pharisees, Farrar supplies him with a lexis of moral antithesis, leaving him no space to formulate his own mode of censure. The author juxtaposes the 'cold, hard cynicism' and 'graceless, pitiless, barbarous brutality' of the Jewish law with the 'stainless Innocence' of Christ. And while not omitting the woman's 'flagrant guilt', we are called upon to appreciate the 'moral torture' and 'superfluous horror' to which the woman is subjected by the religious authorities.[133] The energy and immediacy of the scene and its 'malignant mob' is conveyed through a long series of increasingly fervid questions, moving between reported and free indirect thought:

> Would He then acquit this woman, and so make Himself liable to an accusation of heresy, by placing Himself in open disaccord with the sacred and fiery Law? or, on the other hand, would He belie His own compassion, and be ruthless, and condemn? And if He did, would He not at once shock the multitude, who were touched by His tenderness, and offend the civil magistrates by making Himself liable to a charge of sedition? How could He possibly get out of the difficulty? Either alternative – heresy or treason, accusation before the Sanhedrin or delation to the Procurator [...] would serve equally well their unscrupulous intentions. And one of these, they thought, *must* follow. What a happy chance this weak, guilty woman had given them![134]

When the reader's attention is directed to Christ himself, the prose loses its hectic pace and frantic questions give way to composed certainties:

A sense of all their baseness, their hardness, their malice, their cynical parade of every feeling which pity would temper and delicacy repress, rushed over the mind of Jesus. He blushed for His nation, for His race; He blushed, not for the degradation of the miserable accused, but for the deeper guilt of her unblushing accusers.[135]

In taking care to attribute Jesus's blushing to his shame at his race and nation, and not to any kind of unease at the sexual nature of the sin, Farrar seems to be replying to J. R. Seeley's interpretation of the story in *Ecce Homo*, where the woman's being detected *'in the very act'* [author's italics] is seen to have discountenanced the celibate Jesus so that 'In his burning embarrassment and confusion he stooped down so as to hide his face, and began writing with his finger on the ground.'[136] It was a retelling that had provoked angry reactions in the periodical press, *The Quarterly Review*, for example, denouncing the author for 'the coarseness and latitude of the interpretation' of the incident.[137] Farrar's treatment of the story, then, still carries the shadow of previous treatments by other biographers, an intertextuality that underlines the significance of reader response for the development of the Lives of Jesus genre.

Farrar's predilection for highly emotive writing is nowhere more evident than in his retelling of the Passion narratives. In this description of the scourged Christ, Farrar's highly wrought prose serves to heighten the drama of the ordeal:

Around the brows of Jesus, in wanton mimicry of the Emperor's laurel, they twisted a green wreath of thorny leaves; in His tied and trembling hands they placed a reed for sceptre; from His torn and bleeding shoulders they stripped the white robe with which Herod had mocked Him – which must now have been all soaked with blood – and flung on Him an old scarlet paludament – some cast-off war cloak, with its purple laticlave, from the Praetorian wardrobe. This, with feigned solemnity, they buckled over His right shoulder, with its glittering fibula [...][138]

Here, the anaphoric structure of the lengthy sentence detailing the indignities being inflicted on the victim, along with the two parentheses, serves to emphasize Christ's dignified stillness before the mocking gaze of the spectators; and in the contrastingly short sentence that follows, the adjective 'glittering' is shocking in its incongruous modification of an open wound. A few pages on, the depiction of the actual crucifixion is as grisly and explicit as any to be found in medieval miracle plays:[139]

> His arms were stretched along the cross-beams; and at the very centre of the open palms, first of the right, then of the left hand, the point of a huge iron nail was placed, which, by the blow of a mallet, was driven home into the wood, crushing with excruciating pain, all the fine nerves and muscles of the hands through which they were driven. Then the legs were drawn down at full length: and through either foot separately, or possibly through both together as they were placed one over the other, another huge nail tore its way through the quivering and bleeding flesh.[140]

Perhaps anticipating the criticism this particular passage would receive in the journals of the day, Farrar adds a footnote justifying the violence of the description: 'I write thus because the familiarity of oft-repeated words prevents us from realising what crucifixion really was, and because it seems well that we *should* realise this.'[141] Though the Fourth Gospel is alone in explicitly signalling that Jesus was nailed to the cross, Farrar is content to give it precedence over the other three accounts for the sake of this arresting image of the torture and penetration of the sacred body.[142] And Farrar's fascination with the 'quivering flesh' of Christ continues to reveal itself in his description of the effects of crucifixion. Though ostensibly he itemizes the physical torments of the crucified in general, the reader is encouraged to imagine them as peculiar to the suffering Christ. The author paints in words an image reminiscent of that depicted in the early sixteenth-century painting by Matthias Grünewald of a torn and bleeding Man of Sorrows:

> The unnatural position made every movement painful; the lacerated veins and crushed tendons throbbed with incessant anguish; the wounds, inflamed by exposure, gradually gangrened; the arteries – especially of the head and stomach – became swollen and oppressed with surcharged blood.[143]

Farrar's writing here sensationalizes pain, the dense nature of the sentence serving to enmesh the reader as it recounts every torturous physical detail. Farrar toned down some of the more gruesome descriptions of the crucifixion in the revised edition of 1893, dispensing with some of the more gratuitously graphic images. In making such cuts, Farrar would appear to be practising what he went on to preach in his 1894 work, *The Life of Christ as Represented in Art*, in which he questions whether it 'be lawful to paint this subject at all'.[144] However, the reader already familiar with Farrar's description of the crucifixion cannot help but feel there is a certain irony in the author's admiration of Fra Angelico's restrained visual depiction of the crucified Christ:

> Next we notice the reverence and the good taste which shrank from the attempt at anatomic nudities, as much from the ignorant and ghastly profusion of blood. His object was not to exhibit the Crucifixion as a scene of torture on which men were to gaze with gloating and morbid curiosity [...][145]

If some of Farrar's more purple passages aimed at stirring emotional responses to the story of Christ's life, his liberal sprinkling of lines from the work of British poets, past and present, throughout his work seems intent on rousing a strong sense of national identity.[146] Quotations, some indirect, some direct, are placed within the text, often to reinforce a moral truth or to provide an apt parallel to a thought or deed of Jesus; others form the epigraphs that subscribe each chapter heading. Poets from previous centuries, such as Milton and Pope, share equal space with contemporary poets such as Browning, Clough and Tennyson. But it is Shakespeare who takes pride of place. Speeches from the major tragedies, and even a few of the comedies, find their way into almost every strand of the narrative. In some instances, the sources of these citations are stated; in others, only the playwright's words appear and it is left to the well-educated and literary reader to identify them.[147] This omnipresence of a playwright who had been regarded for over a century as emblematic of Englishness lends Farrar's *Life of Christ* a strong national identity, clearly distinguishing it from its Renanian predecessor.

As the best-selling English Life of Jesus, Farrar's work provided the model for the majority of orthodox studies of Christ up to the close of the century (as well as proving popular as wedding and christening gifts). Farrar had proved beyond any doubt that the public appetite for Lives of Jesus was far from sated, and numerous writers continued to exploit the genre. However, only those authors capable of emulating Farrar's artful fusion of orthodoxy and popular appeal attracted any significant readership. Two such were Cunningham Geikie and Alfred Edersheim, both of whom wrote lengthy studies of Jesus that attracted a wide readership. The first of these to be published, Geikie's *The Life and Words of Christ* (1877), replicates Farrar's *Life* in its evocation of Palestinian landscape, politics, religious ritual and family life, and in its listing of theological authorities. It also follows Farrar in regarding Jesus as part of a literary elite. Geikie insists that 'We all know how lowly a reverence is paid to Him in passage after passage by Shakespere [*sic*], the greatest intellect known', and extends the list of Christ's admirers to include Europeans such as Goethe and Rousseau.[148] And though not quite as extravagant in its style as Farrar's *Life*, it succeeds in rewriting the Gospel stories in a manner guaranteed to appeal more to the reader of historical romance than to the scholar. Geikie's retelling of the Passion narratives in particular owes much to his forefather: the body of his scourged Christ is also a 'quivering' mass of broken flesh and the reader is not spared the graphic detailing of the impact of iron nails being driven through 'sensitive nerves and sinews', and the 'intolerable thirst, and ever-increasing pain' that ensued.[149]

Published six years after Geikie's *Life*, Alfred Edersheim's *The Life and Times of Jesus the Messiah* promised to depart somewhat from Farrar's model in its foregrounding of Judaic cultural, social and religious customs. In the preface to the work he states that 'since Jesus of Nazareth was a Jew, spoke to, and moved among Jews [...] it was absolutely necessary to view that Life and Teaching in all its surrounding of place, society, popular life, and intellectual or religious development'.[150] Of Jewish parentage (Edersheim embraced Christianity in 1846), Edersheim's religious upbringing doubtless provided him with insight and knowledge unavailable to cradle-Christians, and his contextualizing of the life of Jesus gained him high praise from William Sanday, one of the most prominent theologians of the day. Sanday, who undertook the completion of the abridged edition of the work, cut short by Edersheim's death, prefaces the volume with the observation that no one other than the author has shown 'such a profound and masterly knowledge of the whole Jewish background presented in the Gospels'.[151] Yet despite this change of emphasis and the author's denial in the preface to the first edition of 'any pretence [...] to write a "Life of Christ" in the strict sense',[152] it conforms in most senses to the pattern of its forerunners, not least in its evocative prose and liberal use of conjecture, demonstrated in its retelling of the anointing of Christ:

> As she stood behind Him at His Feet, reverently bending, a shower of tears, like sudden, quick summer-rain, that refreshes air and earth, 'bedewed' His Feet. As if surprised, or else afraid to awaken His attention, or defile Him by her tears, she quickly wiped them away with the long tresses of her hair that had fallen down and touched Him [...] And, now that her faith has grown bold in His Presence, she is continuing to kiss those Feet which had brought to her the 'good tidings of peace', and to anoint them out of the *alabastron* round her neck.[153]

So, while Edersheim dismissed Renan's *Life of Jesus* as 'frivolous and fantastic', he, like Farrar before him, owed its author a considerable debt of gratitude for providing a highly successful stylistic model.[154]

Considering the sheer volume of Lives of Jesus, it is unsurprising that a large number of them are undistinguished and formulaic. Indeed, Oscar Wilde's declaration that the quality of a book, like that of wine, can be judged by a brief 'tasting' proves particularly apt when surveying the corpus of Victorian Lives.[155] It is rarely necessary to venture much beyond a Life's preface in order to establish the author's religious stance, the other Lives he intends to flatter, deride or counter, and the image of Christ he intends to project. By the end of the nineteenth century, interest in the historical Jesus, and the innumerable Lives that sprang from it, were in a steady decline. Farrar's *The Life of Lives, Further Studies in the Life of Christ*, published in 1900, did not sell well, despite its author's well-established reputation, and it must have been clear to any writers still intent on presenting the life of Christ that they would need to seek out innovative ways to do so.[156] Alfred E. Garvie, for example, remarks somewhat wearily in the preface to his *Studies in the Inner Life of Jesus* (1907) that 'enough is being written about the scenery, the upholstery and drapery of the life of Jesus', and chooses instead – as his title announces – to concentrate on the psychology of his subject.[157] Likewise, in *The Galilean* (1892), the Unitarian author Walter Lloyd aims 'rather to draw a portrait than to write a history, and, by clearing away the accumulations of centuries, to see what manner of man Jesus of Nazareth was'.[158] This shift in emphasis had already been identified by the Scottish Free

Church pastor James Stalker, in an article entitled 'Our present knowledge of the life of Christ', published in the *Contemporary Review* at the turn of the century.[159] Stalker, himself the author of a brief and uncontroversial Life of Jesus, remarked on how 'study is moving on from the story of Jesus to His mind'.[160] But if approaches to Jesus were changing, interest in him as a person persisted well into the new century. Works such as T. R. Glover's *The Jesus of History*, published in 1917, would continue the tradition of liberal Lives of Jesus, with its clear, readable prose and its appended 'Suggestions for Study Circle Discussions'. Outlined in this appendix are questions such as 'Was Jesus fond of life and Nature?', 'Had Jesus a sense of humour?', and 'What do you imagine Jesus looked like?', answers to which could have been found by looking back to the works of Farrar *et al.*[161]

The first two decades of the twentieth century would see a significant shift in New Testament theology, as form critics such as Rudolf Bultmann moved the emphasis away from the Jesus of history. Yet if theologians turned their attentions away from historical and biographical studies of the Gospels, there were still plenty of non-specialists willing to help the Life of Jesus genre limp into the twentieth century. The by now well-established idea of the Bible as a literary text freed authors with little or no theological training to treat the subject of Christ. John Middleton Murry, for example, pronounces his skills as a literary critic to be the 'equivalent of the more specialised training of the professor of divinity', before attempting to plug the one gap he perceives in the long history of Gospel biography: Jesus as man of genius. Abandoning all scholarly paraphernalia, Murry attempts to dissuade the reader from accepting modernist visions of Jesus as an obscure figure, steeped in an eschatological mode of thought inaccessible to twentieth-century minds. In this, as in several other respects, Murry's work steps back from perceived advances in theological approaches to the Gospels to produce a somewhat universalized figure, removed from his immediate context. Replacing scholarly detail and insight with the artistic licence of the literary writer, Murry abandons the conjectural grammar of the biographer, telling us as if for a certainty that Jesus played in the streets with his friends, watched the dough rise in the family home and learnt the hardships of poverty. And while disassociating himself from the rationalizing tendencies of former Lives, Murry speculates that Jesus's unusually quick death on the cross could be accounted for by his weak constitution, a consequence of poor nourishment as a child. Though striving to write something fresh and original, Murry did little more than produce a work that read like a nostalgic backward glance at over a century's worth of Lives of Jesus: a sure sign that semi-fictional treatments of the Life of Christ had long since had their day.

In *The Quest of the Historical Jesus*, Schweitzer comes to the conclusion that 'There is nothing more negative than the result of the critical study of the Life of Jesus' and that 'the historical Jesus will be to our time a stranger and an enigma'.[162] It is a somewhat bleak, if ultimately judicious, appraisal of the several decades spent attempting to draw the figure of Christ closer to the popular mind. Rather than providing a more realistic portrayal of Jesus, attempts to fill in what James Stalker termed the 'folds and wrinkles' left by the Evangelists' testimonies had developed into a form of biblical fiction, with only the authors' intentions and critical paraphernalia anchoring the work within the realm of non-fiction.[163] In this respect, Lives of Jesus, whatever their theological shortcomings, loosened ethical restraints on the imaginative treatment of the Gospel narratives, preparing the ground for entirely fictional representations of Christ.

Secularists, spiritualists and pseudo-evangelists: some 'alternative' Lives of Jesus

As the popularity of the liberal Lives of Jesus began to wane, so there developed a variety of 'alternative' versions of the New Testament narratives. These can be loosely divided into two main categories: those that were atheist in conviction and highly irreverent in intention, style and presentation, and those that made spurious claims to be recently discovered documents of Christian antiquity. The coincidence in the early 1880s of the decline of Lives of Jesus and the emergence of rather more subversive narratives of Christ springs from a complex combination of factors. First among these was a slow but steady redefinition of the profane, a redefinition that allowed Jesus to become an acceptable figure for debate, imaginative recreation and historical enquiry.

Standing staunchly at the extreme end of the debates surrounding the historical Jesus were Secularists such as G. W. Foote, whose scabrous reworkings of the Bible circulated throughout the 1880s. A Nietzschean *avant la lettre*, Foote characterized Christ as 'a tame, effeminate, shrinking figure', in opposition to the majority of agnostics who still held up the person of Jesus as a pattern of perfection for all men to follow.[164] He subjected both Old and New Testament texts to a variety of generic transformations: Bible stories appeared in the form of cartoons, salacious poems and jokes, and perhaps most memorably, in the grotesque outlines of comic woodcuts.[165] Exuberantly vulgar, Foote's recreation of the Scriptures stripped away all gravity and portentousness. Even the apocalyptic visions of the book of Revelation are reduced to the dream-vision of a terminally ill Jehovah, taking his son to task for only recruiting 'weak, slavish, flabby souls', while Satan manages to attract the 'best workers and thinkers'.[166] One particularly audacious venture of Foote's was his investigation into the 'missing years' of Jesus's youth through an epistolary format. In *Letters to Jesus Christ*, Foote employs relentless comic bathos to mock the very concept of divinity. In these pithily colloquial letters, Jesus is asked to reflect on his early years and answer questions such as 'Did God howl when he was pricked by a nasty pin?', 'Did God kick and squeal in his bath?' and 'Did God play at marbles and make mud-pies?'[167]

What has often gone unacknowledged in studies of Foote's burlesques of the Old and New Testaments is his debt to his Continental counterpart, the French writer, freethinker and conspiracy theorist Gabriel-Antoine Jogand-Pagés who, under the pen-name Léo Taxil, founded an anti-clerical publishing house.[168] His *Vie de Jésus*, first published in 1882, is a crude parody of French Lives of Christ, featuring lewd woodcuts accompanied by a bawdy prose narrative.[169] In its preface, Taxil reduces a century of theological wrangling about the true nature of Jesus to three terse propositions: he was God incarnate; he was a Jewish agitator; or he was a complete invention of his disciples, intent on creating a new religion. Declaring himself unequivocally a supporter of the third position, he sets out to demonstrate that 'l'histoire de Jésus-Christ [...] n'est qu'un tissu de fables immorales et stupides' [the story of Jesus Christ is nothing but a weaving together of stupid, immoral fables].[170] Such impious productions gained some notoriety in Britain and were alluded to with some frequency in prose fictions of the 1880s. In his novel *Thyrza* (1887), George Gissing draws attention to such crude traducing of the Scriptures through one character's account of a ten-year-old girl being sent a biblical burlesque by her atheist working-class father, compelling the reader to consider the effects of such writings on the young and impressionable.[171] Published a year later, Mrs Humphry Ward's novel *Robert Elsmere* makes reference to working men reading *The Comic Life of Christ*, which 'contained a caricature of the Crucifixion, the scroll emanating from Mary Magdalene's mouth, in particular, containing obscenities which cannot be quoted here'.[172] Any reader intent on discovering what such 'obscenities' might have been would have needed to look no further than the writings of Taxil; his illustrated Life of Jesus, for example, pictures the mother of Christ being amorously fondled by the Angel Gabriel, depicting her, a few pages on, heavily pregnant, declaring to her husband 'C'est le pigeon, Joseph!' [Oh, but it was the pigeon, Joseph!] (a joke repeated numerous times in James Joyce's *Ulysses*).

While Secularists pushed the life of Jesus further and further into the realms of fiction, so others endeavoured to return it to historical fact, albeit radically reconfigured. Thanks to the developing field of archaeology, the mid-to-late nineteenth century saw the discovery of a number of early Christian documents, most significantly the *Codex Sinaiticus* in 1859 and, in the 1890s, the Oxyrhynchus Papyri, which provided new extra-canonical writings about the historical Jesus. Such discoveries were amply reported in the periodical press, provoking a good deal of speculation about the potential discovery of hitherto suppressed or discarded accounts of the life of Christ or, indeed, an entire fifth testament. Such a climate was ripe, then, for the circulation of a number of pseudo-gospels, claiming to provide details of those years of Jesus's life unreported in the New Testament accounts. One example, Nicolas Notovitch's *The Unknown Life of Christ*, translated into English from the French in 1895, provided an intriguing, if entirely spurious, account of Jesus's life between the ages of fifteen and thirty.[173] Another, *The Aquarian Gospel of Jesus the Christ* by Levi H. Dowling, related the life of Jesus in 182 chapters, beginning with the birth and childhood of Mary Virgin and ending with the establishment of the 'Christine Church'.[174] While such works offered little to interest the serious biblical scholar, they proved to have a substantial shelf life, their circulation encouraged no doubt by the contemporary fascination with spiritualism and the occult. Where the majority of liberal Lives of Jesus had kept flights of fictional fancy within the borders of the established canonical Gospels, works such as Dowling's and Notovitch's offered readers the opportunity to find out about Christ's supposed travels in India, Tibet, Persia, Greece and Egypt, and his various encounters with Eastern religions. Furthermore, these writings made grand claims to authenticity. Notovitch's account of Jesus's life is purported to have been taken down from a hitherto undiscovered gospel, and Dowling's is based on the 'Akashic Records' transmitted from the Supreme Intelligence thorough the author's own mediumship.

The vast majority of Victorian Lives of Jesus had grappled self-consciously with the historical distance between the time of Christ and that of the contemporary reader; indeed, the desire to revivify the Scriptures for the modern age was often at the heart of these productions, and warmly expressed in their copious prefaces. As far as those works masquerading as ancient sources are concerned, however, we can only conclude that the intentions of the authors were altogether less genuine. Circulating widely in Europe and the United States, these fraudulent publications grew ever more outlandish as the twentieth century wore on. One American scholar, Edgar Goodspeed, dismayed at the increasing number of apocryphal testaments in circulation, took it upon himself to expose the fictitious nature of such texts. Published in 1931, *Strange New Gospels* endeavours to protect those readers 'far removed from scholarly circles' from taking false hope from 'mischievous little books'.[175] Describing the texts that form the focus of his discussion as 'a strange netful, dredged up from obscure depths', Goodspeed brings together a motley collection of writings about various aspects of Jesus's life, outlining their frequently bizarre contents before submitting them to the rigours of academic scholarship. Dealing in the opening chapters with the relatively well-known alternative gospels of Notovitch and Dowling, Goodspeed goes on to discuss some even more outlandish examples of Christian fakery such as the 'Letter of Jesus Christ'. Goodspeed notes that this document appeared in the *Chicago Evening Post* in May 1917, as well as being found 'framed on the walls of people of more piety than intelligence'.[176] While he goes on to explain that he has not been able to find out any details about the letter's provenance, he estimates that it 'seems to have originated in England, forty or more years ago'. In fact, the letter was circulating in published form a good deal earlier than this. Several copies are held by the British Library, one dating as far back as 1724, the introduction to which reads:

And found 18 miles from Iconium, 65 Years after our Blessed SAVIOUR's Crucifixion: Transmitted from the Holy City by a Converted Jew: Faithfully translated from the Original Hebrew

Copy, now in the Possession of the Lady CUBA's Family at Mesopotamia. This Letter was written by JESUS CHRIST, and found under a great Stone both round and large, at the Foot of the Cross, 18 Miles from Iconium, near a Village called Mesopotamia. Upon the Stone was Written and Engraven, 'Blessed is he that shall turn me over'. All People that saw it Prayed to God earnestly, and desired that he would make known to them the Meaning of this Writing that they might not Attempt in vain to turn it over. In the mean time there came a little Child, about six or seven Years old, and turned it over without Help, to the Admiration of all People that stood by; and under this Stone was found a Letter, written by JESUS CHRIST, which was carried to the City of Iconium, and there published, by a Person belonging to the Lady Cuba, and on the Letter was written: The commandment of JESUS CHRIST, Signed by the Angel Gabriel, 98 Years after our Saviour's Birth.

What is represented here is a forgery seemingly borne out of the desire to endow Jesus with his own text, his own 'commandments', which would, once and for all, confirm his status as the son of God. The letter itself, however, falls some way short of living up to the imaginative potential of such a document. The Jesus who speaks out of this jeremiad is a hard and fast Puritan, who exhorts the reader to 'go to Church, and keep the Lord's Day Holy, without doing any manner of Work'; he warns them against the dangers of 'costly Apparel and vain Dresses', and commands fasting on five Fridays in every year 'in remembrance of the five bloody wounds [I] receiv'd for all mankind'. Bearing little resemblance to the meek and mild figure of the Gospels, this Jesus warns unbelievers to expect plagues that will 'consume both him, and his Children and his Cattle'; while those who invest in a copy of the letter to hang in their houses are promised that 'nothing shall hurt them; neither Pestilence, Lightening, nor Thunder [...] And if a Woman be with Child and in Labour [...] she shall safely be delivered of her birth.' Signing off until the Day of Judgement, the letter-writer leaves the recipient with one final piece of advice: 'All Goodness and Prosperity shall be in the house where a Copy of this Letter shall be found.'[177] What this document amounts to is an early eighteenth-century example of pressure-selling, risible in its failure to even attempt to create an authentic voice or any other form of verisimilitude (other than repeating numerous times that it was, indeed, written by Jesus himself). The letter remained in print in Britain throughout

the nineteenth century, inaccurate copying leading to frequent variations on the so-called facts of the discovery. Though a text of such
arrant speciousness would certainly not have passed the increasingly
sceptical scrutiny of biblical scholarship, for the credulous and superstitious it offered a relatively trouble-free means of protecting against
the ills and evils of everyday life.

Also featured in Goodspeed's hall of fakes is *Crucifixion, by an Eye
Witness* (1907). Claiming to be an account of the Passion narratives,
written down seven years after the event, this letter is a somewhat
prosaic reworking of the long-established theory that Christ did not
actually die on the cross but was in truth resuscitated by his followers.
As with all such 'revelatory' writings, the reader looking for a definitive statement on Christ's death and resurrection will find only
historical dubiety, anachronism and a complete lack of scholarly
rigour. In this particular instance, the original document is untrace-
able, its provenance unknown and it is, somewhat improbably, said to
have been composed in Latin. There are places where the editor makes
an ineffectual attempt to convince the reader of its authenticity,
drawing his attention to 'a large vacant place in the document, caused
by the destroying influence of time'.[178] Equally unconvincing is the
editor's contention that the first printed copies of the letter, published
in 1873, were all destroyed, save for one, which 'found its way into the
possession of a prominent Mason in the state of Massachusetts'.[179] It
was a conspiracy theory that would grow more and more outlandish
over time, with the editor of a 1925 publication of the letter claiming
that the document 'created such a stir among the Christian circles that
they seized every available copy and destroyed it'.[180] The contents and
style of the crucifixion account are no more convincing: the narrative
of events seems to rely heavily on the Gospels (even referring directly
to Mark and Luke at one point), though the letter is said to anticipate
these canonical accounts by more than half a century. As Goodspeed
wryly points out, this particular fabrication proves that 'Ignorance is
as difficult to pretend as knowledge.'[181] And though the writer moves
away from the Gospel narratives to pursue the idea that Jesus spent the
six months between his crucifixion and his eventual death living in a
brotherhood of Essenes, a community that had shaped his thinking
and behaviour from childhood, he does so only to follow in the footsteps of early rationalists such as Bahrdt and Venturini, both of whom
had argued that Jesus survived the cross and had lifelong connections
with Essenism.

The rag-bag of documents considered by Goodspeed never found their way into the mainstream of religious discourse. Having only the most tenuous claim to authenticity, they proved no more than a minor irritant to serious biblical scholars, while their often heretical contents ensured that they would never replace the established Lives of Jesus, whose readers tended to cling to the stability and reassurance that they offered. On the other hand, those readers who sought fresh and challenging perspectives on the life of Christ could look to the New Testament novels that entered the literary marketplace in the late 1870s, which, in contrast to the pseudo-gospels, declared their fictitiousness plainly and honestly through their form. Nonetheless, the contribution of these 'alternative' records of the life of Jesus in the development of New Testament fiction was by no means insignificant. Some of them circulated for several decades, helping to keep alive theories and conjectures long since dismissed by the academic community. In this respect they set up a kind of counter-culture, which swam against the tide of both modern theological thought and traditional Christianity, and which would serve as a catalyst to some of the most significant imaginative reconfigurations of the Scriptures published in the late nineteenth and early twentieth century.

Notes

1   The year 1778 is generally regarded as the start of the quest for the historical Jesus; it was in this year that G. E. Lessing published an extract from a work by Hermann Samuel Reimarus, the theologian usually credited with being the first to investigate the historicity of Christ and the Gospels. While Lessing was prevented by the censor from publishing any further extracts, the first publication, '*Von dem Zwecke Jesu und seiner Jünger.' Noch ein Fragment des Wolfenbüttelschen Ungenannten* (Brunswick, 1778), remained a source of inspiration for later writers.

2   Albert Schweitzer, *The Quest of the Historical Jesus*, ed. John Bowden (London: SCM Press, 1st complete edn, 2000). Schweitzer's book is the first major study of the critical research into the historical Jesus carried out in Europe in the nineteenth century. The first edition of the work was published in 1906 (Tübingen) and was translated into English by W. Montgomery (London: Adam & Charles Black, 1910). In the late 1990s John Bowden and Susan Cupitt, in preparing a complete edition of the work, found the translation to be unreliable, and they were obliged to revise it extensively. In the light of this, subsequent citations from *The Quest* will refer to the 2000 edition which includes Schweitzer's extensive additions of 1913, hitherto untranslated.

3   In the Introduction to *Jesus* (Englewood Cliffs: Prentice Hall, 1967), Hugh Anderson states that 'All the Gospel materials bearing on the life of Jesus were so

assiduously studied by liberal Protestant theologians that within the space of a few generations, some sixty thousand biographies, so it is estimated, had been produced' (p. 16). Anderson gives no details regarding the provenance of the estimate, nor does he seem to include the very considerable number of Catholic Lives that were written in the later decades of the century. Both omissions render the figure of 60,000 somewhat dubious. The estimate is, nonetheless, reiterated by Warren S. Kissinger in *The Lives of Jesus* (New York and London: Garland Publishing, 1985), p. xi.

4 Elizabeth Stuart Phelps, *The Story of Jesus Christ* (London: Sampson Low, Marston, 1897), p. vii.

5 For a full account of Strauss's clash with the university authorities, see Chapter 8 of Horton Harris's *David Friedrich Strauss and his Theology* (Cambridge: Cambridge University Press, 1973).

6 David Friedrich Strauss, *The Life of Jesus*, trans. unknown, 4 vols (Birmingham: Taylor, 1842), I, p. vi.

7 Eliza Lynn Linton, *The Autobiography of Christopher Kirkland*, 3 vols (London: Richard Bentley and Son, 1885), III, p. 82.

8 Mrs Humphry Ward, *Robert Elsmere*, 3 vols (London: Smith, Elder, 1888), II, p. 16.

9 George R. Gissing, *Workers in the Dawn*, 3 vols (London: Remington, 1880), I, pp. 301–02.

10 David Friedrich Strauss, *The Life of Jesus Critically Examined*, translated from the fourth German edition [by Mary Ann Evans], 3 vols (London: Chapman, Brothers, 1846), I, p. 19.

11 *Christian Observer*, 'Strauss's Life and Times of Ulrich von Hutten', 74 (October 1874), pp. 892–908 (p. 893).

12 Strauss, *Life of Jesus*, I, p. 84. The term 'fiction' is, of course, a semantically complex one and continues to be a site of considerable dispute, especially in the field of critical theory. It is reasonable to assume that one of the term's meanings – imaginary prose narrative – was settled by the late nineteenth century, when works such as Henry James's *The Art of Fiction*, published in 1884, employed it to signify a stable generic classification. Use of the term in its pejorative sense remained – and remains – common, especially among the more evangelical denominations.

13 Strauss, *Life of Jesus*, I, p. 54.

14 Strauss, *Life of Jesus*, I, pp. 81–82.

15 Strauss, *Life of Jesus*, I, p. 83.

16 Strauss, *Life of Jesus*, I, p. 84.

17 *The Westminster and Foreign Quarterly Review*, 47 (April 1847), pp. 136–74 (p. 138).

18 Frederic W. Farrar, *History of Interpretation* (London: Macmillan, 1886), pp. 413, 417.

19 David Friedrich Strauss, *A New Life of Jesus*, Authorized Translation, 2 vols (London: Williams and Norgate, 1865), I, p. viii; translated from *Das Leben Jesu für das deutsche Volk bearbeitet* (Leipzig, 1864). In the preface, Strauss states: 'I write especially for the use of laymen, and have taken particular pains that no single sentence shall be unintelligible to any educated or thoughtful person; whether professional theologians also choose to be among my readers is to me a matter of

indifference' (I, p. vii).

20 Ernest Renan, *Vie de Jésus* (Paris: Michel Lévy, 1863). The sales of *Vie* outstripped all expectations; one month after its publication in June 1863, Renan's publisher wrote to him: 'La *Vie de Jésus* continue à s'enlever comme du pain! Je compte mettre en vente la 5ᵉ édition avant la fin de cette semaine' [The *Life of Jesus* continues to sell like hot cakes ! I expect to put the fifth edition on sale before the end of the week]. See *Lettres inédites de Ernest Renan à ses éditeurs Michel & Calmann Lévy*, ed. Jean-Yves Mollier (Paris: Calmann-Lévy, 1986), p. 51, n. 4. The work went through 13 editions in the year following its publication, reaching its 61st edition by 1921. The 'édition populaire' sold even more successfully, going through 130 editions by 1921. The most significant revision was that undertaken for the 13th edition of 1864, wherein Renan explained his position on the Fourth Gospel, admitting that his original stance had been flawed. For bibliographical details of Renan's *Vie* and other writings, see *Bibliographie des oeuvres de Ernest Renan*, ed. Henri Girard and Henri Moncel (Paris: Presses Universitaire de France, 1923).

21 The first English translation was *The Life of Jesus*, trans. unknown (London: Trübner, 1864); hereinafter, all citations are taken from this edition. It is evident from Renan's correspondence that the production of the first English translation was fraught with difficulties. The enormous attention afforded to the work on its publication meant that more and more newspapers and reviews began to print unauthorized and inaccurate translations of the original. For this reason alone, Renan was keen to get a sound English translation to press as soon as possible and, fearing his English was not good enough to judge the quality of the translation, he was especially anxious to employ a distinguished man of letters whom he could trust to capture the style of the original work, and who was *au courant* with biblical studies. His first three choices for the job were the English theologian Edward Higginson, the linguist and traveller Sir John Bowring, and the journalist George Augustus Sala, none of whom was able to undertake the work. After a good deal of negotiation, the first English translation was eventually carried out by Henry Harris, an acquaintance of Renan's, who had published several works on religious topics. Renan was keen that this first, rather hasty, translation should not bear the name of the translator and that the door should remain open for future translations by more esteemed literary figures. For fuller details of the negotiations concerning the first English translation of *Vie*, see *Lettres inédites de Ernest Renan*, pp. 50–69.

22 Strauss, *A New Life of Jesus*, I, p. xviii.

23 *Edinburgh Review*, 119 (April 1864), pp. 574–604 (p. 575).

24 In the opening paragraph of *The Quest*, Schweitzer states: 'German theology will stand out as a great, a unique phenomenon in the mental and spiritual life of our time' (p. 3). In a later chapter devoted to Renan, Schweitzer accuses the Frenchman of sacrificing scholarship for the sake of popular appeal (Ch. 13).

25 Ernest Renan, *Studies of Religious History*, trans. Henry F. Gibbons (London: William Heinemann, 1893), p. 119.

26 Renan, *Life of Jesus*, pp. 31, 32. In harmonizing the Gospels, Renan was practising an art that went back as far as the second century when the Syriac *Diatessaron*, compiled by Tatian, incorporated the four accounts of Christ's life into one. For a discussion of Bible harmonies, see R. M. Grant, *The Earliest Lives of Jesus*

(London: SPCK, 1961).

27 The nineteenth-century debates over the generic identity of the Gospels have continued into the present century and current thinking seems to favour Renan's position. In his influential study of the genre of the Gospels, Richard A. Burridge states that 'The study of the genre of the gospels appears to have gone round in a full circle over the last century or so of critical scholarship. The nineteenth-century assumption about the gospels as biographies is explicitly denied by the scholarly consensus of most of the twentieth century. In recent years, however, a biographical genre has begun to be assumed once more.' See Richard A. Burridge, *What Are the Gospels?* (Grand Rapids, MI, and Cambridge: William B. Eerdman's Publishing Company, 2004), p. 3.

28 Strauss, *A New Life of Jesus*, I, p. 3.

29 Indeed, Renan's work is still regarded as one of the finest of its genre. The theologian and cleric Stephen Neill describes Renan's work as 'by far the greatest of all the imaginative lives of Jesus'. See *The Interpretation of the New Testament 1861–1986*, ed. Stephen Neill and Tom Wright (Oxford: Oxford University Press, 2nd edn, 1988), p. 207.

30 Arnold, *Literature and Dogma*, in *Complete Prose Works*, VI, p. 158.

31 For a discussion of the responses to Renan's *Life of Jesus* in Britain, see Daniel L. Pals, *The Victorian "Lives" of Jesus* (San Antonio, TX: Trinity University Press, 1982), pp. 31–39.

32 Cited in Albert L. Guérard's *French Prophets of Yesterday* (London: T. Fisher Unwin, 1913), p. 236.

33 One of Renan's detractors, the artist William Holman Hunt, whose representation of Christ in his painting 'The Light of the World' was one of the best known of the Victorian age, regarded Renan's *Life of Jesus* as revealing a 'lack of imagination concerning the profundity and sublimity of the mind and purpose of Jesus'. See *Pre-Raphaelitism and the Pre-Raphaelite Brotherhood*, 2 vols (London: Macmillan, 1905), II, p. 409.

34 Ernest Renan, *The Hibbert Lectures 1880s*, trans. Charles Beard (London: Williams and Norgate, 1885), p. 210.

35 M. J. Lagrange, *Christ and Renan*, trans. Maisie Ward (London: Sheed & Ward, 1928), p. 1.

36 Edward W. Said, *Beginnings: Intention and Method* (New York: Basic Books 1975), p. 215.

37 Ben Pimlott, 'Brushstrokes', in *Lives for Sale: Biographers' Tales*, ed. Mark Bostridge (London: Continuum, 2004), p. 165.

38 Hans W. Frei, *The Eclipse of Biblical Narrative* (New Haven and London: Yale University Press, 1974), p. 16.

39 As the popularity of Renan's *Life* grew, so such critical apparatus tended to be removed from the text, either to enhance its appeal to the general reader or to fit within the limits set down by the publisher. For example, the translator of the Scott Edition of the work, William G. Hutchison, explains in his preface how the original appendix and notes had been omitted to conform to the limits of the series. See the Translator's Preface in *Renan's Life of Jesus*, trans. William G. Hutchison (London: Walter Scott, 1897).

40 Renan, *Life of Jesus*, p. 53.

41 Renan, *Life of Jesus*, p. 266.

42 Renan, *Life of Jesus*, p. 291.

43 Madame James Darmesteter [Mary F. Robinson], *The Life of Ernest Renan* (London: Methuen, 1897), p. 165.

44 For a detailed survey of evangelical accounts and interpretations of the Holy Land, see John Pemble, *The Mediterranean Passion* (Oxford: Oxford University Press, 1988), pp. 182–96.

45 'The Exploration of Palestine', *London Quarterly Review*, 45 (January 1876), pp. 277–322 (p. 277).

46 Surveying the first nine years of the PEF's work, its Honorary Secretary, Sir George Grove, wrote that the Fund's purpose was to throw light on biblical history so that 'faith is strengthened and reverence increased'. See the Committee of the Palestine Exploration Fund, *Our Work in Palestine* (London: Bentley & Son, 1873), p. 13.

47 Images such as that found in William Holman Hunt's painting *The Scapegoat* (1854–45), which features the rocks of Usdum on the Red Sea, thought to be the site of God's destruction of Sodom and Gomorrah, are bleak representations of the wages of sin and are typical of the evangelical practice of fusing geographical realities with biblical typology. Protestant travel writers often interpreted their observations of the Holy Land in terms of crime and punishment; John Aiton, a Presbyterian minister, described Jerusalem as 'drear and forsaken, blighted and cursed by the Almighty, for the enormous wickedness of which it had been the scene'. See John Aiton, *The Lands of the Messiah, Mahomet, and the Pope* (Edinburgh: A. Fullarton, 1852), p. 173.

48 Renan, *The Life of Jesus*, p. 122.

49 Renan, *The Life of Jesus*, pp. 74–75.

50 Edmond de Pressensé was himself a contributor to the Lives of Jesus genre. In his orthodox *Jesus Christ: His Times, Life, and Work*, trans. Annie Harwood (London: Jackson, Walford & Hodder, 1866), de Pressensé eschews Renanian methods, making little reference to the Eastern landscapes he had himself researched.

51 Edmond de Pressensé, *The Critical School and Jesus Christ: A Reply to M. Renan's Life of Jesus*, trans. L. Corkran (London: Elliot Stock, 1865), p. 32.

52 Renan, *Life of Jesus*, p. 136.

53 John Middleton Murry, *The Life of Jesus* (London: Jonathan Cape, 1926), p. 10.

54 Cobbe, *Broken Lights*, p. 120.

55 Ernest Renan, *La Vie de Jésus*, édition populaire (Paris: Calmann-Lévy, 1893), p. viii.

56 J. S. Mill, 'On Theism', in *Three Essays on Religion* (London: Longmans, Green, Reader, and Dyer, 1874), p. 253.

57 Renan, *Life of Jesus*, p. 84.

58 Renan, *Life of Jesus*, p. 262.

59 Renan, *Life of Jesus*, p. 168.

60 Renan, *Life of Jesus*, p. 249.

61 Renan, *Life of Jesus*, p. 226.

62 Renan, *Life of Jesus*, p. 262.

63 In Emil Ludwig's *The Son of Man*, trans. Eden and Cedar Paul (London: Ernest

Benn, 1928), Christ's thoughts in the Garden of Gethsemane are conveyed by way of free indirect speech: 'Had it all been a mistake? The refuge of women's tender affection, gentle hands to stroke his hair, soft lips to kiss his feet, loving-kindness to cherish him in his daily doings [...] He would have spent his life in the quiet Galilean township, one man among many, and yet different from the rest, for he would have been privileged to hold converse with the Father, on the hillside behind the houses; he could have kept his own counsel about that matter!' (p. 282).

64 Renan, *Life of Jesus*, pp. 137, 221.

65 The biographer Mary Robinson pronounced Renan's Jesus to be 'too Celtic [...] too much like Ernest Renan' (Darmesteter, *The Life of Ernest Renan*, p. 164); William G. Hutchison, a translator of *Vie*, considered the figure of Jesus to have been 'Renanised': see the *Life of Jesus*, trans. William G. Hutchison, p. xxx. A more recent critic, H. W. Wardman, has described the *Life* as 'an idealised portrait of Renan himself'. See *Ernest Renan: A Critical Biography* (London: University of London, The Athlone Press, 1964), p. 86.

66 Schweitzer, *The Quest of the Historical Jesus*, p. 6.

67 Ernest Renan, *The Gospels*, trans. unknown (London: Mathieson, n. d.), p. 53.

68 De Quincey expounds this definition of literature in his essay on Alexander Pope. He explains that 'There is, first, the literature of *knowledge*; and, secondly, the literature of *power*. The function of the first is – to *teach*; the function of the second is – to *move*: the first is a rudder; the second, an oar or a sail.' See Thomas De Quincey, 'Alexander Pope', in *De Quincey as Critic*, ed. John E. Jordan (London: Routledge & Kegan Paul, 1973), p. 269.

69 In a retrospective study of the Life of Jesus genre, Maurice Goguel comments somewhat scathingly that the attractive style of Renan's *Life* caused it to be read by 'hosts of people who were neither initiated into nor even prepared for exegetical research'. See *The Life of Jesus*, trans. Olive Wyon (London: George Allen & Unwin, 1933), p. 50.

70 Christianus [Charles Tilstone Beke], *Jesus the King of the Jews* (London: Robert Hardwicke, 1864), p. 11.

71 Christianus, *Jesus the King*, pp. 10, 11–12.

72 The first edition of *Ecce Homo* was published anonymously by Macmillan, the author fearing the displeasure of his evangelical family at his treatment of a sacred subject.

73 Seeley was elected in 1869 to the post of regius professor of history at Cambridge on Gladstone's recommendation.

74 The *British Quarterly Review* is typical in opening its discussion of *Ecce Homo* by asking if it 'does not compete in fame with Renan's "Vie de Jésus"'; see the *British Quarterly Review*, 43 (January 1866), pp. 229–32 (p. 229). The writer John Addington Symonds is also typical in his drawing of a comparison between the two works: 'I read Seeley's "Ecce Homo". The enthusiasm of humanity in that essay took no hold upon me; just as [...] Renan's seductive portrait of *"le doux Galiléen"* [the gentle Galilean] was somewhat contemptuously laid aside.' See *The Memoirs of John Addington Symonds*, ed. Phyllis Grosskurth (London: Hutchinson, 1984), p. 245.

75 *Ecce Homo: A Survey of the Life and Work of Jesus Christ* (London and Cambridge: Macmillan, 1866), pp. 164, 162. What Seeley termed 'the enthusiasm of

humanity' became one of the work's most repeated phrases. Walter Pater, for example, quotes it in the final paragraph of *Studies In the History of the Renaissance* (London: Macmillan, 1873): 'High passions give one this quickened sense of life, ecstasy and sorrow of love, political or religious enthusiasm, or "the enthusiasm of humanity"' (p. 212).

76 One of Seeley's students, the writer Joseph Jacobs, remarked 'I attended one of his [Seeley's] professorial courses [...] His lectures were clear, but cold.' See Joseph Jacobs, *Literary Studies* (London: David Nutt, 1895), p. 193.

77 Seeley, *Ecce Homo*, p. 89.

78 *Fortnightly Review*, 5 (June 1866), pp. 129–42 (p. 136).

79 *Edinburgh Review*, 'Strauss, Renan, and "Ecce Homo"', 124 (October 1866), pp. 450–75 (p. 468).

80 W. E. Gladstone, *'Ecce Homo' by the Right Hon. W. E. Gladstone* (London: Strahan, 1868), p. 199.

81 *Fortnightly Review*, 5 (June 1866), pp. 129–42 (p. 129).

82 Schweitzer, *The Quest of the Historical Jesus*, p. 515.

83 Gustav Adolf Rein, *Sir John Robert Seeley: A Study of the Historian*, trans. John L. Herkless (New Hampshire, Wolfeboro: Longwood Academic, 1987), p. 90.

84 Seeley, *Ecce Homo*, pp. vi, 328.

85 Seeley, *Ecce Homo*, p. 44.

86 *Westminster Review*, 30 (July 1866), pp. 58–88 (p. 60).

87 'Ecce Homo: a denial of the peculiar doctrines of Christianity; A Review by the Rev. Jas. K. Glazebrook', reprinted from the *Blackburn Times* (Blackburn, 1866), p. 9.

88 Gladstone, *'Ecce Homo'*. Gladstone's review was a staunch defence of Seeley's work and proved extremely influential. The politician's admiration for the book perhaps reflects his own ambivalence towards theological revisionism. Additionally, Seeley's frequent references to the classical world and classical literature may well have appealed to Gladstone, who was engaged in his own study of the classics during the 1860s. See H. C. G. Matthew, *Gladstone 1809–1874* (Oxford: Clarendon Press, 1986), pp. 152–55.

89 'Ecce Homo', *Month: A Catholic Review*, 4 (June 1866), pp. 551–73 (p. 564).

90 One reviewer of Seeley's work remarked: 'There are few, probably, of our readers who are not already well acquainted with the book. For not only has it passed through five or six editions, but it has been reviewed in every periodical, been canvassed in every social circle, and been carried by the angry waves of controversy into unnumbered nooks and corners.' See the *Edinburgh Review*, 124 (October 1866), pp. 450–75 (p. 467). In *The Victorian "Lives" of Jesus*, Daniel Pals states that *Ecce Homo* 'was reviewed extensively not only by the religious press but by nearly every one of the major literary magazines and in essays by several of religious Britain's most distinguished spokesmen' (p. 48).

91 Joseph Parker, *Ecce Deus* (Edinburgh: T. & T. Clark, 1867); Sylva (pseud.), *Ecce Veritas: an Ultra-Unitarian Review* (London: Trübner, 1874); D. Melville Stewart, *Ecce Vir* (London: James Clarke, 1911).

92 One reviewer, severely underestimating the impact that Renan would have in Britain, wrote that 'The shelves that once groaned under his various-sized octavos have now forgotten Rénan [*sic*]'. See *Blackwood's Magazine*, 96 (October 1864),

pp. 417–31 (p. 418).

93 [By a clergyman of the Church of England], *Dr Farrar's "Life of Christ": A Letter to Thomas Scott* (London: Thomas Scott, 1874), p. 9.

94 *Watts Literary Guide*, 39 (15 January 1889), p. 1.

95 Thomas Scott, *The English Life of Jesus* (Ramsgate: Thomas Scott, 1872), p. 320.

96 Scott promises early in his Life that 'The witness of John (so called) will be shown to be nothing more than the unsupported assertions of some unknown writer living, perhaps late, in the second century, and desirous of blending the Alexandrine philosophy of the Logos with a modified Paulinism' (*The English Life of Jesus*, pp. 16–17).

97 Scott, *The English Life of Jesus*, p. 336.

98 William Hanna, *Our Lord's Life on Earth*, 6 vols (Edinburgh: Edmonston and Douglas, 1869), I, pp. v–vi.

99 Hanna, *Our Lord's Life on Earth*, I, p. vi.

100 Hanna, *Our Lord's Life on Earth*, V, p. 157.

101 Hanna, *Our Lord's Life on Earth*, V, p. 158.

102 Hanna, *Our Lord's Life on Earth*, V, pp. 225–26.

103 Hanna, *Our Lord's Life on Earth*, V, p. 226.

104 Hanna, *Our Lord's Life on Earth*, V, pp. 230–31.

105 Hanna, *Our Lord's Life on Earth*, V, p. 328.

106 'The English Life of Jesus by Thomas Scott', *British Quarterly Review*, 56 (July 1872), pp. 269–71 (p. 269).

107 F. W. Farrar, *The Life of Christ*, 2 vols (London: Cassell, Petter and Galpin, 1874), I, p. v.

108 When teaching at Harrow, Farrar wrote *Eric, or, Little by Little* (1858) which achieved great success. In the same period he published two other school stories: *Julian Home; a tale of College Life* (1859) and *St Winifred's, or, the world of school* (1862).

109 Farrar, *The Life of Christ*, I, pp. vii, viii.

110 Farrar, *The Life of Christ*, I, p. ix.

111 *Christian Observer*, 74 (October 1874), pp. 726–46 (p. 731).

112 Reginald Farrar, *The Life of Frederic William Farrar* (London: James Nisbet, 1904), p. 196.

113 *Month: A Catholic Review*, 22 (September 1874), pp. 98–101 (p. 98). That the *Month* had anything complimentary to say about *The Life of Christ* is surprising, given that Farrar's work contains frequent snipes at the Roman Catholic Church.

114 Farrar, *The Life of Christ*, I, p. ix.

115 Frederic W. Farrar, *The Life of Christ as Represented in Art* (London: Adam and Charles Black, 1894), p. 4.

116 Farrar, *History of Interpretation*, p. 419.

117 *Athenaeum*, 27 June 1874, pp. 856–58 (p. 857).

118 *The Life of Frederic William Farrar*, p. 194.

119 'An Adelphi Romance', *Saturday Review*, 82 (12 December 1896), pp. 629–30 (p. 629).

120 F. W. Farrar, 'A Few Words on the Life of Christ', *Macmillan's Magazine*, 31 (March 1875), pp. 463–71 (p. 470).

121 Farrar, *The Life of Christ*, I, p. 58.

122 Farrar, *The Life of Christ in Art*, p. 280.

123 Farrar, *The Life of Christ*, I, pp. 313, 315, 317.

124 In *The Critical School and Jesus Christ*, Edmond de Pressensé writes that Renan 'calls Jesus adorable in the same sense that we apply the word in society to a pretty woman' (p. 5).

125 Farrar, *The Life of Christ*, II, p. 400. In *The Manliness of Christ*, Thomas Hughes considers the life of Jesus from the point of view of his subject's masculinity. He concludes that 'there must be no flaw or spot on Christ's courage, any more than on His wisdom, and tenderness and sympathy'. See Thomas Hughes, *The Manliness of Christ* (London: Macmillan, 1879), p. 151.

126 Farrar, *The Life of Christ*, II, p. 169.

127 Farrar, *The Life of Christ*, II, p. 412.

128 Farrar, *The Life of Christ*, II, p. 7.

129 Farrar, 'A Few Words on the Life of Christ', p. 466.

130 Farrar, *The Life of Christ*, II, p. 72.

131 While there is general agreement that the story of the adulteress is an authentic fragment of early tradition, there is little evidence to support it being Johannine or even evangelical. Its acceptance into the four-fold Gospel can be traced back to the medieval period, when Jerome saw fit to leave it to stand as part of the Fourth Gospel. While Farrar acknowledges the indeterminacy of the text's origin, it is evident that he expects his readers to appreciate the unique qualities of the narrative regardless of its provenance.

132 Wilde asserts that the story of the woman taken in adultery 'was worthwhile living to have said'. See *The Complete Works of Oscar Wilde*, vol. ii, *De Profundis*, ed. Ian Small (Oxford: Oxford University Press, 2005), p. 121. Unless otherwise stated, all references from the works of Oscar Wilde are taken from the Oxford University Press editions, under the general editorship of Ian Small.

133 Farrar, *The Life of Christ*, II, p. 66.

134 Farrar, *The Life of Christ*, II, pp. 67–68.

135 Farrar, *The Life of Christ*, II, p. 68.

136 Seeley, *Ecce Homo*, p. 104.

137 *Quarterly Review*, 119 (April 1866), pp. 515–29 (p. 518).

138 Farrar, *The Life of Christ*, II, pp. 381–82.

139 In *The Crucifixion* from the York pageant, for example, the focus throughout is on the physically violent act of Christ's hands and feet being nailed to the cross by four brutal soldiers who mock him as they carry out their task. See *The Crucifixion*, printed in *Everyman and Medieval Miracle Plays*, ed. A. C. Cawley (London: J. M. Dent, 1974).

140 Farrar, *The Life of Christ*, II, p. 401.

141 Farrar, *The Life of Christ*, II, p. 401, n. 2. Farrar's reasoning here has been echoed recently by the actor and director Mel Gibson, in his defence of the extreme violence depicted in his film *The Passion of the Christ*, released in Britain in March 2004. In an interview given during ABC's *Primetime* programme on 16 February 2004, Gibson justified the graphic nature of his film, stating that it was necessary to 'push [viewers] over the edge so that they see the enormity […] of that sacrifice'. Quoted in the news section of *The Guardian*, 17 February 2004, p. 16.

142 John's Gospel was the subject of fierce critical debate, having been rejected by Strauss as historically invalid. Farrar makes clear in his preface to *The Life of Christ* that he takes an entirely orthodox line on the authorship and authenticity of the Fourth Gospel, and considers it a valid source for his work.

143 Farrar, *The Life of Christ*, II, pp. 403–04.

144 Farrar, *The Life of Christ in Art*, p. 368.

145 Farrar, *The Life of Christ in Art*, p. 407.

146 In *The Bible; Its Meaning and Supremacy* (London: Longmans, Green, 1897), Farrar estimates the significance of the Bible's influence on the nation's great writers: 'All the best and brightest English verse, from the poems of Chaucer to the plays of Shakespeare [...] are echoes of its lessons; and from Cowper to Wordsworth, from Coleridge to Tennyson, the greatest of our poets have drawn from its pages their loftiest wisdom' (p. 244).

147 At times, Farrar's grasp of the plays is somewhat insecure. In his discussion of Christ's Temptation, he quotes approvingly Angelo's lines from *Measure for Measure*, 'Tis one thing to be tempted, Escalus, / Another thing to fall', seemingly unaware of the irony of the words, spoken as they are by a man who goes on to attempt to coerce a novitiate into sleeping with him (*The Life of Christ*, I, p. 126).

148 Cunningham Geikie, *The Life and Words of Christ*, 2 vols (London: Henry S. King, 1877), I, p. 1.

149 Geikie, *The Life and Words of Christ*, II, pp. 558, 565.

150 Alfred Edersheim, *The Life and Times of Jesus the Messiah*, 2 vols (London: Longmans, Green, 1883), I, p. viii.

151 Alfred Edersheim, *Jesus the Messiah* (London: Longmans, 1890).

152 Edersheim, *The Life and Times of Jesus*, I, p. vii.

153 Edersheim, *The Life and Times of Jesus*, I, p. 566.

154 Edersheim, *The Life and Times of Jesus*, I, p. 279, n. 4.

155 *The Complete Works of Oscar Wilde*, vol. iv, *Criticism*, ed. Josephine M. Guy (Oxford: Oxford University Press, 2006), p. 146.

156 See Simon Nowell-Smith, *The House of Cassell 1848–1958* (London: Cassell, 1958), p. 99.

157 Alfred E. Garvie, *Studies in the Inner Life of Jesus* (London: Hodder & Stoughton, 1907), p. vi.

158 Walter Lloyd, *The Galilean* (London: Williams and Norgate, 1892), pp. 3–4.

159 James Stalker, 'Our present knowledge of the life of Jesus', *Contemporary Review*, 77 (January 1900), pp. 124–32.

160 Stalker, 'Our present knowledge of the life of Jesus', p. 125; James Stalker, *The Life of Jesus Christ* (Edinburgh: T. & T. Clark, 1879).

161 T. R. Glover, *The Jesus of History* (London: Student Christian Movement, 1917), p. 243.

162 *The Quest of the Historical Jesus*, p. 478.

163 Stalker, 'Our present knowledge of the life of Jesus', p. 125.

164 G. W. Foote, *What Was Christ? A Reply to John Stuart Mill* (London: Progressive Publishing Company, 1887), p. 13. Foote was particularly dismayed that such a renowned freethinker as Mill could publish a panegyric on Christ in his essay 'On Theism', in *Three Essays on Religion*.

165 On taking over the co-editorship of the *Freethinker* in 1881, Foote introduced a

column to the journal entitled 'Profane Jokes' along with a series of comic wood-cuts, 'Comic Biblical Sketches'. It was the comic sketches in particular that caused Christians great offence and Foote was put on trial for 'wickedly and profanely devising and intending to asperse and vilify Almighty God'. The twelve-month prison sentence that followed brought Foote considerable notoriety, boosting the sales of his journal appreciably.

166 G. W. Foote, *Christmas Eve in Heaven*, reprinted from the *Freethinker* in *Arrows of Freethought*, p. 93.

167 G. W. Foote, *Letters to Jesus Christ* (London: Progressive Publishing Company, 1886), pp. 8, 9.

168 Léo Taxil, *Vie de Jésus* (Paris: Librairie Anti-cléricale, 1882). For more detail about the highly colourful life of Taxil, see *Fictions du Diable: Démonologie et littérature de saint Augustin à Léo Taxil*, ed. Françoise Lavocat, Pierre Kapitaniak and Marianne Closson (Geneva: Librairie Droz, 2007). Taxil's book is mentioned by name in James Joyce's *Ulysses*, suggesting that it circulated for several decades.

169 Orthodox French Lives of Jesus were often sentimental and lacking in any serious engagement with biblical criticism, making them particularly vulnerable to parodic treatments. One of the few to enter into the Higher Critical arena was Father Henri Didon's *Jésus Christ*, published in Paris in 1891, and translated into English in the same year: *The Life of Jesus Christ*, 2 vols (London: Kegan Paul, Trench, Trübner, 1891). While entirely Catholic in spirit, it nevertheless followed Renan in its evocative descriptions of Palestine.

170 Taxil, *Vie de Jésus*.

171 George Gissing, *Thyrza: A Tale*, 3 vols (London: Smith, Elder, 1887), I, pp. 20–21.

172 Ward, *Robert Elsmere*, III, p. 167.

173 Nicolas Notovitch, *The Unknown Life of Christ*, trans. Violet Crispe (London: Hutchinson, 1895). In this modern Apocrypha, Notovitch claims that, during a stay in Tibet, he was given access by the chief Lama to ancient documents recording the life of Jesus. Notovitch insists that Renan had been aware of his findings and was anxious to acquire them for his own purposes and inevitable glory. For this reason, Notovitch insists, the publication of the work had been delayed until after Renan's death. This unlikely scenario, along with the extreme dubiety of Notovitch's evidence, and his translator's refusal to be associated in any way with the work she had undertaken to translate, confirms the account as more fiction than fact.

174 Levi H. Dowling, *The Aquarian Gospel of Jesus the Christ: the philosophic and practical basis of the Religion of the Aquarian Age of the World and of the Church Universal, transcribed from the Book of God's Remembrances, Known as the Akashic Records, by Levi* (London: Cazenove, 1908). In *The Hidden Gospels: How the Search for Jesus Lost its Way* (Oxford: Oxford University Press, 2001), Philip Jenkins writes that 'between 1908 and 1995, the *Aquarian Gospel* [...] went through fifty-two printings in hardbound editions, and thirteen in paperback' (p. 47).

175 Edgar J. Goodspeed, *Strange New Gospels* (Chicago: University of Chicago Press, 1931), p. 7.

176 Goodspeed, *Strange New Gospels*, p. 100.

177 *A Coppy of a LETTER Written by Our Blessed Lord and Saviour Jesus Christ* (London: 1724).
178 *The Crucifixion, by an Eye Witness* (originally published by Indo American Book Co., 1907; repr. Whitefish MT: Kessinger Publishing Company, 2000), p. 57.
179 *The Crucifixion*, p. 13.
180 *Crucifixion, by an Eye Witness* (Muttra: Narayan Swami, 1925), p. vii.
181 Goodspeed, *Strange New Gospels*, p. 36.

CHAPTER 3

The Rise of the Fictional Jesus

> [The novel] is the most elastic, the most adaptable
> of forms. No one has a right to set limits to its range.
> Mrs Humphry Ward, *A Writer's Recollections*

In a survey of British fiction published in 1859, David Masson reported that 'Hardly a question or doctrine of the last ten years can be pointed out that has not had a novel framed in its interest, positively or negatively.' It was an observation never more accurate than in the case of religious debates and controversies.[1] By the middle decades of the nineteenth century, the rapid growth of the Lives of Jesus genre was more than matched by that of the religious novel. One of the first critics to survey the entire body of Victorian religious fiction, Margaret Maison, remarks that: 'Its very abundance is [...] a drawback, for the reader is presented with such an overwhelming *embarras de richesse*.'[2] Whether written from the standpoint of, say, the Broad Churchman, the Tractarian, the Evangelical or the atheist, religious novels responded, with varying degrees of directness, to the contemporary theological and scientific debates that threatened to overturn Christian orthodoxy. Furthermore, they allowed the layman to engage with religious controversies more usually confined to the clergyman or the academic, in a form of discourse hitherto associated with the secular and, to some minds, the profane.

Arguments concerning the morality and aesthetics of the religious novel were underway as early as the 1840s. In the prefatory dedication to *Sir Roland Ashton: A Tale of the Times* (1844), the author, Lady Catharine Long, opines:

> I know there are most excellent people who do not approve of religious sentiments being brought forward through the medium of

fiction, and who think that works of that nature are not calculated to produce good effects. But my experience has taught me decidedly the contrary, for not only have they often been instrumental in awakening and exalting spiritual feelings, but in some instances they have been the means, in God's hands, of conveying vital truth to the soul.[3]

Long's notion of novel-writing being 'in God's hands', with the author as a type of amanuensis, was one that became increasingly familiar as the century wore on, and the medium of fiction, once regarded with suspicion by orthodox Christians, became one of the their most potent weapons in the fight against unbelief. Indeed, by the final decade of the century, there were relatively few voices raised in protest against the fictionalizing of religious issues. Prominent Anglican churchmen, such as Frederic William Farrar, looked to the novel as the most effective means of expressing religious views, albeit with a degree of caution. In the preface to his first religious novel, *Darkness and Dawn* (1891), a story set in Nero's Rome, Farrar is anxious to impress on the reader that 'the fiction is throughout controlled and dominated by historic facts', and that his 'deviations' from precise chronology are 'very trivial in comparison with those which have been permitted to others'.[4] He goes on to insist: 'the book is not a novel, nor is it to be judged as a novel', explaining that 'the outline has been imperatively decided [...] by the exigencies of fact, not by the rules of art'.[5] To all intents and purposes, however, it looked like a novel, read like a novel, and was marketed accordingly. And in the preface to *The Gathering Clouds* (1895), a tale set in the days of the Byzantine Empire, though the author admits that the historic scene he depicts is one 'in which fiction has been allowed free play', he is keen to point out that this is only 'as regards matters which do not affect the important facts'.[6] It would seem from Farrar's defensiveness, then, that while acknowledging the novel to be the most expedient route to a wide audience, he is still keenly aware of fiction's former associations with deception and impiety.

As the role of novelist was taken on ever more frequently by the likes of Farrar, so those sensitive to the aesthetics of prose fiction grew increasingly perturbed. The sheer volume of religious novels produced in the second half of the nineteenth century clearly indicates that there was something of a fiction bandwagon, with writers of diverse denominations eager to jump on it. The speed at which religious fiction was produced militated against experimentation or time-consuming redrafting, and literary quality was inevitably compromised; moreover, a large majority of those penning it were decidedly amateurish, convinced that the importance and urgency of what they had to convey would more than make up for any limitations they might have as writers. Just two years after the publication of *Sir Roland Ashton*, George Eliot launched a scathing attack on such works in an article published in the *Westminster Review* under the waspish title 'Silly Novels by Lady Novelists'.[7] Categorizing contemporary religious novels by women writers under the facetious labels of 'oracular' (High Church) or 'white neck-cloth' (Low Church), Eliot regrets that 'in novel-writing there are no barriers for incapacity to stumble against, no external criteria to prevent a writer from mistaking foolish facility for mastery'.[8]

Several decades and hundreds of religious novels later, Andrew Lang, one of the most influential journalists and authors of the late nineteenth century, followed Eliot in bemoaning the fact that 'writers, not gifted with skill in narrative, or with that skill not fully developed, are driven into attempting narrative. They must preach in fiction, or preach to empty pews.'[9] For critics like Lang the religious novel had not *replaced* the tract, it had *become* one. As well as regretting the use of poor-quality fiction to strengthen faith, Lang also deplored the late-Victorian tendency to explain theological scholarship through didactic novels, declaring that he preferred to take his 'Higher Criticism "neat", and from the fountain heads'.[10] This chapter considers four novels that, on aesthetic grounds alone, would have been unlikely to find their way onto Lang's bookshelf: Samuel Butler's *The Fair Haven* (1873), Edwin Abbott Abbott's *Philochristus* (1878), Joseph Jacobs's *As Other Saw Him* (1895) and Marie Corelli's *Barabbas* (1893). What they lack in literary merit, however, they more than make up for in terms of their significance for the development of New Testament fiction. Written from radically divergent perspectives, they each offered the lay public a means of engaging with some of the central debates in modernist theology, taking the genre of the religious novel away from contemporary sectarian struggles over doctrine and dogma into the more distant days of the historical Jesus. Placed side by side, they help to chart the relaxation of those boundaries of religious fiction laid down in the first half of the nineteenth century by largely conservative publishers and their readers.

Fictionalizing the Higher Criticism:
Samuel Butler's *The Fair Haven* (1873)

In a decade when religious novels of all persuasions were flooding the literary marketplace, one that stood out from the rest was Samuel Butler's *The Fair Haven*, the first sustained attempt at arguing Higher Critical ideas through the medium of fiction. Butler's engagement with theological revisionism, and with the writings of D. F. Strauss in particular, can be traced back to the mid-1860s when he published a pamphlet entitled *The Evidence for the Resurrection of Jesus Christ as Given by the Four Evangelists, Critically Examined.*[11] Coinciding with the publication of the first English translation of Strauss's *A New Life of Jesus* (an event that revived interest in the original work), Butler's pamphlet examines – and finds wanting – the German theologian's theory that belief in Christ's resurrection came about through the hallucinatory visions of his disciples. Just as a decade or so later Butler would fly in the face of expert opinion in asserting the superiority of the evolutionary theories of Lamarck over the later theories of Darwin, so he chooses here to promote the reasoning of early theological rationalism over the later mythopoeic reasoning of Strauss. Butler argues that Jesus did not die on the cross but, having fallen into a cataleptic trance, was presumed dead and taken away for burial by Joseph of Arimathea and Nicodemus who, on discovering their mistake, kept secret the real nature of Christ's 'resurrection'. This hypothesis, commonly known as the 'swoon theory', was by no means new, as Butler readily admits in the pamphlet's preface:

> I have no doubt that the line of argument taken in the following pages is a very old one, and familiar to all who have extended their reading on the subject of Christianity beyond the common English books. I do not wish to lay claim to any originality whatsoever.[12]

Yet, as Butler goes on to explain in justification of his having written the pamphlet, such ideas were not generally to be found in English works. To encounter the 'swoon theory' the Victorian lay reader would have had to undertake a thorough study of major works such as Strauss's *Life of Jesus* or *A New Life of Jesus*, where it is outlined for the sole purpose of being discredited. That Continental scholarship such as this was slow in reaching Britain is borne out by Charles Darwin's remark in a letter of 1865, thanking Butler for sending him a copy of the Resurrection essay, that the 'main argument is to me quite new'.[13]

The Evidence for the Resurrection made little impact, yet Butler's eagerness to promulgate his heterodox views to a wider public persisted. As is evident from his correspondence with his great friend and confidante, Miss Savage, it took him some time to fix on prose fiction as the best way of achieving such an ambition. In a letter dated June 1872, he wrote:

> But I am very doubtful about a novel at all; I know I should regard it as I did *Erewhon*, i.e., as a mere peg on which to hang anything that I had a mind to say [...] the only question is whether after all that matters much, provided the things said are such as the reader will recognize as expressions of his own feelings, and as awakening an echo within himself, instead of being written to show off the cleverness of the writer [...][14]

Still endeavouring in the early 1870s to make his mark as a painter, there is, in fact, little to suggest that Butler had any ambitions at this time to contribute to the burgeoning genre of the religious novel, and it is plain here that literary concerns take second place to the promotion of his views on the New Testament narratives. That it is not to say, however, that he was indifferent to the pitfalls of religious fiction. Never one to mince his words, he wrote to Miss Savage that he hated Eliza Lynn Linton's immensely popular novel *The True History of Joshua Davidson*, published in the year when *The Fair Haven* was taking shape, and it is certainly difficult to imagine a writer as predisposed to mordant irony as Butler emulating the oversimplification and sentimentality of such writing.

The Fair Haven might easily stand as an antidote to works by the likes of Linton. As the lengthy sub-title to the book announces, competing biblical theories are to be debated not though the usual medium of stock characters in action, but through a highly complex narrative framework featuring two fictional brothers, William Bickersteth Owen and John Pickard Owen. The first section of the book is a kind of fictional biography entitled 'Memoir of The Late John Pickard Owen', written by the subject's younger brother, a devout member of the Church of England. In this Memoir, William recounts John's journey through the orthodoxy of his youth and the heterodoxy of his early adulthood, with a speed and compression that seems to parody the trajectory of so many heroes in so many religious novels of the day:

> He [...] joined the Baptists and was immersed in a pond near
> Dorking. With the Baptists he remained quiet about three months,
> and then began to quarrel with his instructors as to their doctrine of
> predestination. Shortly afterwards he came accidentally upon a
> fascinating stranger [...] who turned out to be a Roman Catholic
> missionary, landed him in the Church of Rome, where he felt sure
> that he had found rest for his soul. But here, too, he was mistaken;
> after about two years he rebelled against the stifling of all free
> inquiry [...] and he was soon battling with unbelief.[15]

While John Pickard Owen's unbelief proves only temporary, the
recovery of his faith takes a heavy toll on his mental health. The
Memoir concludes with John's death 'from some obscure disease of
the brain brought on by excitement and undue mental tension' (*FH*
49) and the revelation that a collection of his papers has been discovered, extracts from which go to form the remainder of the novel.
Leaving behind the intimate fraternal style of the Memoir, the work
moves into the autobiographical voice of the deceased brother
recounting his arduous quest for truth and, in the process, engaging
the reader in the religious controversies of the day. One of his main
contentions is that orthodox Christians, in pusillanimously refusing
to take on the challenges of biblical criticism, have helped to
strengthen the position of their opponents. Drawing strength from his
own religious journey, John takes it upon himself to refute what he
regards as the speciousness of anti-Christian arguments, a task he sees
as vital in saving mankind from the inevitable wrath of God.

In the introduction to the New Edition of *The Fair Haven*, Richard
Streatfeild, Butler's literary executor, asserts that the author 'provided
an ironical framework for his arguments merely that he might render
them more effective than they had been when plainly stated in the
pamphlet of 1865'.[16] Doubtless Butler chose to create the individual
voices of the Owen brothers as a means of conveying Higher Critical
ideas to a lay public more accustomed to the language of the novelist
than that of the theologian. Indeed, John Pickard Owen may be seen
to state the view of his own creator in his introductory commentary:

> We are bound to adapt our means to our ends, and shall have a
> better chance of gaining the ear of our adversaries if we can offer

them a short and pregnant book [...] We have to bring the Christian religion to men who will look at no book which cannot be read in a railway train or in an arm-chair. (*FH* 53)

Yet if the individuality of these two fictional voices helps to give the work a novelistic tone, they by no means lend it the familiarity and accessibility more usually associated with the realist novel. Thanks to what Miss Savage described as the novel's 'sanglant' satire, the reader is rarely able to engage in any straightforward way with issues such as the reliability and authorship of the Gospels, changing notions of historicity or the facts of the resurrection; instead, they have to grapple with the novel's ever-shifting voices, tones and satirical targets.[17] The ironical edge of the work derives from Butler's invention of a character who, though capable of presenting the ideas of writers such as Strauss, Jowett and Arnold in a detailed and convincing manner, is signally incapable of putting up a convincing counter-argument on behalf of the traditionalists. To create such a paradox, Butler affords his chief narrator a perplexing variety of registers and idioms so that, within a paragraph or two of his treatise, he can move from the moderate view that 'men will not seriously listen to those whom they believe to know one side of a question only' (*FH* 59) to the rather more fanatical view that 'Infidelity is as a reeking fever den' (*FH* 60). The opinions of those 'infidels' he seeks to undermine are presented in a scrupulously detailed and reasoned manner, whereas the arguments he manages to muster to counter them are formed from all manner of fallacious reasoning: false dilemmas, false analogies and circuitous arguments. The reader is left to infer that John's explanations of revisionist theology are clear and persuasive because of their validity and, conversely, that the arguments of the traditionalists are indefensible because they are fundamentally flawed.

To lend authenticity to his fictional persona's discourse on the Gospels, Butler supplements the text with lengthy quotations from the writings of well-known theologians, ranging from the orthodox William Paley and Henry Alford to the heterodox Strauss. John engages most frequently with the works of Henry Alford, Dean of Canterbury, whose Greek Testament and Old and New Testament commentaries had earned him a reputation as a biblical scholar. As one of those clergy willing to take up the gauntlet and confront Higher Critical ideas head on, he would have seemed the likely hero of John's treatise. Yet any such expectations are confounded as lengthy citations from Alford's *New Testament for English Readers* are closely examined, only to be deemed inadequate.[18] Having summarized Alford's views on the Fourth Gospel's much-debated account of the sword piercing Christ's side, Owen comments:

> With this climax of presumptuous assertion these disgraceful notes are ended. They have shown clearly that the wound does not in itself prove the death: they show no less clearly that the Dean does not consider that the death is proved beyond possibility of doubt *without* the wound; what therefore should be the legitimate conclusion? Surely that we have no proof of the completeness of Christ's death upon the Cross – or in other words no proof of his having died at all! Couple this with the notes upon the Resurrection considered above, and we feel rather as though we were in the hands of some Jesuitical unbeliever, who was trying to undermine our faith in our most precious convictions under the guise of defending them [...] (*FH* 137–38)

Demonstrated here is the complexity of Butler's satire as he states his own heretical belief that Christ survived the cross through the voice of a fictional believer even more orthodox than the 'real life' Dean Alford, the mere insertion of the exclamation mark after the crucial statement fusing two voices, that of the author and that of the authored. Butler clearly relishes the irony of comparing Alford to 'some Jesuitical unbeliever', a comparison much more compatible with his own mischievous intentions, and one that a reader in tune with the satirical tone of the work might appreciate. In a similar vein, Butler concludes the book's prolix and repetitive examination of the Resurrection narratives (some of it taken directly from his 1865 essay) by stating his own heterodox convictions through the anguished voice of the orthodox Christian:

> The case, therefore, of our adversaries will rest thus: – that there is not only no sufficient reason for believing that Christ died upon the Cross, but that there are the strongest conceivable reasons for believing that he did not die; that the shortness of time during which he remained upon the Cross, the immediate delivery of the body to friends, and, above all, the subsequent reappearance alive, are ample grounds at arriving at such a conclusion. (*FH* 183–84)

As John's treatise draws to a close, his repeated insistence that 'ideals gain by vagueness' (*FH* 199) builds into an obvious mockery of those Christians who shy away from scientific challenges to their belief system and from the numerous discrepancies to be found in the Gospel records. Taking the somewhat sophistic approach of some of the authors of Lives of Jesus, who had long given up trying to harmonize the four evangels, he argues that they lose nothing from their inconsistencies but should be thought of as having 'the error distributed skilfully among them, as in a well-tuned instrument wherein each string is purposely something out of tune with every other' (*FH* 202). The satirical bite of John's celebration of the vague and the undefined is continued in *The Fair Haven*'s penultimate chapter entitled 'The Christ-Ideal'. It is here that Butler chooses some rather less likely targets for satire: agnostics like Renan and John Stuart Mill who, while denying Jesus's divinity, continued to esteem him as the pattern of all humanity; and those contemporary novelists who bent the image of Christ to suit their own ideological stance, be it Christian Socialist, High Church or Unitarian. In addition, he ridicules those who, like Matthew Arnold, 'regarded the whole New Testament as a work of art, a poem, a pure fiction from beginning to end, and who revered it for its intrinsic beauty' (*FH* 203). In this final section, John explains how the 'blurring of no small portions of the external evidences whereby the Divine origin of the ideal was established' (*FH* 201) has lent an irrevocable indistinctness to the figure of Christ, allowing it to be moulded to suit any man in any epoch. Essentially under attack here is what Butler seems to have regarded as the respectable face of unbelief which, as a self-professed *enfant terrible*, he clearly felt the urge to rail against; in so doing, he anticipates the Nietzschean notions of a pale and sickly Jesus that would emerge a little later in the century.

Given the polyphonic nature of the narrative, its numerous interpolations, its predilection for the double and triple negative and its frequent use of author's italics, it is unsurprising that readers struggled – and still struggle – to make sense of *The Fair Haven*. On its publication it met with diametrically opposed responses from readers, luring some of its reviewers into accepting it as an entirely orthodox work by a devout Christian. Butler revelled in such misinterpretations, quoting them verbatim in a mischievous preface written for the novel's second edition. In this, he adopts the satirical voice of the main work, putting himself forward as 'the champion of orthodoxy' (*FH* xiii) and feigning surprise that his work had ever 'been suspected of a satirical purpose' (*FH* xiv). Yet it would be a mistake to assume that respondents to Butler's text divided neatly into those sophisticated enough to perceive its irony and those who were not: some of the best contemporary minds were left perplexed by its quirky manner of presenting religious controversy. Charles Darwin, for example, having received a copy of *The Fair Haven* from Butler, wrote to him that, if he had not known him personally, he would 'never have suspected that the author was not orthodox'.[19] And even a literary critic as experienced and perceptive as Edmund Gosse absolved those taken in by Butler's book from all charges of credulity, placing the blame for such misunderstandings firmly at the feet of the author:

> His religious polemic was even more disagreeable than his scientific, and the lumbering sarcasm of the attack on Christianity, called *The Fair Haven*, is an epitome of all that is most unpleasing in the attitude of Butler. Unctuous sarcasm so sustained as to deceive the very elect [...][20]

Butler's ambition to communicate his resurrection theories to a wide audience was to remain unfulfilled. According to the author's own estimate, only 442 copies of *The Fair Haven* were sold, a paltry number after the success of *Erewhon*, which had sold almost ten times this number.[21] Butler's disappointment is evident from his correspondence with his friend and fellow writer, Edward Clodd. In one letter Butler writes: 'I venture to send you [...] one of the many unsold copies of *The Fair Haven*', and in another he quips: 'If you know any one else who you think would like a *Fair Haven* he can have it [...] I ought to pay any one for taking it.'[22] As someone also engaged with biblical scholarship, Clodd would have had a particular interest in Butler's book, and its failure to impress may well have influenced his own decision to select the safer option of a rationalist biography to expound his ideas on the life of Christ. His own *Jesus of Nazareth: Embracing a Sketch of Jewish History to the Time of His Birth*, in common with *The Fair Haven*, endeavoured to be 'of service to those [...] unable to follow in detail the methods of modern criticism', and while not a best-seller, its more familiar generic identity ensured that it reached a wider readership than Butler's more hybrid work.[23] *The Fair Haven*'s failure to engage the Victorian reader could be put down to a number of reasons, the most compelling being its author's insistence on mimicking the religious discourse of his time. In this respect,

Butler is a victim of his own success. By so authentically capturing the circumlocutions, repetitions and involved grammatical phrasing of the Higher Criticism, the author does his reader no favours, with even someone as erudite as Charles Darwin remarking that it 'was not light reading' – an admirably tactful meiosis.[24] Though Butler had originally considered the Memoir to be the novel's 'stupidest part',[25] he was quick to realize that it was, in fact, its most successful element, and he advised Clodd to confine his reading to this section in the hope that this, if not the rest, would 'amuse' him.[26] It was, in fact, the energy and pace of the Memoir that made the satire that followed seem all the more heavy-going by comparison. Partly based on his own family experiences, the Memoir takes the reader through the early life of John Pickard Owen with comic brio. John's first awakenings of religious doubt, for example, come not from a text or a sermon but from spying on his mother's friend undressing, and realizing, as she peels away numerous undergarments, that she is not 'all solid woman', from which revelation he extrapolates that 'The world itself was hollow, made up of shams and delusions' (FH 6). That readers were gripped by the Memoir and bemused by what followed is clear from the responses of some of Butler's correspondents, who encouraged him to drop the theology and concentrate on the human interest. Darwin detected a 'dramatic power' in the early stages of The Fair Haven, advising its author to 'write a really good novel';[27] Miss Savage felt similarly, telling Butler: 'I am […] sure you would write such a beautiful novel.'[28] The wisdom of such friendly advice would not become fully apparent until 1903 when Butler's finest fiction, The Way of All Flesh, one of the most iconoclastic of Victorian novels, was posthumously published.

While numerous commentators, from the early twentieth century to the present day, have remarked on the autobiographical elements of the Memoir, and its anticipation of The Way of All Flesh, not much attention has been paid to the equally self-referential nature of the remaining portion of the novel and its significance as a prototype of what the Edwardian Stephen Reynolds termed 'autobiografiction'. In its treatment of elements of the author's own life, particularly his struggle with Christianity, through a fictitious editor and his equally fictitious subject, The Fair Haven stands as the forerunner of works such as The Autobiography of Mark Rutherford, where the inner conflict of the author, Hale White, is conveyed through its fictional subject and his editor-friend, Reuben Shapcott. Careful reading of

The Fair Haven, alongside Butler's *Notebooks*, reveals more than just superficial affinities between John Pickard Owen and his creator. The contradictoriness of John's narrative, often blamed for impeding the clarity of the satire, is also an expression of Butler's own confliction. While his primary motivation in writing *The Fair Haven* may have come from an attraction to rationalism, there is also a part of him that reserves judgement. He writes in his *Notebooks*:

> the attempt to symbolise the unknown is certain to involve inconsistencies and absurdities of all kinds and it is childish to complain of their existence unless one is prepared to advocate the stifling of all religious sentiment, and this is like trying to stifle hunger or thirst. To be at all is to be religious more or less.[29]

For Butler, then, the road to apostasy was not a straightforward one, and uncertainty and the unknowable were inescapable elements of human existence.

The Fair Haven is an intriguing anomaly among the religious fiction of its time, often defined by what it fails to be: a successful satire, an engrossing novel, a coherent account of contemporary biblical scholarship. As a work of fiction, it was a brave if ultimately unsuccessful attempt to bring Continental scholarship to a Victorian audience without recourse to voluminous Lives of Jesus or tract-like novels. There can be no doubt that Butler had seriously underestimated the difficulties inherent in fictionalizing theory, difficulties that writers would continue to grapple with in the closing years of the century. In *A Writer's Recollections*, Mrs Humphry Ward explains how she endeavoured to deal with 'the reading and the argument which had been of necessity excluded from the novel [*Robert Elsmere*]' in the form of a fictional dialogue that she claims to have made 'as living and as varied' as she could.[30] Published in the *Nineteenth Century*, 'A New Reformation, A Dialogue', though bearing a formal resemblance to Oscar Wilde's agonistic writings 'The Critic as Artist' and 'The Decay of Lying', is entirely lacking in their intellectual sparkle, wit and epigrammatic grace.[31] Indeed, it is forced and cumbersome specimens of Victorian 'dumbing-down' such as this which explain why Andrew Lang preferred to take his Higher Criticism 'neat'.

Yet if *The Fair Haven* is a failed synergy of theory and fiction, it went some way to carving out what could be regarded as an anticipation of Modernism in its use of masking personae and its exploration of the self. If the evangelical narrator of the Memoir, William, serves as Butler's superego, so his elder brother, John, serves as his alter ego. John travels Butler's own spiritual journey from evangelicalism to unbelief but, unlike his creator, returns to the orthodoxy of his youth, and at great cost. John's eagerness to record his tempestuous spiritual journey leads him into a state of exhaustion and 'religious melancholy', resulting in his death 'on the 15th of March, 1872, aged 40' (*FH* 49). Looking beyond the immediate facetiousness of the actual date (the Ides of March), Butler's decision to kill his fictional counterpart at the same time that *The Fair Haven* is being written, and at much the same age as the author himself, confirms his inability to return to the securities of religious orthodoxy. For Butler, the rekindling of Christian faith was an idea he could only countenance in fictional terms.

The Fair Haven is best seen as a fictional playing out of the human struggle to find truth and certainty. Ultimately, it offers no one overarching theory, unless it be that knowledge and truth will always be provisional, what Butler described in his *Notebooks* as 'best guesses at truth that could be made at any given time'.[32] In some respects, the novel foretells Karl Popper's conviction that the refutation of a theory will always bring us closer to the truth, as Victorian belief systems – or 'best guesses' – as disparate as Millenarianism, Broad Church liberalism and agnosticism all come under the author's sceptical regard. That the focus of the satire in *The Fair Haven* is not steady or monoperspectival can be put down to Butler's main intellectual position, insisting as it does that inconsistencies, contradictions and error will always form the outcome of mankind's attempts to make sense of what he called the 'unseen world'.[33] Yet if the novel is generally true to its law of falsification, there is one theory that proves the exception: that Christ did not die on the cross. Totting up his achievements in his *Notebooks* towards the end of his life, Butler lists his Resurrection pamphlet as one of his most interesting endeavours. While the 'swoon theory' that the pamphlet champions belonged to a much earlier period of rationalism, and would never again carry any theological weight, it would continue to circulate well into the twentieth century, providing the foundation for some radical and imaginative retellings of the Scriptures.

Philochristus: Edwin A. Abbott's 'Disciple of the Lord' (1878)

One of the many readers to be perplexed by *The Fair Haven* was
Edwin A. Abbott, a contemporary of Butler's at St John's College,
Cambridge, and a well-established writer on both secular and religious topics. Recalling their reunion in London, some years after
leaving the university, Butler writes:

> By and by he asked me to dinner and I went. I found him a dull
> fellow [...] and a dull, pedagogical fellow into the bargain. There
> was a man named Seeley there, who had written *Ecce Homo* – trash
> which Mr Gladstone had had a fit over [...] Then I wrote *The Fair
> Haven* and was asked again.[34]

It easy to imagine why Butler might have felt somewhat out of place
at such a dinner table and why he felt moved to recount the occasion
with quite such splenetic force. His host, Abbott, and his fellow diner
J. R. Seeley had a close friendship, dating back to their time as pupils
at the City of London School and both were prominent members of
the Advanced Broad Church, to which Butler – somewhat waywardly
– declared an allegiance.[35] Yet a church would have had to have been
very broad indeed to have contained such contrasting spirits as Butler
and Abbott. Where Butler was addicted to polemic, satire and iconoclasm, Abbott was intent on thoughtful adaptation, earnest debate and
breaking down what he saw as false dichotomies in religious thinking.
Such contrasts in attitude and manner are evident in their dealings
with Higher Critical ideas. Butler's instinct was to wrestle with
modernist theology for the sake of intellectual probity; Abbott's was
to stop unbelief in its tracks by demonstrating how the arguments of,
say, Strauss or Darwin could be entirely compatible with Christian
belief. Most telling of all contrasts, perhaps, was that between Butler's
refusal to enter holy orders and Abbott's life-long devotion to the
Church of England and his role as priest and preacher.

Abbott's acquaintance with the great and the good of liberal
theology, such as Benjamin Jowett, William Sanday and J. Llewelyn
Davies, ensured that he was always at the heart of the debates
surrounding the changing face of Christianity; and, though certainly a
more moderate and cautious man than Butler, he was equally
committed to promulgating what were, by the standards of the day,
highly heterodox views. He believed passionately in what he termed

the 'natural worship' of Christ and what he felt others might dub 'Christian positivism'. For him, Jesus was the ideal form of human being, the supreme object of love, trust and awe; Christianity did not subsist in the historical truth of the Virgin Birth or the Resurrection, but in a force of the imagination that enabled the believer to appreciate the spiritual, rather than the material, body of Christ. Little wonder, then, that Butler recalls Abbott's being both bemused and discomfited on learning that the 'Christ-Ideal' chapter of *The Fair Haven* was entirely insincere, and that his own fictional response to the Higher Criticism should present Jesus in a rather more reverential light.

1878 saw the publication of Abbott's first fictional writing and the first British novel to feature Jesus as its central character: *Philochristus: Memoirs of a Disciple of the Lord*.[36] Told from the viewpoint of a fictional disciple, this re-imagining of the Gospels was Abbott's bold attempt to put into story form ideas that, a year earlier, he had expounded in *Through Nature to Christ* (1877), a scholarly monograph. The main aim of this work was to communicate the author's vision of a non-miraculous Christianity to those who, while inclined to heterodoxy, were not yet confirmed agnostics. Though entirely reverent in tone, its argument was far from orthodox and the author expected his work to cause a stir. If Butler positively encouraged controversy, Abbott was not similarly inclined, a difference that came as much from the exigencies of economics as temperament. As a bachelor of independent means, Butler was relatively unburdened by financial responsibility. Abbott's circumstances were rather more precarious, as his letter regarding the imminent publication of *Through Nature to Christ* makes clear:

> If I do not lose my present position I shall be quite willing [...] that the book should be published on our usual terms [:] half profits, you taking the risk [...] But if I lose my post I shall have next to nothing to live on [...] Now of course I could not be turned out of my post for this book, without attracting a great deal of attention to the book and making it commercially a great success. Therefore [...] I will take all risk, pay all bills, and receive all profits, paying you the usual commission.[37]

Abbott did not lose his job – though the book did indeed provoke some harsh criticism – and the author was undeterred from translating his unorthodox version of Christianity into fiction, potentially an even more daring venture.

In some respects, *Philochristus* could be regarded as more transitional than ground-breaking. The author himself described it as 'half fiction, half religious' and even a cursory glance at the work reveals it as a strange hybrid of the conventional Life of Jesus and autobiographical fiction.[38] The paratext, though kept within the fictional framework of an imaginary scribe and editor, appears identical to the table of contents and critical paraphernalia of the typical Life and, when the printer made the mistake of omitting these sections from the first published edition, Abbott was most anxious that the error should be rectified with all speed. His correspondence with Macmillan also indicates that he viewed his work very much in terms of the biographical mode. Writing to the company in early 1874 to advise them that he had completed *Philochristus*, he added that he had 'carefully compared it with *Ecce Homo*'; in addition, he pointed out that the publication of Farrar's *The Life of Christ* that same year was a compelling reason to delay the launch of his own version of the Gospels.[39] Publishing a work by a relatively unknown author to coincide with that of the celebrated Dean Farrar, and on the same topic, would, of course, have made little commercial sense; it is also likely that Abbott feared his text would appear all the more heterodox if placed alongside the work of someone as uncontroversial as Farrar.

Yet Abbott's decision to abandon the speculative mood of the biographer for the intimacy of a fictional autobiographical narrator was in itself a bold move. To date, British novels treating the story of Christianity had dealt with the first five centuries or so *after* the crucifixion and not with the actual life and times of Jesus. As Abbott no doubt realized, depicting the life of Christ through the more direct mimetic structures of fiction was a good deal more contentious. In imagining Jesus through the eyes of one of his contemporaries, Abbott was venturing on a form of fiction that, though quite new to Britain, was already well established in the United States. Here, fictional versions of the Gospels had started to replace narratives of Christian martyrdom a good twenty years earlier. One particularly popular American New Testament fiction – so popular that a baseball team was named after it – was *The Prince of the House of David* (1855), written by Joseph Holt Ingraham, an Episcopalian minister from Mobile, Alabama. An epistolary religious romance, the novel relates the life of Christ through a series of letters written by Adina, a young Jewess, to her father in Alexandria. While Ingraham's writing differs starkly from Abbott's in its lack of erudition and unremittingly purple prose, he shares with him the technique of presenting Jesus from the point of view of a fictional eyewitness, referring to it in the preface as 'a new aspect [...] a new point of view'.[40] And, if Abbott feared the wrath of the faithful on the publication of *Philochristus*, so Ingraham, two decades before him, had felt moved to introduce his work with the defensive statement: 'There can be no charge of irreverence where none is intended.'[41]

Abbott's decision to take on the challenge of presenting his views on Christianity through prose fiction can be put down to a number of factors. He may well have sensed that the fashion for Lives of Jesus appeared to be reaching its peak and that a new, more vital mode of expression was required to keep wavering Christians from falling into a hardened state of agnosticism. He was also a writer of considerable literary sensibility who moved in fashionable artistic circles (on one occasion in the 1870s dining with George Eliot and George Henry Lewes in the company of Trollope and Turgenev), and he may have found the prospect of writing his first imaginative work a source of some excitement and challenge. By the time he embarked on *Philochristus*, he had already shown his interest in imaginative literature through his work as headmaster at the City of London School. One of the features of his distinguished career at the school (which was also his *alma mater*) was his introduction of English Literature to the curriculum in all years, including the compulsory study of one Shakespeare play each term for sixth-formers; he also published several works on literary subjects, including *A Shakespearean Grammar* (1869) and *English Lessons for English People* (1871), co-authored with Seeley.

Whatever Abbott's motivation for writing *Philochristus* might have been, there is no doubt that the work meant a great deal to him. In a letter to Macmillan, the involved syntax and frequent parentheses of which betray his nervousness at the prospect of the novel's going public, he explains that it is 'the result of many years of labour' and his only chance of 'being remembered for a generation'. What is also revealed in the letter is that he was fully prepared to risk offending the orthodox. In a paragraph double underlined as 'private', he explains:

> I shall publish it anonymously: but shall carefully let it be known that I am the author: for there are reasons why (though I may not like to be abused by *name* in the religious papers) I have no right to shirk the odium of heterodoxy, for the book is heterodox.[42]

Indeed, with Seeley as his dedicatee, it was likely that its author could be easily identified and that readers would not expect an orthodox work.

Abbott's version of the Gospels is told through the frame narrative of Philochristus, once a youthful disciple of Jesus and now an old man established in his church in London. Having witnessed the destruction of Jerusalem, but not the second coming that was prophesied to follow, Philochristus is prompted to record his memories of Christ for posterity before death overtakes him. In introducing his account of Jesus, the narrator seems to articulate Abbott's own misgivings about whether such a great figure can ever be adequately portrayed through writing:

> But when I adventured to write, behold, it was an hard matter and well-nigh impossible, to set forth an image of the Lord Jesus as should be at once according to the truth, and yet not altogether too bright for mortal eye to look upon and love. (*P* viii)

It was a sentiment frequently expressed in the prefaces to Lives of Jesus and one that Abbott seemed to have felt quite sincerely. The tone of gentle reverence established here at the start of the work never falters, as Abbott's fictional fifth Gospel takes the reader through his own very nineteenth-century account of Jesus's ministry, already clearly outlined in *Through Nature to Christ*. The reader is told of Jesus's emergence as a leader of the Galileans, partly through his power of instantaneous healing, but also through the people's mistaken expectation that he would take up arms in a quest to liberate Israel. As his ministry progresses, his followers become increasingly alienated by his breaking down of barriers between Jew and Gentile, his disregard for the Mosaic Law and his fondness for society's dispossessed. Some of his closest disciples become more and more bemused by his often opaque and metaphorical language and stories, and by his insistence on strict standards of morality obtained through inner, rather than outer, righteousness. So Philochristus's story pushes through Abbott's conviction that Jesus was a fully human being, an ideal pattern for all mankind and a leader who brought the promise of spiritual resurrection and immortality into the world.

There is no denying that Abbott's first fiction is heterodox in its quiet but persistent denial of Christ as a miracle worker and of his bodily resurrection, yet its tone is unwaveringly devout and respectful. The figure of Christ is introduced into the text in a tentative manner, as Philochristus announces that he will portray Jesus 'as in a mirror […] seen as by reflexion' (*P* viii), a technique that guarantees that a seemly distance is maintained between reader and holy subject. His first direct reference to Christ is as 'the stranger' (*P* 38), whose compassionate treatment of a young boy possessed by spirits leaves a lasting impression upon him; but this stranger is not identified as Jesus until almost a fifth of the way through the novel. And even when Philochristus lives amidst Jesus and his disciples, the reader is only allowed to glimpse the master from a distance. Not counted among the chosen twelve, Philochristus is usually positioned on the peripheries of significant events. When Jesus addresses the people of Bethsaida, for example, Philochristus recalls how he 'could not come nigh unto him for the press' (*P* 171); and even when he manages to catch the actual words of his leader, on one of the many occasions when he heals the sick, he 'could not see the countenance of Jesus' (*P* 152).

While insisting on the humanity of Jesus through his narrator's yearning for 'a man, or some similitude of a man' (*P* 69) on which to focus his religious passion, we hear little of his leader's actual physical self. Philochristus's memories of Jesus are phrased in language that, while avoiding implications of the supernatural, creates an aura of alterity around him. He recalls being drawn towards Jesus 'as by an enchantment' (*P* 98), and from then on associates him with images of celestial light. As time moves on, Jesus is defined in increasingly beatific terms until, just before his arrest, he takes on the 'countenance of an angel' (*P* 368). In employing such imagery, Abbott shies away from describing the bodily reality of Christ, a tendency also evident in his handling of the crucifixion. Where the likes of Farrar seem almost to relish the corporeal agonies of the cross, Abbott's employment of a single narrator allows him to offer a muted, though nonetheless evocative, account of human sacrifice:

> a deep silence fell on the crowd; and I could hear the blows of the hammer upon the nails; and every man held his breath, if perchance there might come the sound of a shriek or a groan. But no such sound came to the place where we stood. (*P* 386)

Unable to see the face of Jesus, 'for his head was bowed forward and his hair, hanging over his forehead, hid his eyes' (*P* 386), and oppressed by the baying of the crowd, Philochristus flees the scene, returning only to witness the crucified man's final moment.

As Abbott insists on turning away from the flesh and blood realities of Jesus, so he omits events or details that place his subject in a less than perfect light. Recalling, perhaps, the opprobrium heaped on Renan for depicting Christ's increasingly morose temper in the final stages of his ministry, he ensures that his Jesus remains 'gentle and tender' (P 337). He accomplishes this by the careful redaction of his source materials, choosing, for example, to put into the mouth of his narrator Luke's parabolic rendition of the story of the barren fig tree (13:6–9) rather than the accounts given by Matthew (21:18–23) and Mark (11:12–14), which tell of Christ's actual cursing of the tree and the resulting physical damage. This particular choice of one Gospel account over another is more than one man's preference; it reflects a more general unease to be found in Victorian readers, puzzled by this snapshot of an angry and vengeful Jesus. Indeed, Farrar devotes several pages of his Life of Christ to a discussion of the fig tree miracle and why so many Bible readers considered it 'an untrue and mistaken story'.[43] Abbott also shows a sharp awareness of the sensibilities of his potential readers in his steering clear of references to Jesus's sexuality. His decision only to include events recorded in all three Synoptic Gospels obliges him to exclude John's story of the woman taken in adultery – always a minefield for biographers of Jesus – and where Renan dared to suggest that Jesus must have reflected on the sexual life he had sacrificed for his ministry, Abbott goes no further than hinting that he might regret his childless state when, after hearing the proverb that 'they that die and leave no children [...] die indeed', he is left 'strangely moved' (P 204).

Readers who had grown tired of the imaginative excesses of some Lives of Jesus may well have welcomed Abbott's more reticent portrait of his subject. Ultimately, though, the Jesus of Philochristus leaves no lasting impression, lending weight to the theologian J. Llewelyn Davies's opinion that it is 'beyond the reach of human and Christian art, that the introduction of our Lord in a work of fiction should be so managed as not to create disappointment and a sense of inadequacy in the minds of readers of the Gospels'.[44] Much of the disappointment and inadequacy of Abbott's depiction of Christ comes from his privileging of theology over the demands of narrative. If the reader is left with only the vaguest sense of Jesus, he is left with a much clearer understanding of Abbott's theological stance. Areas of

New Testament studies treated in *Through Nature to Christ* are amplified in *Philochristus*. Abbott was particularly concerned with the existence of what he termed a 'Common Tradition' (a narrative of the words and deeds of Jesus that predates the Gospels), now commonly referred to as the 'Synoptic problem'. Part of this 'problem' was ascertaining the existence and provenance of a common source text used by both Matthew and Luke to supplement the record of Mark, a hypothetical body of writing that came to be labelled 'Q' (from the German 'Quelle' or 'source') by twentieth-century scholars. Abbott's selection of the sayings and deeds of Jesus that go to form *Philochritus* serves to underline his ideas about the Common Tradition, and if the reader fails to pick up on this editorial strategy – and if his interest is sufficient to get him to the end of the novel – he has the point spelt out to him in the 'Scholia' of the final pages: 'But Anchinous the son of Alethes maketh conjecture that Philochristus had in his mind a certain Original Gospel [...] of exceeding antiquity; whence also the holy Evangelists drew that part of their several relations which is common to the first three Gospels' (*P* 437).

Rather less heavy-handed is Abbot's treatment of the truth, or otherwise, of miracles: one of the key theological debates of the nineteenth century. Where Seeley had side-stepped miracles entirely, and Renan had dismissed them as 'tediously enumerated' illusions, Abbott pays them extensive attention.[45] In *Through Nature to Christ*, he asserts his position on the subject with conviction:

> But while I have no doubt or misgiving at all as to the divine nature of Christ, I have grave doubts as to the historical accuracy, or as to the correctness of the literal interpretation of the miraculous element in the narrative of the New Testament. Not that I deny the possibility of a miracle, or that I should decline to believe in a miracle upon sufficient evidence: but the evidence usually accepted as sufficient appears to me quite insufficient [...][46]

It is a view of the miraculous very much in evidence in *Philochristus*. Christ's healing of the sick is seen as the result of a mutual act of faith within the laws of nature; the feeding of the four thousand and the five thousand is related only in terms of their figurative significance, the bread having a purely symbolic existence; and the Transfiguration is presented as a vision witnessed by disciples in between sleep and waking, the story of which is passed around the community, with the implication that it will vary with each retelling. While never doubting the veracity of Christ's miraculous works, Philochristus comes to understand that he 'was not drawn unto Jesus by his signs and wonders, but by reason of [...] love for him and trust in him' (*P* 247), a conclusion in keeping with Abbott's belief that 'it is quite possible to reject the miraculous as essentially non-historic, and yet to retain the worship of Christ'.[47] His friend J. Llewelyn Davies was perplexed by Abbott's approach to the miraculous, pointing out that 'whilst he goes thus far with the naturalizing critics, he believes heartily and frankly in Christ as the Word and Son of the Father'.[48] It was, certainly, a somewhat questionable stance, but one that Abbott would go on to defend in some detail, both in his non-fiction writing and in his other two Early Christian novels: *Onesimus: Memoirs of a Disciple of Paul* (1882) and *Silanus the Christian* (1906).

Abbott, then, manages to clarify his particular perspective on Gospel miracles by a gradual unfolding of a series of illustrative events, embedded in the everyday life of Philochristus and his circle. Much more forced and obtrusive, however, is his exploration of the diverse viewpoints and expectations of those directly affected by Jesus and his teachings. In this case, characterization is sacrificed to scholasticism, with biblical and extra-biblical figures serving as mere mouthpieces for a diversity of first-century attitudes and philosophies. Out of the twelve disciples, Judas and Nathanael are selected to stand for two diametrically opposed interpretations of Christ's words. Judas is the literalist who regards Jesus as a potential conqueror of the Romans, only to turn against him on realizing his 'kingdom' has nothing to do with 'war, nor vengeance, nor military matters' (*P* 203). Nathanael, by way of contrast, has 'a discerning Spirit' (*P* 176), offering Philochristus a more spiritual explication of Jesus's teaching. Appearing only in the Fourth Gospel, it is fitting that this disciple's understanding of Christ's mission is strongly Johannine. As the fictional editor explains in the Scholia that append the novel: 'Philochristus, although he make no mention of any acts, nor of the long discourses nor set dialogue of that Gospel, nevertheless useth the doctrine of that Gospel as the foundation of the whole of the history.' Here, the author's own theological perspective is writ large. Abbott considered John's Gospel as the best expression of his Christianity, approving of its privileging of poetry over history and spirit over fact. To further press home such preferences, he moves beyond the Gospel records to include the historical figure of Philo of Alexandria, the most significant representative of the Greco-Judaic tradition that flourished at the time of Christ, and strongly influential in the development of the doctrine of the Logos, so crucial to Johannine thought. Philo appears fleetingly in the novel when Philochristus visits him to talk over his religious doubts and confusions. In an episode that takes up most of Chapter Five – and is better suited to the lecture hall than the novel – Philochristus listens to his teacher's explanation of the Logos: 'all men have in themselves a ray of light from the archetypal Light, the Word of the Supreme Being' (P 67). For the theologically well-informed, these references to the 'Word' and the 'Light' would signal the ongoing debate over John's Gospel and its Hellenistic underpinnings, an area that Abbott continues to explore through the invented character of Quartus, whose very name associates him with the Fourth Gospel. An Alexandrine merchant of a Greek father who 'had caused him to be trained in the Greek learning and philosophy' (P 117), and a Jewish mother who had ensured that her son was circumcised and 'conformed himself to the worship of Israel' (P 117), Quartus represents the dual influences of the Hellenic and Judaic worlds, acting as the comparative philosopher of the novel through whose insights Philochristus is helped to judge the doctrines of Jesus.

As the novel progresses, Abbott's imaginary disciple is constantly torn between the old and the new, the literal and the metaphorical, the textual and the spoken. He has to evaluate the contrasting epistemologies of the Pharisaic-Rabbinic tradition embodied in Eliezer, son of Arak, with his insistence on the primacy of 'the Law, whereby was created all that is' (P 115), alongside those of Judas and Quartus. In this respect, the novel looks forward to Walter Pater's *Marius the Epicurean*, a work that also explores competing religious systems through the experiences of its central character. Both Abbott and Pater set up the dilemmas faced by their fictional heroes in a way that mirrors the dilemmas of their actual contemporaries, and both produce densely allusive and erudite writing. Yet the success with which the two handle these elements is by no means equal. Though Pater adopts a third-person narrative for his work, he manages to convey Marius's subjective mind, with all its shifts and equivocations, through an elegant and sophisticated prose, adroitly exploiting a number of narrative techniques such as free indirect discourse. Abbott, in contrast, despite choosing the more ostensibly subjective autobiographical narrator, fails to convey any real sense of his hero's interiority. Philochristus's search for religious truth is rarely expressed through the inner workings of his mind; instead, his memoir is crowded with the direct or reported speech of its numerous representative figures, rendering him little more than a device for bringing together various strands of first-century thought about Jesus. The inner life of the hero is also subordinated to the author's desire to demonstrate current trends in biblical criticism. Philochristus's often self-conscious unreliability is a narrative means to a theological end and not, as could have been the case with a more adventurous writer, a way of exploring the complexities of memory, perception and story-telling. Through the observations of his eponymous hero, Abbott informs the reader about contemporary debates concerning the Gospel records and their various discrepancies and contradictions. Frequently absent from key events, such as the Transfiguration or Christ's quelling of the storm at sea, Philochristus is obliged to rely on hearing about them from the chosen few, emphasizing the likelihood that New Testament writings were based on second-hand accounts. At other times he is positioned as a distant onlooker, unable to hear Jesus's words with any real clarity, thus underlining the unreliability of recorded speech (a situation memorably exploited in the film *The Life of Brian*, where the Beatitudes are misheard with hilarious results). Ultimately, Abbott's choice of an autobiographical narrator amounted to little more than a perfunctory shift in pronoun. While the first-person voice enabled him to distinguish his account of Jesus from those biographical lives that had gone before it, it contributed little to its appeal as a work of fiction.

If Abbott and Pater are unevenly matched in their manipulation of narrative perspective, so are they in their management of intertextuality. Where Pater weaves allusion, quotation and citation deftly into his prose, Abbott's handling of texts tends to impede the fluency of the narrative and to break through the illusion of a fictional world. *The Times* described the prose of *Philochristus* as 'Elizabethan English', a view arising no doubt from the fact that a high proportion of the text is taken up with the language of the Authorized Version.[49] Resisting the challenge of inventing a *vulgaris eloquentia*, Abbott extracts the direct speech of Jesus from the Synoptic Gospels, supplementing it with a few sentences that, according to a footnote, are traditional sayings, approved by the venerated theologian F. B. Westcott as 'in a more or less altered form, traces of words of our Lord' (*P* 437, n. 1). As a consequence, Abbott has to create and sustain a style that blends unobtrusively with these biblical quotations, an effort that results in a somewhat stilted prose, weighed down by awkward syntactical inversions and formal anachronisms such as 'it came to pass', 'perchance' and 'methinks'. Perhaps aware of the need to compensate for these stylistic inadequacies, Abbott pursues the characteristically mid-Victorian route of uniting the language of Shakespeare and the Bible, weaving familiar lines from the major tragedies into his own prose. Philochristus takes up the language of Hamlet in defining his pre-Christian vision of the world as 'flat and unprofitable' (*P* 52) and his Greek friend, Xanthias, in responding to Christ's teaching, echoes Desdemona's response to Othello's exotic past: 'it was strange, it was passing strange' (*P* 228). Abbott's attempts to recreate the grand rhythms of the King James Bible and the verse of Shakespeare no doubt served to take the edge off what some of the more traditionalist readers would have found heterodox material, but they added little to its aesthetic appeal. Abbott may well have found the more modern idiom of the Revised Version, published in the decade following *Philochristus*, rather more amenable to fictional manipulation.

Matthew Arnold's verdict on *Philochristus* was that it suffered from 'being neither quite a work of art, nor quite a direct treatment of its subject'.[50] It is an astute judgement of a work that tries – and ultimately fails – to break free of its forefathers: mid-Victorian Lives of Jesus. Given that Abbott was attempting the first intentionally fictional treatment of the Gospels, it is somewhat of an irony that he retains the most scholarly elements of the Lives of Jesus genre, while avoiding their tendency to employ imaginative speculation, domestic detail and evocative descriptions of Palestine. J. Llewelyn Davies believed that *Philochristus* ranked 'rather with "Ecce Homo" than with Canon Farrar's "Life of Christ"', and Abbott's prose style certainly bears more resemblance to the measured tones of Seeley than it does to the hyperbole of Farrar.[51] Indeed, Abbott's novel reads rather less like a work of fiction than many of the Lives that predate it. Farrar's speculations about the colour and texture of Jesus's hair, Renan's depiction of his mood swings, or Geikie's evocation of the domestic routine of his childhood read more like fiction than anything to be found in over 400 pages of Abbott's *Philochristus*. In a letter to Macmillan of 1912, concerning a possible reissue of the novel, Abbott writes: 'I should not like to reprint it without some attempt to improve it, not as to the theological views which I retain unaltered and strengthened, but as to the literary form and expression.'[52] While Abbott does not go on to explain how he might alter the novel's 'form and expression', it is likely that he had in mind changing its diction. Writing in the preface to *Silanus the Christian*, he states that 'No attempt has been made to give the impression of an archaic or Latin style', suggesting that he had come to realize, through the process of writing his first two novels, that refining a prose style to capture successfully the spirit of the early Christian period was nigh on impossible.[53]

Abbott clearly had high expectations of *Philochristus*, both in terms of the place it would hold in his own body of work and the impact it would have on public opinion. In some respects these expectation were met. In the preface to a later publication, *The Kernel and the Husk* (1886), Abbott recalls receiving a letter from a terminally ill man who, having read *Philochristus*, felt able to turn from what he terms his 'reverent agnosticism' to embrace a form of Christianity revealed to him by the novel.[54] Invited to visit him, Abbott discovered that the dying man's faith had long since been damaged by being taught to believe too much, too young. Motivated by this revelation, Abbott began work on *The Kernel and the Husk*, a series of anonymous letters debating various Christological issues from an unorthodox, though entirely reverent, standpoint. If *Philochristus* itself had not brought quite the traditionalist backlash that Abbott had anticipated, this work, indirectly inspired by it, most certainly did. Less than a year after its publication, *The Kernel* was denounced from an Oxford pulpit on Trinity Sunday by the conservative clergyman Charles Gore, who objected vehemently to Abbott's denial of the literal meaning of the creeds and his conviction that belief in the Virgin Birth and the Resurrection was not a prerequisite for ordination. *Philochristus* never incurred such hostility from its readers, nor did it enjoy a place on the best-sellers list alongside novels of a similar persuasion, such as *Robert Elsmere*. Abbott resisted any desire to republish the work until 1916, when he received a letter from a school-teacher, Miss E. M. Farr, expressing her desire to use *Philochristus* as a teaching text. This third and final edition of the novel was published by Macmillan in the same year. More by accident than a desire to protect the author's identity, the novel was once again published anonymously, Abbott having omitted his name from the new preface by mistake. That *Philochristus* had acquired the absolute respectability of a school textbook was a sure sign that, in the forty years that separate the first and final editions, Jesus had become a perfectly acceptable subject for fictional treatment.

Viewing Abbott's work as a whole, there can be no doubt that the author was a more committed and able theologian than he was a man of literature. In a review of the first English translation of Albert Schweitzer's *The Quest of the Historical Jesus*, the writer expresses surprise at Abbott's omission from the volume, remarking on how the 'originality and boldness' of his religious writings made them wholly deserving of a place in such an encyclopaedic and seminal work.[55] No one ever came forward to stake such claims for his fiction. Yet for all Abbott's limitations as an imaginative writer, his *Philochristus* holds an important place in the history of fictional retellings of the Gospels. Vestiges of its narrative form, and its practice of blending theology and New Testament narrative, can be traced in numerous biblical novels of the twentieth century. Now largely written out of both literary and theological history, his most enduring influence is to be found in *Flatland: A Romance of Many Dimensions* (1884), a slim volume that operates both as a satire on Victorian society and an introduction to the geometry of higher dimensions, and that continues to enjoy a certain cult status in the realms of mathematics and science.

Shifting perspectives: Joseph Jacobs's *As Others Saw Him* (1895)

The fictionalizing of the Gospel records was to undergo another notable development before the nineteenth century was out when Joseph Jacobs took on the task of presenting the life of Jesus from a Jewish perspective. His novel, *As Others Saw Him: A Retrospect A.D. 54*, appears at first glance to follow Abbott's *Philochristus* in its use of the autobiographical narrator and its presentation of key Gospel episodes in their first-century religious context. Furthermore, Jacobs, like Abbott, seems to insist on the semi-fictional nature of the work in his provision of sporadic footnotes to identify the provenance of some of Christ's non-canonical sayings. Yet where *Philochristus* is written from the viewpoint of a convert to Christianity, *As Others Saw Him* is told from the perspective of one who fails to be convinced by Jesus's teachings and remains faithful to the Judaic Law. Presuming that the implied reader is a British Christian, the titular 'other' is, ostensibly at least, Meshullam Ben Zadok, a Jewish scribe who recounts his witness of Christ and his ministry to a fictional addressee, Aglaophonos, a Greek physician. On the other hand, as a former member of the Sanhedrin and one of those who voted for Christ's execution,

Meshullam is very much part of the majority of the community his story describes, so potentially shifting the followers of Jesus – and by implication the Christian reader – to the position of 'other' by the novel's conclusion. While Abbott's Philochristus recounts his youthful quest for religious truth, and his eventual conversion to Christianity, Jacobs's Meshullam never wavers from his strict observance of the Mosaic Law, his use of the plural possessive pronoun throughout the novel emphasizing his faithful adherence to 'our custom', 'our nation' and 'our way of thinking'. Telling his story at a time when Paul's missionary activities were beginning to make an impact, the novel's narrator is compelled to counter the apostle's good news of the resurrection with an alternative version of Jesus's life, ministry and what he considers to be his 'shameful death'.[56]

As Others Saw Him was Jacobs's only work of fiction in a writing career encompassing the disciplines of history, literature and science.[57] Born in New South Wales, educated at the universities of Sydney, Berlin, London and Cambridge, and later a resident of the United States, Jacobs was a cosmopolitan figure and a true polymath. A folklorist of some renown, he published collections of English, Celtic and Indian fairy tales, and held the post of honorary secretary of the International Folklore Council. His literary endeavours included editing works by authors such as Goldsmith, Austen and Thackeray, and publishing studies of Tennyson, Browning and George Eliot. But it was in the field of Jewish history and civilization that Jacobs was best known. An orthodox Jew who held strictly to the morality of his faith, he devoted much of his life to researching Jewish race and culture. As president of the Jewish Historical Society of England, editor of the *Jewish Year Book*, and revising editor of the *Jewish Encyclopaedia*, Jacobs made an immense contribution to Jewish studies. His work in this area included sociological and anthropological research into the Jewish race (he was at one time a student of Francis Galton), the recovery of documents relating to Spanish Jewry, and a letter-campaign in *The Times* protesting against the persecution of Jews in Russia.[58] Placed in the context of Jacobs's prolific range of publications, there has been a tendency for *As Others Saw Him* to be overlooked; it is scarcely mentioned by his obituarists, and Anne J. Kershen's entry on Jacobs in the *Oxford Dictionary of National Biography* makes no comment on it.[59] But it is the work that, according to the Jewish scholar Israel Abrahams, Jacobs considered to be his finest composition.[60] Uniting as it does his interests in literature and Jewish religious and cultural history, it is understandable that the author might have regarded it as a significant achievement.

In the 'Afterwards' of an American edition of *As Others Saw Him*, Jacobs explains how his novel 'may be regarded as a sort of Apologia of the Jewish people for their so-called "rejection" of Jesus', a statement that clearly designates the addressee as Christian.[61] Indeed, the very title of the work seems to indicate that it is mainly intended for non-Jews: the British Christian majority rather than the Semitic 'others'. Throughout the nineteenth century, the perceived 'otherness' of the Jews stemmed largely from the notion that, in rejecting Christ, they had been cast out of God's kingdom, forfeiting any chance of immortality. In the first half of the century, evangelical Christians put strenuous efforts into saving their Jewish neighbours from such a desolate end, establishing organizations such as the London Society for the Promotion of Christianity Amongst the Jews and supporting publications with a conversionist agenda. One such work was *Both One in Christ* by A. M. Myers, published in 1838. In its preface, the author states that he has 'undertaken to write the following pages with a view to dispel [...] the doubts, the fears, and the false notions which have hitherto slackened the exertions made to promote Christianity amongst my brethren', and the rest of the work is devoted to recounting his emergence from 'the darkness of Judaism into the light as it is revealed in Jesus'.[62] This confessional conversion narrative was also available in an abridged version for children, wherein the young reader could learn more about the 'truth' of the Jewish Diaspora:

> Where can the child be found who has never seen a Jew? The Jews are to be seen in every land. What is the reason for this? Why do they not live in their own country as we do? The reason is, that they were disobedient to God [...] they would not believe in Jesus when he came, nor listen to the preaching of the apostles; so their city was destroyed, their land was taken away from them, and they were scattered among all people.[63]

As this unashamedly punitive version of history would have it, the chosen people of the Old Testament had denied the fulfilment of the prophecies and incurred the righteous wrath and punishment of God.

While in some respects political legislation and public attitudes towards the Jews had grown more liberal by the end of Victoria's reign (Britain had, after all, elected its first Jewish-born prime minister),

Jacobs, as an orthodox Jew living and working in London, was acutely aware of the prejudice that continued to inform many people's attitudes towards his faith. Moreover, in the twenty years or so leading up to the publication of *As Others Saw Him*, the immigration of Jews from Poland and Russia had created a rapid rise in the Anglo-Jewish population. Jacobs was personally engaged with the consequences of this movement of peoples from Eastern Europe, carrying out statistical research on its impact on the population of London, the findings of which were published in a brief pamphlet of 1894. A heightened awareness of a surge of anti-Semitic feeling in the 1890s no doubt contributed to his decision to add a work of fiction to an already lengthy list of historical and anthropological works on the Jews. Jacobs's interest in the representation of the Jew in the novel is evident as early as 1877, when he published his first literary essay, an impassioned defence of George Eliot's *Daniel Deronda* in *Macmillan's Magazine*. In this, Jacobs attributes the hostility of reviewers to the Jewish elements of the novel to a 'lack of sympathy and want of knowledge on the part of the critics', applauding the character of Mordecai as 'the finest representative of [his] religion and race in all literature'.[64] In the year following the publication of *As Others Saw Him*, Jacobs noted the impact of *Daniel Deronda* on his own work:

> When it appeared, I was just at that stage which comes in the intellectual development of every Jew [...] when he emerges from the Ghetto, both social and intellectual, in which he was brought up [...] George Eliot's influence on me counterbalanced that of Spinoza, by directing my attention, henceforth, to the historic development of Judaism.[65]

Though Jacobs would eventually worry that his praise for Eliot had been rather too effusive, he had clearly realized that she had accomplished what Dickens never could: an imaginative portrait of a Jew that was both aesthetically accomplished and free from the prejudice of the day. Eliot's artistic success may well have convinced him that fiction was one way to bridge the gap in understanding between Christian and Jew, leading him to try his own hand at imaginative writing. In choosing the novel form, Jacobs may also have sought to reach the type of Christian reader accustomed to Lives of Jesus and novels set in the times of the Early Church. Both these genres and their authors were familiar to Jacobs: he was acquainted with J. R.

Seeley, attending some of his courses while at Cambridge, and later writing an appraisal of *Ecce Homo*;[66] he also knew Abbott, who worked and socialized in the same north-west London circles as he did. In choosing the Early Christian novel over the biography to present the Jewish Jesus, Jacobs is true to his conviction that 'the highest truth can only be expressed in art' and to his belief that the current tendency of the public was to 'fly for relaxation to the Something-other-than-the-Here-and-Now'.[67]

Jacobs's combining of a familiar form of religious fiction with a relatively unfamiliar perspective lends the work a radical edge, making it read in places like a counterblast to a great number of the Lives of Jesus that antedated it. Jacobs seems determined to break down the anti-Semitic dichotomy built up in liberal Lives of Jesus whereby Christ is sweet-natured and unfeasibly Gentile in appearance and attitude, and the Jews are untrustworthy, cruel and hook-nosed. Judging these distortions to have originated with the Gospel records, Jacobs aims to set the record straight. The Christian stereotyping of the Jewish nation as bloodthirsty and vengeful is challenged throughout the novel. In relating Jesus's encounter with the woman taken in adultery to his Greek correspondent, Meshullam presents a very different version of events from that found in John. He explains that 'for a long time among us there has been an increasing horror of inflicting the death penalty' (*AOSH* 60–61), adding that 'No Jewish woman in my time has been stoned as the Law commands for this sin' (*AOSH* 61). Here, then, Jacobs seeks to exemplify how the Law of Leviticus had undergone, and would continue to undergo, Rabbinic adaptation according to the needs and opinions of contemporary Jewry. In the novel's account of the Passion, the crown of thorns, that iconic image of suffering perpetuated through centuries of Christian art and literature, is downgraded to a 'faded rose-wreath of some reveller' (*AOSH* 194) which, though still tearing into the flesh, is placed on Christ's head on the spur of the moment rather than being specifically crafted with a cruel intention in mind. As Jacobs points out in a somewhat literal-minded endnote to a later edition of the novel, 'No one desiring to torture another would first torture himself still more, as any one [*sic*] would have to do to make a crown of thorns.' [68]

An even more egregious distortion of the historical truth that Jacobs endeavours to put right is the Christianized figure of a merciful Pontius Pilate, forced into killing Christ by a Jewish mob baying for blood. The figure of Pilate as recorded by Jewish historians, such as

Josephus and Philo, is a good deal less sympathetic than that found in the records of the Evangelists. Meshullam's vivid memory of the Roman procurator's slaying 'of wanton cruelty, certain Galileans, even while they were making sacrifices' (*AOSH* 172) relates to a detail mentioned only once in the New Testament, in the Gospel of Luke – the one and only trace of the more brutal Pilate of the historical records, and one that seems to have escaped the blue pencil of the author. It is the Sanhedrin's fear of the consequences of Pilate's wrath should Jesus lead an abortive uprising against the Romans that prompts them to press for the rebel's arraignment, as Jacobs drives home the importance of reviewing the Christian story through the eyes of the 'other'.[69] The story of the villainous Barabbas, released in preference to the sinless Jesus, is also given an alternative slant in Jacobs's retelling. From Meshullam's point of view, the choice is not an example of the fickleness of the Jewish mob, but one that is entirely rational:

> And shortly afterwards there came forward the man Jesus Bar Abba of Jerusalem [...] Now he had been very popular among the folk, and had lost his liberty in a rising against the Romans [...] And there stood the two Jesuses – the one that had risen against the Romans, and the one that had told the people they should pay tribute to their Roman lords. (*AOSH* 194–95)

Not only does Jacobs invite readers to reconsider the events of the New Testament from a Judaic perspective, he also immerses them fully in the everyday life of the Jew. Later Lives of Jesus, such as that by Alfred Edersheim, had already attempted to place Jesus in his original cultural, religious and geographical context, but this was largely so as to emphasize his *difference* from – and superiority to – his surroundings. As a Jewish writer, Jacobs insists on the essential Jewishness of Jesus, showing his hero as inseparable from the context in which he was born and grew up. The daily customs of Jesus's world are captured in precise detail through the description of a feast at the house of one of the leading Pharisees; the reader is taken from the early stages of the meal when the host 'saw that each of the guests had a piece of bread dipped in salt' (*AOSH* 97) to the 'last course of salted olives, lettuces, and radishes' (*AOSH* 98). In addition to this domestic verisimilitude, Jacobs endeavours to educate the Christian reader in first-century Judaic thought and practice, and in so doing, correct some of the distortions of the four-fold Gospel. The story of the Good Samaritan, for example, becomes the story of the Good Israelite, a shift in emphasis that corrects the Christian assumption that the moral centre of Christ's parables could never be found in orthodox Jewry. In supplementary notes to an American edition of the work Jacobs explains:

> Jewish society was divided into three castes, Priests, Levites, and the ordinary Israelites, and the distinction is kept up even to the present day [...] There would be no point in referring to two of the castes if they were not to be contrasted with the third, the ordinary Israelite of the time. The point of the parable is against the sacerdotal classes, who were indeed Jesus' chief opponents and ultimately brought about his execution.[70]

Jacobs also tempers the Evangelists' depiction of the Pharisees as religious pedants determined to destroy any who stand to oppose them, an unflattering image perpetuated throughout the nineteenth century by popular works such as Renan's *Life of Jesus*. Meshullam insists that 'Jesus had seemed to incline more to the sect of the Pharisees than to any other section of the house of Israel' and, while he accepts that some of them were undoubtedly hypocritical, asks 'of what man can it be said that all his acts and words go together?' (*AOSH* 148).[71]

Given the complexity of Jewish attitudes regarding the historical Jesus and how he should be positioned within Judaism, Jacobs's project was a formidable undertaking. Talmudic literature had relatively little to offer in the way of description or opinion about Jesus, and polemical writings such as the *Toledat Jeshu*, which emerged in the Middle Ages as a defence against Christian anti-Semitism, presented far too harsh and scurrilous a view of the subject for it to form the basis of a work intended to engage both Jews and Christians.[72] However, Jacobs's choice of the novel form enabled him to weave together various strands of Christian and Jewish literature with his own surmises, and to steer a course mid-way between the two belief systems. A case in point is the dramatic opening of the story, where Jacobs binds Gospel narrative and elements of Jewish folklore together with his own imaginative insights. After scourging the money-lenders of the Temple, an irate Jesus is hounded by a crowd shouting '"*Mamzer! Mamzer!*" which [...] signifieth one born out of wedlock' (*AOSH* 4), an incident that echoes the *Toledot Jeshu*, in which Christ is presented as a man stigmatized by his status as a bastard.[73] Readers of the Secularist press may have encountered this source text in a translation edited by G. M. Foote and J. M. Wheeler under the title *The Jewish Life of Jesus*, published with the intention of impugning the veracity of the Gospels.[74] But for those unfamiliar with the notion of Jesus as a figure reviled for the sexual improprieties of his parents, Jacobs's introduction to his subject must have proved disquieting; as one reviewer pointed out 'On the birth of Jesus he is compelled to write in a manner which, though indirect, is perfectly frank, even at the risk of wounding the religious susceptibilities of most of his readers at the very outset.'[75]

As the novel unfolds, the 'susceptible' reader encounters several other threats to his equilibrium. Where all four Gospels record Jesus consenting willingly to baptism, Jacobs's novel presents him as a much more reluctant figure who at first refuses, but then submits to the ritual purely so that his own power might be released. At no point in the novel is Jesus portrayed as an innocent victim of a malign and vengeful Jewish community; rather, he is shown to be a man entirely responsible for what Meshullam terms a 'sublime suicide' (*AOSH* 213). From the start of his chronicle, Meshullam makes clear that Jesus's behaviour is unlikely to endear him to his fellow Jews. Haughty, and capable of anger that leaves 'the vein throbbing on his left temple' (*AOSH* 99), he speaks harshly to all but his disciples. In the final week of his life, his 'stubborn conduct' (*AOSH* 183) at the trial and his refusal 'with words of menace, to take the draught of myrrh and wine which the ladies of Jerusalem [...] prepare for all men condemned to capital punishment' (*AOSH* 198) cause the people to lose all sympathy for him. Nor is he any more conciliatory towards his own relatives. Where Christian Lives of Jesus had presented a variety of arguments to exonerate Jesus from the charge of being unaffectionate towards his family, Meshullam attempts no such defence, stating simply that he has 'heard things told of this Jesus which seem to show some harshness in his treatment of them, and even of his mother' (*AOSH* 18). Not for Jacobs the idealized image of sweetness and grace popularized by the likes of Renan and Farrar; his Jesus is a rough-mannered peasant who, in common with his fellows, gives 'no thought to the beauties and grandeur of nature' (*AOSH* 201), and whose volatility is reflected in eyes equally capable of 'flashing with scorn' or 'melting with tenderness' (*AOSH* 40).

Jacobs's task of portraying an authentically Jewish Jesus to correct the Europeanized image that had grown out of centuries of Christian thought and practice required more than a mere revision of his subject's character. If non-Jewish readers were to appreciate the complexities of why Jesus was put to death, an educated and knowledgeable narrator was required to guide the way. As a member of the Sanhedrin, Meshullam has the rank and background necessary to present an overview of the community in which Christ moved, unlike the disciples, whose vision of their leader is inevitably restricted by their lack of education and limited experience of the political world. Meshullam adumbrates the diverse expectations his society had of Jesus:

> Most of the lower orders were hoping for a rising against the Romans to be led by this Jesus. Shrewder ones among the Better thought that the man was about to initiate a change in the spiritual government of our people. Some thought he would depose the Sadducees, and place the Pharisees in their stead. Others feared that he would carry into practice the ideals of the *Ebionim*, and raise the Poor against the Rich. Others said, "Why did he not enter by the gate of the Essenes, for he holdeth with them?" (*AOSH* 126–27)

With such conflicting interpretations of Jesus and his role, the novel suggests, it was inevitable that a great number of his followers would be disappointed and would refuse to take his part against the authorities when he was eventually brought to trial. Alert to the rhythms of fiction, Jacobs chooses just one event to dramatize the people turning away from Christ: that which culminates in his command to 'Render to Caesar the things that are Caesar's' (*AOSH* 159). Here, Jacobs captures the reaction to Jesus's subtle reasoning by creating a striking contrast between the noisy jubilation of the Jewish crowd as they anticipate an insurrectionary response from a potential rebel leader, and the 'deep silence of mortification' (*AOSH* 160) that falls upon them on hearing what they consider to be a wholly compliant answer. That the reader is expected to identify this episode as the turning point in Christ's ministry is clear, not only from Meshullam's evocation of the scene, but also from the illustration of two Roman coins on the front cover of the novel's first edition, super-inscribed with the quotation 'They say unto him, "Caesar's"'. Jacobs continued to insist on the significance of the coin incident in his scholarly writings, commenting in an entry on 'Jesus of Nazareth' in the *Jewish Encyclopaedia*: 'It is only this incident which accounts historically for the contrast between the acclamations of Palm Sunday and the repudiation on the succeeding Friday.'[76] Unfolding the New Testament narratives from an entirely Jewish perspective also obliged Jacobs to overturn what was axiomatic for the majority of nineteenth-century Christians: that Jesus was divine, and that he brought into the world a religious order that was entirely new. Meshullam describes the profound distaste with which he and his fellow Jews responded to the idea of an incarnate deity:

> Alone among the nations of men we refuse to make an image of our God. We alone never regarded any man as God Incarnate. Those among us who have been nearest to the Divine have only claimed to be [...] messengers of the Most High. Yet here stood this man [...] claiming to be the Very God, and all my Jewish feeling rose against the claim. (*AOSH* 113–14)

It is in the light of this idea that Jacobs asks his Christian readers to think themselves into the mind of a Jew: to appreciate blasphemy from the other side of the religious divide. Indeed, one Jewish critic considered this brief moment in the novel to be 'a healthy sign of a real *Other*' [author's italics] in a novel otherwise too disposed to seek out the *via media*.[77]

Jacobs's determination to correct some of the distortions of the Evangelists is matched only by his desire to assert the centrality of the Hebrew Scriptures to any real understanding of Jesus and the New Testament accounts of his life. Christian attitudes to the Old Testament ranged from the evangelicals, who regarded it as holding a crucial place in the narrative of Christianity, to Broad Church Anglicans who regarded it as more or less obsolete, a mere stepping stone in God's overall plan for mankind. An example of the latter school of thought is Baden Powell's stridently titled *Christianity without Judaism*, which argues that Christ's teaching should be regarded as a complete rupture with Judaism, pointing the finger at the biblical literalists for keeping the Old Testament in its hallowed place for so long. Published two years later in the notorious *Essays and Reviews*, Frederick Temple's article 'The Education of the World' expressed a similarly patronizing attitude towards the Hebrew Scriptures; such ancient texts, he argues, mirror a state of childhood with its 'positive rules, which we cannot understand, but are bound implicitly to obey', and which, once maturity is reached, can be safely set aside. Such an attitude was anathema to Jacobs and not only because he was, as Israel Abrahams put it, a 'stalwart son of the synagogue'.[78]

In a posthumously published volume entitled *Jewish Contributions to Civilization*, Jacobs holds up the Hebrew Bible as crucial to the enduring unity and survival of the Jewish people. In the same way that Christians tended to extol the felicities of the Authorized Version and its influence on great works of literature, so Jacobs illustrates how Old Testament phraseology is to be found deeply embedded in European languages. In the richly intertextual *As Others Saw Him*, Jacobs employs materials from the Old and New Testaments, the extra-canonical sayings of Jesus and the Talmud, not with the intention of asserting the primacy of any one source, but to insist on their absolute interconnectedness. The weaving of these various texts throughout the narrative serves to underscore how, without an understanding of the Judaic writings, there can be no true grasp of the New Testament Jesus. In the foreword of the second edition of *As Others Saw Him*, Jacobs insists that Christians need to appreciate 'how little novelty to Jews there is in the notes struck by Jesus'. It is a point he reinforces several times in the novel itself. Meshullam attributes the saying 'The Sabbath was made for you, not you for the Sabbath' (*AOSH* 36) to the Hebrew sages, confounding the traditional Christian assumption that it is a memorably original and pithy saying of Jesus. That it is impossible to separate the doctrines of Christ from those derived from the Old Testament is further illustrated when, after his baptism, Jesus is reported to have 'spake of the fatherhood of God as if it had to him a deeper sense than to most of us Jews, though [...] it is the central feeling of our faith' (*AOSH* 24). His teachings about the righteousness of the poor are, likewise, placed squarely in the Judaic tradition, with Meshullam pointing out to Aglaophonos, at one stage in his epistle, how the yoking of poverty and goodness, wealth and wickedness, is in evidence throughout the Psalms and in the daily prayers of the Jewish community.

In spite of its resolutely Jewish standpoint, *As Others Saw Him* refrains from offending all but the most orthodox Christians. While drawing the reader's attention to the essential Jewishness of Jesus's teaching, Jacobs also acknowledges his unique qualities, such as his sympathy for women, a tendency that would have had particular resonance in the 1890s, a crucial decade for feminist thought and action. The figure of Christ is shown to be charismatic enough to attract not only a loyal following of women, but also a highly educated and experienced man such as Meshullam, who is thrilled by his voice and admits that 'He looked and spake as a king among men' (*AOSH* 110). So strong is the impact of Jesus on the narrator that he experiences visions of him while studying the Torah, and is entranced by his eyes which 'shone forth as if with tenderness and pity' (*AOSH* 90). In allowing his narrator visionary moments, Jacobs is also fictionalizing – and endorsing – one of the commonest explanations for the resurrection: that the appearance of Christ after his crucifixion was no more than a hallucination on the part of his followers, a natural consequence of a heightened emotional state. Yet if Jesus has the power to move Meshullam in the same way that he moved his disciples, he fails, ultimately, to persuade him away from his Judaic roots. The reader experiences one moment of suspense as the narrator hesitates to vote for the deliverance of Jesus to the authorities, and seems set to follow in the footsteps of Abbott's Philochristus. But the suspense is short-lived. Meshullam concludes that Israel is greater than any of its sons, and the novel closes with an impassioned apostrophe to Christ: 'But [...] the day will come when he [Israel] will know thee as his greatest. And in that day he will say unto thee, "My sons have slain thee, O my son, and thou hast shared our guilt"' (*AOSH* 215).

It is a resolution that seems determined to forge a link between Judaism and early Christianity, capturing the prevailing spirit of the work. Some of Jacobs's Jewish readers were disturbed by such religious tolerance, one of his obituarists observing that 'at times it [...] seemed that, in order not to show any Jewish bias, he went too far in his effort to understand and defend the Church and its representations in their treatment of the Jews'.[79] A similar reservation was expressed by a reviewer who regarded Meshullam as coming dangerously close to being a convert to Christianity, and wondered why 'his editor took the trouble at all to publish his account and did not at once refer us to the narrative of the Gospels, or rather to some modern *réchauffée* of it, as the "Philo-Christus" or some other semi-rational life of Christ'.[80] That Jacobs's religious fiction appeared much like Abbott's to its Jewish readers is not entirely unexpected, given that its representation of Jesus is, in most respects, respectful and admiring. Indeed, a review of the novel that appeared in the *Athenaeum* demonstrated next to no awareness that this anonymous work had been written by anyone other than a believer in Christ. Rather, it considered the author's depiction of Jesus to be in no sense 'hostile, or even critical' and that he was 'brought the nearer as a pattern and example'.[81] The *Athenaeum* review confirmed Jacobs's potential as a novelist, commending his 'lively imagination' and his 'remarkable gift for romance', and though such praise was a little too generous – Jacobs was a regular contributor to the journal and likely to have been looked upon favourably – it was not entirely unmerited. [82]

Jacobs's novel presents an impressive amount of erudite material in a relatively unobtrusive fashion, recreating Jesus's authentic environment in a way that both engages the imagination of the reader and makes clear to him the essentially Jewish roots of Christianity. Hitherto, such contextual details had congregated in the dense footnotes of Lives of Jesus, or had been employed by Christian writers (some with but a feeble knowledge of the first-century Judaic world) to lend their work some Middle Eastern charm. Resisting the lure of the picturesque, Jacobs chooses instead to employ a Gentile addressee, Aglaophonos, Meshullam's one-time tutor in Hellenic culture and traditions. This simple framing device, used in a somewhat redundant and cursory manner in Abbott's *Philochristus*, is more gainfully employed by Jacobs. At the outset of the novel, the relationship between Meshullam and Aglaophonos is firmly established as one of mutual respect, based on a shared interest in each other's cultures. While the reader is reminded only intermittently of the presence of the addressee, through the use of the second person and the occasional personal comment inserted parenthetically mid-sentence, it is enough to give Meshullam's explications of Jewish writings and practice a more or less convincing purpose. Consequently, what in *Philochristus* reads like interpolations from a scholarly work fares rather better under Jacobs's pen, settling more naturally into the texture of the narrative. In addition, as the Jewish scholar Israel Abrahams points out in his preface to the novel, 'The charm of Jacobs's presentation derives from his admiration of Jesus on the one hand and, on the other hand, his appreciation of what Jesus owed to his Jewish ancestors and contemporaries', a balance that ensured it received equal amounts of praise and criticism from Jewish and Christian readers.[83]

If nothing else, *As Others Saw Him* attempted to bring the Old Testament and New Testament faiths a little closer together, and to a great extent it succeeded. It should also be considered as a work of fiction that looked forward to early twentieth-century debates about 'thoroughgoing eschatology', centred on the fundamental Jewishness of the historical Jesus. A staunch opponent of this development in

New Testament criticism, Abbott, while situating the hero of *Philochristus* in his immediate Judaic context, leads him to be sufficiently excited by the newness of Jesus's teaching to break from his original faith. In contrast, Jacobs's Meshullam, fully aware of the derivative nature of so much of this teaching, defines Jesus as no more than 'the best of our Sages' (*AOSH* 209) and keeps to a more orthodox route.

Marie Corelli's reign of orthodoxy

Butler, Abbott and Jacobs all endeavoured to present contemporary theological and historical studies of the Gospels through fiction, and while their literary imaginations and religious motivations may have differed, they were as one in promoting scholarly enquiry into the sacred past. Despite the best efforts of all three, however, sales of their work were, to say the least, modest, limiting the circulation of their ideas to a fairly narrow range of readers. In complete contrast stood the enormously popular – and populist – novelist, Marie Corelli. If the religious convictions of the authors discussed above were sometimes difficult to pin down, Corelli's were quite the reverse. In an article entitled 'A Question of Faith', she outlined the tenets of her belief in phraseology closely aligned with the Apostles' Creed:

> If you are a Christian, your religion is to believe that Christ was a human Incarnation or Manifestation of an Eternal God, born miraculously of the Virgin Mary; that He was crucified in the flesh as a criminal, died, was buried, rose again from the dead, and ascended to heaven as God and Man in one [...] Remember, that if you believe this, you believe in the PURELY SUPERNATURAL. [Corelli's capitalization][84]

And it is these items of faith that Corelli insists on spelling out and enforcing in her religious novels, often in somewhat outlandish ways. Strongly hostile to liberal thinking about Christianity and its texts, Corelli approached her fiction writing with a missionary zeal; her prose, so she believed, would revivify and endorse the Scriptures, which she considered to have been 'very much mis-read [...] and even in the Churches [...] only gabbled'.[85] Furthermore, so she believed, her work would counteract the 'constant output of decadent and atheistical literature' that she publicly declared was plunging the nation into a state of heresy and ignorance.[86]

Corelli's most significant – and most controversial – contribution to the fight against unbelief was *Barabbas: A Dream of the World's Tragedy*. Published in 1893, the novel dilates the Gospel accounts of Christ's trial, crucifixion and resurrection to amply meet the requirements of the Victorian triple-decker. Where Abbott and Jacobs produced earnest, sober fiction to put forward what for the time were relatively radical ideas, Corelli chose to convey deeply conservative ideas through a highly sensational version of the Scriptures, full of sexual intrigue, lurid visions and, most daring of all, through a direct presentation of Christ himself. This paradoxical mix of religiosity and scriptural liberty-taking gathered similarly paradoxical responses. Denounced by some as offensive and blasphemous, it was at the same time held up by others as a tonic for the times, a formidable fictional strike against half a century's undermining of orthodox Christianity. After a more than usually savage mauling by the critics, *Barabbas* went on to enjoy phenomenal success, romping through numerous editions and being translated into several languages, and scholar-novelists endeavouring to disseminate the results of decades of Higher Critical study must have felt the ground slipping away from beneath their feet.

Barabbas placed Corelli in the league of Victorian best-sellers, its success stemming largely from the author's undoubted popular appeal and her intuitive sense of the public mood. Writing in 1888 to her then publisher, Richard Bentley, Corelli asks 'Do you notice what an *immense* [Corelli's italics] eagerness there is at the present day to read anything connected with religion and psychology?'[87] Five years later, *Barabbas* would satisfy such eagerness, no thanks to the over-cautious Bentley, who turned it down as too daring, a decision he no doubt regretted when the first set of sales figures came in. What frightened Bentley was exactly what gave the novel its mass appeal: Corelli's rearrangement, re-angling and, most importantly of all, supplementing of its foundation texts. A prime example of the author's willingness to exploit the imaginative possibilities of the novel form is her choice of eponymous hero. Taking up a handful of verses in the Gospels, the role of Barabbas is extended to fill over 700 pages in Corelli's recasting. Unperturbed by the variations in the Evangelists' descriptions of her hero, Corelli lists verses from all four Gospels on the novel's frontispiece, before harmonizing them to model a more sensational figure than one single version could provide. Under such authorial control, Barabbas becomes at once a jealous lover, a robber, a murderer and an insurrectionist, a depth of immorality that renders his eventual rehabilitation through the power of Christ all the more miraculous. Traditionally thought of as no more than the luckiest escapee in biblical history, Corelli's Barabbas is given a much more sympathetic persona, taking on the qualities of the penitent thief of Luke's Gospel. The novel opens with a lurid description of his incarceration in a dank and suffocating prison and of his mental torment on account of unrequited love for the temptress Judith, sister of Judas. After his unlooked-for release, he continues to suffer the pangs of unfulfilled longing and sexual jealousy, at the same time undergoing a gradual conversion to Christianity. The novel concludes with his being sentenced to death, after being falsely accused of stealing the body of Christ from the tomb, only to die peacefully just prior to his execution thanks to an appearance of 'the shining Figure, the radiant Face of the Divine "Man of Sorrows!"'.[88]

In developing Barabbas from a sketchy Gospel figure to an early Christian convert, Corelli satisfies her traditional Christian reader's sense of the redemptive power of Christ and his love for society's underclass, at the same time providing an epilogue to the Gospel story. With a name signifying no more than 'Son of the father', Barabbas seems a fitting candidate for development. In Corelli's vision, he is no longer a shadowy criminal but a deeply sensitive soul, driven to theft and murder by his obsessive love for a manipulative and deceitful woman. Pulling out all the stops of the sentimental writer, Corelli invites the reader to contemplate the image of Barabbas sleeping in his prison, attempting to soften their hearts by asking if 'it was possible to imagine what this unkempt and savage-looking creature might have been in boyhood' (B I, 22). After his release, we are frequently reminded of the extenuating circumstances of his crimes: he is an insurrectionist in the cause of the poor and disenfranchised, a robber and a killer thanks to the wiles and temptations of a woman. Perhaps aware that her readers would only go so far in accepting Barabbas's transformation into a man more sinned against than sinning, the post-resurrection stage of the novel sees him take on the role of doubting Thomas. As the token rationalist of the novel up until his conversion to Christianity, Barabbas is taxed with seeking out answers to two of the most energetically debated questions in theology: was Christ born of a virgin and did he rise again from the dead? His quest for the truth sees him not only seek out Jesus's mother for confirmation of her chastity, but also the aged Joseph who, he is relieved to hear, had no congress with Mary Virgin 'by look or word or touch or breath!' (*B* III, 202). It was a scene singled out by critics as particularly unseemly, one reviewer commenting that it 'should never have been written', let alone published.[89]

In choosing Barabbas as her focus for imaginative development, Corelli seems to reject the more conventional option of Judas. An equally sketchy figure, Christ's treacherous disciple was, along with the Magdalene, the most likely character to feature prominently in works of biblical drama, poetry and fiction. While some writers chose the predictable route of painting him as the villain of the piece, others treated him more sympathetically, allowing some form of redemption. Matthew Arnold's poem 'St Brendan', for example, depicts a Judas who, while doomed to suffer everlasting torment for his betrayal, is allowed one hour's respite from his suffering every year from a merciful Jesus, a scenario that took its inspiration from Renan's account of the legend in the *Poetry of the Celtic Races*. As time went on, so compassion for Judas increased. The final stanza of Robert Buchanan's *The Ballad of Judas Iscariot* (1904) sees the outcast soul find a resting place with Christ himself, and Coulson Kernahan's dream vision *A World Without the Christ* (1934) concludes with Judas falling at Christ's feet and being granted remission for his sins. Corelli takes a similarly redemptive line with Judas, shifting the burden of guilt to his sister Judith, who is persuaded by her lover, Caiaphas, to use her brother's influence to trap the Messianic troublemaker.

Seemingly uninterested in developing the character of Judas much beyond that of the manipulated brother, Corelli's main interest lies in creating the entirely fictional figure of Judith, the novel's centre of sexual intrigue. In addition to departing from the basic plot line of the Gospels, she also departs from the tradition perpetuated by the majority of biblical fiction and drama writers of choosing Mary Magdalene as the focus of male desire. The framework of Corelli's story demands a rather more sober and celibate figure, featuring as it does a Mary Magdalene who has already found a new life in Christ. The invention of Judith provides a means by which she can retain the sensational figure of the *femme fatale* without compromising the newly inspired celibacy of the Magdalene. A Delilah, Salome and Mary Magdalene all rolled into one, Judith moves swiftly through the novel, leaving a trail of unrequited desire and sexual jealousy in her wake. Corelli writes at her melodramatic best when describing her flawed heroine, whether holding her jewel-encrusted toy dagger to Barabbas's chest in order to test the extent of both his courage and his passion, or soliloquizing in front of the mirror, like the wicked queen in Snow White:

'For such as I am the world is made!' she exclaimed – 'For such as I am, emperors and kings madden themselves and die! For such as I am, proud heroes abase themselves as slaves. No woman lives who can be fairer than I, – and what shall I do with my fairness when I am weary of sporting with lovers and fools? – I will wed some mighty conqueror, and be the queen and mistress of many nations!' (B II, 166–67)

Though a sworn enemy of the 'fleshly school' of poetry, Corelli has no qualms about adopting its imagery to paint Judith as the very epitome of decadence:

Nature, in a picturesque mood, had done wondrous things for her [...] To nature therefore the blame was due, for having cast the red glow of a stormy sunset into the bronze-gold of her hair, – for having melted the blackness of night and the fire of stars together and set their mingled darkness and dazzle floating liquidly in her eyes, – for having bruised the crimson heart of the pomegranate-buds and made her lips the colour of the perfect flower [...] (B I, 196)

Corelli is at her most outrageous in her depiction of Judith's intense hatred of Christ. Considering Jesus a vulgar carpenter's son, given to consorting with the poor and leprous, Judith deeply resents his power over her brother. She rejoices at the prospect of his crucifixion, vowing to laugh at his torture and rejoice in his agony. All of this railing against Christ is erotically charged. Even as she looks down at Jesus prostrate on the cross, prior to being lifted up to hang, 'her jewelled vest rose and fell lightly with the gradual excited quickening of her breath' (B I, 216), suggesting a perverse excitement at the prospect of physical violence.

Judith's flagrant violations of female decorum do not go unpunished. The reader follows her through a series of dire misfortunes: from her brother's suicide to her own descent into madness. In a scene reminiscent of the death of Emily Brontë's Heathcliff, Judith suffers the horrific sight of her brother's corpse:

> Such fixed impenetrable eyes! – they gave her wondering stare for stare, – and as she stooped down close, and closer yet, her warm red lips went nigh to touch those livid purple ones, which were drawn back tightly just above the teeth in the ghastly semblance of a smile. (*B* II, 172–73)

Subsequently haunted by a vision of a 'Cross of light, deep red and dazzling as fire' (*B* II, 201), Judith falls into a state of madness, singing 'broken scraps of melody, sweet and solemn and wild' (*B* III, 129), reminding the reader, somewhat inappropriately, of the final hours of Shakespeare's grief-maddened Ophelia. Yet, just as there was a certain reason in Ophelia's madness, so there is in Judith's, as she comes to realize the greatness of Jesus and the error of her ways. In place of Ophelia's flowers, Corelli's mad woman carries a makeshift cross, lifting it aloft as she approaches her former lover, Caiaphas, to form 'a mystic barrier dividing them for ever!' (*B* III, 62). Recoiling at the sight in true vampiric fashion, Caiaphas attempts to wrench the offending symbol from her grasp, snapping it in two in the struggle. Such a violation of the sacred object by the very man who had sought Christ's execution rouses Judith to such a violent fury that she stabs her former lover with the dagger formerly used only for display. Later finding that the damage she had inflicted has not proved fatal, Judith takes a turn for the worse. Her face assumes a 'dusky pallor as of death' (*B* III, 183), before becoming lit up with the rapture of finally witnessing 'the King' and receiving forgiveness both for herself and her brother. Corelli's evocation of Judith in death, still clutching a small cross to her bosom, confirms for the reader that the novel's Eve has regained paradise.

Corelli's portrait of Jesus contrasts starkly with the novel's earthy tales of sexual liaisons and endemic venality. If writers of Lives of Jesus had tended to stress Christ's humanity, Corelli insists on his otherworldliness. Jesus appears as an 'angelic white Figure' that shines with 'a thousand radiations of lightening-like glory!' (*B* I, 44), seemingly charged with the electric force featured in her first novel, *A Romance of Two Worlds*, in which 'God's Cable is laid between us and His Heaven in the person of Christ'.[90] Closer to a Greek god than a mere human, he is likened to 'a crowned Apollo' (*B* I, 98) and bears a 'mighty muscular force as would have befitted a Hercules' (*B* I, 37–38). And he is no more lifelike in his speech than he is in his physical appearance. Just as Lew Wallace, American author of *Ben Hur: A Tale of the Christ* (1880), had been 'religiously careful that every word He uttered should be a literal quotation from one of His sainted biographers', so Corelli's Jesus speaks only in Gospel verses, clearly indicated in italics.[91] Such reverential treatment of the hero's speech contrasts strongly with Corelli's prodigal use of melodramatic dialogue, resulting in an incongruity of tone that makes Jesus appear, in the words of one critic, like 'a puppet among raving women and moonstruck men'.[92] Yet Corelli does not create a Christ so super-human that he does not bleed, and her description of the physical torments he endures during his last days on earth is anything but respectful. One such episode is built up from John's brief statement 'Then Pilate took Jesus and scourged him' (John 19:1). By disregarding the fact that Pilate would not have carried out the punishment himself (the New English Bible makes this explicit by phrasing the verse 'Pilate took Jesus and *had him flogged*' [my italics]), Corelli heightens the drama by bringing the two men into close physical contact. Pilate's scourging of Christ is unrelentingly bloody and brutal:

> … he turned away his eyes and,… lifted the lash. It dropped heavily with a stinging hiss on the tender flesh, – again and again it rose,… again and again it fell,… till the bright blood sprang from beneath its iron points and splashed in red drops on the marble pavement. [Corelli's ellipses] (*B* I, 109)

Here, Corelli's evocation of 'tender flesh', 'bright blood' and the undulating rhythm of the prose suggest a lurid fascination with the body of Christ; and the transferred epithet in the subsequent description of how 'the scourge caught in its cruel prongs a strand of the Captive's gold-glistening hair' (*B* I, 110) adds a final rousing touch. Corelli insists both here and in the later crucifixion scenes on Jesus's remarkable physical courage. He remains 'tranquil' as the crown of thorns is placed on his head, and 'stirred not' as the nails are hammered through his hands and feet. Careful not to fall prey to the docetic heresy, whereby Christ's divinity prevents him from feeling the pain suffered by humanity, Corelli insists that it is sheer courage and force of will that prevent the victim from crying out in his agony.

Employing yet more transferred epithets such as 'pained blood' (*B* I, 117) and 'hurt veins' (*B* I, 226), she insists on the victim's ability to cut off mind from body, to render powerless the harm inflicted on the material flesh, leaving the spirit free and unscathed.

Yet for all Corelli's insistence on the otherworldliness of Jesus, there is an undeniably erotic undercurrent that constantly threatens to undermine such an image. Unlike those authors of Lives of Jesus who had suggested that Christ felt sexual desire, Corelli – some might argue unwittingly – makes him the *object* of desire. Throughout his trial and crucifixion, Jesus remains an imposing and regal presence. As Pilate stands before his victim, scourge in hand, the reader is invited to gaze on Christ's 'bared shoulders and arms, dazzling in their whiteness, statuesque in their symmetry' (*B* I, 106–07); later, on the road to Calvary, the focus closes in to dwell on how his 'lips parted a little [...] trembled and were dewy' (*B* I, 168); and in a final show of preternatural physical courage, his 'firmly composed limbs' require no bonds to prevent his struggling on the cross, as he faces the worst of ordeals in a manner entirely fitting his 'marvellously heroic mould' (*B* I, 224). To be sure, Corelli's lingering emphasis on every portion of Christ's body would lend weight to Q. D. Leavis's suggestion that the author 'had – for reasons best explained by a psycho-analyst – discovered the novel as a means of satisfying [...] suppressed desires'.[93] With its unsettling fusion of eroticism and the supernatural, the Christ of *Barabbas* left even Corelli's hagiographers somewhat bemused; the co-authors of *Marie Corelli: the Writer and the Woman* explained in somewhat hesitant prose how he embodies 'much of the human – the human that is divinely magnetic, almost, if not quite, indefinable, yet not exclusive, not idolatrous, but simply and gently *human*'.[94]

One of the main didactic aims of *Barabbas* is to separate Jesus once and for all from what Corelli appears to regard as the taint of Jewishness. Pilate seems to voice the sentiment of the author in wondering whether 'this young Preacher, so unlike the Jewish race in the fair openness and dignity of His countenance, the clear yet deep dark blue of His eyes' (*B* I, 90) might turn out to be an exiled monarch, 'notwithstanding the popular report of His Plebeian origin' (*B* I, 91). The Roman executioner is equally sceptical about his birthplace, declaring that 'He hath the air of an alien to this land.' But it is not until after the crucifixion that the first concrete 'evidence' of Jesus's true origins comes to light. Joseph of Arimathea confirms that Christ's mother was Egyptian which, with the Virgin Birth as a given of the novel,

firmly establishes the son's non-Jewish roots. Showing no concern for
the historical realities of the foundation and development of the primitive church, Corelli goes all out to strip Christ's disciples of any trace
of Jewishness, more or less overnight. Peter – often regarded as the
disciple most firmly rooted in Judaic thought and culture – declares
himself a 'Stranger [...] to the Jews', following his conversion statement with a diatribe against his former people's 'filthy worship of
Mammon and the ways of usury' (*B* II, 182).

Recent critics have made a case for an open, non-judgemental
reading of Corelli's work, free, as far as possible, from twenty-first-
century values and attitudes. It is, however, difficult for a modern
reader to regard her as anything other than an anti-Semite, even by the
standards of her own age. Corelli panders to views that are
unashamedly anti-Jewish and that belong to the kind of Christian
mindset Joseph Jacobs endeavoured to enlighten through his writing
of *As Others Saw Him*. From the start of the novel, she leaves the
reader in no doubt that she considers the Jews to be totally responsible
for Christ's death. Though the insurrectionist Barabbas of the Gospel
records is clearly a rebel against Roman oppression, Corelli draws him
as a rebel against the tyranny of the Jewish priesthood, and she spares
no energy in painting these authorities as depraved, bloodthirsty and
corrupt. Well-known for her anti-clericalism, it is perhaps unsurprising that she chooses the chief priest, Caiaphas, as the arch-villain
of the novel or, as one of her characters describes him, 'a self-
professing Priest of the Divine who crucifies Divinity!' (*B* II, 84). The
Romans, by way of contrast, emerge rather well from Corelli's
rewriting. In contradistinction to Caiaphas, Pilate is throughout a
sympathetic figure, impressed and attracted by Jesus, and repelled by
the Jewish crowd's 'morbid engrossment in the work of cruel torture
and blood-shedding' (*B* I, 235). In *As Others Saw Him* Jacobs sought
to demonstrate what he believed to be a Christianizing of the figure of
Pilate by the Christian community, and Corelli is an extreme example
of this process at work as she reinvents the brutal ruler of historical
record as an early convert to Christianity. Pilate's wife, who appears
only once in the Gospels, undergoes similarly sympathetic treatment.
Awarded the aptronym Justitia, she is a passionate defender of
Christ's innocence, whose dramatic vision of 'a blazing Cross of
Light' (*B* II, 144) seems to anticipate the conversion of one of the great
founding fathers of the faith, the Emperor Constantine.

Corelli's antipathy towards the Judaic context of Christ's life and ministry demonstrates her complete disregard for several decades of scholarly enquiry into the New Testament narratives. Several reviewers seized upon this dismissal of scholarship, pointing out errors that remained in the critical consciousness well into the twentieth century. Writing in 1906, one commentator enumerated what he terms the 'serious blunders' of *Barabbas*:

> There is no Roman name Galbus [...] Volpian is not antique, and is rather more modern Italian than Roman. The vocative case of Peter could never be Petrus, and Pilate's wife would never have addressed him as Pontius. Her name, Justitia, is impossible, for it is an abstract noun. Judith Iscariot is a misnomer, and Miss Corelli is touchingly simple in believing that the Hebrews had family names like Brown or Robinson, and that Iscariot was one of them.[95]

While Corelli defended herself with characteristic arrogance and pugnacity on the final point, it was clear that she had little real interest in historical accuracy.[96] Nor did she have much time for extolling the evocative beauties of Palestine. What for Renan had conjured up a 'fifth Gospel' appears in *Barabbas* as a geographical reflection of a decadent state:

> Jerusalem lay staring up at the brilliant glare, its low white houses looking almost brittle in the blistering flames of noon [...] the large loose leaves of the fig-trees lolled lazily, spreading wide and displaying on their branches, ripe fruit ready to break into crimson pulp at a touch. (*B* I, 151–52)

Nature here, like everything else in the novel, is made to serve Corelli's highly reactionary agenda: it blisters, lolls and threatens to burst with excess, mirroring what the writer clearly regards as a nation in urgent need of a new religious order.

Inevitably, given the novel's sensitive subject and Corelli's distinctive prose style, *Barabbas* provoked strong reactions from both the general reader and the critics, with views on its religious and aesthetic value tending to polarize. Despite taking far more liberties with the sacred texts than had many of the 'atheistical' writers she so reviled, Corelli found favour among certain of the more orthodox clergy. Canon Wilberforce praised the author of *Barabbas* for her 'high-minded and very powerful effort to revivify [...] a time-honoured history',[97] and the Dean of Westminster read out its resurrection scene as part of his Easter Sunday sermon.[98] As far as the critics were concerned, however, it was a novel that would have been better left unwritten. The *Saturday Review* deemed it a 'blunder', wondering why Corelli did not 'regard her descriptions, her interpolations, her fantastic embroideries, her pretentious inventions as irreverent'.[99] Its gaudy sensationalism prompted Ealing Public Library to ban it and all other works by Corelli;[100] and the editor of the *Nineteenth Century*, after refusing to publish a review of *Barabbas* by Canon Wilberforce, vowed never again to mention Corelli or her work in the journal.[101] The prolific sales of *Barabbas* were no doubt encouraged by some of the newsworthy controversies surrounding its publication, as readers flocked to read what all the fuss was about. Yet the cult status that the author had acquired by the close of the century was built up from more than idle curiosity, or a taste for controversy. Writing retrospectively, Q. D. Leavis outlines how Corelli reached a readership that extended throughout all social classes, permeating the national consciousness:

> She was not merely the idol of the man in the street; Tennyson, Theodore Watts-Dunton, Queen Victoria, and the Prince of Wales were equally enraptured [...] the Dean of Gloucester wrote expressing his admiration, Dean Wilberforce and Dean Farrar testified that her novels made for sweetness and light [...][102]

Corelli's appeal at the end of a century that had witnessed the overturning of the inerrancy of the Scriptures, the demise of organized religion and the steady growth of scientific technology lay in her creation of fictions that refused to acknowledge that Christianity had been in any way compromised by such developments. The popularity of *Barabbas* was overwhelming proof that the general public and a fair number of clergy had accepted that, if sensational works of fervid religiosity were the most effective way of seizing the attention of doubters, any charge of irreverence could be waived aside. Corelli's decision to turn down one publisher's invitation for her to write an account of Christ's life was an astute one: she had a canny instinct for the popular taste, and was no doubt fully aware that the Life of Jesus genre had had its day, and that her true *métier* lay in fiction-writing.[103] As sales of *Barabbas* mounted – it went through 14 editions in its first year – the literary world scoffed at its aesthetic and academic shortcomings, and those of a sensitive religious disposition recoiled at the glaring disparity between Corelli's sensationalist prose and the sonority of her source text. Ultimately, the nineteenth century had failed to produce a writer who could transform academic studies of the historical Jesus into a compelling and aesthetically appealing literary form, and biblical fiction looked in danger of being dominated by what George Eliot had dubbed silly novels by lady novelists.

Notes

1   David Masson, *British Novelists and their Styles* (Cambridge: Macmillan, 1859), pp. 264–65.
2   Margaret Maison, *Search Your Soul, Eustace* (London and New York: Sheed & Ward, 1961), p. 7.
3   Lady Catharine Long, *Sir Roland Ashton: A Tale of the Times*, 2 vols (London: James Nisbet, 1844), I, pp. v–vi.
4   F. W. Farrar, *Darkness and Dawn*, 2 vols (London: Longmans, Green, 1891), I, pp. vii, viii.
5   Farrar, *Darkness and Dawn*, I, p. viii.
6   F. W. Farrar, *The Gathering Clouds*, 2 vols (London: Longmans, 1895), I, pp. ix–x.
7   George Eliot was one of the few novelists of the period who managed to explore the diversity and complexity of Christian faith in Victorian Britain in a subtle and challenging manner, without resorting to sentimentality, caricature or sensationalism.
8   George Eliot, 'Silly Novels by Lady Novelists', *Westminster Review*, 10 (October 1856), pp. 442–61 (p. 461).
9   Andrew Lang, 'Theological Romances', *Contemporary Review*, 53 (June 1888), pp. 814–24 (p. 815).
10 Cuthbert Lennox, *George Douglas Brown* (London: Hodder and Stoughton, 1903), p. 5.
11 Samuel Butler, *The Evidence for the Resurrection of Jesus Christ as given by the Four Evangelists, Critically Examined* (London, 1865).
12 Butler, *The Evidence for the Resurrection of Jesus Christ*, p. v. For an early twentieth-century discussion of rationalist theorizing about Christ's survival of crucifixion by theologians such as Karl Bahrdt, Karl Venturini, Heinrich Paulus and Friedrich Schleiermacher, see Schweitzer, *The Quest of the Historical Jesus*, chapters 4, 5 and 6.
13 See 'Correspondence with Charles and Francis Darwin', BL Add. MS 34486, ff. 56–86, f. 58.
14 *Letters Between Samuel Butler and Miss E. M. A. Savage 1871–1885*, ed. Geoffrey Keynes and Brian Hill (London: Jonathan Cape, 1935), p. 27.
15 Samuel Butler, *The Fair Haven* (London: Watts, 1938), pp. 15–16. Hereafter cited in the text as *FH*. First published in 1873 by Trübner and Co., London.

16 Samuel Butler, *The Fair Haven*, New Edition (London: A. C. Fifield, 1913), p. x.

17 *Letters Between Samuel Butler and Miss E. M. A. Savage*, p. 36.

18 Henry Alford, *New Testament for English Readers*, 2 vols (London: Rivingtons, 1863–66). Butler seems to have had no qualms about launching a merciless attack on the writings of Alford, despite the fact that he had died only a year before the novel's publication.

19 Letter from Charles Darwin to Samuel Butler, 1 April 1873, BL Add. MS 34486, f. 60.

20 Edmund Gosse, *Aspects and Impressions* (London: Cassell, 1922), p. 73.

21 *The Notebooks of Samuel Butler*, ed. Henry Festing Jones (London: The Hogarth Press, 1985), p. 368.

22 Cited by Edward Clodd in *Memories* (London: Chapman and Hall, 1916), p. 261.

23 Edward Clodd, *Jesus of Nazareth: Embracing a Sketch of Jewish History to the Time of His Birth* (London: C. Kegan Paul, 1880), p. vi.

24 Letter from Charles Darwin to Samuel Butler, 1 April 1873, f. 61.

25 *Letters Between Samuel Butler and Miss E. M. A. Savage*, p. 34.

26 Clodd, *Memories*, p. 261.

27 Letter from Charles Darwin to Samuel Butler, 1 April 1873, f. 61.

28 *Letters Between Samuel Butler and Miss E. M. A. Savage*, p. 36.

29 *The Notebooks of Samuel Butler*, pp. 346–47.

30 Ward, *A Writer's Recollections*, p. 259.

31 Mrs Humphry Ward, 'The New Reformation, A Dialogue', *Nineteenth Century*, 25 (March 1889), pp. 454–80.

32 *The Notebooks of Samuel Butler*, p. 347.

33 *The Notebooks of Samuel Butler*, p. 347.

34 Quoted in Henry Festing Jones, *Samuel Butler: Author of Erewhon*, 2 vols (London: Macmillan, 1919), I, p. 182.

35 In the preface to *Erewhon Revisited* (London: Grant Richards, 1901), Butler wrote: 'I would say that I have never ceased to profess myself a member of the more advanced wing of the English Broad Church [...] No two people think absolutely alike on any subject, but when I converse with advanced Broad Churchmen I find myself in substantial harmony with them' (pp. vi–vii).

36 [Anon.], *Philochristus: Memoirs of a Disciple of the Lord* (London: Macmillan, 1878). Hereafter cited in the text as *P*.

37 Letter from Edwin A. Abbott to Macmillan, 23 January 1877, ff. 32–33. All letters from Abbott cited in this chapter are taken from the Macmillan Archive, vol. CCCXXIX, BL Add. MS 55114.

38 Letter from Edwin A. Abbott to Macmillan, 6 January 1874, f. 19.

39 Letter from Edwin A. Abbott to Macmillan, 6 January 1874, f. 19.

40 J. H. Ingraham, *The Prince of the House of David* (New York: Pudney & Russell, 1856), p. v.

41 Ingraham, *The Prince of the House of David*, p. vi.

42 Letter from Edwin A. Abbott to Macmillan, 6 January 1874, f. 19.

43 Farrar, *The Life of Christ*, II, p. 215.

44 *Contemporary Review*, 31(March 1878), pp. 804–20 (p. 807).

45 Renan, *The Life of Jesus*, p. 190.

46 Edwin A. Abbott, *Through Nature to Christ* (London: Macmillan, 1877), p. 26.

47 Abbott, *Through Nature to Christ*, p. 27.

48 *Contemporary Review*, 31 (March 1878), p. 817.

49 *The Times*, 13 October 1926, p. 19.

50 Quoted from a letter to the Reverend Charles Anderson in Edward Clodd's *Memories*, p. 249.

51 *Contemporary Review*, 31 (March 1878), p. 804.

52 Letter from Edwin A. Abbott to Macmillan, 3 July 1912, f. 139.

53 Edwin A. Abbott, *Silanus the Christian* (London: Adam & Charles Black, 1906), p. 12.

54 Edwin A. Abbott, *The Kernel and the Husk* (London: Macmillan, 1886), p. vi.

55 *The Spectator*, 104 (11 June 1910), pp. 978–99 (p. 978). Schweitzer rectified his omission by including a brief discussion of Abbott's work in one of the additional chapters of the 1913 German edition of the *Quest of the Historical Jesus*, entitled '1907 to 1912'.

56 *As Others Saw Him: A Retrospect A.D. 54* (London: William Heinemann, 1895), p. vi. Hereafter cited in the text as *AOSH*.

57 For the most detailed bibliography of Jacobs's writings, see Mayer Salzberger's obituary article on the author printed in *Publications of the American Jewish Historical Society*, no. 25 (Baltimore: The Lord Baltimore Press, 1917), pp. 156–73.

58 For a recent study of Jacobs's work in the area of race science, see John M. Efron's *Defenders of the Race: Jewish Doctors and Race Science in Fin-de-Siècle Europe* (New Haven, CT, and London: Yale University Press, 1994), pp. 58–90.

59 Anne J. Kershen, 'Jacobs, Joseph (1854–1916)', *Oxford Dictionary of National Biography*, ed. H. C. G. Matthew and Brian Harrison, 61 vols (Oxford: Oxford University Press, 2004), XXIX, pp. 565–66.

60 See the preface by Israel Abrahams to *Jesus: As Others Saw Him* (New York: Bernard G. Richards, 1925), p. 5. It is interesting to note the addition of the prefix 'Jesus' to the title of later editions of Jacobs's work. Making the book's subject matter immediately obvious from its title may have been recommended by Jacobs's American publishers.

61 Jacobs, *Jesus: As Others Saw Him*, p. 220.

62 Alfred Moritz Myers, *Both One in Christ* (London: L. and G. Seeley, 1840), pp. viii, ix.

63 A. M. Myers, *The History of A Young Jew* (London: Wertheim and Macintosh, 1857), pp. 1–2.

64 Joseph Jacobs, 'Mordecai: a Protest Against the Critics', *Macmillan's Magazine*, 36 (June 1877), pp. 101–11 (p. 111).

65 Joseph Jacobs, *Jewish Ideals and other Essays* (London: David Nutt, 1896), pp. xii–xiii.

66 Jacobs, *Literary Studies*. The final chapter of this work is devoted to J. R. Seeley.

67 Jacobs, *Literary Studies*, p. xix.

68 *Jesus: As Others Saw Him*, p. 230.

69 The figure of Pontius Pilate as recorded by Jewish historians, such as Josephus and Philo, is certainly less sympathetic than that of the Gospels. Lives of Jesus tended to follow the Christian tradition of viewing Pilate as the civilized 'other' of the Jews. In Charles Dickens's *The Life of Our Lord*, written in the 1840s especially for his children, the author underscores this distinction through parenthesis: 'Pilate

(who was not a Jew) said to Him "your own Nation, the Jews, and your own Priests have delivered you to me. What have you done?" Finding that He had done no harm, Pilate went out and told the Jews so...'. See *The Life of Our Lord* (London: Associated Newspapers, 1934), p. 100. For a succinct and authoritative account of the Christianizing of Pontius Pilate, see Paul Winter, *On the Trial of Jesus* (Berlin: Walter de Gruyter, 2nd edn, 1974), pp. 70–89.

70 *Jesus: As Others Saw Him*, p. 226.

71 Hostile views of the Pharisees were perpetuated by popular works such as Renan's *Life of Jesus*. The freethinker J. M. Robertson pointed out in *Ernest Renan* (London: Watts, 1924): 'Renan, instead of trying [...] to save Jesus from the discredit of the wholesale vilification of Scribes and Pharisees, undertook to demonstrate that these were in the mass as black as they are painted' (p. 54).

72 For a detailed discussion of Jewish attitudes to Jesus, see Thomas Walker, *Jewish Views of Jesus* (London: G. Allen & Unwin, 1931).

73 The conviction that the historical Jesus would have been taunted for his illegitimacy is still held by some modern Jewish scholars. Gerd Lüdemann, for example, asserts that 'From the very first, people in his home town of Nazareth bombarded him with comments that he was a bastard without a proper father. Hence the taunt "son of Mary".' See *Jesus After Two Thousand Years* (London: SCM Press, 2000), p. 688.

74 *The Jewish Life of Christ*, ed. G. W. Foote and J. M. Wheeler (London: Progressive Publishing Company, 1885).

75 *Athenaeum*, 22 June 1895, p. 797.

76 Joseph Jacobs, 'Jesus of Nazareth', *The Jewish Encyclopaedia*, ed. Isidore Singer, 12 vols (New York and London: Funk and Wagnalls, 1904), VII, p. 165.

77 S. Schechter, 'As Others Saw Him', in *Studies in Judaism*, 3rd Series (Philadelphia: The Jewish Publication Society of America, 1924), p. 45. This review first appeared in the *Jewish Chronicle of London*, 10–17 May 1895.

78 *Jesus: As Others Saw Him*, p. v.

79 *Essays in Jewish Biography*, ed. Alexander Marx (Philadelphia: The Jewish Publication Society of America, 1948), p. 252.

80 Schechter, 'As Others Saw Him', p. 31.

81 *Athenaeum*, 22 June 1895, p. 797.

82 *Athenaeum*, 22 June 1895, p. 797.

83 *Jesus: As Others Saw Him*, p. iii.

84 Marie Corelli, *Free Opinions* (London: Archibald Constable, 1905), p. 40.

85 Corelli, *Free Opinions*, p. 46.

86 Marie Corelli, *'The Vanishing Gift': An Address on the Decay of the Imagination* (Edinburgh: The Philosophical Institution, 1901), p. 14.

87 Quoted in Annette R. Federico, *Idol of Suburbia* (Charlottesville, VA, and London: University Press of Virginia, 2000), p. 130.

88 Marie Corelli, *Barabbas: a Dream of the World's Tragedy*, 3 vols (London: Methuen, 1893), III, p. 227. Hereafter cited in the text as *B*.

89 *Saturday Review*, 76 (November 1893), p. 546.

90 Marie Corelli, *A Romance of Two Worlds*, 2 vols (London: Richard Bentley and Son, 1886), II, p. 128. In a chapter entitled 'The Electric Creed', Corelli expounds the theory that Jesus was electrified, a quality that enabled him to carry out mira-

cles, including that of the Resurrection. In the same chapter, she provides a list of textual proofs of this theory, aimed at marrying contemporary science with orthodox Christianity. It is a theory that also appears in non-fiction writing of the time. Bernard Lucas, for example, writing in *The Fifth Gospel*, explains that 'Christ's injunction to Mary not to touch Him may indicate the presence in His body of forces which would have proved fatal, like the shock occasioned by contact with a body highly charged with electricity' (p. 194).

91 Lew Wallace, *An Autobiography*, 2 vols (New York: Harper & Brothers, 1906), II, pp. 933–34.

92 'A Note upon Marie Corelli', *Westminster Review*, 166 (December 1906), pp. 680–92 (p. 684).

93 Q. D. Leavis, *Fiction and the Reading Public* (London: Chatto & Windus, 1932), pp. 167–68.

94 Thomas F. G. Coates and R. S. Warren Bell, *Marie Corelli: The Writer and the Woman* (London: Hutchinson, 1903), p. 147.

95 'A Note upon Marie Corelli', p. 686.

96 The derivation of the name Iscariot is still considered uncertain by New Testament scholars. For an up-to-date summary of the various hypotheses put forward on the subject, see William Klassen, *Judas: Betrayer or Friend of Jesus?* (London: SCM Press, 1996).

97 Letter from Canon Wilberforce to Marie Corelli, quoted in Brian Masters, *Now Barabbas was a Rotter* (London: Hamish Hamilton, 1978), p. 129.

98 See Eileen Bigland, *Marie Corelli: The Woman and the Legend* (London: Jarrolds, 1953), p. 145.

99 *Saturday Review*, 76 (November 1893), p. 546.

100 For details of the novel's reception and sales, see Chapter 8 of Masters, *Now Barabbas was a Rotter*.

101 See William Stuart Scott, *Marie Corelli: The Story of a Friendship* (London: Hutchinson, 1955), p. 170.

102 Leavis, *Fiction and the Reading Public*, p. 166.

103 Bertha Vyver, Corelli's friend and lifelong companion, records how the author received a letter from a publisher asking her to write a Life of Christ which he assures her 'would be an enormous factor for good'. See *Memoirs of Marie Corelli* (London: Alston Rivers, 1930), p. 165.

CHAPTER 4

The Fifth Gospel of Oscar Wilde

> When I think about religion at all, I feel as if I would like
> to found an order for those who *cannot* believe: the
> Confraternity of the Faithless one might call it [...]
> Oscar Wilde, *De Profundis*

By the final decade of the nineteenth century, no stone of the Christian faith had been left unturned by writers of the religious novel, and pious protests against imaginary versions of the Gospels were increasingly few and far between. Yet despite the loosening of ethical constraints bringing greater freedom to the creative writer, the quantity of religious fiction continued to far outweigh its quality. One writer who was particularly exercised by the genre's literary shortcomings was Oscar Wilde. Whether it be the populist prose of Marie Corelli, or the earnest theorizing of Mrs Humphry Ward, Wilde, a self-declared 'Professor of Aesthetics', found it quite unpalatable.[1] In *Men and Memories*, William Rothenstein recalls Wilde telling him of how, on being asked his opinion of Corelli while in jail, he retorted that 'from the way she writes *she ought to be here*';[2] and his low opinion of Ward's *Robert Elsmere* is set down in 'The Decay of Lying', where Vivian hails it with comic bathos as 'a masterpiece of the "genre ennuyeux", the one form of literature that the English people seem to thoroughly enjoy'.[3] Working as a critic for the influential *Pall Mall Gazette* between 1885 and 1890, Wilde encountered abundant examples of well-meaning religious fiction and verse, the majority of which he dismissed as trite, ugly and anachronistic. Yet, however caustic Wilde's criticisms of his contemporaries might appear, he was generally more disposed to hate the sin than the sinner. In 1888, reviewing an especially unhappy attempt at versifying the Gospel narratives, he remarked on how 'the worst work is always done with the best intentions', an *aperçu* he would endorse almost a decade later in *De Profundis*.[4] In spite of – or perhaps even thanks to – encountering so many lamentable examples of religious fiction and verse in the 1880s, Wilde would develop his own ambitions in the genre. There is ample evidence in early biographical studies of Wilde, and in his own non-fiction writings, that, from the late 1880s onwards, he was preoccupied with the idea of composing his own evangel. Coulson Kernahan, for example, records in his memoirs how Wilde had plans to write what he termed the 'Epic of the Cross, the Iliad of Christianity', and Guillot de Saix in his commentary to *Le Chant du Cygne* [*Swan Song*],[5] a collection of Wilde's oral tales, states how 'Oscar Wilde se plaisait à dire: "Je suis le treizième apôtre du Christ, et je dois écrire le Cinquième Évangile"' [Oscar Wilde liked to say 'I am the thirteenth disciple of Christ and I am to write the fifth Gospel'].[6] While such declarations must be accepted on trust, both being set down in print some years after Wilde's death, they certainly seem in accord with his inclination towards iconoclasm and the merging of the sacred and the secular.

If England provided Wilde with a plethora of examples of how *not* to refashion the New Testament narratives, France offered him a more aesthetically interesting range of biblical transformations. Paris was Wilde's second literary home in the early 1890s and, according to John Middleton Murry, without his frequent voyages to the city, the British would 'never have heard so much of the so-called French influence'.[7] One of Wilde's most esteemed biographers, Richard Ellmann, pinpoints Flaubert's *Trois Contes* [*Three Tales*] as the likely inspiration for his agnostic revisions of Gospel stories, though his more immediate literary circle is at least as credible an influence.[8] Wilde was acquainted with the poet and novelist Catulle Mendès, whose *Contes Évangéliques* [*Gospel Tales*] were published in *L'Écho de Paris* in 1894.[9] Anatole France, another prominent literary figure in Wilde's Paris circle, experimented with recreating biblical texts in his two volumes of short stories, *Balthasar* (1889) and *L'Étui de Nacre* [*Mother of Pearl*] (1892). Perhaps even more significant was Wilde's friendship with André Gide, whom he first encountered in 1891. This relationship afforded Wilde the opportunity to rehearse a number of his heterodox New Testament parables, several of which were later transcribed by the French writer. Gide, though, was more than just an auditor: like Wilde, he had an extensive knowledge of the Bible and appreciated its potential as a foundation for fiction. Engaged with the idea of writing his own drama *Saul* as early as 1894, he is another likely influence on Wilde's plans for revising the New Testament narratives. Paris, then, provided Wilde with a literary milieu in which his ideas for remoulding the Scriptures for an increasingly sceptical age were stimulated and refined.

Wilde, theology and the 'fifth Gospel'

Wilde's aspiration to write what he frequently referred to as a 'fifth Gospel' might well strike a twenty-first-century reader as typically Wildean, combining as it does a certain audacity with a spirit of playful inventiveness; yet to Wilde's original audience, the 'fifth Gospel' would have been a familiar phrase, initiated and popularized by Renan's *Life of Jesus*. In the introduction to this seminal work, the author evaluates the significance of his extensive travels in Palestine for the presentation of his subject:

> I have traversed, in all directions, the country of the Gospels; I have visited Jerusalem, Hebron, and Samaria [...] All this history, which at a distance seems to float in the clouds of an unreal world, thus took a form, a solidity, which astonished me. The striking agreement of the texts with the places, the marvellous harmony of the Gospel ideal with the country which served it as a framework, were like a revelation to me. I had before my eyes a fifth Gospel, torn, but still legible, and henceforward, through the recitals of Matthew and Mark, in place of an abstract being [...] I saw living and moving an admirable human figure.[10]

Renan's conviction that witnessing the Holy Land at first-hand could reveal a hitherto 'unread' testament to Jesus's life, a 'fifth Gospel' as he terms it, was one that would be shared by numerous biographers after him. A fervent admirer of Renan's, it is his life of Jesus that Wilde reveres in *De Profundis* as 'that gracious fifth gospel, the gospel according to St Thomas'.[11] For him, Renan had established a doubter's testament that liberated the Scriptures from the accretions of ecclesiastical dogma and the figure of Jesus from the supernatural trappings of divinity.

The meaning of the term 'fifth Gospel' was not, however, limited to Renan's initial conception of the term. In an effort to counter the attacks on the historical accuracy of the Evangelists' accounts of Jesus that had driven so much of nineteenth-century theology, some orthodox Christian writers argued for the establishment of a Pauline fifth Gospel. One such author, Bernard Lucas, writing in *The Fifth Gospel: being the Pauline Interpretation of the Christ*, insisted that:

> The Gospel according to Paul is the earliest Gospel which has come down to us, and the one whose historicity is practically beyond question. Its right to the title of Gospel is based upon the fact that, although it was not an attempt to record the life and ministry of Jesus, it was and is the fullest attempt which we possess to explain the significance of that life and ministry.[12]

And it was not only established New Testament writings that provided scope for an additional evangel. Archaeology's transformation from a crude method of plundering foreign treasures into a scientific study of antiquities opened up the possibility of uncovering scriptures hitherto unread. In 1886, for example, French archaeologists uncovered fragments of a manuscript purporting to have been written by the apostle Peter. While theologians were quick to dismiss these writings as, at best, a slender supplement to the New Testament, their discovery signalled that the canon might not be definitive.[13] Indeed, the spirit of discovery that prevailed in both Britain and the United States seems to have tempted one prominent New England minister and translator, Dr James Freeman Clarke, to pass off his fictional fifth Gospel, *The Legend of Thomas Didymus: the Jewish Sceptic*, as a translation of a recently unearthed Syriac manuscript. An unfinished preface to the work, not brought to light until the 1940s, revealed the author's intention to publish fiction as fact, and to proffer the additional testimony of Jesus's most sceptical disciple in the hope of strengthening the case for the authority of the established four.[14] Yet if by the 1890s the appellation 'fifth Gospel' was being applied to a diverse range of religious writings, its familiarity did not guarantee its acceptability.[15] Predictably opposed to Renan and all his works, the Catholic journal the *Month* insisted in a review of 1874 that it 'did not in the least believe that "Galilee is a fifth Gospel"'[16] and, almost twenty years on, J. M. P. Otts's decision to incorporate the term into the title of his thoroughly devout work *The Fifth Gospel: The Land Where Jesus Lived* (1892) attracted some controversy. Otts makes clear in his preface that Renan's thirty-year-old phrase was still by no means neutral: 'Objection has been raised against our title, The Fifth Gospel, as implying, or suggesting, a thought that is irreverent and almost sacreligious [sic]'.[17]

As the term continued to provoke debate, the ambition to actually write a fifth gospel came to be shared by writers of all shades of the religious spectrum. Most prominent among these was Marie Corelli whose conviction that the '"Divine Spirit" of the Christian Religion should be set forth in "a new vehicle and vesture" to *keep pace with the advancing enquiry and research of man*' [Corelli's italics], expressed here through the voice of her fictional *alter ego* Theos Alwyn, was typical of its time.[18] If Corelli and Wilde were not natural literary soulmates, it is nonetheless true to say that the former's desire to revivify the Scriptures did not differ substantially from the latter's view that 'If Theology desires to move us, she must re-write her formulas.'[19] However, their motivations were most certainly at odds. Whereas Corelli was motivated to write religious fiction by a burning desire to keep the ideas of the Higher Criticism at bay, Wilde – constitutionally averse to literature written for a didactic purpose – had no such intention. Nor, though, did he have any strong inclination to engage in any sustained way with the modernist theology of his day. The historicism that had dominated New Testament studies throughout the Victorian period seems to have held little appeal for Wilde, its insistence on placing Christ in his religious, social and historical contexts perhaps coming too close to the literary realism against which he so regularly inveighed. For Wilde, the narrative force and aesthetic grace of the Scriptures would always prevail over the vexed question of their provenance, as demonstrated in his comment to Robert Sherard: 'How beautifully artistic the little stories are [...] one pauses to consider how it all came to be written.'[20] Theological questions of textual authorship and composition were, then, only worthy of a brief pause in the process of appreciating the aesthetics of the text, and the contempt expressed in 'The Critic as Artist' for the 'sordid and stupid quarrels of [...] third-rate theologians' (C 204) would seem to have been as much Wilde's as Gilbert's. That is not to say, however, that Wilde was uninformed about the biblical scholarship produced by some of the leading theologians of the day. He had, after all, studied at Oxford, a major site of theological scholarship and debate. The 1860s in particular had seen the university at the very centre of religious controversies. John Addington Symonds, recalling his undergraduate years at Balliol College, Oxford, in the same decade, writes of how 'Theology penetrated our intellectual and social atmosphere. We talked theology at breakfast parties and at wine parties, out riding and walking, in college gardens, on the river, wherever young men and their elders met together.'[21] While the controversies raised over the publication of works such as Seeley's *Ecce Homo*, Renan's *Vie de Jésus* and *Essays and Reviews* had abated by the time Wilde reached Oxford in the 1870s, he is nonetheless likely to have found there a high level of interest in all things theological.

That Wilde continued to take an interest in religious questions once away from the university is evident from even the most cursory reading of his work. Whether it be the decadent, often derivative, religious imagery of the early *Poems* (1881), the symbolist re-imagining of the Gospels in *Salomé* (1893), the mockery of the established church in *The Importance of Being Earnest* (1895) or the expression of more conventional Christian values in *The Ballad of Reading Gaol* (1898), his particular fascination with Christianity and its texts is plain to see. Wilde's engagement with religious writings and ideas has led numerous critics to attempt to define his religious temperament once and for all. This has sometimes resulted in certain aspects of his *oeuvre* being ignored or sidelined so that what is an essentially untidy matter can be neatly labelled. As Wilde's prison reading indicates, he had an enduring interest in a diverse range of theological perspectives, his selection of writings by authors such as F. W. Farrar, Henry Hart Milman, Cardinal Newman and Ernest Renan suggesting an openness of mind incompatible with any one of the various religious positions he has been seen to occupy: devout agnostic, inveterate Protestant, decadent Roman Catholic.[22] The writings discussed in this chapter demonstrate a constantly shifting relationship with the religious, fired by an abiding fascination with the Bible and with the person of Christ in particular. While the chapter closes with a discussion of *De Profundis*, the text most frequently examined in discussions of Wilde and Christianity, its foremost concern is with the biblical oral tales and prose poems, which are much more likely to be overlooked.

Poems in Prose (1894)

In 1894, the *Fortnightly Review* published a small collection of Wilde's prose poems, two of which, 'The Doer of Good' and 'The

Master', provided fresh perspectives on the New Testament narratives.[23] In striving to revivify the words of the New Testament in a striking and original manner, Wilde was no doubt attracted by the *frisson* generated by couching heterodox ideas in a prose that emulated the diction and cadences of biblical versification.[24] At the same time, Wilde's choice of the prose poem underlines how strongly he inclined towards French literary style at this point in his career. Charles Baudelaire, whose influence weaves its way through so many of Wilde's works, was the foremost exponent of this putative genre, and the first to use the phrase 'poème en prose'. Though not the first writer to experiment with the form, his 50 prose poems, first published together in the collection *Le Spleen de Paris: Petits Poèmes en prose* [*Paris Spleen: Prose Poems*] (1869), placed it on the literary map.[25] J.-K. Huysmans, another important influence on Wilde's art, imitated Baudelaire's prose poems in his first published work, *Le Drageoir à épices* [*The Spice Jar*],[26] and elaborated on the merits of this literary innovation through the persona of Des Esseintes in *À Rebours* [*Against Nature*]:

> Bien souvent, des Esseintes avait médité sur cet inquiétant problème, écrire un roman concentré en quelques phrases qui contiendraient le suc cohobé des centaines de pages toujours employées à établir le milieu, à dessiner les caractères, à entasser à l'appui les observations et les menus faits [...] En un mot, le poème en prose représentait, pour des Esseintes, le suc concret, l'osmazome de la littérature, l'huile essentielle de l'art.

> [Many were the times that Des Esseintes had pondered over the fascinating problem of writing a novel concentrated in a few sentences and yet comprising the cohobated juice of the hundreds of pages always taken up in describing the setting, drawing the characters, and piling up useful observations and incidental details [...] In short, the prose poem represented in Des Esseintes' eyes the dry juice, the osmazome of literature, the essential oil of art.][27]

The linguistic concentration so revered by Huysmans' high priest of sensation and aesthetics offered Wilde the perfect medium through which to counteract the contemporary inclination towards prolix rewritings of the Scriptures, some of which inflated one or two Gospel episodes into a novel of several hundred pages. Indeed, the glaring disparity so often apparent between the spare source text and its Victorian adaptations calls to mind Vivian's complaint in 'The Decay of Lying' that 'The ancient historians gave us delightful fiction in the form of fact; the modern novelist presents us with dull facts under the guise of fiction' (C 75–76). There is no doubt that Wilde wanted to return to the 'delightful fiction' of the Gospels, and settled on the prose poem as an ideal form to carry his intentions through. However, it is equally certain that he anticipated no such return to the 'facts' of the narratives.

Ever the creative borrower, Wilde's employment of the Baudelairean model was far from a slavish imitation. Where the French poet had taken the modern city as the subject to be distilled into prose poem form, his successor took a sacred text, an act of reverence and radicalism in equal measure.[28] In some respects Wilde was conventionally Victorian in his reverence for the language of the King James Bible, evincing his contempt for the text of the Revised Version of the 1880s.[29] He had particular admiration for what he described as the 'four prose poems' of the New Testament, and his delight in encountering the '*ipsissima verba*, used by Christ' (*DP* 118) when reading his Greek Testament suggests a traditionalist's reverence for historical origin and faith in the Evangelists' reliability as chroniclers. On the other hand, he was disapproving of the 'uncritical admiration of the Bible' (C 250) that he identified in the English, deeming it a barrier to artistic experimentation, and his desire to rewrite the Gospels was more an impulse of radicalism than conservatism. Perhaps heeding Pater's oft-quoted credo from the conclusion of *The Renaissance* that 'failure is to form habits', Wilde attempted to breathe fresh life into texts that he believed had become 'wearisome and meaningless through repetition'.[30] Rejecting the options of revamping or elaborating on Gospel accounts, Wilde chose instead to build up entirely new episodes, as if picking up scraps from the Evangelists' cutting-room floor and working them into fully realized narratives, increments, perhaps, of his own 'fifth gospel'.

In an introduction to a volume of Wilde's works, W. B. Yeats relates how, on returning to London after a long stay in Ireland and enquiring what his fellow writer was up to, he was told that 'he is very melancholy, he gets up about two in the afternoon, for he tries to sleep away as much of life as possible, and he has made up a story which he calls the best story in the world'.[31] The story that Yeats then goes on to record is an oral variant of 'The Doer of Good', one of the prose poems published a year prior to Wilde's arrest. In the published version, he revisits some of the episodes of the New Testament, imagining the trajectories of some of the key characters' lives after the miraculous moments on record had passed.[32] Freed from the stanzaic and metrical restraints of what Wilde labelled 'the Tate and Brady school of poetry', he manipulates the prose poem form to imitate the text of the Authorized Version.[33] The retention of the upper case for the Lord's pronoun and the breaking of the prose into short verses ensure that the piece is visually close to biblical text, while extensive use of grammatical parallelisms and polysyndeton helps to recreate its cadences. Yet while 'The Doer of Good' might resemble its Gospel origins in a formal sense, its mention of 'halls of chalcedony and jasper' and a young man 'whose hair was crowned with red roses and whose lips were red with wine' invites us into a world akin to that of Wilde's *Salomé*. There is a nightmarish element to this world of vivid colours and precious stones, more in tune with the book of Revelation than the Gospels. Characters approach each other from behind, adding an unnerving edge to the narrative; lutes produce 'loud noise' rather than music, and the senses seem amplified through isolated parts of the body as the sound of 'the tread of the feet of joy' mingles with 'the loud laughter of the mouth of gladness'. Departing radically from the Evangelists' message of good news, the prose poem provides a kind of cynic's epilogue to Christ's miracles of healing: the former leper has become a man mired in sloth and gluttony; the man whose sight has been restored has given himself up to lechery, so that the once-blind eyes now burn 'bright with lust'. The object of his lust is the woman once saved by Jesus from death by stoning, who has since gone against his injunction to 'sin no more'. With her painted face and fine clothing, she is as far removed from the pattern of the repentant fallen woman as Wilde's own Mrs Erlynne. Even more disturbing for the orthodox reader is the description of her feet 'shod with pearls'. With this one simple detail Wilde exploits the New Testament symbolism of the pearl as both representative of sacred wisdom and female vanity to underline the woman's recidivism, providing a shocking visual sign that Christ has failed to heed his own warning not to 'throw [...] pearls before swine, lest they trample them underfoot' (Matthew 7:6). Most disturbing of all, though, is the resuscitated Lazarus who is locked in a life of despair, seemingly tormented by the prospect of looking death in the face for a second time. A prime example of Wilde's taste for paradox, the title of this prose poem becomes increasingly ironic with each fallen character's encounter with Christ, inviting the reader to agree with Gilbert's observation in 'The Critic as Artist' that 'Charity [...] creates a multitude of evils' (C 148).

Just as 'The Doer of Good' envisages the 'aftermath' of Christ's time on earth, urging readers to take their imaginations *beyond* the New Testament narratives so familiar to them, so 'The Master' (*PP* 175–76) asks them to contemplate a type of encounter that might have taken place and gone unrecorded. It pictures a meeting between Joseph of Arimathea and a young man who 'had wounded his body with thorns and on his hair [...] set ashes as a crown', performed miracles and healed the sick yet, he complains, 'they have not crucified me'. A highly polyvalent tale, it has sustained a number of critical interpretations. Some readers have viewed it as a kind of subversive *imitatio Christi*, linking it to Wilde's warning in the 'The Soul of Man' that 'All imitation in morals and in life is wrong' (C 243). Yet while there is a strong implication in the prose poem's title that the distraught young man is slavishly mimicking a superior, the text refuses to make such imitation explicit; it is equally possible to read the story as conveying the idea of a Jerusalem swarming with any number of prophets and thaumaturges, perhaps illustrating Renan's point that 'The faculty of performing miracles was regarded as a privilege frequently conferred by God upon men, and it had nothing surprising in it.'[34] The second reading is certainly the more heterodox, suggesting as it does that Jesus was by no means an original, and that his death on the cross was more a matter of chance than divine preordination: given different timing and circumstances, the weeping young man could have hung in his place. Whichever interpretation of the prose poem is preferred, what remains a constant is Wilde's inclination to aestheticize the life and person of Jesus. Like Arnold before him, who believed that the death on the cross was the 'perfecting' of the victim, so Wilde suggests in 'The Master' that Christ's life is a work of art because of its narrative perfection; without the crucifixion, the young man's actions are as nothing, and his life remains artistically incomplete.[35]

The exiguous number of prose poems fixed in print suggests that Wilde was not entirely at ease with the results of his experiments with the form, and the six pieces have continued to hold a somewhat uncertain place in his *oeuvre*. Wilde's contemporaries were divided in their judgements of *Poems in Prose*. Arthur Symons, himself an exponent of the prose poem form, compared them to 'a shallow pool, trying to look as if it had some deep meaning',[36] and Marie Corelli dismissed them as 'ludicrously bad', no doubt offended by their unorthodox sentiments.[37] A decade or so later, by way of contrast, the artist and designer of many of Wilde's books, Charles Ricketts, selected them as one of only five late works in which could be found 'a hint at the power of thought, sardonic insight, and wit which characterized the man himself',[38] and the literary historian Holbrook Jackson considered them (along with a small selection of his more substantial work) to be worthy of 'a definitive place in English literature as the expression and explanation of the type Wilde represented'.[39] What his contemporaries did agree on, however, was that this slim collection was more prose than poetry. It was published first in book form in 1908 in *Lord Arthur Savile's Crime and Other Prose Pieces*, appearing a year later in the volume titled *Essays and Reviews* in Ross's edition of Wilde's collected writings, rather than the poetry volume of the same series.[40] Only in the most recent edition of Wilde's collected works are the prose poems awarded the same status as the verse poems, being placed in chronological order of composition and included in the title of the volume. Yet however slight a place they might be considered to hold in Wilde's complete works, they are highly significant in revealing his vision for transforming the Scriptures into secular literature. If, as there is every reason to believe, Wilde was serious in his ambitions to compose a fifth Gospel, then the prose poems must be considered as small steps towards the larger project.

Le Chant du Cygne: Wilde's oral testament

Both of the New Testament prose poems had started their creative lives as spoken tales, going through a number of variations both before and after being fixed in writing. Several of these oral versions were recorded by Wilde's literary friends and acquaintances. André Gide, for example, transcribes Wilde's spoken version of 'The Master' in *In Memoriam*,[41] and 'The Doer of Good' is set down from memory by W. B. Yeats in *Autobiographies*.[42] It was inevitable that Wilde's primary audience, used to hearing the tales from his own mouth, crafted to suit the individual listener and accompanied by inflections and gestures impossible to capture in writing, would find their published equivalents wanting.[43] W. B. Yeats's response to the written version of 'The Doer of Good' is a case in point: 'Wilde published that story a little later, but spoiled it with the verbal decoration of his epoch, and I have to repeat it to myself as I first heard it, before I can see its terrible beauty.'[44] Protean in their oral form, likely to be modified not only on the whim of the teller but in the context of every new listener, the ever-changing dynamics of the spoken narrative inevitably suited Wilde's sense of playfulness and his love of performance.[45] His reputation as a skilled raconteur was, after all, central to his public image and Gide's remark to him that 'Le meilleur de vous, vous le parlez' [The best of you is what you speak] epitomizes the tendency, both then and now, to regard him as a better talker than writer.[46] Indeed, Wilde himself appears to have encouraged such an appraisal, once declaring to Richard Le Gallienne that he 'gave only his talent to his writings, and kept his genius for his conversation'.[47] Wilde's oral fluency also chimed – and perhaps still does – with notions of Irishness. As Deirdre Toomey argued in her influential article, 'The Story-Teller at Fault: Oscar Wilde and Orality', Ireland is 'the most oral culture in Western Europe', a phenomenon brought very much to the fore in the latter part of the nineteenth century through the gathering together of Irish folklore by nationalists such as Sir William Wilde, W. B. Yeats, Lady Augusta Gregory and Douglas Hyde.[48]

Wilde had a wide and varied repertoire of oral tales, a substantial number of which were transcribed and assembled into one volume by the author and translator Guillot de Saix, under the title *Le Chant du Cygne*. Of course, a collection of this sort raises questions regarding the provenance of each tale, the authenticity and quality of the French in which they are recorded, and how far the versions selected for publication are 'definitive'.[49] Guillot de Saix goes some way to answering these concerns by supplying details of the contexts in which each tale was delivered, and appending a section entitled 'Le jeu des variantes' [the play of variants]. Inevitably, though, the uncertain nature of such a collection has led to differences of opinion regarding how far they deserve critical attention. Fong and Beckson, in their edition of Wilde's poetry, include them in an appendix headed 'Questionable Texts';[50] and Ian Small classifies them as 'apocrypha and dubia', casting doubt on the methodologies of literary scholars such as Toomey, who uses them to illustrate the vital role played by the oral mode in the Wildean aesthetic.[51] However, one distinguished Wilde scholar, John Stokes, makes a convincing case for paying the spoken tales serious attention, not least for the light they cast on the interrelatedness of the author's speech and writing:

There are stories that Wilde never wrote, but most certainly told. There is an oral Wilde, who is at least as well known as the written Wilde, and who even conditions the way we read him now. So there's an aural Wilde as well.[52]

Certainly, the recollections of Wilde's tales to be found in the various writings of those who had shared his company strongly corroborate those published by Guillot de Saix, and to ignore such a substantial portion of his work – albeit one not securely extant in any traditional sense – would allow textual scrupulousness to preclude several fruitful areas of investigation, not least that of the author's fifth Gospel ambitions.

Guillot de Saix groups together Wilde's biblical reworkings under the heading 'L'Évangile de Minuit' [The Midnight Gospel], an organization that allows the reader to appreciate them as a complete work.[53] Immediately striking is how effectively the transcriptions capture the oral qualities of the tales. Thanks to their iterative phrasings, colloquial dialogue and memorable punch-lines, the reader is able to sense the modulations of tone, the appropriations of different voices and accents and the carefully managed pauses that would have lent full impact to their transgressive qualities. 'Simon le Cyrénéen' [Simon of Cyrene] (CC 117–18), for example, contrasts the subdued and somewhat bemused tone of Simon with the hectoring strains of his wife as she berates him for missing out on the opportunity of becoming 'gardien à la porte du Temple!' [guardian of the temple gate]. Concluding the tale with what the wife intends as a rhetorical question, 'Mais toi, vieux benêt radoteur […] tu passeras vite à l'oubli, car qui donc jamais quand tu seras mort, qui entendra parler de Simon de Cyrène?' [But you, you drivelling old half-wit […] you'll quickly sink into oblivion, for who'll ever hear the name of Simon of Cyrene after you're dead?], the listener is left to savour its proleptic irony.[54] Moreover, the transcribed versions of the tales convey a vivid sense of the literariness and polish of the spoken originals, as reported by auditors such as Yeats: 'I noticed […] that the impression of artificiality that I think all Wilde's listeners have recorded came from the perfect rounding of the sentences and from the deliberation that made it possible.'[55] And if the style of the transcriptions helps the reader recreate the original performance of the tales, so their contents suggest the identity of those who first heard them. The intertextuality of Wilde's versions of the Gospel narratives indicates that his listeners were *au courant* with the theological debates of the day and the different media through which they were conducted. Wilde takes issues that had preoccupied the writers of Lives of Jesus, such as the nature of the Gospel miracles, Christ's relationship with his mother and the motivations of Judas, and presents them from his own irreverent perspective. Where Christ's biographers had tended to present one 'true' interpretation of the Gospel stories, in keeping with their particular religious standpoint, Wilde seems to embrace their indeterminacy. We are invited in 'Jean et Judas' (*CC* 113–14) to consider the view that Judas's betrayal was born out of the agonizing jealousy he feels when John becomes 'le préféré' [the favourite] of the disciples;[56] whereas, in 'Les Trente Deniers' [The Thirty Pieces of Silver] (*CC* 120–21), we have a traitor more motivated by money than love, who hangs himself not from shame but from the despair he experiences on discovering that his blood-money is counterfeit currency.[57]

It is not only the scholarly or devout Lives of Jesus that Wilde seems to have had in mind when playing to his audience. Some of the more colloquially phrased apologues, such as 'Simon le Cyrénéen' and 'Les Trente Deniers', bear a striking resemblance in tone to Léo Taxil's savagely impious *Vie de Jésus*, and seem particularly well suited to Wilde's predominantly male coterie. Likewise, Wilde's retelling of the raising of Lazarus, 'Le Ressuscité' (*CC* 104), owes something to Taxil's unholy reworking. In his crude burlesquing of the miracle, the raising of Lazarus is revealed as a cheap trick. Jesus or, as Taxil describes him, 'le fils du pigeon' [the pigeon's son], keen to prove himself as the true Messiah, persuades the grieving sisters to overcome their fear of 'une odeur repoussante' [a repellent smell] and allow him to open the tomb and revive the 'dead' Lazarus.[58] Taxil turns the biblical original into a narrative of deception, playing on the model reader's vulgar fascination with the body with detail after detail of the physical effects of spending four days entombed. Jesus is given the idiom of the streets, yelling 'Bougez donc [...] nom d'un chien!' [Get out of the way [...] damn you] as curious onlookers get under his feet, and the story closes with the image of Lazarus scratching his buttocks to counteract the havoc wreaked on his skin by 'les vers qui avaient déjà commencé à le grignoter' [the maggots which had already started to nibble away at him].[59]

In 'Le Ressuscité' Wilde manages to retain something of the audacity of the French anti-clerical version while abandoning its vulgar focus on the flesh. The tale imagines a dialogue between

Lazarus and Jesus in which the resurrected man responds to his saviour's question concerning what lies beyond the grave with the blunt sentence: 'Rabbi, il n'y a rien' [There's nothing there, master]; gesturing to those around them, Jesus then whispers in the ear of the newly resurrected man 'Je le sais, ne leur dis pas!' [I know, but don't tell anyone!]. So, the miracle generally regarded as an anticipatory sign of the resurrection, confirming the true meaning of Christ, becomes in Wilde's version a means of affirming the absence of any such meaning. Yet if Wilde seems to be at his most sceptical in having Lazarus deny the existence of an afterlife, he is entirely at odds with the atheist Taxil in casting no doubt on the miracle itself. Those rationalist theories that argued that the raising of Lazarus was mere trickery would have held little imaginative appeal for Wilde. His version of the story has the deception lie in a Christ figure who, while capable of raising the dead, knows there is no afterlife, and who seems to have quite knowingly perpetuated a myth of a world existing beyond the tomb for reasons that are left to the listener to contemplate.

Wilde was by no means alone in his desire to re-imagine the Lazarus story. The brief biblical text was a source of endless fascination for the Victorians, not so much for the miracle it unfolded but for the silence its subject keeps concerning his unique experience both in and beyond the tomb.[60] Devout Christians, such as Wilde's friend Coulson Kernahan, regarded this silence as holy, citing it as compelling evidence for his fervent opposition to the rise of spiritualism:

> One cannot believe that Lazarus went all unquestioned; and had he made a statement of any sort, that statement would [...] surely have been recorded. But Lazarus is silent as his Lord is silent, and their silence seems to be a tacit condemnation of what goes by the name of spiritualism.[61]

Tennyson captures the heart of the mystery Coulson so reveres in just four lines of *In Memoriam*:

> Behold a man raised up by Christ!
> The rest remaineth unreveal'd
> He told it not; or something seal'd
> The lips of that Evangelist.[62]

Wilde was a great admirer of the poem (ranking it alongside Shakespeare's *Hamlet* in a youthful letter to a university friend), and his own retelling of the story presumes to unlock what Tennyson describes as 'something sealed'. Paradoxically, however, the response with which he chooses to break the silence of Lazarus only serves to intensify it, the revenant's 'il n'y a rien' seeming to confirm that, after death, the rest really is silence. Related in the 1890s, a decade in which the relations between high and low cultures were very much under debate, Wilde's resurrection tale demonstrates his own predisposition to mix the palettes of the literary with the popular, the bawdy with the refined, the canonical with the marginal, creating a hybrid that encourages first laughter and then quiet contemplation from the listener.[63]

Another example of a New Testament story that had already undergone extensive reworking by both visual artists and literary authors before coming under Wilde's imaginative manipulation is that of Salome. The contemporary fascination with this most deadly of dancers is accordingly well represented in Guillot de Saix's volume, which includes three different treatments of this relatively minor Gospel figure.[64] Not only are these tales interesting as possible ur-texts of Wilde's 1891 drama, *Salomé*, they also testify to his fascination with the legends that had grown out of the four-fold Gospel. One of the three Salome stories Wilde is reported as telling has the princess banished to the desert by Herod as punishment for her kissing of the Baptist's head; after years of exile, living on locusts and wild honey, she witnesses and recognizes Jesus as the Messiah, only to have her mission to spread the news aborted when she falls through the ice of a frozen lake, resulting in her decapitation (*CC* 135–36). To a modern reader, this tale seems typically Wildean in its multiple ironies and dramatic treatment of the heroine but, as Wilde reminds his listeners, its origins lie in the writings of 'Nicéphore, le vénérable Patriarche de Byzance' [Nicephorus, the venerable Patriarch of Constantinople]: an ancient version of the Salome story that would have been familiar to some of Wilde's 1890s' audience.[65] Here, then, the story of the princess takes on the quality of a palimpsest, as Wilde overwrites a tale that is in itself a reworking of the original.

If the success of Wilde's oral tales depended to some extent on their being heard in their immediate cultural and literary contexts, this is not to say that they amount to little more than creative borrowing and contemporary allusiveness. These spoken parables demonstrate Wilde putting into practice his theory that, if art is to express the complexities of modern life, it must adopt 'strange perspectives' (*DP* 86). Each one sees him marry the familiar with the strange, obliging the listener, or reader, to reach imaginatively beyond the Gospel accounts. In some instances they are asked to consider what might have transpired after recorded events had taken place, as in the case of Lazarus or Simon of Cyrene; in others they are asked to consider well-known New Testament moments from quite different angles, such as in 'Jésus et les Femmes' [Jesus and the Women] (*CC* 115) where the Jewish women crying out for Christ to be crucified are simply afraid to acknowledge his Messiahship lest they lose entirely 'le merveilleux espoir de porter dans ses flancs Celui-là qui doit naître' [the wonderful hope of carrying in their wombs the Messiah that is to be born].

Certainly, Wilde's desire, as expressed to Coulson Kernahan, to recast the story of Christ 'with new and divine vision, free from the accretions of cant which the centuries have gathered around it' seems at the heart of these tales, embodying as they do the agnostic spirit of the age.[66] Nowhere is this spirit more perfectly captured than in Wilde's version of the story of Thomas: 'La Puissance du Doute' [The Mightiness of Doubt] (*CC* 128–29). In this, Wilde takes the idea of Thomas's twin-hood (mentioned only in the Fourth Gospel) and expands it to explore the idea of doubleness. Thomas's habit of thought looks forward to the religious dilemmas of the nineteenth century:

C'est que vous tous, toi, Pierre, avec Nathanaël, et le frère de Zébédée, et les autres disciples, vous croyez simplement que Jésus est le fils de Dieu, mais moi je dois me dépenser doublement, et doublement souffrir, parce que je crois qu'il est peut-être le Fils de Dieu.

[It's that all of you, you yourself Peter, Nathaniel, and the brother of Zebedee, and the other disciples, believe unquestioningly that Jesus is the son of God, whereas I have to go through double the suffering and anguish because I believe he might be the son of God, and he might not be.]

Wilde's interest in the division of the self, so memorably worked out in *The Picture of Dorian Gray* and in the 'Bunburying' motif of *The Importance of Being Earnest*, expresses itself here in Thomas's being 'in two minds', a permanent state of uncertainty. Through a characteristically Wildean inversion 'la puissance aveugle de la foi' [the blinding mightiness of faith] is transformed into 'la puissance du doute' [the blinding power of doubt] and the vacillations of the doubter, traditionally perceived as weakness, take on associations of great strength.

Re-imagining Jesus in a scientific age

The majority of Wilde's biblical tales are speculations on the afterlife of Gospel events and moments, intriguing glimpses of what might have escaped the notice of the Evangelists, or what might have taken place decades after the death and resurrection of Christ. Wilde was by no means alone in being tantalized by such speculations. In his *Life of Jesus* Renan imagines how Pilate 'In his retirement [...] probably never dreamt for a moment of the forgotten episode, which was to transmit his pitiful renown to the most distant posterity.'[67] Anatole France would go on to fictionalize the same idea in his short story 'Le Procurateur de Judée' [The Procurator of Judea], in which Pilate, when asked if he remembers Jesus of Nazareth, replies in the negative, a moment of memory lapse that forms the climax of the story. In Guillot de Saix's collection, two of Wilde's tales create highly contrasting alternative versions of the post-crucifixion Jesus. The first of these, 'L'Inutile Résurrection' [The Useless Resurrection] (CC 170–72), is the author's vision of the second coming of Christ and his ultimate rejection by a people given over to a creed of scientific rationalism. In some respects it resembles an increasingly popular sub-genre of fiction dealing with the return of Jesus in a modern age.[68] Such fictions were Europe-wide and Wilde would certainly have been familiar with works such as Balzac's short story 'Jésus-Christ en Flandre' [Christ in Flanders] (1831), which tells of a stranger (Jesus) helping fellow ferry passengers to safety when they are caught up in a violent storm; he may also have known Alphonse Louis Constant's collection of imaginary legends *La Dernière Incarnation* [*The Last Incarnation*], which place Jesus in various modern settings, witnessing the iniquities of modern society (1846).[69] Closer to home, and published around the time that Wilde's spoken tales were in circulation, was William T. Stead's *When Christ Came to Chicago* (1894), which served the double purpose of raising Christian awareness and exposing the corrupt practice of certain Chicago businessmen and politicians.[70]

'L'Inutile Résurrection' opens with the discovery of Christ's tomb, complete with mummified corpse, by 'un terrassier arabe au service d'un entrepreneur de fouilles qui ne recherchait que des monnaies anciennes' [an Arab labourer, in the employ of an archaeological entrepreneur, who was looking solely for ancient coins]. Here, Wilde engages with a particularly topical issue: the integrity of the relatively new discipline of archaeology and its affiliations with biblical scholarship. Having been associated with plunder and money-making in its infancy, archaeological excavations had, by the later part of the century, taken on a much more respectable image. Thanks largely to the setting up of the Palestine Exploration Fund (PEF) in 1865, with its strongly evangelical leanings, excavations of the Bible lands came to be regarded as a means by which the literal truth of the Scriptures could be revealed, helping to effect a peaceful coalescence of science and faith. As far as the PEF was concerned, the primary purpose of excursions to the Near East was to authenticate the four-fold Gospel, mainly through the identification of sacred sites – not to help the traveller imagine a fifth evangel. Wilde's own father, Sir William Wilde, had contributed to the archaeological researches into the Bible lands, visiting important holy sites during his stay in Palestine in the late 1830s, and recording his experiences in a travel book that included his own map of Jerusalem.[71] Written in an engaging conversational style, the work proved popular and enjoyed healthy sales. Wilde was certainly influenced by his father's work in this field, considering archaeology to be one of the main areas in which the family name had gained honour and recognition.

Proud though Wilde was of his father's archaeological achievements, his Parousia tale appears to mock excavation in the Lord's name by having Christ's mummified corpse – the most significant find imaginable – discovered quite accidentally by an Arab labourer. Such a seemingly random discovery stands in ironic contrast to the purposeful and well-documented endeavours of evangelical Christians such as General Gordon, whose claims to having identified the place of the crucifixion and of the Holy Sepulchre were something of a talking point in the late decades of the nineteenth century. Gordon's identification of these two sites while visiting Palestine in 1883 was based entirely on literal readings of the Bible and, despite the paucity of scientific evidence to support his claims, 'Gordon's Calvary' and 'Gordon's Tomb' soon became established sites, finding a fixed place on maps and in guide books. Following Gordon's death in 1885, there was an enormous outpouring of hagiographical works about him, among them 'Gordon in Africa', the 1888 winner of the Newdigate Prize Poem, an award taken by Wilde a decade earlier. Widely acclaimed as a hero, a saint and a Christian soldier, his theories about biblical sites were widely accepted by the majority. Yet while Wilde's story is in accord with the evangelical Gordon in placing the tomb 'au flanc de la montagne du Calvaire' [on the slope of Mount Calvary], it departs radically from the Christian message by placing within it the 'unrisen' body of Jesus Christ in all its inanimate gruesomeness: 'un corps momifié, portant évidentes, encore ourlées d'un sang desséché, noirâtre et craquelant, des plaies aux poignets, aux pieds et au flanc' [a mummified corpse, still bearing clear wounds on the wrists, feet and side, edged in dried, blackened, cracking blood]. In circulating such a destabilizing idea in the 1890s, when the energies and optimism of the PEF were in a steady decline, Wilde seems to have been playing on current fears that, for traditional Christians at least, biblical archaeology was a double-edged sword, having the potential to affirm, but also to refute, the historical 'facts' of the Scriptures.

Having opened on a resolutely rationalist note, the tale continues to pursue the increasingly commonplace notion that centuries of Christian domination could be put down to mere delusion, originating with that of 'les saintes femmes et les premiers disciples' [the holy women and the first disciples].[72] Yet just as the triumph of the doubters seems to be confirmed in the setting up of 'une sorte de temple de la Vérité Scientifique où l'on exposa sous verre [...] le cadavre par qui le mensonge séculaire avait été assassiné' [a kind of temple dedicated to Scientific Truth wherein lay, under glass, the corpse which had killed the centuries-old lie], Wilde begins to expose the inadequacies of this new age of materialism. Reflecting the ambivalence of many turn-of-the-century Victorians at the prospect of a future dominated by science, the exhibiting of the erstwhile saviour as a museum piece brings with it 'un triste dimanche sans cloches' [a dreary Sunday, without bells], as the liturgy dating back hundreds of years is abandoned. And it is at this point in the narrative that the possibility of a third age comes into view and, as Deirdre Toomey points out, 'Wilde's Joachimism can be detected'.[73] After relating the passing of the religious era, and depicting the arid scientific age that ensues, Wilde's tale goes on to offer the brief hope of a glorious new stage in religious faith as Christ 'reprit la vie, brisa les vitres de son cerceuil transparent et, devant les visiteurs et les gardiens prosternés, traversant d'un essor glorieux la Voûte Vaticane, disparut à leurs yeux' [came back to life, burst through the glass of his transparent coffin and, after soaring gloriously through the Vatican vault in full view of prostrated visitors and guards, disappeared from their sight], an image already contemplated by the author in his 'Sonnet: On the Massacre of the Christians in Bulgaria'.[74] The tenets of this tertiary religion are firmly rooted in Wilde's own philosophy: the resurrected Christ espouses a view of the world where 'il n' y aurait plus ni riches, ni pauvres, ni luttes de classes, ni guerres' [there would be neither rich nor poor, nor class conflict, nor wars], echoing the vision of the perfect state put forward in 'The Soul of Man Under Socialism' and, in particular, Wilde's protestation that 'A map of the world that does not include Utopia is not worth even glancing at' (C 247). As the parable draws to a close, Jesus exhorts each individual to 'Sois toi-même', a dramatization of Wilde's assertion, in the same essay, that Christ's message to man 'was simply "Be thyself"' (C 240). Yet the promised Utopia is not to be. The second coming of Christ and his revelations are explained away by the bespectacled men of science, and the world falls back into 'l'apathie des jours sans croyance et sans joie' [the apathy of the days without belief and without joy].

Wilde's misgivings about scepticism and his reluctance to relinquish entirely the miraculous in life are elegantly captured in 'L'Inutile Résurrection'. In this exemplary parable of agnosticism, an outright rejection of either the religious or the scientific is steadfastly resisted: the rejection of Christ's 'révélation suprême' [supreme revelation] cannot be viewed simply as the triumph of modernity over an outdated supernaturalism. Instead, it leaves the listener to ponder what might be in an ideal future when, as is proposed in 'The Soul of Man', science can make machinery serve man, leaving the individual free to pursue a life of creativity and imagination. For a reader rather than a listener, the title that heads the transcribed version frames the tale in such a way as to heighten its agnostic temperament. The title's adjective, while gesturing towards a cynical rejection of the cornerstone of Christianity, shifts in meaning as the story develops: the first resurrection was useless because it was false, and ushered in a false religion; the second resurrection is true, and holds the potential for great change, but useless in its failure to make a lasting impact on a society too deeply entrenched in scientific rationalism. A reader well acquainted with other aspects of Wilde's writing will also discern in the title a gesture towards the Gauterian notion that 'All art is quite useless' and, indeed, the tale's Third Age Christ with his 'culte de beauté' [cult of beauty] aligns very closely to the Christ of *De Profundis*, regarded by many as the ultimate expression of the author's Christology.[75]

Equally concerned with the tensions between rationalism and supernaturalism is 'Le Miracle des Stigmates' [The Miracle of the Stigmata] (*CC* 126–27). A resolutely heterodox story, it tells of how Jesus is taken down from the cross by Joseph of Arimathea while still alive, and nursed back to health. After living some years as a humble carpenter, the arrival of Paul shatters his peaceful existence, and he finds himself ostracized by the community, the one man who refuses to believe in the apostle's creed of the Resurrection. On his death, a group of early Christians come to prepare him for burial and witness for the first time the marks of the cross, concealed by the victim for so many years. On the discovery of such 'proof', all rejoice in the conversion of the community's most immovable unbeliever and in the miracle of the first stigmatic. Fictionalizing as it does the 'swoon theory' of rationalist theology, the tale demonstrates Wilde's ability to engage his listeners in the concerns of biblical scholarship in a spare and memorable narrative that, according to W. B. Yeats, he would announce as 'a Christian heresy' delivered in the 'style of some early Father', a fusion of heterodox content and biblical style that no doubt delighted his 1890s audience.[76] As has been established in previous chapters, theories proposing that Christ survived crucifixion and regained enough strength to appear before his disciples were several and varied. Wilde would certainly have encountered the gist of one of the most prominent of these theories through his reading of Matthew Arnold's *Literature and Dogma* in which the author discusses – and discredits – Friedrich Schleiermacher's 'fancy of the death on the cross having been a swoon, and the resurrection of Jesus a recovery from this swoon'.[77] While by the last decade of the century such theories were no longer regarded as academically respectable by the theological establishment, those set on discrediting the Gospels continued to exploit them with some abandon.[78] In a work of 1883, for example, one of a small number of female authors of Lives of Jesus, Constance Howell, took the 'swoon theory' as the basis of her dissident counter-narrative of Christ's final days on earth, building it up into a somewhat grisly scenario wherein Jesus, enfeebled by his sufferings on the cross and deserted by his followers, walks into the wilderness and dies 'from exposure, want of proper food, distress of mind, and the bodily effects of all that he had gone through'.[79] Not content with revealing the falsity of the resurrection, and with inventing a lonely and humiliating death for the failed Messiah, Howell goes on to describe how 'vultures ate the flesh from his skeleton, and thus his remains were never found and recognised'.[80]

Indifferent to the dicta of received theological wisdom, Wilde seems to have identified in this rationalist explanation of the resurrection the potential for a fiction that could be both aesthetically interesting and topical. In choosing to centre the story on the physical wounds of Christ, Wilde's tale connects to the field of anatomy, a rapidly developing area of scientific enquiry. Given Sir William Wilde's prominence in the medical world, and his editorship of the *Dublin Quarterly Journal of Medical Science*, it is likely that his younger son would have been more than usually alert to developing trends in the field of anatomy and the potential they held to unlock some of the mysteries of the Passion narratives. Aided by the Anatomy Act of 1831, which made corpses more readily available for experiments, questions concerning Jesus's expiration after only six hours on the cross were investigated with all the rigour that nineteenth-century medicine could offer.[81] A biblical verse that stood at the centre of ongoing speculation about Christ's death on the cross came from the Fourth Gospel: 'one of the soldiers pierced his side with a spear, and at once there came out blood and water' (John 19:34).[82] Anatomy afforded heterodox and orthodox alike a means of glossing this troubling text; sceptics could present the blood and water as evidence that Christ had not actually died on the cross as dead bodies did not bleed; believers, by the same token, could argue that the effusion of blood and water was scientifically feasible. Published in 1847, William Stroud's lengthy *Treatise on the Physical Cause of the Death of Christ* set out to prove, through anatomical exactness, that the effusion of blood and water from Christ's side was medically sound. In so doing, he hoped that his treatise might 'furnish Christians with additional motives to engage with energy in missionary exertions, both at home and abroad'.[83] The author of one of the most popular Lives of Jesus, William Hanna, based his argument that Jesus died on the cross on Stroud's work, as did several clergyman after him, and its authority lasted well into the twentieth century. In *The Days of His Flesh* (1905), for example, the author, David Smith, quotes from Stroud's treatise to prove his point that: 'medical science has confirmed the Evangelist's testimony [...] Jesus died literally of a broken heart [...] In that awful hour when He was forsaken by the Father, His heart swelled with grief until it burst, and then the blood was "effused into the distended sac of the pericardium".'[84] Developments in anatomy also encouraged scientific enquiry into the exact nature of Roman crucifixion, the practicalities of driving nails through the hands and feet of the victims being a common area for investigation. In a postscript to *The Crucifixion of Jesus Christ Anatomically Considered*, Abner Phelps describes the experiments he had carried out on dead bodies in order to ascertain whether a nail the size of a man's finger could be driven through an average male hand without it breaking. Phelps had in mind, of course, John's verse 'Not a bone of him shall be broken' (John 19:36), with its typological allusion to Exodus (12:46): a particularly telling example of how empirical science could be employed to serve those who believed in the supernaturalism of the Gospels.[85]

As well as raising questions about current interactions between anatomy and theology, 'Le Miracle des Stigmates' also engages with the contemporary fascination with the figure of the stigmatic. With the rapid advance of science and the growing sophistication of medicine, the phenomenon of stigmata became a focus of interest for both doctors and psychologists. The Belgian stigmatic Louise Lateau was particularly well known, and continued to be the subject of close medical scrutiny until her death in 1883.[86] One of the physicians who undertook a close observation of Lateau was Antoine Imbert-Gourbeyre who, inspired by his experience, produced the first data on stigmatics, listing all known cases century by century.[87] The sub-title of the resulting work, *La Stigmatisation, L'extase divine, et les miracles de Lourdes. Réponse aux libres-penseurs* [*Stigmatization, Divine Ecstasy, and the Miracles of Lourdes: a Response to Freethinkers*], clearly announces that his census is by no means disinterested, and demonstrates the continuing conflict between rationalists and supernaturalists. Yet despite the best efforts of religiously devout physicians such as Imbert-Goubeyre to prove the verity of stigmatics, the Catholic Church's attitude towards them was growing more cautious. Prior to the nineteenth century, stigmatization was common grounds for beatification; however, of the 29 nineteenth-century stigmatics listed by Imbert-Goubeyre, none was declared a saint, suggesting that the Church had started to draw up a set of criteria for sainthood that would be able to stand the scrutiny of an increasingly scientific age.

At the same time as stigmatics came under forensic examination from a sceptical medical profession, so they proved to be figures of fascination for literary authors such as J.- K. Huysmans, whose captivation with the sufferings of the flesh grew more and more intense as he made his well-documented journey back to the Church of Rome. For Huysmans, physical suffering was capable of bringing about spiritual revelation and refinement, a relationship most tellingly demonstrated by the case of Anna Katharina Emmerich, an early nineteenth-century visionary, who came to be known as 'the living Crucifix'. Describing her in a letter to a friend as 'the most complete example of a stigmatist', he refers to her frequently in his fictions.[88] Emmerich's stigmata first appeared in 1812, so it was claimed, when she was 38 years old, and stayed with her until her death in 1824. Her dream-visions of Jesus and his life were told to the poet Clemens Brentano as he sat at her bedside, his notes forming the basis of *The Dolorous Passions of Our Lord Jesus Christ* (1834), a work recently drawn upon by Mel Gibson for his film, *The Passion of the Christ*. Outside of his novels, Huysmans pursued his interest in stigmatics in his 1901 hagiography of Saint Lydwina of Schiedam in which, recounting the history of this fourteenth-century saint, he seems to revel in descriptions of suppurating flesh:

> en outre de ses ulcères dans lesquels vermillaient des colonies de parasites qu'on alimentait sans les détruire, une tumeur apparut sur l'épaule qui se putréfia [...] le menton se décolla sous la lèvre inférieure et la bouche enfla [...] enfin, après une esquinancie qui l'étouffa, elle perdit le sang, par la bouche, par les oreilles, par le nez, avec une telle profusion que son lit ruisselait.

> [In addition to these ulcers, crawling with colonies of parasites, which were fed without being destroyed, a tumour appeared on the shoulder and putrefied [...] Her chin dropped away from under her bottom lip and her mouth swelled up [...] finally, after a quinsy which choked her, she lost blood from her mouth, ears and nose with such profusion that the bed streamed with it.][89]

While Wilde would eventually forge a relationship between pain and the spirit in his endeavour to make some kind of sense of his physical suffering as an inmate of Reading Gaol, his religious temperament was of a quite different sort from Huysmans'. So, too, was his interest in the stigmatic. Whereas Huysmans considered the writing of a life of

Saint Lydwina an 'act of penance [...] the literary equivalent of fasting', Wilde had no real taste for such acts of self-castigation and aesthetic deprivation.[90] Nor did he share Huysmans' interest in the physical realities of the body. Indeed, there is a certain fastidiousness that characterizes much of his work, not least that dealing with religious subjects. Of course, for some critics, Wilde's stigmata tale would stand as an apt illustration of his fascination with Roman Catholicism, stigmata being generally regarded as a Catholic phenomenon.[91] Yet 'Le Miracle des Stigmates' is singularly lacking in the kind of religious aestheticism that typified the decadent Catholicism in vogue in the 1890s.[92]

The tenor of 'Le Miracle des Stigmates' is resolutely agnostic. In the course of the story, the very word 'stigmata', deriving as it does from the Greek word for 'sign', takes on a sharply paradoxical quality. Far from being physical signs of mystical union with Christ, the marks of the cross become literal proof that the divinity of Christ is a fallacy and the revelation that there is no divine doctrine of substitution renders fraudulent, or deluded, the several hundred surrogate sufferers down the ages. Ranked first among such hundreds was St Francis of Assisi: the type of divine stigmatics. Wilde's unreserved admiration for the Italian friar followed that of Renan. For the Frenchman, St Francis was 'a faithful mirror of Christ';[93] for Wilde he was 'the true *Imitatio Christi*' (*DP* 123). For Renan, though, he was also a counterfeit stigmatic, whose wounds were invented by a close companion, Elias of Cortona, immediately after his death, and 'would not have borne a close examination'.[94] In 'Le Miracle des Stigmates', Wilde's substitution of Christ for St Francis as the first false stigmatic is quite audacious. While the tale commences with the reassuring presence of Joseph of Arimathea come to take the body of his master to the tomb, it soon develops an unorthodox trajectory. Just a little way into the story, we are confronted with a failed Messiah, taking refuge 'dans une ville obscure où il reprit son ancien métier de charpentier' [in an out-of-the-way town where he resumed his former trade as a carpenter], the teller being unable to resist adding the mischievously irreverent detail that 'nul n'était plus habile à construire des crèches et des croix' [no one was more handy at making cribs and crosses]. Christ's life, so Wilde's tale suggests, has gone into reverse: a man who once went from the obscurity of Nazareth to the courts of Jerusalem is now in retreat from the world. We are told how, when Paul comes preaching the Gospel of Christ crucified, 'Jésus baissa la tête en rentrant les mains dans les manches de sa tunique' [Jesus lowered his head and pulled his hands inside the sleeves of his tunic], gestures that suggest both shame and an emotional and physical recoiling from society. While the Jesus of the Fourth Gospel displays his wounds to Thomas as proof of his divinity, the Jesus of Wilde's version knows his marks to be proof of 'la fausseté de la religion nouvelle' [the falseness of the new religion], and hides them away. And while the Gospel Christ can command Mary Magdalene not to touch him, Wilde's sad and disillusioned figure has no such power after death. Scrutinized and touched by those who prepare him for burial, his scars are laid bare, appearing to provide incontrovertible evidence for the miracle that has changed the lives of those gathered round him.

Yet Wilde's parable is more than a simple inversion of the Gospel original, offering a muted materialist reading of the resurrection. In contrast with some of the rationalist theories that circulated throughout the nineteenth century, Wilde withholds all physical details of the post-crucifixion body and its recovery, perhaps sharing the view expressed by Thomas Scott in his rationalist biography of Jesus that 'there is something [...] revolting in suppositions that Jesus was only apparently dead'.[95] While he might have asserted in 'The Soul of Man' that 'the mediaeval Christ is the real Christ' (C 266), the gruesome putrescence of Matthias Grünewald's Crucifixion, so revered by Huysmans, would have held rather less attraction for Wilde, incompatible as it was with his anti-realist aesthetic. In 'Le Miracle des Stigmates', the physicality of Jesus is barely remarked upon, save for the five scars that distinguish him as 'Sauveur du Monde' [Saviour of the world]. We are told nothing of the physical torments of the cross; instead, the tale bridges an awkward narrative gap by transforming the hyssop of John's Gospel into 'une essence magique qui, mêlée au sang, donnerait au condamné l'apparence de la mort' [a magic potion which, when it entered the bloodstream, would give the condemned man the appearance of death], calling to mind that administered to Juliet by Friar Lawrence in Shakespeare's Romeo and Juliet. Here, Wilde steers a mid-course between rationalist and supernaturalist thinking: on the one hand, the detail recalls the rationalist theory recorded by D. F. Strauss that accused Jesus's disciples of 'a preconceived plan of producing apparent death by means of a potion'; on the other hand, the tale's insistence on the magical nature of the draught preserves an element of the mysterious and the inexplicable.[96]

The tale continues in this spirit of openness, reaching a conclusion that, though never allowing for any possibility that Jesus was anything other than an ordinary man, nevertheless refuses to entirely affirm or deny the power of the miraculous. In *The Eclipse of Biblical Narrative*, Hans Frei observes:

> What is so striking and revealing about Schleiermacher's inference that Jesus probably underwent a *Scheintod* on the cross is not his disbelief in the resurrection. Skepticism about physical miracles, especially that one, is, after all, a typically modern attitude. Far more remarkable is the fact that, no matter what he may have chosen to believe about the facts of the case, it never occurred to him that there is something unfitting, indeed ludicrous, about rendering the story of Jesus in a way that makes such a thundering anticlimax possible.[97]

The ending of 'Le Miracle des Stigmates' suggests that Wilde, too, had understood the inherent bathos of this well-known rationalist theory, and had endeavoured to prevent his own fictionalizing of it from concluding on an entirely flat note, devoid of any sense of the spiritual. In the final line of the tale, the joy felt by the early Christians on discovering the wounds of Jesus is clearly expressed in their exclamation 'C'est un miracle, un grand miracle!' [It's a miracle, a great miracle!], and while this cry of rapture could be dismissed as naïve and foolish, its positioning at the very close of the story allows it to remain open to other less sceptical interpretations. Wilde seems to suggest here that an intense spiritual or emotional experience generated by a falsehood should be considered no less genuine or meaningful than one based on truth. Just as Antony's grief at what Shakespeare's audience knows is Cleopatra's faked death is not rendered less affecting by the fact that he is being deceived, so the numinous quality of the early Christians falling to their knees 'comme devant les stigmates d'un saint' [as before the marks of the cross on a saint], for all its ironic anachronism, is not diminished by the listener's knowledge of the illusory nature of the oblations.

Wilde wrote in his Oxford notebook that 'To define a miracle as a violation of the Laws of Nature is absurd; Nature is all which is: it is the series of phenomena of which the alleged miracle is one.'[98] In *De Profundis*, he reveals a similar approach to the miraculous, explaining how one of the most contentious of the New Testament miracles, the changing of water into wine, was achieved through the power of

Jesus's personality, so that for those who ate with him 'the water had the taste of good wine' (*DP* 112), while its physical properties remained the same. Similarly, in 'Le Miracles des Stigmates', while the falseness of the resurrection holds fast, Paul's fervent faith in its supernatural truth gives him transformative power: power to create joy and unity and to stimulate what, in 'The Decay of Lying', Vivian describes as 'that mythopoeic faculty which is so essential for the imagination' (*C* 99). It was a view of the miraculous that would be echoed three decades later in George Bernard Shaw's dramatization of the life of St Joan where the Archbishop of Rheims explains to his Lord Chamberlain that 'A miracle [...] is an event which creates faith', adding that, even if the event can be traced back to entirely natural causes, 'if they feel the thrill of the supernatural, and forget their sinful clay in a sudden sense of the glory of God, it will be a miracle and a blessed one'.[99]

One other version of Wilde's stigmata story is recorded in *Le Chant du Cygne* in the section headed 'Le jeu des variantes', its transcription attributed to the writer Georges Maurevert (*CC* 299–300). This later version differs significantly from that which Guillot de Saix presents as (for want of a better term) the 'standard'. Its setting in 'le quartier juif de Rome' [Rome's Jewish quarter] is more contextually specific and reflects the tendency of certain Lives of Jesus published in the last two decades of the century to emphasize how Jesus was a Jew, living among Jews. In the standard version, the central character is never explicitly named and, rather like in Monty Python's *The Life of Brian*, the onus is put on the audience to conspire with the teller's own blasphemy in identifying the hero as the Jesus of the Gospel stories. In this variant rendering, however, Jesus is immediately announced by his Jewish appellation 'Ieschou-ben-Iossef'. A more domestic telling of the tale, it goes on to present a married Jesus who converses with his wife, Valéria, in colloquial tones; we are told the exact dates of key events and given the precise cause of Ieschou's death from 'une pleurésie' [pleurisy]. The effect of these realistic details is to detract from the mystery of the Christ-figure. Ieschou lacks the withdrawn and brooding quality of the Jesus of the other version; his crucifixion marks are not hidden from sight but described bluntly as 'les rouges cicatrices' [red scars]. When attention is drawn to these wounds by Balbus, his father-in-law and employer, he explains them away in a matter-of-fact manner as 'Un accident, jadis' [an accident long past]. Any attentive listener would have been puzzled, then, at Valéria's only discovering Ieschou's wounds while preparing him for burial. That a wife could live with her husband without being aware of the physical marks pointed out by a less intimate relative strains the listener's credulity, especially given that the naturalistic style of the tale is more likely to invite a literal-minded response.

Another noticeable change in this variant of the stigmata tale comes from its replacing Paul with Peter. By placing Peter in Rome, Wilde engages his listener in what Renan described as a 'curious historical question'.[100] While according to some extra-Biblical traditions, Peter was martyred in Rome in 64 CE, during the reign of Nero, the historical facts of his appearance – or otherwise – in the city were a subject of fierce debate during Wilde's lifetime.[101] Never overly concerned by the exigencies of historical accuracy, Wilde may well have considered the apostle 'entrusted with the gospel to the circumcised' a more suitable choice for his explicitly Jewish version of his story, regardless of its factual validity.[102] Yet this shift in apostle renders the tale less successful than the standard version where the shadowy presence of Paul, for whom the death and resurrection of Jesus were even more significant than his life and ministry, creates an acute irony in a scenario that exposes the absolute falsity of such a doctrine. Indeed, taken as a whole, this revision lacks the spare and haunting qualities of its Pauline counterpart. Its final line: 'Et le coeur et l'esprit de Valéria sont ravis en étonnement...' [and Valeria's heart and mind stand still, seized in astonishment...] loses the impact that direct speech brings to the other rendering of the miraculous moment and, though the concluding ellipsis might solicit a questioning response, a glimpse into the future, the listener is limited to one viewpoint, and the symbolic force of an anonymous gathering of first-generation Christians, falling to their knees in worship, is lost.

Notwithstanding their qualitative differences, examining the two versions of Wilde's stigmata story side by side throws light on Wilde's approach to theology and the Bible. Whereas the Pauline version operates outside the theological debates of the day, the Petrine variant shows a much keener awareness of contemporary perspectives on the Gospels. The very existence of the two accounts suggests that Wilde might have alternated between them in such a way as to play out in fictional form the theoretical stance of Ferdinand Baur and the Tübingen School, who regarded a conflict between Pauline and Petrine traditions as crucial to an understanding of early Christianity. Ultimately, though, the pair reveals that he was both interested in, and indifferent to, the theological revisionism of his day, embracing it and ignoring it as the fancy took him.

De Profundis: Wildean Christology

Rich in literary potential and contemporary appeal, the majority of Wilde's spoken tales were never fixed in writing. His two years of imprisonment would take him away from the stimulus of friends and acquaintances who had once listened so attentively to his biblical stories and would keep him at a distance from the constantly evolving theological controversies of the day. They were also years in which he would evolve a Christology far removed from any developed in his oral tales. Wilde's prison writings have proven to be all things to all men: an apologia, a *confessio peccati*, an autobiography, a love letter and, most significantly for this study, a secular Gospel.[103] As Wilde's most sustained writing on Christ, there is, indeed, a case to be made for *De Profundis* representing the culmination of the author's ambition to compose a fifth Gospel, though the work's uncertain textual status prevents any definitive judgement. Like the spoken tales, it hovers somewhat beguilingly between the private and the public; if Wilde's oral parables can be regarded as improvised private performances, never intended for publication, so the religious portion of the prison manuscript can be viewed as one man's musings on the New Testament narratives that had so captured his attention during his term of imprisonment. Yet the oral tales can equally well be seen as work in progress, improvisatory gestures towards a written text, and so, correspondingly, can Wilde's prison letter be seen as a first draft of a published work, to include the author's final vision of Christ. Like Cecily's diary in *The Importance of Being Earnest*, then, *De Profundis* can be regarded as at the same time intimate and public, introspective and self-publicizing.

What is certain, however, is that *De Profundis* offers a more refined and stable vision of the figure of Christ than that sketched out in the oral parables. Superficially at least, the letter reads like the author at his most conventionally Christian. The tenor of the piece is less colloquial, less shifting, than the oral tales; there are fewer allusions to contemporary theological debates and its style is redolent of the prose poems published a year or so before his imprisonment. The reader notices frequent echoes of Gospel imagery and paradox, and encounters a Christ who is hailed as the cynosure for all ages, sometimes described in language so reverential as to be reminiscent of one of the more devout Lives of Jesus. Yet though the Christ passages in *De Profundis* are ostensibly more orthodox than his biblical apologues in tone and spirit, closer reading uncovers them as the author's most outright rejection of anything approaching traditional Christianity and, most especially, the Christian ethos of humility. In filtering his interpretation of the Gospels through the autobiographical frame of his own Golgotha, Wilde follows visual artists such as Ensor, Gauguin and Van Gogh, all of whom depicted themselves as Christ figures in paintings of the 1880s. Showing little real regard for the Jesus of history, Wilde gives us an entirely solipsistic vision of the man and his ministry. Countering the Victorian tendency to shape the figure of Jesus to fit one of the social categorizations of the age, such as 'an ordinary philanthropist' (*DP* 113), he recreates him instead in his own image as 'the most supreme of individualists' whose 'place indeed is with the poets' (*DP* 110). This identification of Christ with the figure of the poet is already evident in Wilde's early poetry, where the 'brawlers of the auction mart', selling off Keats's love letters, are likened to the Roman soldiers of the Passion narratives, casting lots 'for the garments of a wretched man' (*PP* 165–66). Yet, whereas in this early work Wilde looks to familiar biblical parallels to express the sacred nature of the great artist and the callous indifference of those who fail to recognize his greatness, in *De Profundis* the two sides of the analogy coalesce: Jesus is not merely a fitting *comparison* to the poet, he *is* the poet himself, and the author's identification with Christ becomes at once an affiliation with the betrayed and suffering artist. By the same token, Lord Alfred Douglas takes on the role of Judas to Wilde's Jesus. Described at the time of Wilde's entering his term of imprisonment as 'a golden-haired boy with Christ's own heart' (*CL* 651), he is subsequently upbraided for his 'terrible lack of imagination' (*DP* 66), a failing that places him in the role of the betrayer.

If *De Profundis* is indeed a confessional work, it does not conform in any way to late-Victorian expectations of the repentant sinner. Rather than atoning for his violation of society's moral codes, Wilde declares that the 'Sins of the flesh are nothing', confessing only to his betrayal of aesthetics. He protests to Bosie:

> While you were with me you were the absolute ruin of my art, and in allowing you to stand persistently between Art and myself I give

to myself shame and blame in the fullest degree […] One half-hour with Art was always more to me than a cycle with you. Nothing really at any period of my life was ever of the smallest importance to me compared with Art. (*DP* 40)

The ideal nature of Jesus is redefined to suit his own aesthetic creeds rather than any that would fit into the Victorian mainstream. That said, his proclaiming of Christ as the type of the poet was, by the last decade of the century, a fairly familiar notion, to be found in the writings of Ernest Renan and Matthew Arnold and those of less well-known authors such as Edgar Saltus, whose depiction of Jesus as someone who 'gave the world a fairer theory of aesthetics, a new conception of beauty' predates *De Profundis* by almost a decade.[104] What *does* stand out as original in Wilde's Christology, however, is his insistence on Jesus being an autogenous creation. Where most agnostic studies of Christ called on historical, social and religious contexts to explain how and why he might have come to be considered divine, Wilde insists that 'out of his own imagination entirely did Jesus of Nazareth create himself' (*DP* 117). For him, the significance of Isaiah's prefiguring of the Man of Sorrows inheres in its being the catalyst for Christ's act of self-creation, rather than in its validity as Old Testament prophecy. Just as Wilde keeps in place the traditional relationship between sinner and saviour, at the same time describing Jesus in highly heterodox terms, so here he preserves the typological habit of the Christian mind while simultaneously denying Christ's divinity. If 'The Song of Isaiah […] had seemed to him to prefigure himself', then Christ's suffering on the cross, so Wilde suggests, shadows forth the trials of the artist 'despised and rejected of men' (*DP* 115).

In *De Profundis*, Wilde holds firm to his belief that meaning can only inhere in the individual. He holds the mirror up to Jesus and sees his own self reflected – or at least his preferred version of himself: the individualist, the antinomian, the artist, the rejected and the betrayed. Christ's story provides an analogue through which Wilde can regard his own personality and experiences, illustrating Schweitzer's contention that throughout the nineteenth century, 'each individual created Jesus in accordance with his own character'.[105] Unsurprisingly, considering how neatly the Gospel narrative is made to fit Wilde's own predicament, one of the first reviewers of *De Profundis*, E. V. Lucas, declared it 'a dexterously constructed counterfeit';[106] and three

years later, on the publication of the 1908 *Collected Works*, Harold
Hannyngton Child remarked even more caustically that 'There is a
looking-glass, it seems, even in the depths.'[107] Yet Wilde's invocation
of Christ in *De Profundis* goes beyond the mere posturing and narcis-
sism of which it has been so frequently accused. Examined in the
context of his earlier fictional versions of the New Testament and his
non-fiction writings about the Bible and theology, it articulates a more
refined and individual vision of a potential fifth Gospel. Staying true
to Gilbert's dictum in 'The Critic as Artist' that 'Aesthetics are higher
than ethics' (*C* 204), Wilde lifts the figure of Jesus out of the domains
of theological debate, historical enquiry and religious practice, placing
it squarely in the realms of art. Just as Renan identified in Jesus 'that
great instinct of futurity which has animated all reformers',[108] so Wilde
identifies in him the 'palpitating centre of romance' (*DP* 117), which
animates the artists of future ages. We are told to look for him 'in
Romeo and Juliet, in the *Winter's Tale*, in Provençal poetry, in *The
Ancient Mariner*, in *La Belle Dame sans Merci*, and in Chatterton's
Ballad of Charity' (*DP* 116). Accordingly, he is defined through
predominantly literary allusions: his 'flamelike imagination' (*DP* 110)
recalls Pater's *Marius*, and the Mass spoken in his honour is likened to
the Greek chorus (*DP* 112). Indeed, the Christ figure of *De Profundis*
seems to mirror the Third Age Christ of 'L'Inutile Résurrection' with
his 'culte de beauté' and his exhortation to the people to 'Sois toi-
même'. Wilde follows William Blake in shifting authority from the
biblical texts to the poet of genius and in reshaping the Gospel texts to
create his own system of belief, whereby sin is transformed into a
means of self-knowledge quite unreachable by those who simply keep
within the bounds of society and practise self-restraint.

As Wilde's last published writing on Christ, it is perhaps inevitable
that *De Profundis* has come to dominate critical discussions of his religious temperament and theological views. However, there is
compelling evidence to suggest that Wilde had plans to commit a good
deal more of his religious imagination to paper after his release from
prison, and to extend his range of source material beyond the New
Testament. Richard Ellmann records how he 'continued his higher
criticism of the Bible by reworking the story of Ahab and Jezebel,
with the idea that it might be made into a play like *Salome*'.[109] This
shift of focus from the New to the Old Testament was a potentially
shrewd move on Wilde's part. In the first decade of the twentieth
century there was a growing trend for dramatic adaptations of Old

Testament stories to be treated more leniently by the Examiner of Plays than those based on the Gospels, and Wilde's choice of subject was particularly prescient, given that Gwendolen Lally's *Jezebel* (1912) would become the first overtly biblical play to be passed by the censor in England.[110] And there is nothing to suggest that he was dissatisfied with the prose poems he had already composed. Writing in the preface to *Essays and Lectures*, Robert Ross expresses the opinion that '*Poems in Prose* were to have been continued' and that the hostile reception they received had not deterred him from writing more.[111]

Yet if Wilde continued to hold an ambition to complete a fifth Gospel for the 'Confraternity of the Faithless' (*DP* 98) he imagines in *De Profundis*, it would never be realized. Recording his memories of a meeting with Wilde at Dieppe in 1897, Gedeon Spilett recalls Wilde's outlining to him 'the scenario of a satiric play in three scenes which he planned to write but has given up, at least for the present', and transcribes the author's own description of the proposed drama, based largely on 'The Doer of Good', already much reworked – if not overworked.[112] Having once told Yeats that he considered this 'the best short story in the world', it is perhaps understandable that he would continue to explore its potential in other creative forms; at the same time it is clear that, by this stage in his writing career, any further work on fictionalizing the Scriptures would be more a matter of remodelling past ideas than inventing any new ones. Even the numerous oral tales he already had at his disposal would remain unwritten, perhaps with good reason. There is no doubt that Wilde's publishing prospects were substantially diminished after his release from prison and, perhaps more significantly, he no longer enjoyed the public acclaim that had once guaranteed that his oral tales would find captive audiences.[113] One of Wilde's biographers, Hesketh Pearson, explained how 'Wilde would often repeat his stories, trying them out in various guises, testing their effect on different people, until he had achieved the form that satisfied himself'.[114] The creative interdependence of the spoken and written elements of Wilde's work that Pearson identifies here was inevitably damaged in his post-imprisonment years, as his social and economic circumstances grew ever more impoverished and narrow. Moreover, given the abrupt change in the public's attitude towards him after his conviction, he must have found the prospect of publishing undeniably heterodox stories to an already censorious readership immensely daunting.

Looking beyond the merely practical, Wilde's failure to record his

oral tales in writing is in many ways in keeping with his often ambiva-
lent attitude towards the Gospels. While admiring their 'simple
romantic charm' and acknowledging their literary qualities in referring to them as 'four prose poems' (*DP* 118), he nevertheless
recognized how their canonical authority brought with it the stulti-
fying effects of repetition and literalism. In keeping his own stories
about Jesus free of the limitations that come with a typographic form,
Wilde left them open for extemporizing with each new audience, with
each new theological theory, and with each new stage of the creator's
own life. In Wilde's *oeuvre*, then, fictional representations of Jesus
remain primarily in the oral domain, in keeping with his view of
Christ as the world's eternal mouthpiece, whose place among the
poets is earned not from what he *writes* but what he *says*.[115] Wilde's
declaration to Laurence Housman that 'It is enough that the stories
have been invented, that they actually exist; that I have been able, in
my own mind, to give them the form which they demand' suggests
that the oral version of a tale was, for him, every bit as valuable as a
textual version.[116] Such ambivalence towards textuality is clearly articulated in his best-known work, *The Importance of Being Earnest*. In
this satirical take on the ruling classes, characters are restricted both
socially and imaginatively by the tyrannical rule of texts, whether it be
seating plans, school books, legal documents, society papers or
maternal lists of eligible bachelors. Even Cecily's invented diary,
though potentially a creative outlet, is revealed as yet another document upholding Victorian expectations of a young woman's life and
conduct.

Though many of Wilde's retellings of the Gospels would remain
unwritten, some of those who heard them were quick to recognize
their artistic potential. With Wilde to all intents and purposes
excluded from society following his release from prison, some of his
literary contemporaries found the temptation to appropriate his oral
stories and fix them in written form irresistible. In the two decades or
so following the death of their creator, Wilde's biblical apologues
would find new life under new ownership.

Notes

1 In his 1916 biography of Wilde, Frank Harris recalls how his subject 'described himself on leaving Oxford as a "Professor of Aesthetics and a Critic of Art"'. See *Oscar Wilde: His Life and Confessions*, 2 vols (New York: printed and published by the author, 1916), I, p. 56.

2 William Rothenstein, *Men and Memories* (London: Faber & Faber, 1931), p. 311.

3 *The Complete Works of Oscar Wilde*, vol. iv, *Criticism*, ed. Josephine M. Guy (Oxford: Oxford University Press, 2007), p. 78. Hereafter cited in the text as *C.*

4 Oscar Wilde, 'The Poet's Corner', *Pall Mall Gazette*, 6 April 1888, reprinted in *The Collected Works of Oscar Wilde*, ed. Robert Ross, 15 vols (London: Routledge/Thoemmes Press, 1993), XIII, p. 316; originally published as *The First Collected Edition of the Works of Oscar Wilde* (London: Methuen, 1908–22).

5 Coulson Kernahan, *In Good Company* (London: John Lane, The Bodley Head, 1917), p. 223.

6 Guillot de Saix, *Le Chant du Cygne: contes parlés d'Oscar Wilde. Recueillis et rédigés par Guillot de Saix* (Paris: Mercure de France, 1942), p. 95. Hereafter cited in the text as *CC.*

7 John Middleton Murry, 'The Influence of Baudelaire', *Rhythm*, 2 (March 1913), pp. xxiii–xxvii (p. xxvii).

8 Richard Ellmann, *Oscar Wilde* (London: Penguin Books, 1987), pp. 80–81.

9 In the editorial commentary Guillot de Saix relates how Mendès's *Contes Évangéliques* started to appear shortly after the publication of Wilde's *Poems in Prose* in 1894 (CC 97).

10 Renan, *The Life of Jesus*, p. 31.

11 *The Complete Works of Oscar Wilde*, vol. ii, *De Profundis*, ed. Ian Small (Oxford: Oxford University Press, 2005), p. 175. Hereafter cited in the text as *DP.*

12 Lucas, *The Fifth Gospel*, p. v.

13 See W. E. Barnes, *Canonical and Uncanonical Gospels* (London: Longmans, 1893), for a contemporary discussion of the Petrine manuscript and a translation of the text. For a modern scholarly work on extra-canonical gospels, see Philip Jenkins, *The Hidden Gospels: How the Search for Jesus Lost its Way* (Oxford: Oxford University Press, 2001).

14 See J. Wesley Thomas, 'The Fifth Gospel', *Modern Language Notes*, 62 (November 1947), pp. 445–49, for an account of how Freeman Clarke's plans to publish a spurious Gospel were uncovered.

15 The term 'fifth Gospel' persisted well into the twentieth century. In an article concerning the cult of Marie Corelli, the author avers that 'only the most infatuated of reviewers could have called the first-named book [*Barabbas*] "a fifth gospel"'. See 'A Note Upon Marie Corelli', *Westminster Review*, 166 (December 1906), pp. 680–92 (p. 687).

16 See the *Month*, 22 (September 1874), pp. 98–101 (p. 99).

17 J. M. P. Otts, *The Fifth Gospel: the Land where Jesus Lived* (Edinburgh and London: Oliphant, Anderson and Ferrier, 1892), p. i.

18 Marie Corelli, *Ardath*, 3 vols (London: Richard Bentley and Son, 2nd edn, 1889), III, p. 147.

19 *The Collected Works of Oscar Wilde*, ed. Ross, XIII, p. 315.

20 Robert Harborough Sherard, *The Life of Oscar Wilde* (London: T. Werner Laurie, 1906), pp. 381–82.

21 See *The Memoirs of John Addington Symonds*, p. 244.

22 For details of the books that Wilde requested during his imprisonment, see *The Complete Letters of Oscar Wilde*, ed. Merlin Holland and Rupert Hart-Davis (London Fourth Estate, 2000), pp. 660, 673, 682. Hereafter cited in the text as *CL*.

23 *Fortnightly Review*, 56 (July 1894), pp. 22–29. 'The House of Judgment' and 'The Disciple' were first published in the Oxford undergraduate journal, the *Spirit Lamp*, 17 February 1893.

24 Baudelaire's description of the prose poem as 'une prose poétique, musicale sans rythme et sans rime, assez souple et assez heurtée pour s'adapter aux mouvements lyriques de l'âme' [A poetic prose, musical without the aid of rhyme and rhythm, with exactly the right amount of flexibility and dissonance to express the lyrical movements of the soul], given in the dedication of *Petits poèmes en prose*, could apply equally well to the prose of the Authorized Version of the Bible.

25 Aloysius (Louis) Bertrand appears to have been the first writer to establish the prose poem as a genre with a collection entitled *Gaspard de la nuit: Fantaisies à la manière de Rembrandt et de Callot*, posthumously published in Paris in 1842. Arsène Houssaye, the dedicatee of Baudelaire's *Petits poèmes en prose* and founder of the journal *L'Artiste*, also composed prose poems.

26 J.-K. Huysmans, *Le Drageoir à épices* (Paris, 1874).

27 J.-K. Huysmans, *À Rebours* (Paris: Bibliothèque Charpentier, 1891), pp. 264–65. The English translation is taken from *Against Nature*, trans. Robert Baldick (London: Penguin Books, 1959), p. 199.

28 It is possible that Wilde was aware of Arthur Rimbaud's *Proses évangéliques*, rewritings of episodes from John's Gospel, which convey the poet's vehemently anti-Christian sentiments. See *Arthur Rimbaud: Collected Poems*, trans. Martin Sorrell (Oxford: Oxford University Press, 2001), pp. 206–09.

29 Wilde parodies the Revised Version in a letter to E. W. Godwin. See *CL*, p. 260.

30 *The Collected Works of Oscar Wilde*, ed. Ross, XIII, p. 315. Elsewhere, Wilde describes such repetitions of the Scriptures as 'anti-spiritual' (*DP* 118).

31 W. B. Yeats, *The Complete Works of Oscar Wilde* (New York, 1923); reprinted in *Oscar Wilde: The Critical Heritage*, ed. Karl Beckson (London: Routledge & Kegan Paul, 1970), p. 398.

32 *The Complete Works of Oscar Wilde*, vol. i, *Poems and Poems in Prose*, ed. Bobby Fong and Karl Beckson (Oxford: Oxford University Press, 2000), pp. 174–75. Hereafter cited in the text as *PP*.

33 Wilde used this label in a review of a verse poem 'The Story of the Cross' in the *Pall Mall Gazette*, 6 April 1888, in *The Collected Works of Oscar Wilde*, ed. Ross, XIII, p. 316. Tate and Brady were the authors of *A New Version of the Psalms of David*, which versified the language of the Old Testament into rhyming quatrains. The work went through over 500 editions between 1696 and 1860.

34 Renan, *The Life of Jesus*, p. 189.

35 Arnold, *Literature and Dogma*, in *Complete Prose Works*, VI, p. 318.

36 *Athenaeum*, 16 May 1908, pp. 598–600 (p. 599).

37 Cited from a letter from Corelli to Madame Remé in Bigland, *Marie Corelli*, p. 149.

38 Cited in the postscript of a letter to William Antony Pye, reprinted in Beckson, ed., *Oscar Wilde, The Critical Heritage*, p. 324.

39 Holbrook Jackson, *The 1890s* (London: Grant Richards, 1913), p. 106.

40 *Lord Arthur Savile's Crime and Other Prose Pieces* (Leipzig: Bernhard Tauchnitz, 1909).

41 André Gide, *In Memoriam* (Paris: Mercure de France, 1910), pp. 20–21.

42 W. B. Yeats, *Autobiographies* (London: Macmillan, 1955), p. 286.

43 In *The Romantic '90s* (London: G. P. Putnam's Sons, 1925), Richard Le Gallienne recalls how 'One secret of the charm of Wilde's talk … was the evidently sincere interest he took in his listener' (p. 246); however, Henri de Régnier takes a somewhat different view: 'He needed more someone to listen to him, than someone to speak with. One felt he could even have managed without the former.' See E. H. Mikhail, *Oscar Wilde: Interviews and Recollections*, 2 vols (London: Macmillan, 1979), II, p. 464.

44 *Autobiographies*, pp. 286–87. The phrase 'terrible beauty' is, of course, to be found in Yeats's canonical poem 'Easter 1916'; that he should use the same phrase of Wilde's spoken tale as that articulating his response to the Easter Rising emphasizes the power of its effect on him.

45 Writing in an article on Wilde's spoken tales, Henry-D. Davray describes how their impact was heightened by the setting in which they were related: 'Il lui fallait aussi le cadre, le milieu, – la mise en train d'un repas aux mets excellents, aux vins de choix, avec l'élégance du linge, de l'argenterie, des cristaux, de la porcelaine' [He also needed the right setting, the right milieu: the preliminaries to a meal with excellent dishes, with fine wines, elegant table linen, silverware, crystal glass and china]. See 'De Quelque "Poèmes en Prose" D'Oscar Wilde', *Mercure de France*, 189 (15 July 1926), pp. 257–77 (p. 266).

46 Gide, *In Memoriam*, p. 31, n. 1.

47 *The Romantic '90s*, p. 268.

48 Deirdre Toomey, 'The Story-Teller at Fault: Oscar Wilde and Orality', in *Wilde the Irishman*, ed. Jerusha McCormack (New Haven and London: Yale University Press, 1998), p. 25. In his classic work, *Orality and Literacy* (London: Routledge, 2002), Walter Ong describes Ireland as 'a country which in every region preserves massive residual orality' (p. 68). Wilde himself regarded orality as a national characteristic, telling Yeats that the Irish were 'the greatest talkers since the Greeks'. See Yeats, *Autobiographies*, p. 135.

49 Henry-D. Davray, who undertook the translation of several of Wilde's works, gave this assessment of the author's French: 'Il possédait admirablement notre langue, dans laquelle son vocabulaire était étonnamment étendu' [He had an impressive command of our language, with a surprisingly extensive vocabulary]. See *Mercure de France*, 189 (15 July 1926), p. 271.

50 Fong and Beckson describe the stories in *Le Chant du Cygne* as 'virtuoso performances but thoroughly unreliable' (*PP* 218).

51 Ian Small, *Oscar Wilde Revalued* (Gerrards Cross: Colin Smythe, 1993), p. 206. Small expresses these doubts in *Oscar Wilde: Recent Research* (Gerrards Cross: Colin Smythe, 2000), pp. 56–57. In a footnote to 'The Story-Teller at Fault', Toomey points out that Small's labelling of Wilde's oral stories as 'apocrypha' 'assumes a chirographic-typographic mind-set'; see 'The Story-Teller at Fault', p.

178, n. 10. See also Paul K. Saint-Amour's *The Copywrights: Intellectual Property and the Literary Imagination* (Ithaca, NY, and London: Cornell University Press, 2003), wherein the author uses Toomey's argument as a foundation for his own contention that 'Wilde contributed during his career to a counterdiscourse with private print culture' (p. 95).

52 John Stokes, *Oscar Wilde: myths, miracles and imitations* (Cambridge: Cambridge University Press, 1996), p. 23.

53 A large majority of these tales had appeared previously in *Mercure de France*. See Guillot de Saix, 'Le Cinquième Évangile selon Oscar Wilde: Dix-neuf Contes Inédits' [The Fifth Gospel according to Oscar Wilde: Nineteen Hitherto Unpublished Tales], *Mercure de France*, 296 (1 February 1940), pp. 257–73.

54 'Simon le Cyrénéen', along with several others of the biblical tales collected by Guillot de Saix, has the tone and structural rhythm of a narrative joke. Wilde's sense of the comic in the Gospel narratives would have earned the approbation of theologians such as Adolf Jülicher (1857–1938), who argued that Christ frequently used comic stereotypes and exaggerations in his parables, elements that had been obscured by the Church's insistence on divorcing the stories from their cultural contexts and reading them as wholly allegorical. For a discussion of Jülicher's interpretation of the parables, see Joachim Jeremias, *The Parables of Jesus*, trans. S. H. Hooke (London: SCM Press, 1954).

55 Yeats, *Autobiographies*, p. 130.

56 This particular interpretation of Judas's motivation draws on the detail found in John's Gospel (13:23–26) that it is the 'beloved disciple' (assumed by Wilde to be John) who asks Jesus to name his future betrayer.

57 Ellmann includes an English translation of this tale in his biography of Wilde, explaining that it 'was recounted to André Gide soon after his [Wilde's] release from prison' and that it was one of several stories which 'grandly paralleled his conviction that he was being betrayed in money matters by Adey and Ross, by Ernest Leverson, and others' (*Oscar Wilde*, p. 488). The image of Judas as a shallow-minded money-grabber was, of course, a traditional one, originating from Matthew's mention of the 'thirty pieces of silver' (Matthew 27:3), and John's account of him as a corrupt treasurer, whose personal greed leads him to berate Martha for wasting ointment to anoint the feet of Jesus (John 12:4–6).

58 Taxil, *La Vie de Jésus*, pp. 275, 279.

59 Taxil, *La Vie de Jésus*, p. 279.

60 The abiding fascination with the figure of Lazarus is exemplified in J. Paterson-Smyth's *A People's Life of Christ* (London: Hodder & Stoughton, 1921): 'Often in this history we have wished to know the further life of men who have for a moment crossed the stage with Jesus. Above all others Lazarus [...] Why did he not tell of that world which Jesus pictured in His story of Dives as a world of vivid conscious life and thought and memory?' (pp. 260–61).

61 Coulson Kernahan, *Spiritualism: A Personal Experience and A Warning* (London: Religious Tract Society, 1919), p. 14.

62 Alfred, Lord Tennyson, *In Memoriam*, ed. Erik Gray (New York: W. W. Norton, 2004), Section 31, ll. 13–16, p. 22. One other poet whom Wilde admired, Robert Browning, had also treated the Lazarus story in 'An Epistle containing the Strange Medical Experience of Karshish, the Arab Physician' (*Men and Women*, 1855).

63 James Joyce would continue the tradition of Lazarus jokes in *Ulysses*, punning on the text of the Fourth Gospel: 'Come forth, Lazarus! And he came fifth and lost the job.' See *Ulysses* (Harmondsworth: Penguin, 1987), p. 87.

64 In a recent work, Charles Bernheimer states: 'In poems, stories, plays, paintings, posters, sculptures, decorative objects, dance, and opera, well over a thousand versions of the Judean princess were made in Europe between 1870 and 1920.' See *Decadent Subjects; The Idea of Decadence in Art, Literature, Philosophy, and Culture of the Fin de Siècle in Europe* (Baltimore and London: Johns Hopkins University Press, 2002), p. 104. Never actually named in the Gospels, Salome's precise identity is to be found in Josephus.

65 In *The Life of Christ*, F. W. Farrar provides the following footnote: 'For the traditional death of "the dancing daughter of Herodias," by falling through, and having her head cut off by the ice, see Niceph. i. 20'. See *The Life of Christ*, I, p. 394, n. 1.

66 Kernahan, *In Good Company*, p. 223.

67 Renan, *The Life of Jesus*, p. 297.

68 For a detailed discussion of this sub-genre of biblical fiction, see Ziolkowski, *Fictional Transfigurations of Jesus*, pp. 17–22. The creative tradition of placing the historical Jesus in a modern-day setting continued throughout the twentieth century; Jerome K. Jerome's drama *The Passing of the Third Floor Back* (1910), Charles Causley's poem 'The Ballad of the Bread Man', published in *Underneath the Water* (1968), and Stanley Spencer's painting *Christ Preaching at Cookham Regatta* (1953–59) are but three of many examples.

69 After 1851, Constant published under the name of 'Eliphas Levi' and turned his attention to occultism; this later work found a great admirer in Catulle Mendès.

70 W. T. Stead was editor of the *Pall Mall Gazette* from 1883 until 1890, and Wilde would have known him through his reviewing work for the journal.

71 See W. R. Wilde, *Narrative of a Voyage*, 2 vols (Dublin: William Curry, Jun., 1840).

72 Wilde follows Renan, and several other biblical scholars, in regarding Jesus's resurrection as a figment of the imagination of Mary Magdalene and the disciples.

73 Toomey, 'The Story-Teller at Fault', p. 31. For an account of the influence of Joachimism on nineteenth-century authors, including Wilde, see Warwick Gould and Marjorie Reeves, *Joachim of Fiore and the Myth of the Eternal Evangel in the Nineteenth and Twentieth Century* (Oxford: Oxford University Press, rev. edn, 2001).

74 'Sonnet: On the Massacre of the Christians in Bulgaria' was first published in *Poems* (London: David Bogue, 1881). Wilde had previously sent the poem to Gladstone, hoping for his approval (*CL* 46–47). In some ways Wilde's choice of reader is unsurprising: Gladstone had recently written two pamphlets on the Eastern question and his ardent defence of J. R. Seeley's *Ecce Homo* (1865) associated him with the Broad Church movement and its openness to reading the Scriptures in new ways. Nevertheless, Wilde was taking quite a risk in sending this poem to a man who, for all his engagement with contemporary ideas about Christ, was a lifelong High Churchman. The sonnet's mood is certainly agnostic, questioning as it does whether Christ had really 'burst the tomb' or whether his bones were 'Still straitened in their rock-hewn sepulchre?' Furthermore, Wilde's uncritical citing of Renan's description of Mary Magdalene's account of the risen Christ as 'the

divinest lie ever told', in his second letter to Gladstone (*CL* 48–49), would not have endeared him to the statesman. It is likely that Wilde, along with many others, made the mistake of regarding Seeley as the English Renan, and that he took Gladstone's approval of the English writer as an indicator of his acceptance of the views of his French counterpart.

75 Wilde, of course, had already asserted Gautier's aesthetic credo, as professed in the preface to *Mademoiselle de Maupin* (1835), in several of his works, most famously in his preface to *The Picture of Dorian Gray*.

76 Yeats, *Autobiographies*, p. 136.

77 Arnold, *Literature and Dogma*, in *Complete Prose Works*, VI, p. 268. Wilde was certainly well acquainted with this work, referring to it frequently in his non-fictional writings and quoting from it in *De Profundis* .

78 William Sanday, the Lady Margaret Professor of Divinity and Canon of Christ Church, Oxford, wrote that 'No one now believes that the supposed death was really only a swoon, and that the body laid in the tomb afterwards revived.' See *Outlines of the Life of Christ* (Edinburgh: T. & T. Clark, 1905), pp. 180–81.

79 Constance Howell, *A Biography of Jesus Christ* (London: Freethought Publishing Company, 1883), p. 56.

80 Howell, *A Biography of Jesus Christ*, p. 56.

81 For details of the development of anatomy in the nineteenth century, see Ruth Richardson's *Death, Dissection and the Destitute* (London: Phoenix Press, 2nd edn, 2001).

82 With this Gospel example in mind, Frank Kermode points out that 'some commentators continue to insist that the realism of John's narrative is easily explained' and that anatomical arguments are still advanced by those 'who cannot accept that the historical account is an invention, founded on a repertory of texts brought to fulfillment by a literary narrative'. See *The Genesis of Secrecy: On the Interpretation of Narrative* (Cambridge MA: Harvard University Press, 1979), pp. 104, 105.

83 William Stroud, *A Treatise on the Physical Cause of the Death of Christ* (London: Hamilton and Adams, 1847), p. 356.

84 David Smith, *The Days of His Flesh* (London: Hodder and Stoughton, 1905), p. 506.

85 Abner Phelps, *The Crucifixion of Jesus Christ Anatomically Considered* (Boston, MA, 1853).

86 There was interest in Lateau throughout Europe. In England, George E. Day wrote an article entitled 'Louise Lateau, A Biological Study', which was published in *Macmillan's Magazine*, 23 (April 1871), pp. 488–98. In a footnote, he states that 'Dr Lefebvre […] took upwards of a hundred medical friends to examine the phenomena', p. 488, n. 1.

87 Antoine Imbert-Gourbeyre, *La Stigmatisation, l'extase divine, et les miracles de Lourdes. Réponse aux libres- penseurs*, 2 vols (Clermont-Ferrand, 1894).

88 See *The Road from Decadence: Selected Letters of J.-K. Huysmans*, ed. and trans. Barbara Beaumont (London: The Athlone Press, 1989), p. 60.

89 *Sainte Lydwine de Schiedam* (Paris: P.-V. Stock, 1901), pp. 83–84.

90 Huysmans, *The Road from Decadence*, p. 207.

91 In *The Myth of the Resurrection*, Annie Besant discusses the tendency to equate

belief in modern miraculous events with Catholicism: 'The English Protestant turns up his nose at the Popish miracles at Lourdes and at Knock, although they are a good deal better authenticated than those at Nain and at Bethany' (p. 134). In a footnote to his article on Louise Lateau, George E. Day explains the word 'stigmata' for what he clearly expects to be a Protestant readership: 'this term is applied by Roman Catholic writers to the marks of the wounds on our Saviour's body as shown in most pictures of the Crucifixion'. See *Macmillan's Magazine*, 23 (April 1871), p. 489, n. 1.

92 W. B. Yeats refers to the 1890s' 'tradition' of converting to Roman Catholicism in his introduction to *The Oxford Book of Modern Verse 1892–1935* (Oxford: Clarendon Press, 1936), pp. x–xi.

93 Ernest Renan, *Studies in Religious History*, Authorized English Edition (London: Richard Bentley and Son, 1886), p. 315.

94 Renan, *Studies in Religious History*, p. 326.

95 Scott, *The English Life of Jesus*, p. 336.

96 Strauss, *The Life of Jesus Critically Examined*, III, p. 362.

97 Frei, *The Eclipse of Biblical Narrative*, p. 313.

98 *Oscar Wilde's Oxford Notebooks: A Portrait of a Mind in the Making*, ed. Philip E. Smith II and Michael S. Helfand (New York: Oxford University Press, 1989), p. 163.

99 Bernard Shaw, *Saint Joan* (Harmondsworth: Penguin Books, 1946), pp. 70, 71.

100 Renan, *The Hibbert Lectures 1880*, p. 64.

101 In 1880 Renan delivered a Hibbert lecture on the establishment of the Jews in Rome, and Peter's and Paul's respective roles in the founding of the Roman Church; this was later published in *The Hibbert Lectures 1880*. Wilde may well have known this work.

102 This distinction between Peter and Paul is explained in Galatians 2:1–10.

103 While acknowledging the complexities of Wilde's prison writing, I have chosen to refer to it by its most commonly known title, *De Profundis*, and not, as some critics would prefer, 'the prison manuscript'. For the purpose of this chapter, there are no significant variations between the text that appears in Ian Small's Oxford University Press edition and that edited by Wilde's literary executor, Robert Ross, under the title *De Profundis* (London: Methuen, 1905).

104 Edgar Saltus, *The Anatomy of Negation* (London: Williams and Norgate, 1886), p. 79. Wilde saw a good deal of Saltus during the American's visits to London. In an account of her husband's life, Marie Saltus relates how a discussion between Wilde and Saltus about fictionalizing the Bible initiated the writing of *Salomé* and *Mary of Magdala* respectively. See *Edgar Saltus, the Man* (Chicago: Pascal Covici, 1925), p. 51. Wilde would later praise *Mary of Magdala* for being 'so pessimistic, so poisonous and so perfect' (*CL* 453).

105 Schweitzer, *The Quest of the Historical Jesus*, p. 6.

106 *Times Literary Supplement*, 24 February 1905, pp. 64–65 (p. 64).

107 *Times Literary Supplement*, 18 June 1908, p. 193.

108 Renan, *The Life of Jesus*, p. 206.

109 Ellmann, *Oscar Wilde*, p. 488. Guillot de Saix recorded Wilde's version of the Ahab and Jezebel story, 'Le Vigne de Naboth' (*CC* 56–60), and reconstructed the tale into the form of a one-act drama. See 'Oscar Wilde et Le Théâtre: Jézabel,

Drame Inédit en un acte' [Oscar Wilde and the Theatre: Jezebel, a hitherto unpublished one-act play], *Mercure de France*, 279 (1 November 1937), pp. 513–49.

110 Gwendolen Lally, *Jezebel* (London: Arthur L. Humphreys, 1918). The copyright performance of the play was given at the Comedy Theatre in March 1912.

111 Oscar Wilde, *Essays and Lectures* (New York and London: Garland Publishing, 1978), p. xi, first published by Methuen, London, 1909.

112 Gedeon Spilett, 'An Interview with Oscar Wilde', published for the first time in English in Mikhail's *Oscar Wilde: Interviews and Recollections*, II, p. 356.

113 After his release from Reading Gaol, Wilde found a sympathetic publisher in Leonard Smithers. For a study of the relationship between Wilde and Smithers and the complex history of the publication of the *Ballad of Reading Gaol*, see James G. Nelson, *Publisher to the Decadents: Leonard Smithers in the Careers of Beardsley, Wilde, Dowson* (University Park: The Pennsylvania State University Press, 2000), pp. 173–223. See also *The Early Life and Vicissitudes of Jack Smithers* (London: Martin Secker, 1939), which includes an extremely partial account of Smithers' dealings with Wilde by the publisher's son, Jack Smithers.

114 Hesketh Pearson, *The Life of Oscar Wilde* (London: Methuen, 1946), p. 217. Walter Pater's comment that 'There is something of an excellent talker about the writing of Mr. Oscar Wilde' also underlines the interconnectedness of Wilde's spoken and written work. See 'A Novel by Mr Oscar Wilde', *Bookman*, November 1891, pp. 59–60 (p. 59).

115 Wilde's appreciation of Jesus's freedom from textuality concurs with Renan's view that 'His doctrine was so little dogmatic that he never thought of writing it or of causing it to be written'. See his *Life of Jesus*, p. 302.

116 Laurence Housman, *Echo de Paris* (London: Jonathan Cape, 1923), p. 34.

CHAPTER 5

The Afterlife of Oscar Wilde's Oral Tales

[A] story wanders far like thistle-down, and somebody hearing
it [...] might unexpectedly feel himself called upon to write it.
George Moore

In his 1912 study of Oscar Wilde, the writer and journalist Arthur
Ransome wrote that 'the flowers of his [Wilde's] talk bloom only in
dead men's memories, and have been buried with their skulls'.[1] This
somewhat romantic notion was by no means the case, especially as
regards Wilde's oral stories, a range of which were recorded in
memoirs and biographical sketches about him, with some being developed into imaginative fictions of somewhat dubious literary merit.
Two of the biblical tales, 'L'Inutile Résurrection' and 'Le Miracle des
Stigmates', considered in some detail in the previous chapter, under-
went extensive refashioning in writings published well into the
twentieth century, gradually losing all connection with the original
teller. This chapter examines how three writers, Coulson Kernahan,
Cyril Ranger Gull and Frank Harris, developed Wilde's spoken
heterodoxies into their own forms of fiction and to serve their own
literary and ethical purposes. These three authors were connected
through their professional lives: Gull worked for the *Saturday Review*
under Harris's editorship, and published several of his novels with
Ward Lock, a company that for many years employed Kernahan as
principal reader. They also had associations of varying degrees of
closeness with Wilde himself. Gull, the youngest of the three, was not
one of Wilde's immediate circle, being barely twenty the year Wilde
was tried and imprisoned. However, his close and abiding friendship
with Leonard Smithers, one of the principal publishers of 1890s'
writing and of Wilde's work in the years immediately following his
release from prison, ensured that he was very much in touch with the

world of the British decadents.[2] Kernahan was rather more closely acquainted with Wilde thanks to his work for Ward Lock. Liaising with Wilde in the early 1890s over the publication of *The Picture of Dorian Gray*, he came to be on friendly terms with the author, devoting a substantial chapter to him in his book of reminiscences, *In Good Company*. However, of the three authors it is undoubtedly Frank Harris who would be most immediately associated with Wilde, not least because of the highly colourful account he gives of their years of friendship in *Oscar Wilde: His Life and Confessions* (1916).

In tracing the relationship between Wilde's biblical tales and the later fictions of his friends and acquaintances it is crucial to bear in mind contemporary notions of literary ownership and borrowing. In recent years, one of the consequences of a rapidly expanding internet has been the perils of plagiarism, with students in all sectors of education using – or misusing – the work of others. At the same time, the very concept of plagiarism has become an increasingly compelling focus for academic consideration, with Wilde as one of its major authors. In a recent study of intellectual property and the literary world, Paul K. Saint-Amour gives this analysis of the creative borrowing in Wilde's circle:

> Wilde not only plagiarized, but created a community of plagiarists; by scattering his literary ideas and expressions around him for others to seize freely, he united writers in theft. In doing so, he endowed a private print culture with the dynamics of an idealized oral culture: stories received as gifts were passed on as gifts; narratives branched in abundant retellings, limning a community through circulation rather than reinforcing private ownership through accumulation.[3]

Saint-Amour's description of Wilde 'scattering his literary ideas' echoes Richard Ellmann's comment that the 'ideas and themes he scattered were sometimes reaped by his young admirers'.[4] Yet, as Ellmann suggests in an anecdote following this statement, not all of Wilde's ideas were available for others to 'seize freely':

> The novelist W. B. Maxwell [...] had heard many stories from Wilde, and wrote one of them down and published it. He confessed to Wilde, whose face clouded, then cleared as he mixed approval with reproach, 'Stealing my story was the act of a gentleman, but

not telling me you had stolen it was to ignore the claims of friendship.' Then he suddenly became serious, 'You mustn't take a story that I told you of a man and a picture […] I fully mean to write it, and I should be terribly upset if I were forestalled.'[5]

It is a story that alerts us to the complexities of what Saint-Amour terms an 'idealized oral culture' at a time when publishing practices were becoming increasingly regulated and complex.[6] Of the texts examined in this chapter some – to use Julia Kristeva's memorable metaphor – smell more strongly of Wilde's texts than others, yet all share with him an equally pressing desire to explore Christian ideas through imaginative writing.

Bringing Wilde back to faith:
Coulson Kernahan and Guy Thorne

In the penultimate chapter of *In Good Company*, Kernahan recollects:

My friendship with Wilde was literary in its beginnings. Flattered vanity on my part possibly contributed not a little to it, for I was young and – if that be possible – a more obscure man even than I am now, Wilde, already famous, was one of the very first to speak an encouraging word.[7]

While the contrast here between the youthful Kernahan and the famous Wilde is somewhat overstated (Wilde was Kernahan's senior by a mere four years), the master–disciple relationship it implies rings true: Kernahan was an aspiring writer and journalist, doubtless in awe of a literary author approaching the height of his celebrity.[8] Yet it is clear from Kernahan's mature reflections on his friendship with Wilde that, with respect to religious belief, and Christian morality in particular, the younger man considered himself the more enlightened. Though by insisting that his friend was 'not an irreligious man' Kernahan resists the image of the 'pagan' Wilde propagated by the likes of Gide and Harris, it is evident that he is uncomfortable with what he clearly regards as the deceased author's immorality.[9] The more Kernahan extenuates, the more obvious this discomfort becomes; he conjectures that though Wilde 'talked and wrote much nonsense […] about there being no such thing as a moral or an immoral book', such sentiments were mere 'pose', and he views his homosexuality as coming from 'powers and forces of darkness outside himself' that propelled him into 'a sort of Jekyll and Hyde life'.[10] While Kernahan may have entered the world of the decadents in writing about Swinburne and managing the publication of *The Picture of Dorian Gray*, his devout Christianity ensured that he would always be on the outside looking in, and that the treatments that Wilde's oral tales would receive under his authorship would draw back from the heterodoxy of the originals.

In Good Company tells of how, during a discussion about religion, Wilde related the opening of a scenario featuring the 'finding to-day of the body of the Christ in the very rock-sepulchre where Joseph of Arimathea had laid it'.[11] Though Kernahan claims not to have heard the story – presumably 'L'Inutile Résurrection' – through to its conclusion, his later writings suggest that he was eventually acquainted with at least one complete version of it.[12] Kernahan had the heightened awareness of literary ownership that comes with the experience of working in the world of publishing, and had already been punctilious in asking Wilde's permission to use a phrase of his in one of his collections of short stories, published in 1893, three years before his reworking of the resurrection story appeared under the title *The Child, the Wise Man, and the Devil*.[13] In the same spirit of honesty, he directly addresses the question of Wilde's influence in his account of their relationship:

> The idea appears to have occurred to both, but whereas, in Wilde's mind, it was clear and defined, in mine it was then no more than an idea. I sometimes wonder whether his words did not make vivid to me what before was vague. Of one thing at least I am sure, that he was the first to speak of such an opening scene, which fact in itself constitutes some sort of previous claim.[14]

Given the public attention that biblical archaeology was attracting at this time, Kernahan's claim that the idea of the tale might have occurred to them both at the same time is not unreasonable. However, his religious fiction is more deeply interconnected with Wilde's story than he would have the reader believe, and while his relationship with Wilde might only have lasted a few years, the ideas that emerged from it endured in publications spanning three decades.

The Child, the Wise Man, and the Devil (1896) takes the form of a series of dream-visions, a choice of form that places its author within the literary tradition of 'Bishop Bunyan' and signals a desire to rein in Wilde's heterodoxy. In this *Pilgrim's Progress manqué*, Kernahan conducts his narrative through the voices of allegorical figures reacting to the discovery of Christ's body in 'the rock hewn sepulchre whither it was borne nineteen hundred years ago by Joseph of Arimathea'.[15] The end of Christ's dominance is marked by a great ceremony in which the long-established rituals of Christianity are destroyed and the 'Reign of Sorrow' is replaced with the 'Reign of Joy'. However, the new order is short-lived as members of this post-Christian society begin to realize what they have lost; life without Christ is described by one despairing man as akin to being 'held captive at the will of an Unknown Gaoler' (*CWD* 54), and the token fallen woman laments that she can no longer live without the hope of forgiveness. Kernahan wastes little time in bringing out the ultimate *deus ex machina*: God himself, who berates the people for their unbelief and leaves them in a world described by the anonymous dreamer in imagery reminiscent of Arnold's great poem of agnosticism, 'Dover Beach': 'Below me, as on a midnight plain, that stretched away into infinite darkness, lay the wounded in life's battle – the widowed, the orphaned, the friendless, the sick, the halt, and the sin bound' (*CWD* 42–43). In a sentimental final scene, the desolate grief of a father at the death of his small child prompts the reappearance of Christ, whose 'streaming eyes' (*CWD* 80) confirm that he is, indeed, God made flesh and whose promise never to forsake the earth again, however many times he is despised and rejected, ensures that the tale ends on a note of peaceful optimism in contrast to the joyless, hopeless apathy that prevails at the close of Wilde's version. And where the rationalism of the bespectacled scientists of Wilde's story succeeds in driving away the figure of Christ for all eternity, Kernahan's equivalent 'wise men' are clearly marked out as of the Devil's party, and left in a state of delusion, believing themselves to have destroyed the 'Religion of Sorrow' for all time, and not realizing that 'many a little child was wiser [...] than they' (*CWD* 82) and ultimately invincible.

'L'Inutile Résurrection' and *The Child, the Wise Man, and the Devil* are both typically *fin-de-siècle* texts: the former in its emphasis on art, beauty and the individual consciousness, the latter in its contemplation of a future stripped of the old certainties of Christianity and looking to the potential problems of democratization and scientific development. Whereas Wilde's tale ends with a world doomed to unrelenting scientific materialism, having rejected the worship of beauty and individualism, Kernahan's concludes with a stark warning of the consequences of rejecting the more traditional Christ. Where Wilde conjures up an image of perpetual limbo, Kernahan presents the reader with an image of hell averted. The narrator of the tale might have seen terrifying glimpses of a dystopia where 'a mob, scrambling and fighting' (*CWD* 55), deprived of the moral restraints of Christianity, grows ever more vicious and threatening, but the reader can rest safe in the knowledge that it is only a nightmare vision from which any true believer is free to wake up.

Perhaps inspired by the relative success of Kernahan's dreamvision, the journalist and popular novelist Ranger Gull, writing under the pseudonym 'Guy Thorne', would further develop the central idea of Wilde's resurrection tale into a novel entitled *When It Was Dark*.[16] It was a work of fiction straddling several popular genres, offering elements of mystery, crime and sensationalism; it was also a work of Christian propaganda on a par with that of Marie Corelli, a writer Gull considered 'a great modern force'.[17] Indeed, it was just the kind of orthodox writing that might have been expected from the son of a Church of England clergyman. Yet Gull was by no means the typical vicar's son. Described by the poet and novelist Richard Aldington as a 'tubby little *bon vivant* who never refused a double whisky', he moved in fashionable decadent society, as likely to be attending a dinner at the Café Royal as a church service.[18] Gull's taking on a *nom de plume* would seem, then, to be in keeping with his Janus-like character, enabling him to be both Guy Thorne, the minister's son on a mission to save men from the 'apathy of despair' by way of his fiction, and Ranger Gull, the fast-living man about town.[19]

Inevitably, though, bearing two such contrasting identities brought its difficulties, and Gull's self-confliction is apparent in both his fiction and non-fiction writings. Not yet publishing under a pseudonym, his first attempt at religious fiction was a selection of Bible stories from both the Old and New Testaments, adapted for a modern audience and collected under the title *From the Book Beautiful: Being Some Old Lights Relit* (1900). Gull insists in the preface that he has written in the 'reverent and proper spirit' of the best fictional treatments of the Scriptures, and follows in the footsteps of Corelli in his desire 'to clothe [...] living facts with a picturesque dress', so that his readers might appreciate the 'aesthetic pleasure that can be found in the narratives of Holy Scripture', too often lost through over-familiarity.[20] Yet he also warns that he has allowed 'a certain *modern* note to creep into them here and there' and the reader does not have to venture too far into the work to discover that what the author defines as 'modern' in his writing could be more accurately defined as *fin-de-siècle* decadence. In 'The Slave's Love', for example, the erotic allure of Potiphar's wife is clearly modelled on that of the Salome figure that flourished in the literary imagination of the 1890s, her jewelled tortoise attached 'by a tiny silver thread to one of the gold rings fastened in her breasts' recalling Des Esseintes' ill-fated turtle in the fourth chapter of Huysmans' *À Rebours*.[21] Paterian influence is also evident in 'The Young Man with Many Possessions', a retelling of the Synoptists' story of the aspiring disciple unable to obey Jesus's instruction that he must give up all his wealth before joining his followers. Gull's rich young man seems like a poor parody of Pater's Marius. He shrinks from the idea of having to renounce the delights of good wine and fine books in order to share the company of unedu-cated illiterates, who are unable to appreciate 'the beauty of art or discuss a hexameter'.[22] Having enough self-knowledge to realize that he could never survive a life of dirt, poverty and 'horribly vulgar [...] fat' women, he settles on what he terms a 'third way': a beautiful suicide.[23]

From the Book Beautiful would seem to mark a turning point in Gull's writing career in its blend of orthodoxy and aestheticism. In an essay published in 1907, he dismisses his affiliation with the decadents as a youthful infatuation and confirms his allegiance to the wisdom of his father, to traditional Christianity and to Guy Thorne, his second self:

> The theory of modern criticism is that Art is a thing by itself and owes no duty to Ethics. The reason for Art, is art. Ten years ago I think I would almost have gone to the stake for this doctrine [...] I well remember the indignant anger with which I repudiated the suggestion of my father, a clergyman, that when I grew older [...] I should think very differently. He was perfectly right. Art is the essential part of fiction, but it is not destroyed because it is employed as the handmaid of an ethical standpoint.[24]

However, notwithstanding such public disavowals, Gull continued to take a keen interest in the decadents. Writing under yet another pseu-donym, Leonard Cresswell Ingleby, Gull authored two lengthy, if otherwise undistinguished, monographs on Wilde, one largely concerned with the work (*Oscar Wilde*, 1907) and one with the man (*Oscar Wilde: Some Reminiscences*, 1912);[25] and 1915 saw the publication of his translation of Théophile Gautier's *Charles Baudelaire*, with the addition of a lengthy essay on Baudelaire's influence on British writers, a substantial part of which concentrated on the literary life of Wilde.[26]

When It Was Dark was perhaps Gull's way of pursuing his interest in Wilde's work while at the same time keeping at a safe distance from it. That he managed to keep any decadent influences at bay is confirmed in Albert Guérard's *Art for Art's Sake*, a polemic decrying aestheticism in literature, and in religious literature in particular, in which Gull's novel is singled out as a shining example of a 'thrilling and most edifying tale'.[27] The story begins in what was for Gull a most familiar setting: a vicar's study. The vicar in question is Ambrose Byars, a broad-minded and well-read minister of the Church of England, whose bookshelves allow for the peaceful co-existence of works by the heretical Renan and the devout Edersheim. In his initial portrait of the clergyman, Gull goes out of his way to convince the reader that not all members of the Church are blinkered and old-fashioned, and that a strong Christian faith need not be shaken by the claims of the Higher Criticism:

> As year by year his knowledge grew greater, and the scientific criticism of the Scriptures undermined the faith of weaker and less richly-endowed minds, he only found in each discovery a more vivid proof of the truth of the Incarnation and the Resurrection.[28]

But the faithful are soon to be sorely tested. The villain of the novel, Constantine Schaube, a wealthy Jew, and his sidekick, Sir Robert Llwellyn, an eminent biblical historian and expert on the Holy Sepulchre, conspire to prove that the resurrection was an egregious fraud. A new tomb is discovered by a member of the PEF, bearing the inscription: 'I, Joseph of Arimathea, took the body of Jesus, the Nazarene, from the tomb where it was first laid and hid it in this place' (*WIWD* 197). The newspaper world is quick to disseminate the discovery and, as the news goes public, so the whole of the civilized world is thrown into a state of chaos. The novel, too, loses its equilibrium at this point, taking on a heady mix of omniscient narration and a variety of inserted texts: newspaper articles, letters, song lyrics, speeches and cables.

Gull's depiction of the response of various Christian denominations to the crisis is a prime example of his unashamed exploitation of crass stereotypes. The Church of England publishes a mealy-mouthed statement, confirming its removal of twelve words from the Thirty-nine Articles and citing the words of Matthew Arnold as a declaration of its future ethos; the Roman Catholics close ranks, put their head in the sand and stifle all debate with the publication of a Papal Bull; the Non-Conformists, thanks to their heterogeneity, go in various directions, with the Methodists and Wesleyans best preserving the faith by organizing revival meetings nationwide. Yet the best efforts of the various Churches around the globe are not sufficient to keep moral order, and the mayhem and disorder only hinted at in Kernahan's dream-vision become fully realized. With the Virgin Mary and the Magdalene no longer held in saintly esteem, reverence for the female is abandoned and fallen women, once rescued from a life on the streets, fall back into prostitution; sexual morality is rapidly over-turned, leading to 'Unmentionable orgies' (*WIWD* 305) in the inner cities of Chicago and New York. Those remaining true to Christianity are persecuted; Catholics are hunted down by mobs of rationalists and, in Bulgaria, the followers of Islam threaten to expel all Christians from the state. As with all moral fables, of course, the havoc is arrested in the nick of time, good triumphs over evil, and the Christian world is restored to a state of faith and harmony.

That Gull does a very thorough job of bringing Wilde's agnostic parable back to orthodoxy is beyond doubt, yet echoes of Wilde's 'L'Inutile Résurrection' continue to resonate.[29] Gull's emphasis on the power of the press in spreading the news of the archaeological discovery chimes with Wilde's brief but powerful comment that 'Les journaux s'emparèrent de l'événement' [The newspapers got hold of the event]. Christian faith is replaced in Wilde's version by 'des explications rationnellement scientifiques' [rational scientific explanations], and in Gull's by 'the religion of common sense' (*WIWD* 259); and just as the discovery of the tomb in the oral tale results in the pope being chased from the Vatican, so in the novel the Catholic Church undergoes 'a storm of persecution and popular hatred' (*WIWD* 241). Yet if, by the end of the book, we cannot doubt the religiously orthodox sentiments of the author, as the sceptical elements of 'L'Inutile Résurrection' are well and truly overpowered by Christian fortitude, we can nonetheless perceive traces of the former decadent. The main appeal of Gull's work resides not in its hackneyed pieties but in its lurid and sensationalist exploitation of Wilde's rather more muted and haunting vision of 'l'apathie des jours sans croyance et sans joie' [the apathy of the days without belief and without joy]. And it is not only traces of Wilde's imagination that can be found in the novel: features of the author himself are represented in Gull's portrayal of Sir Robert Llwellyn. A 'man of purple, fine linen, and the sparkling deadly wines of life' (*WIWD* 398), Sir Robert's hedonistic lifestyle strongly resembles that popularly associated with Wilde. Likewise, the physical consequences of his debauchery, manifested in cheeks that have 'lost their firmness and [begun] to be pendulous and flabby' (*WIWD* 394), recall descriptions of Wilde's appearance in his final years.[30] Sir Robert's downfall, like Wilde's, is rapid and degrading; his crime is revealed by his lover and he eventually flees to the wife he hitherto neglected and mistreated. Trapped in their London apartment, surrounded by an angry mob, his body ceases to function; however, his mind remains unimpaired, allowing him to fully realize and repent of his sins. As he breathes his last, his still faithful and loving wife, angelic in a flowing white gown, lifts the crucifix to his lips in a gesture reminiscent of the faithful Ross bringing Father Dunne to Wilde's deathbed to administer the sacraments of baptism and extreme unction. It would seem, then, that for Gull both Wilde and Llwellyn are creators of fraudulent resurrection stories, the former in the real world, the latter in a fictional one, and both are accordingly punished and redeemed.

Published a few years after the discovery of the 'Sayings of Jesus' (the Oxyrhynchus Papyri) and one year after the English translation of Paul Vignon's influential study of the Turin shroud, Gull's crude propagandist fiction was perfectly suited to the talking points of the day, its popularity proving a testament to the author's unwavering conviction that 'Fiction will find those that can be reached by no other means.'[31] Indeed, his obituary in *The Times* singled out *When It Was Dark* as his most memorable achievement, recording how it 'formed the subject of sermons by popular preachers, headed by the Bishop of London and [...] had a sale of over half a million copies'.[32] While the novel's success was beyond dispute, responses to Gull's imposition of a traditional Christian resolution on a powerfully agnostic scenario were divided. The Bishop of London might have given it his *imprimatur*, but views outside the metropolis were rather more hostile. Richard Aldington, who grew up in the same Cornish village as that in which Gull took up residence, recalled how the small community there was of the 'general opinion [...] that it [the novel] was blasphemous and that one definitely should not call'.[33] To mollify such disgruntled readers Gull wrote *When It Was Light: A Reply to 'When It Was Dark'* (1906), publishing it anonymously. Set in a rural parish rather than the metropolis, *When It Was Light* features parishioners who refuse to believe in the inscription supposedly proving the resurrection to be a fake, holding tight to their faith until good prevails and the hoax is exposed. Responses to the 1919 film version of the novel were equally mixed, one reviewer writing that 'one is rather repelled by the idea of a film play based upon a plot to destroy Christianity [...] with scenes showing newspaper boys rushing through the streets with such posters as "Resurrection proved a myth"'.[34] Released just one year after the end of the First World War, the novel's scenes of chaos, violence and moral mayhem may well have been the very last thing some viewers wanted to see on the cinema screen.[35]

After the enormous popular success of Gull's novel, the *donné* of Wilde's resurrection tale would seem to have been fully exploited, if not exhausted. However, fifteen years after Kernahan's rather more moderate success with *The Child, the Wise Man, and the Devil*, and despite declaring in its preface that it was very unlikely he would write another book on religion, he returned to the same theme in *The Man of No Sorrows* (1911), the Wildean inversion of the title suggesting a continuing connection between the author and his former friend. In this prose fiction treatment of Wilde's story, Kernahan focuses more emphatically on the idea of a New Age Messiah, inventing an entirely human leader in the 'Man of No Sorrows' whose tempting promise of a world without pain and suffering ensures his ready acceptance by the people. Claiming that Jesus misrepresented the will of God by setting up 'the worship of Sorrow', the new leader inaugurates his own 'Reign of Joy', much to the delight of the masses.[36] As in Kernahan's earlier work, the dream grows increasingly nightmarish, as the Christ-forsaking people fall into 'feasting, lusting, and debauch'.[37] In this evocation of degeneracy the author departs entirely from his source, looking instead to Gull's apocalyptic vision in *When It Was Dark* for inspiration.[38] Like Gull, Kernahan extends the action world-wide, showing the spread of bestiality from London to Jerusalem where 'the blackened corpses of men, women, and little children lay roasting and smoking among the embers',[39] and the prurient sensationalism of Gull's chapter entitled 'What it meant to the world's women' is echoed in Kernahan's reference to the horrible fate 'of any young girl

[...] who fell into the hands of that drink-maddened, lust-inflamed, and bestial crew' roaming the Sodom and Gomorrah that is now Jerusalem.[40] Having shown the devastating consequences of Wilde's 'culte de beauté', order is restored by the return of the true Christ who, forgiving his usurper, reasserts his reign as the 'vast and colossal Shadow of a Cross' appears in a flame-like sky: a replaying of Emperor Constantine's fourth-century moment of conversion.[41]

The Man of No Sorrows is not a literary success: its various voices are better suited to a morality play than to the dialogue of a novella and its blatant didacticism seems to belong to an earlier century. Even less successful is *A World without the Christ* (1934), the final chapter of Kernahan's engagement with Wilde's resurrection tale. In this brief allegory, the fictional device of the dream-vision is transformed into an autobiographical account of an *actual* dream Kernahan claims to have had in a church, shortly after recovering from a serious illness. Once more he repeats the opening of Wilde's tale, but departs from it entirely as the work develops into a Manichean struggle between the forces of good and evil. It is a work that never rises above the level of a crude fire-and-brimstone warning of the consequences of unbelief, where 'tortured forms of men and women' writhe in the mouth of hell, before being restored to the bosom of Christ.[42] In short, it is the work of a man of declining years who has long exhausted his theme. It becomes clear on examining Kernahan's three religious fictions in sequence that his motivations for adapting Wilde's original tale had more to do with ethics than aesthetics. As if attempting to undo a malevolent spell, he seeks to restore to rights Wilde's most unsettling ideas: the new Messiah preaching his aesthetic creed is restored to the meek and gentle figure found in orthodox Lives of Jesus, and the promise of freedom and individuality implicit in 'L'Inutile Résurrection' is exposed as an impossible and dangerous ideal.

Frank Harris's second-hand tales

Wilde's resurrection tale offers a glimpse of a world in which the individual and the imagination are freed from external restraints. Gull and Kernahan developed it into works that confirm humankind as irredeemably fallen and dependent on the moral checks of Christianity for its survival. The deeply conservative nature of their writing transforms Wilde's radical and thought-provoking vision of the Gospels into a series of dull, tract-like warnings of the consequences of denying the truth of the resurrection. Rather more mindful of preserving the spirit of the spoken parables was the author and journalist Frank Harris, who drew on a number of Wilde's tales in his own short fiction. Twelve years after Wilde's death, a collection of Harris's short stories entitled *Unpath'd Waters* was published to a mixed critical response. A brief review in *The Times Literary Supplement* praised all but one story for striking 'an original note',[43] and in what amounts to an encomium to Harris in the arts periodical *Rhythm*, John Middleton Murry proclaimed 'The Miracle of the Stigmata' to be 'among the supreme creations of art', and its author to be 'the greatest artist living among the English-speaking people'.[44] Other reviewers were less convinced of Harris's creative genius and, focusing mainly on the early Christian stories, treated them as unremarkable examples of an already well-established European genre of scripturally based fiction. 'The Miracle of the Stigmata' was singled out by the *Saturday Review* as a work very much in the mode of Continental writers such as Anatole France and Maurice Maeterlinck, a mode that had 'already been worked for all it is worth';[45] and *The Nation*, though selecting it as the most impressive story of the volume, considered it 'not so original in conception as Audreieff's "Judas"'.[46] Yet, however alert some critics were to Harris's numerous literary influences, his borrowings from Wilde's oral tales seem to have escaped their notice.

The title *Unpath'd Waters*, a phrase taken from the fourth act of Shakespeare's *The Winter's Tale*, offers the promise of fiction writing which is both new and adventurous. Yet out of its nine stories, at least five are adaptations of works by other authors. Harris acknowledges the provenance of only two of these, suggesting a somewhat inconsistent attitude to the rights of the author: 'The Irony of Chance' bears the sub-title 'After Oscar Wilde' and 'The Holy Man', first published in *Rhythm*, is clearly denoted as 'After Tolstoi'. No such attribution is attached to 'The Miracle of the Stigmata' nor to the short play-script 'The King of the Jews', though both bear a close resemblance to Wilde's oral fables.[47] The longest story in the collection, 'An English Saint', also stands free of a named literary forefather, though, as Middleton Murry recounts in his autobiography, it owed much to Stendhal:

Suddenly, in a volume of his [Stendhal's] comparatively unknown stories I came upon the unmistakable original of 'An English Saint'.

I kept my discovery to myself, but my attitude to Harris was changed in a moment. I did not trust him any more; for the shock of that discovery came at a final moment. I had just written and published in *Rhythm* a tremendous dithyramb about him.[48]

Middleton Murry was not the only critic of Harris's short stories who had cause to rethink his opinions of the author. In a work of 1921, Hesketh Pearson praised *Unpath'd Waters* for containing 'more real genius, a larger humanity, a deeper comprehension, a wider vision' than any other collection he had read,[49] only to acknowledge years later that 'Several of Wilde's apologues have appeared in a volume of short stories called *Unpath'd Waters*.'[50] One of Harris's biographers, Hugh Kingsmill, also noted that the prose of the volume's biblical stories was 'reminiscent of Wilde's parables'.[51] As time wore on, though, biographers and critics of Harris with no first-hand knowledge of their subject either omitted to mention, or failed to perceive, their subject's debt to Wilde. E. Merrill Root, for example, in his near-hagiographical work on Harris, states how '"The Miracle of the Stigmata" develops a favourite idea of Harris's: that Jesus did not die upon the cross.'[52] Writing a decade or so later, Vincent Brome describes the same story as 'original, ironic and written with a spare beauty', praise that might have been more justly bestowed on Wilde's oral version.[53]

Harris's failure to put Wilde's name to 'The Miracle of the Stigmata' could be put down to a regrettable oversight; after all, he acknowledges him as the originator of one of the stories in the volume. Guillot de Saix was of the opinion that Harris bought from Wilde the rights to both 'The Miracle of the Stigmata' and 'The Irony of Chance', presumably prior to his ill-fated purchase of the *Mr and Mrs Daventry* scenario.[54] Certainly, the relative poverty endured by Wilde during his post-prison years makes it highly probable that he would have put some of his imaginative property on the literary market; but the sale of an entirely oral composition is clearly problematic. Considering that 'Le Miracle des Stigmates' is slight enough for Harris to have committed it to memory for later use, it is possible that he appropriated the tale as a kind of compensation for the *Mr and Mrs Daventry* fiasco; but, ultimately, the question as to whether Harris bought or stole 'Le Miracle des Stigmates' is difficult to resolve with any certainty.[55] However, his well-documented dispute with the Anglo-Irish author George Moore over the rightful ownership of the stigmata story attests to the fact that he fully intended to pass the story off as his own invention.[56] Harris was, in fact, an inveterate plagiarist, whose magpie tendencies are remarked upon in the published writings of both his friends and enemies. In his biography of Wilde, Hesketh Pearson includes William Rothenstein's account of Harris's prolix retelling of a tale by Anatole France and Wilde's caustic response: 'What a charming story, Frank [...] Anatole France would have spoiled that story', an anecdote that indicates that Harris's plagiarism was common knowledge.[57] Enid Bagnold, employed by Harris during his editorship of the periodical *Modern Society*, recalls in her autobiography: 'I rewrote stories from Maupassant and signed them myself (needless to say, at my chief's suggestion).'[58] And in *Bernard Shaw, Frank Harris and Oscar Wilde*, Robert Sherard accuses Harris of translating André Gide's transcriptions of Wilde's oral tales into English and quoting them as his own in his biography of Wilde.[59]

While the weight of evidence would seem to confirm Harris as a purloiner of Wilde's stigmata tale, there is room for recognizing that the transference of ideas was not exclusively one way. Wilde is, after all, a writer noted for his creative recycling of both his own and others' writing, with the impact of his work often depending on the audience's recognition of the old within the new and vice versa. The genesis of Wilde's spoken tale 'L'Ironie du Hasard' is a relevant case in point. Harris's letter in reply to Hesketh Pearson's enquiry as to whether the story 'The Irony of Chance' (published in *Unpath'd Waters*) had originated with Wilde throws an interesting light on prevailing attitudes to the ownership of ideas:

> Yes, the first idea of the story came from Wilde but the ending of it, that the boy was *not* in the ball, was my idea. Wilde told it me one night very casually, saying he had a story. I said of course the boy must not be in the ball at the end, so that the man could have worsted his critics if he only had had the self-confidence of virtue, but his cheating had weakened *him* and so he came to grief. The moment I said it, Oscar jumped at the idea and said: 'Oh! Frank, what a splendid ending; but that makes the story yours; I have no more interest in it; you must write it.' He never wrote it, I believe, but I heard him telling it once afterwards with my addition, saying at the end laughing: 'This is *our* story, Frank.'[60]

Though the reliability of Harris's version of a long-past conversation cannot go unquestioned, the reported speech of Wilde carries a tinge of that arch irony frequently found in his comments to and about his friend, lending a degree of authenticity to the account. It would seem from this anecdotal case at least that co-ownership of the story was a perfectly tenable state of affairs, so long as it remained in its spoken form; it is only when Harris commits the story to the page that the sub-titular attribution 'After O.W.' is deemed necessary. This demarcation between oral and literary cultures is further underlined if, as Guillot de Saix claims, Harris purchased the rights to the story from Wilde before committing it to print.

'The Miracle of the Stigmata'

In the third volume of *My Life and Loves*, Harris writes: 'I must confess that the chief influence in my life, in the first years of the nineties, was Oscar Wilde.'[61] The publication of 'The Miracle of the Stigmata', first in the *English Review* in 1910, and then in *Unpath'd Waters*, serves as proof that Wilde's ideas held sway over Harris's literary endeavours for some considerable time after the close of the 1890s. There are several possible reasons why Harris was so keen to exploit Wilde's biblical revisions. On a purely personal level, his predilection for shocking the moral majority may well have been a driving force. Enid Bagnold remembered how he 'talked loudly of his three companions, Christ, Shakespeare and Wilde [...] and heads were raised to listen'.[62] And, recalling a similar occasion, Hesketh Pearson wrote how Harris 'talked with amazing fluency [...] and when he caught sight of a dean or an archdeacon sitting near us, his terribly audible question "Did Jesus Christ wear gaiters?" horrified me'. Publishing a written version of Wilde's stigmata story must have seemed to Harris an ideal way of gaining attention from a less immediate, but more extensive, public. In a postscript to a letter dated December 1908, Harris asks Arnold Bennett whether he knows of anyone interested in publishing his short story 'The Magic Glasses' and continues 'Of course no one will look at "The Miracle of the Stigmata"', a strategically placed afterthought that suggests he was already anticipating future notoriety.[63] Just one month later, negotiations over the publication of his stories were already in motion, and Harris reported to Bennett, with something akin to pride, that 'Hueffer has lunched with me and told me that his partner, Marwood, regarded

"The Miracle of the Stigmata" as a piece of blasphemous profanity which no right-thinking man would publish anywhere.'[64] Notwithstanding such objections, the publication of his heterodox tale in *Unpath'd Waters* went ahead, launching Harris's venture into biblical fiction.

If Harris's braggadocio is partly responsible for prompting his prose treatment of Wilde's stigmata tale, so was his wish to be taken seriously as a biblical scholar. His account of an interview with Ernest Renan, first published in *The English Review* in 1911, is written in a style that flaunts the writer's easy familiarity with his subject.[65] Harris presents himself as a knowledgeable theologian, undaunted by the fame and reputation of his interviewee, whom he presents as insufferably self-regarding and eager for praise and admiration. All in all, the portrait reads like an exercise in wish-fulfilment: Harris is much more likely to have held this interview in his own head than in Renan's sitting room. Indeed, one of his biographers, Hugh Kingsmill, writes that 'Harris's subjects may be arranged in three classes', estimating that Renan fits into the second of these: 'those whom there is either a certainty or a reasonable presumption that he met between once and half a dozen times'.[66] Yet however insubstantial the friendship may have been, Harris liked to give the impression that the two were on sufficiently intimate terms for him to take Renan to task for his portrayal, in the *Life of Jesus*, of a sweet-natured and handsome Christ, and to upbraid him for filling in the gaps of the Gospel stories with his own imagination. Harris continued to regard Renan's *chef-d'oeuvre* as deeply flawed, its having 'missed Jesus at his highest', and set himself the task of bettering it.[67] As early as 1910, he informed Arnold Bennett that his dealings with Renan had made him 'eager to write about Jesus' and to compose 'a gospel according to St. Thomas'.[68] Far from feeling awed and intimidated at the thought of following in Renan's footsteps, he seems to have been spurred on by a certain competitive urge to compose better scriptural fiction than his contemporaries. The novelist Louis Marlow, who contributed to *Pearson's* while it was under Harris's editorship in New York, observed that Harris 'rarely if ever wrote disinterestedly, but with an eye to the main chance and in the competitive spirit'.[69] Such competitiveness is clearly demonstrated in Harris's warning to Bennett not to tell anyone of his plans for a scriptural fiction 'or some clerical Shaw will probably exploit the idea', and in his boast to the same correspondent that Anatole France, in composing the short story 'The

Procurator of Judea', had 'spoiled a fine thing' and that he had written '"The Stigmata" to beat that thing of his'.[70]

The literary and theological climate of the day was certainly conducive to Harris's venture into biblical fiction. Spurred on by the discoveries of extra-canonical gospels, theological studies in the early years of the twentieth century were increasingly dominated by interest in early Christianity. Having identified the era of the Primitive Church as a compelling subject for fiction, Harris transferred his literary interests from the figure of Shakespeare to the figure of Christ, his critical study *The Women of Shakespeare*, published in 1910, marking the point of transition. In this work, following in the tradition built up over decades in Lives of Jesus, he yokes together Christ and Shakespeare, drawing the reader's attention to a number of verbal similarities between the sayings of Jesus and lines from Shakespeare's plays, finally declaring his preference for the words of the Man of Sorrows who 'gave himself a little more absolutely than Shakespeare to the divine inspiration'.[71]

Harris's development of Wilde's stigmata tale into short-story form is remarkable only in its lack of literary ambition. Despite moving in the same circles as writers such as Middleton Murry and Katherine Mansfield, Harris does not seem to have shared their interest in narrative innovation. Foregoing the opportunity of exploring the psychology of the resuscitated Jesus by daring means such as free indirect speech or interior monologue, he opts in 'The Miracle of the Stigmata' for an unwaveringly omniscient narrative, staying well within the boundaries of classic Victorian realism. As far as content was concerned, Harris no doubt selected from whichever version – or versions – of Wilde's tales best suited his purpose. So, for example, he opts for a married Jesus, enabling him to pursue ideas concerning the relationship between sexuality and character, and to explore, through the wife figure, the role played by women in the Early Church. The apostle Paul is chosen over the apostle Peter, allowing Harris to explore a character that he seems to have found infinitely more interesting than Jesus himself. His choice of location, Caesarea Philippi, a city in the northernmost area of Israelite territory known for its worship of graven images, emphasizes Jesus's estrangement from Jerusalem, once destined to be the site of his glorious resurrection; furthermore, as the site where Peter acknowledged Jesus as 'the Son of the living God' (Matthew 16:16), it provides a particularly ironic retreat for a failed Messiah.

Harris's Christ-figure closely resembles that of Wilde's tale: he is reclusive and withdrawn, tolerated by his companions because 'his shrinking self-effacement flattered vanity and disposed them in his favour'.[72] Building on Wilde's brief but resonant description of Jesus as 'le seul homme sur la terre à connaître la fausseté de la religion nouvelle' [the only man on earth to knew the falseness of the new religion], Harris presents a disenchanted idealist, whose superior understanding derives from surviving the agonies of the cross and living to tell the tale that there is no tale to tell.[73] A leader and a charismatic preacher in his former life, his only labour now is to conceal his tortured past and to speak 'very little, and never about himself' (*UW* 4). Harris's decision to name him 'Joshua', the Jewish equivalent of 'Jesus', serves not only to insist on his Semitic roots but also to underline his self-division: he has, in the reader's mind at least, two names and two identities. Once Paul's teachings take hold of the community, its discussions revolve almost entirely around the miracle of Christ's Resurrection, and Joshua is made even more acutely aware of the distance between his former self and present self, fielding painful rhetorical questions such as 'what do you know of Jesus that you should contradict His apostle?' (*UW* 17). As the story progresses, so the reader is made increasingly aware of the linguistic adjustments Joshua is obliged to make to conceal his true identity. The verbal estrangement from his earlier self is most emphatically underlined when he disputes Paul's interpretation of Christ's teachings and puts forward what he knows to be the authentic version:

'Paul has made doctrines of belief and rules of conduct; but Jesus wanted nothing but love: love that is more than righteousness ... He may have been mistaken,' he went on in a voice broken by extreme emotion; 'He trusted God, cried to Him in his extremity, hoping for instant help – in vain ... He was forsaken, cruelly forsaken, and all his life's work undone.' (*UW* 19–20)

Here, Joshua's emotional fragility when remembering his anguish on the cross impedes his fluency; his halting speech rhythms threaten a lexical breakdown and the reader half-expects him to shift from the third person to the first person in a dramatic moment of revelation that Christ's resurrection is merely an illusion. The situational irony of Joshua hearing his own supposed death and resurrection spoken about by Paul and his followers, his own wife included, is also fully exploited to add tension to an otherwise leaden narrative. A Christ-figure turned rationalist theologian, Joshua questions whether Jesus's death on the cross was genuine:

> 'But sometimes,' Joshua went on, 'men are thought to be dead who have only fainted. Jesus is said to have died on the cross in a few hours; and that, you know, is very strange; the crucified generally live for two or three days.' (UW 10)

Similarly, he applies materialist arguments to explain away Paul's Damascene vision, positing the theory: 'It may have been the sun [...] the noonday sun; his blindness afterwards seems to show that it was sunstroke' (UW 11). Yet in so frequently drawing the reader's attention to the fact that the supernatural figure worshipped by Paul and his followers is one and the same as the sole rationalist and unbeliever in their community, Harris blunts the ironical edge of Wilde's version of the tale and coarsens its tone.

In most respects Harris's presentation of Christ is considerably more conventional than Wilde's, and he takes care to perpetuate the familiar image of a meek and gentle Jesus, so beloved of orthodox Christians. While his name and appearance might distinguish him immediately as a Jew, his 'silence [...] more stimulating than the speech of other men' (UW 4) sets him apart from his 'loud, high-coloured, grasping compatriots' (UW 3).[74] However, somewhat less conventionally, and in contrast to Wilde, Harris seeks to explore Jesus's sexuality. As the art historian Leo Steinberg points out in his highly illuminating study, *The Sexuality of Christ in Renaissance Art and in Modern Oblivion*, 'the sexual component in the manhood of Christ [...] was normally left unspoken, suppressed originally by the ethos of Christian asceticism, ultimately by decorum'.[75] While questions arising from the relationship between godhead and sexuality lose their significance in an agnostic story of a purely human Jesus, questions of decorum still remain. Harris tackles the issue with a fair degree of caution, examining it mainly from the perspective of his two female characters. For them, Joshua's alterity derives not so much from his withdrawn manner but from his lack of masculinity. Tabitha is ill at ease in his company, declaring him to be 'soft and affectionate by nature, like a girl' (UW 5). The story suggests that Joshua's ignoble defeat on the cross has led inexorably to sexual impotence and a child-less marriage, a fictional variation on Harris's own conviction that 'everything high and ennobling in our nature springs directly out of the sex instinct'.[76] This is not the elective celibacy of a spiritual leader but the inevitable sexual failure of a broken man who, as Tabitha remarks, 'has a lot of the woman in him' (*UW* 6).

Harris's emphasis on Christ's lack of masculinity is, in fact, a crass reshaping of mid-to-late Victorian traditions to suit the realistic mode of his fiction. Images of an effeminate Jesus were to be found in both orthodox and heterodox depictions of Christ in the Victorian period. As the theologian Norman Pittenger points out in *Christology Reconsidered*, traditional Christianity produced 'the anaemic, lifeless, almost effeminate Christ of the Victorian stained-glass windows'.[77] As the Victorian era wore on, the effeminacy of Christ was given increasingly heterodox interpretations, such as that found in Algernon Swinburne's *Poems and Ballads* (1866), the image of the 'pale Galilean' in 'Hymn to Proserpine' proving particularly influential on contemporary writers. It was also an emphasis very much in keeping with Harris's own habit of psycho-sexual theorizing. His most recent biographer, Philippa Pullar, suggests that 'As Frank's sexual competence diminished, so he became more obsessed with other men's sexual weaknesses – especially in those men whom he had admired', adding that 'As Frank's physical and intellectual incompetence grew, so did his preoccupation with Jesus.'[78] Harris's version of the 'The Miracle of the Stigmata', then, is not without its autobiographical elements.

However, it is not Joshua's effeminacy but his opposition to Paul and his teachings that eventually ostracizes him from the entire community. The more Joshua hears reports of the missionary's preaching, the more he realizes that his own words have been distorted; as he insists to his wife, Judith, the apostle's teaching 'is not the teaching of love; and Jesus came into the world to teach love, and nothing else' (*UW* 19). Harris sentimentalizes Wilde's vision of a failed saviour by stressing Joshua's boundless capacity for love and forgiveness, transforming a hauntingly agnostic tale into a story closer in tone to Unitarianism. Joshua's capacity for love is seen to have expanded as a consequence of his suffering on the cross, helping him to realize the error of his former declaration that 'no earthly ties should fetter us who are called to the service of the divine Master' and to accept that 'the higher love ought to include the lower and not exclude it' (*UW* 21). When Judith abandons the marital home, it is with the conviction that she is obeying the exhortation of Christ, little suspecting its origin to lie in words spoken by the very husband she is deserting. And so, in yet another example of Harris's less than sophisticated handling of irony, Joshua is hoist with his own petard: the only aspect of his teaching accurately transmitted by Paul is the very one he would most like to retract.

In fleshing out Wilde's original story, Harris seems less interested in fictionalizing the character of Jesus than in exploring the historical figure of Paul. The apostle's presence dominates the story, his overwhelming success throwing Joshua's failings into sharp relief. The two men are contrasted throughout: where Joshua is reserved and laconic, Paul is bold and eloquent; where Joshua's 'great eyes made [...] flesh creep' (*UW* 5), Paul's 'eyes are wonderful' (*UW* 12). This interest in the relation between Jesus and Paul is very much of its time, the prevailing theological trend being to regard Paul as a unique thinker who had succeeded in breaking with an outmoded Judaic tradition and inaugurating a new and permanent spiritual order.[79] Whereas in Wilde's version Paul is but a shadowy presence, referred to only fleetingly as being 'au cours de sa première tournée évangélique' [in the course of his first missionary tour], Harris's story pays close attention to the Acts of the Apostles, detailing the missionary's progress from unknown preacher to one recognized as the greatest of the apostles.[80] By adding brief details of the evangelical ministries of the apostles Philip and Peter, and stressing the limits of their success, Harris presses home his own conviction that, without Paul, 'Christianity [...] might have perished in obscurity.'[81] The brief appearance of these two original disciples also makes the point that their first-hand knowledge of the Messiah does not render their preaching any more authoritative or compelling. Paul, on the other hand, whose Achilles' heel is commonly held to be that he was not in the original band of disciples, seems to acquire spiritual authority through force of personality and strength of conviction. In the community, it is only Joshua who thinks to ask 'Did he know Jesus...? He was not one of the disciples, was he?' (*UW* 11), a question answered with ironic force at the story's conclusion when Paul fails to recognize Joshua's corpse as that of the crucified Jesus. Following the general tendency to regard Paul as the figure who brought about a rupture with the Judaic law, Harris depicts him as a man with a seemingly boundless capacity for innovation; those who hear him are thrilled by the 'new creed' (*UW* 9–10) and Joshua is dismayed by the manner in which Paul has reinvented his own words, shaping them into 'doctrines of belief and rules of conduct' (*UW* 19–20). While the more devout Jews had rejected

Peter's teaching on account of the fact that Jesus was crucified, violating the statute laid down in Deuteronomy that 'a hanged man is accursed by God' (21:23), Paul manages to convince them that the crucifixion, far from being a disgrace, is 'the crowning proof [...] that Jesus was indeed the Messiah' (*UW* 9). As fast as Judaic law is overturned, new Pauline law is established. Judith's quitting of the marital home in obedience to Paul's decree 'Be ye not unequally yoked together with unbelievers' (*UW* 18), which Harris takes verbatim from II Corinthians (6:14), is an emphatic example of how quickly the apostle's word becomes law. Known as 'the Pauline privilege', the granting of a divorce to a man or woman whose partner refuses to convert to Christianity still forms part of the canon law of the Roman Catholic Church, and Harris's own complex marital history would no doubt have drawn him to this relatively minor detail. For the sake of his storyline, Harris conveniently ignores Paul's words given in I Corinthians (7:13–14): 'If any woman has a husband who is an unbeliever, and he consents to live with her, she should not divorce him [...] But if the unbelieving partner desires to separate, let it be so.' Joshua, of course, does not want to separate from Judith, and her decision to leave him goes against the apostle's advice quoted above.

Paul is shown to bring about a profound shift in the community's eschatological beliefs and even one of its most sceptical members, Simon, is won over by 'Paul's idea that the kingdom promised to us Jews is to be a spiritual kingdom, a kingdom of righteousness, and not a material kingdom' (*UW* 13). Clearly regarding Paul's declaration in II Corinthians (11:6) that he is 'unskilled in speaking' as no more than the rhetorician's use of *diminutio*, Harris suggests that his centrality to Christianity is thanks in no small part to his linguistic facility rather than his privileged position as witness to a divine revelation. Paul's ability to talk 'of Jesus beautifully' convinces his audience that he is 'filled with the very Spirit of God' (*UW* 11) and, as a result, 'Conversion followed conversion' (*UW* 13). Allied to Paul's sophisticated articulation is his gift for reinterpreting the words of others. Perhaps having in mind Paul's admission in I Corinthians (15:3) that the good news he delivers of Christ's resurrection comes only second-hand, Harris frequently reminds the reader that the original words of Christ were inevitably distorted by those who carried them forward. And Harris has no compunction in wrenching quotations from their New Testament contexts to press home Paul's shortcomings as a conduit of Christ's word. In one instance, Harris presents Mark's recording of

Christ's response to being accused of casting out demons in the name of Beelzebub, 'He that is not against us is on our part' (*UW* 17), as the opposite of Matthew's version 'He that is not with me is against me.' While the two accounts are, when read in their immediate scriptural contexts, complementary, Harris chooses, for the purpose of his characterization, to present them as conflicting. The seemingly more moderate words from Mark are presented as the authentic words of Christ, whereas Matthew's harsher version is delivered through the reported speech of Paul (*UW* 15–16), underlining the apostle's habit of misrepresenting Christ's teaching to suit his own rather vengeful nature.[82] In footnoting these Gospel verses in the text of the story, Harris is impressing on the reader his awareness of the ongoing theological debate over which of the two Gospels was written first. While Matthew's Gospel had been traditionally regarded as the first account of Christ's life, the case for Marcan priority started to assert itself in the 1870s and, by the late 1800s, Mark was widely accepted as the primary source for the life and ministry of Christ.[83]

As the narrative advances, Harris explores current opinions that Paul was the falsifier of Jesus and his teaching. Most extreme among such views were those of Friedrich Nietzsche, whose vituperative assaults on the personality and ministry of Paul featured strongly in his late work, *The Antichrist*, the first English translation of which appeared in 1896.[84] By 1909, the year when Harris was formulating a picture of Paul for his stigmata story,[85] Nietzschean philosophy was very much in vogue among his contemporaries, most notably George Bernard Shaw, a friend of Harris's since the mid-1890s and one of the earliest and most active popularizers of Nietzschean ideas.[86] Harris's portrayal of the Early Church in 'The Miracle of the Stigmata' accords with Nietzsche's view that Christianity is a 'purely *fictitious world*' [translator's italics].[87] Paul is the consummate storyteller, constructing a new religion from the compelling narrative of a resurrection that has not actually taken place. His preaching begins with a crucifixion that he has not witnessed and that is later proclaimed as the 'chief doctrine of the new creed' (*UW* 9), consistent with Nietzsche's opinion that the apostle 'could not use the life of the Saviour at all, – he needed the death on the cross...'[88] An important part of Paul's resurrection fiction is his offering up of his own personal account of Damascene conversion as one of the sacred texts of the new faith. His followers consider it 'a wonderful story' (*UW* 11), appearing to value it more for its narrative qualities than as a testament to Christ. The Paul of 'The

Miracle of the Stigmata' also bears a close resemblance to Nietzsche's 'genius of hatred'. An advocate of vengeance and punishment, he stirs up the crowds with his citation of vengeful Old Testament texts, twisting the teachings of Jesus to form a doctrine that prefers exclusion to inclusion, division to unity.[89] Even the holy stigmata he perceives on the corpse of Joshua are interpreted as marks of punishment for unbelief, placed there as a sign of divine retribution.

The logic of the stigmata story leads inexorably to an absence at the centre of Christianity: there is no risen Messiah, there are no holy stigmata, and the Primitive Church is founded on a figment of the community's imagination, most especially that of the impressionable female.[90] While Harris characterizes the story's male Jewish community through scraps of dialogue spoken by a few unnamed men, the women of the story are given names, described in detail and play crucial roles in the domestic life of Joshua and in the Pauline mission. Harris's foregrounding of the apostle's female followers is, in some regards at least, true to what we learn from certain of Paul's letters: women are promoted to serve the Christian community on an equal footing with their male peers.[91] Joshua's wife, Judith, and her aunt, Tabitha, are among Paul's first converts and 'it was only natural that their zeal should grow when they found their example followed by the priests and Levites and other leaders of the people' (UW 14).[92] Judith, in particular, is 'treated by Paul with great tenderness, as one who had suffered much for the faith' (UW 24) and is constantly by his side at meetings. When Joshua's death is discovered, Judith and Tabitha lay out his body, a travestying of the task that the female disciples set out to perform in the Synoptic accounts of Jesus's death and burial and, just as Mary Magdalene is one of the first witnesses of the resurrected Christ, so these two are the first to see the marks of the cross on Joshua's corpse.

Yet if the surface details of the story seem to represent the women of the community as the most energetic and loyal leaders of the new faith, a closer inspection reveals the author's strong reservations about the female religious temperament. For Judith, the initial attraction of Paul's preaching is the relief it brings from the monotony of 'the wretched loneliness of her life' with Joshua (UW 8). When she returns from a meeting with the apostle, we are told that she 'seemed like a new creature; her cheeks were red and her eyes glowed, and she was excited, as one is excited with the new wine' (UW 9), from which we are invited to infer that her devotion to Paul stems more from displaced physical desire than religious fervour. Both the barrenness of Judith's marriage and her feeling that she could have respected Joshua more if 'he had turned on her and mastered her' (*UW* 6) hint at her husband's impotence, the latter phrase reinforcing what was undoubtedly Harris's own belief: that women are naturally disposed to desire male domination. The unseemly haste with which Tabitha and Judith are received into the new faith is set against the more circumspect behaviour of Simon, the only male convert to be named. He looks on cautiously as Tabitha and her niece rush to be baptized, stating that 'for his part, he meant to wait: he would hear more, and do nothing rashly' (*UW* 12). And while his conversion to Pauline ways is not long in coming, he retains a strong affection for Joshua throughout the story, being the only one to reprove Judith for deserting her husband, telling her: 'He was too good for you' (*UW* 24). It is an accusation that, once more, carries the author's own criticism: women lack the discernment of men and cannot distinguish quiet truth from loud falsehood. In depicting the women of the story as led by sexual and social needs, rather than by the more noble pull of the spirit, Harris follows Renan's view that the 'female conscience, when under the influence of passionate love, is capable of the most extravagant illusions', perpetuating the tradition of centuries of male writing on the shortcomings of female religious devotion.[93]

In developing Wilde's lapidary parable into a story of considerable length, Harris seems to have concentrated more on substance than style, prompted perhaps by his desire to be regarded as a biblical expert. The text abounds with direct quotations from the Pauline Epistles and laboured attempts to dramatize what were, by this time, rather commonplace theological issues. Harris's involvement with scriptural study, and with the person of Jesus in particular, persisted for a few years following the publication of *Unpath'd Waters*. Several of his biographers put this continuation of interest down to his brief incarceration in Brixton prison in 1914 for contempt of court. Elmer Gertz and A. I. Tobin, in their 1931 study of Harris, wrote that:

He drew parallels between himself and the Divine One, who was crucified at Calvary. 'I am being punished that I may teach more efficaciously,' he said. It was then that the words of Jesus began to take on a personal note. They became his words, too, and constantly they flowed from his lips, infecting him with what were virtually messianic illusions.[94]

Given that Harris was deeply involved in writing a life of Wilde during this period, it is highly likely that the author identified his own prison experiences with that of his subject's, and that his increasing engagement with the Man of Sorrows was a genuine instance of life imitating art. More and more, his vision of Christ came to resemble that expounded in *De Profundis* as he took on Wildean phraseology, such as his description of Christ as an 'artist of the noblest'.[95] Furthermore, he followed Wilde in his disregard for the historical Jesus and in his contempt for those who endeavoured to 'prove his existence by the testimony of Paul, or by the references to the crucifixion in Tacitus and Josephus'.[96] Yet, though Harris admits in his life of Wilde that he and his friend shared a passion for the Gospels, and especially for the figure of Jesus, he is also anxious to stress that they approached the subject 'from opposite poles'; Harris presents himself as a believer in Jesus as a 'divine spirit', characterizing Wilde as a thoroughgoing pagan.[97] That Harris lived out an image of himself as an ardent worshipper of Christ is evident from contemporary accounts of his behaviour. Recalling a visit from Harris, Augustus John writes how, on reading the manuscript of the Wilde biography, he discovered 'the text interlarded with pious sentiments and references to our Saviour', which were only toned down after considerable resistance from the author.[98] Indeed, as Harris aged, his vision of Jesus grew increasingly sentimental, more in line with the Christ of Renan's *Life of Jesus*, a portrait he continued to dismiss as inadequate.

Harris's inclination as an older man was to look back to the liberal theology of the nineteenth century for his ideal image of Christ, refusing the challenge of writing a Jesus for the twentieth century by means of a more modernist fiction. *Unpath'd Waters*, with its four biblically based stories, is the nearest Harris came to completing a fifth Gospel. His 1924 volume of short stories, *Undream'd of Shores* (a title also taken from *The Winter's Tale*), included one fiction based directly on the New Testament entitled 'St Peter's Difficulty'.[99] Closely resembling a comic tale related to him by Shaw in a letter of 1918, this brief story of how Jesus's mother allows the deformed and wretched into the gates of heaven when Peter's back is turned is yet another example of Harris's reliance on the inspiration of others.[100] A rather more arresting story in the volume is 'A Temple to the Forgotten Dead', a series of tales within a frame-tale, one of which explores the possibility of light rays transmitting pictures of Jesus back to earth two thousand years after his death. Though of no particular literary merit, and indebted in parts to H. G. Wells's *The Time Machine*, the story is an early example of the Gospels meeting the world of science fiction, a combination that would be more fully exploited in the second half of the twentieth century. One other intriguing detail of the story lies in the character of Mr Collinson, a storyteller who entertains travellers in a pub on the outskirts of Brighton. Fascinated by Collinson and his brilliant facility for storytelling, the first-person narrator builds up an image of a character bearing considerable resemblance to Wilde. In the final sentence of the story, the narrator tells the reader: 'Collinson has left a memory as a story-teller that I have sought to perpetuate', and it is tempting to detect here the autobiographical voice of Harris himself.[101]

In 1915, Harris boasted in a letter to Shaw: 'one of these days you will see what these fifteen years of study of him [Jesus] has brought me'.[102] Such a boast was to sound decidedly empty just one year later when George Moore's biblical novel, *The Brook Kerith*, was published to considerable critical acclaim. Harris responded to Moore's success by accusing him of having plagiarized his own stigmata story and by launching splenetic attacks on the literary qualities of the novel. The intemperance of the response suggests that he was becoming painfully aware that he was losing the race to compose the evangel for modern times. By the time he came to complete the fourth and final volume of his memoirs in the late 1920s, he had to admit defeat: 'If I had another life to live, I would learn Aramaic and Hebrew and try to do what Renan failed to do: give a real portrait of the greatest man who ever wore flesh.'[103] Whether, if granted another life, Harris could have fulfilled such soaring ambitions must remain uncertain. That his long-time adversary, George Moore, had come closer to achieving them in his own lifetime was, however, beyond dispute.

Notes

1 Arthur Ransome, *Oscar Wilde* (London: Martin Secker, 1912), p. 209.
2 For accounts of Thorne's close friendship with Smithers, see Smithers, *The Early Life and Vicissitudes of Jack Smithers*, and Nelson, *Publisher to the Decadents*.
3 Saint-Amour, *The Copywrights*, p. 96.
4 Ellmann, *Oscar Wilde*, p. 292.
5 Ellmann, *Oscar Wilde*, p. 292.
6 For a succinct overview of turn-of-the-century publishing practices, see *An Introduction to Book History*, ed. David Finkelstein and Alistair McCleery (New York

and London: Routledge, 2005), pp. 78–80.

7   Kernahan, *In Good Company*, p. 194.

8   In a *Times* obituary of 19 February 1943, Kernahan is defined as 'a versatile writer' (p. 7). Long-lived, he produced novels and poetry, and essays on topics as diverse as spiritualism, Victorian poets, cricket, dogs and the value of National Service; his interest in religion was no doubt fostered by his father, a biblical scholar. Five of Kernahan's 'Triolets' are included in a volume dedicated to 'Humour' in the eleven-volume series *The Poets and the Poetry of the Nineteenth Century*, ed. Alfred H. Miles (London: George Routledge & Sons, 1905–07), X. In his introduction to Kernahan's work, Miles describes him as 'one of the group of younger writers from whom much is to be expected' (p. 596).

9   Kernahan, *In Good Company*, p. 222.

10 Kernahan, *In Good Company*, pp. 221, 222, 231.

11 Kernahan, *In Good Company*, p. 223.

12 Wilde's story doubtless took on various forms during its years in circulation. While it appears in *Le Chant du Cygne* in the form of a short apologue, Kernahan states in *In Good Company* that it formed 'the opening scene in a sort of religious drama which he intended one day to write' (p. 223). In a note to her article 'The Story-Teller at Fault' (p. 179, n. 35), Deirdre Toomey points out that 'The genesis of Wilde's tale can be dated since it responds directly to a controversy of January 1895. Ferdinand Brunetière published, in the *Revue des Deux Mondes* [...] an article, "Après une visite au Vatican". He attacked the cult of science and denounced the failure of science either to understand human nature or to develop a new morality.' However, if Kernahan's claim that he never saw Wilde after the spring of 1892 is true (*In Good Company*, p. 215), we must assume that the story was circulating in some form prior to 1895.

13 See *The Complete Letters of Oscar Wilde*, pp. 474–75.

14 Kernahan, *In Good Company*, p. 224.

15 Coulson Kernahan, *The Child, the Wise Man, and the Devil* (London: James Bowden, 1896), p. 14. Hereafter cited in the text as *CWD*.

16 *The Child, the Wise Man, and the Devil*, along with an earlier dream-vision, *God and the Ant* (1895), enjoyed combined sales exceeding 100,000. See Sarah Kemp, Charlotte Mitchell and David Trotter, *Edwardian Fiction: An Oxford Companion* (Oxford: Oxford University Press, 1997), p. 223.

17 Guy Thorne, *'I Believe'* (London: F.V. White, 1907), p. 297.

18 Richard Aldington, *Life for Life's Sake* (New York: The Viking Press, 1941), p. 46.

19 Thorne, *'I Believe'*, p. 19.

20 C. Ranger Gull, *From the Book Beautiful: Being Some Old Lights Relit* (London: Greening, 1900), pp. ix, x, xiii.

21 Gull, *From the Book Beautiful*, p. 79.

22 Gull, *From the Book Beautiful*, p. 177.

23 Gull, *From the Book Beautiful*, pp. 179, 182.

24 Thorne, *'I Believe'*, p. 299.

25 According to a brief manuscript note written by Stuart Mason [Christopher Millard], Wilde's first bibliographer, on the fly-leaf of *Oscar Wilde: Some Reminiscences*, Leonard Cresswell Ingleby is another of [Cyril Arthur Edward Ranger] Gull's pseudonyms, his better known one being Guy Thorne, under which he

wrote some of his best-selling fiction.

26 See Théophile Gautier, *Charles Baudelaire*, trans. Guy Thorne (London: Greening, 1915).

27 Albert Guérard, *Art for Art's Sake* (New York: Lothrop, Lee and Shepard, 1936), p. 205.

28 Guy Thorne, *When It Was Dark* (London: Greening, 1903), p. 9. Hereafter cited in the text as *WIWD*.

29 See *Le Chant du Cygne*, pp. 170–72.

30 Coulson Kernahan, for example, describes Wilde in his later years as having 'a flabby fleshiness of face and neck, a bulkiness of body, an animality about the large and pursy lips'. See *In Good Company*, p. 191.

31 Thorne, '*I Believe*', p. 33. The Oxyrhynchus Papyri, uncovered in Egypt, added to the increasing number of 'logia' or extra-canonical sayings of Jesus; Paul Vignon's *The Shroud of Christ*, trans. unknown (Westminster: Archibald Constable, 1902), argued forcefully for the authenticity of the shroud, based on the hypothesis that the materials used to embalm Christ's body acted as a type of photographic plate onto which was recorded the 'very features of the Saviour Himself' (p. 84).

32 *The Times*, 10 January 1923, p. 7.

33 Aldington, *Life for Life's Sake*, p. 46.

34 *The Times*, 6 October 1919, p. 11.

35 The film version, also entitled *When It was Dark*, was directed by Arrigo Bocchi and produced by the Walturdaw-Windsor film company; during the filming of one of the novel's more riotous scenes, in the coliseum at Rome, a military guard was called out with loaded rifles and bayonets to quell the mob. *The Times* reported that 'Explanations relieved the tension'. See *The Times*, 23 May 1919, p. 4.

36 Coulson Kernahan, *The Man of No Sorrows* (London: Cassell, 1911), pp. 28, 32.

37 Kernahan, *The Man of No Sorrows*, p. 37.

38 Kernahan refers to the popularity of Thorne's novel in *Celebrities: Little Stories about Famous Folk* (London: Hutchinson, 1923), p. 145.

39 Kernahan, *The Man of No Sorrows*, p. 47.

40 Kernahan, *The Man of No Sorrows*, p. 46.

41 Kernahan, *The Man of No Sorrows*, p. 59.

42 Coulson Kernahan, *A World without the Christ* (London: Hodder and Stoughton, 1934), p. 50.

43 *The Times Literary Supplement*, 5 June 1913, p. 247. The only named story charged with being derivative was 'An English Saint'.

44 John Middleton Murry, 'Who is the Man?', *Rhythm*, 1 (July 1912), pp. 37–39 (pp. 39, 38). 'The Miracle of the Stigmata' was first published in *The English Review*, 5 (April 1910), pp. 12–26.

45 *Saturday Review*, 115 (21 June 1913), p. 781. Harris's somewhat turbulent time as editor of the *Saturday Review* may account for this particularly scathing appraisal of his work.

46 *The Nation*, 13 (21 June 1913), pp. 470–72 (p. 470).

47 See 'Le Miracle des Stigmates' and 'Simon le Cyrénéen', in de Saix, *Le Chant du Cygne*, pp. 126–27, 117–18.

48 John Middleton Murry, *Between Two Worlds* (London: Jonathan Cape, 1935), p. 179.

49 Hesketh Pearson, *Modern Men and Mummers* (London: George Allen & Unwin, 1921), p. 103.

50 Pearson, *The Life of Oscar Wilde*, p. 184.

51 Hugh Kingsmill, *Frank Harris* (London: Jonathan Cape, 1932), p. 234.

52 E. Merrill Root, *Frank Harris* (New York: The Odyssey Press, 1947), p. 180.

53 Vincent Brome, *Frank Harris* (London: Cassell, 1959), p. 142.

54 In *Le Chant du Cygne*, Guillot de Saix introduces Wilde's stigmata story by explaining that 'Le sujet du conte qui va suivre avait été vendu par Oscar Wilde à Frank Harris et développé différemment par ce dernier dans *Le Miracle des Stigmates*, nouvelle publiée dans [...] *Unpath'd waters* [sic]' [The main idea of the following tale had been sold by Oscar Wilde to Frank Harris and given a different treatment by the latter author in the short story, *The Miracle of the Stigmata*, published in *Unpath'd Waters*] (p. 124). Likewise, he introduces *L'Ironie du Hasard* by outlining how 'Oscar Wilde avait vendu le sujet de ce conte à Frank Harris, qui le transforma et le publia dans son recueil: *Unpath'd Waters*, sous le titre *The Irony of Chance*' [Oscar Wilde sold the main idea of this tale to Frank Harris, who then transformed it and published it in his collection: *Unpath'd Waters*, under the title *The Irony of Chance*] (p. 215). While there is a great deal of discussion regarding *Mr and Mrs Daventry* in Wilde's correspondence with Harris, there is no mention of the sale of either tale. It is tempting to conclude that de Saix was confusing the sale of the stories with the sale of *Mr and Mrs Daventry*; however, this seems unlikely, given that de Saix was left the draft of the play in the will of Cora Brown Potter (the first person to whom Wilde sold the scenario) and must, therefore, have been aware of its complex history. For a comprehensive account of the history of Wilde's unfinished play, see H. Montgomery Hyde's introduction to *Mr and Mrs Daventry* (London: The Richards Press, 1956), p. 39.

55 Guillot de Saix suggests that Gabriel Trarieux's three-act drama *Joseph d'Arimathée*, first performed at the Théâtre Antoine in 1898, was another work that took its inspiration from 'Le Miracle des Stigmates'. However, in its treatment of the last week of Christ's life, culminating in the eponymous hero's revelation that Christ's body had not emerged from the tomb by supernatural means but had been removed by Nicodemus, it seems more to resemble 'L'Inutile Résurrection'. See *Le Chant du Cygne*, p. 125.

56 Harris's disagreement with George Moore is outlined in a series of letters collected by Guido Bruno – an ardent admirer of Harris – under the title *Moore Versus Harris* (Chicago: privately printed, 1925). In *The Private Life of Frank Harris* (New York: William Faro, 1931), Samuel Roth recalls how, when 'The Miracle of the Stigmata' was published, George Moore denounced it as 'unconscionable plagiarism of a novel which he was in the course of writing' (p. 154). At no stage in this ongoing dispute is Wilde's name associated with the story.

57 Pearson, *The Life of Oscar Wilde*, p. 184.

58 *Enid Bagnold's Autobiography* (London: Heinemann, 1969), p. 91.

59 Robert Harborough Sherard, *Bernard Shaw, Frank Harris and Oscar Wilde* (London: T. Werner Laurie, 1937), pp. 138–40. Certainly, a parallel reading of the two writers' versions of 'The Master' would, give or take a few minor variations, bear out Sherard's claim, though his further allegation that Harris persuaded Henry-D. Davray, the translator of the French edition of the work, to put in 'a few

clumsy words of his own concoction' (p. 139) to make the theft less obvious to French readers would seem wide of the mark. Indeed, Davray appears to have opted for a direct translation of the published version of the prose poem; it is an irony that, in writing a book that purports to put the record straight about certain facts of Wilde's life, Sherard should fail to recognize the published work of his subject.

60 Pearson, *Modern Men and Mummers*, pp. 122–23.

61 Frank Harris, *My Life and Loves*, 4 vols (Paris: Obelisk Press, 1945), III, p. 104.

62 *Enid Bagnold's Autobiography*, p. 87.

63 *Frank Harris to Arnold Bennett: Fifty-Eight Letters 1908–1910* (Pennsylvania: privately printed, 1936), p. 14.

64 *Frank Harris to Arnold Bennett*, p. 17.

65 Frank Harris, 'Renan: The Romance of Religion', *The English Review*, 7 (March 1911), pp. 610–27; the interview was subsequently published in *Contemporary Portraits*, First Series (London: Methuen, 1915).

66 Kingsmill, *Frank Harris*, p. 190.

67 Harris, *Oscar Wilde: His Life and Confessions*, I, p. 136.

68 *Frank Harris to Arnold Bennett*, p. 39. Harris is here, of course, borrowing Wilde's phrase from *De Profundis*.

69 Louis Marlow, *Seven Friends* (London: The Richards Press, 1953), p. 27. Louis Marlow was the pen name of Louis Umfreville Wilkinson, author of numerous novels. As an adolescent, he had taken it upon himself to write to Wilde while he was incarcerated in Reading Gaol, and the correspondence between them continued until just a few months before Wilde's death. *Seven Friends* is an account of his friendship with various characters, including Wilde and Harris.

70 *Frank Harris to Arnold Bennett*, pp. 39, 14.

71 Frank Harris, *The Women of Shakespeare* (London: Methuen, 1911), p. 278.

72 Frank Harris, *Unpath'd Waters* (London: John Lane, The Bodley Head, 1913), p. 3. Hereafter cited in the text as *UW*.

73 De Saix, *Le Chant du Cygne*, p. 127.

74 Harris has frequently been accused of anti-Semitism; one of the stories in *Unpath'd Waters*, 'Mr Jacob's Philosophy', is often cited in evidence. Certainly, his depiction of the Jews in 'The Miracle of the Stigmata' also lays him open to the charge of anti-Semitism: they are presented as base, money-grabbing and argumentative and his description of 'a red Jew, with head of flame' (*UW* 15) is reminiscent of the stereotypical Jew of medieval Passion plays, as well as echoing the figure of Fagin in Dickens's *Oliver Twist*. However, such stereotyping is commonly found in writing of the period, Guy Thorne's *When It Was Dark* being a case in point.

75 Leo Steinberg, *The Sexuality of Christ in Renaissance Art and in Modern Oblivion* (London: Faber & Faber, 1983), p. 15.

76 Harris, *My Life and Loves*, I, p. 14.

77 Norman Pittenger, *Christology Reconsidered* (London: SCM Press, 1970), p. 61.

78 See Philippa Pullar, *Frank Harris* (London: Hamish Hamilton, 1975), pp. 346–47.

79 The German theologian Adolf von Harnack was an influential exponent of the view that Paul delivered whole communities from the yoke of Judaism. In a collection of popular lectures, he argues: 'Someone had to stand up and say "The old is done away with" [...] he had to show that all things were become new. The man

who did this was the apostle Paul, and it is in having done it that his greatness in the history of the world consists.' See *What is Christianity?*, trans. Thomas Bailey Saunders (London: Williams and Norgate, 1901), p. 175. The ready availability of English translations of Harnack's work meant that his ideas had considerable influence on British theological thought. One of the most important theologians to counter Harnack's view was Albert Schweitzer, whose major survey of Pauline studies, *Paul and his Interpreters*, trans. W. Montgomery (London: Adam & Charles Black, 1912), was published shortly before Harris's *Unpath'd Waters*. He spoke against viewing Paul as a Hellenizer, seeing him instead – as he saw Jesus – as part of an apocalyptic Judaism.

80 De Saix, *Le Chant du Cygne*, p. 126.

81 *Contemporary Portraits*, First Series, p. 59.

82 An American acquaintance of Harris's, Mary Austin, shows Paul in a similar light, writing in her study of Christ: 'by the time the book of Mark was written it was not only believed that Jesus rose from the dead, but many other things were believed about him which were no part of his teachings, but were owed to Paul of Tarsus [...] Paul [...] would have cut off the manuscript of Mark with his own hand if he thought it contradicted in any particular that understanding of the teachings of Jesus which he claims openly to have received.' See *The Man Jesus* (New York and London: Harper & Brothers, 1915), pp. 187–88. A heavily annotated copy of Austin's book was found among Harris's possessions after his death. Although 'The Miracle of the Stigmata' was published four years before *The Man Jesus*, there are a number of similarities between them, suggesting that the two writers had debated the topic of Jesus and Paul in the course of their friendship. See Pullar, *Frank Harris*, pp. 347–48.

83 In *The Life of Christ in Recent Research* (Oxford: Clarendon Press, 1907), William Sanday writes that 'It should be remembered that all critics in a greater or less degree [...] are agreed in starting from the Gospel of Mark' (p. 92).

84 This translation by Thomas Common was published by H. Henry & Co. in 1896, as part of what was intended to be a complete edition of Nietzsche's works. However, the project was abandoned after four volumes when the company went bankrupt. In the same year, three articles by Havelock Ellis, discussing Nietzsche's life and works, appeared in *The Savoy* (Nos. 2, 3, 4), stimulating considerable interest in the philosopher. As Holbrook Jackson points out in *The 1890s*, 'It was not until 1896 that any general interest in Nietzsche's ideas began in this country' (p. 155); from this time on, articles on his life and work started to appear in the more established journals. For example, a detailed survey of Nietzsche's life and work, by A. Seth Pringle Pattison, appeared in the *Contemporary Review*, 73 (May 1898), pp. 727–50. The publication of extracts from Nietzsche's major writings in *Nietzsche as Critic, Philosopher, Poet and Prophet. Choice Selections from his Works*, compiled by Thomas Common (London: Grant Richards, 1901), also encouraged interest in his work.

85 In December 1908, Harris wrote to Arnold Bennett that he was just about to 'add the portrait of Paul' to his stigmata story. See *Frank Harris to Arnold Bennett*, p. 11.

86 In *Nietzsche in England 1890–1914* (Toronto: University of Toronto Press, 1970), David S. Thatcher estimates that the tide began to turn in 1907 with Dr Oscar

Levy's series of English translations of Nietzsche's works, and that Nietzsche 'was the philosopher *à la mode* in England between 1909 and 1913' (p. 42).

87 *The Works of Friedrich Nietzsche: The Case of Wagner, Nietzsche Contra Wagner, The Twilight of the Idols, The Antichrist*, trans. Thomas Common (London: H. Henry, 1896), p. 257.

88 *The Works of Friedrich Nietzsche*, p. 304.

89 In *The Antichrist*, Nietzsche defines Paul as 'the antithetical type of the "bearer of glad tidings" [...] the genius in hatred' (p. 303). Harris follows suit in presenting Paul as an inciter of hatred and retribution, in stark contrast to the peace-loving Jesus.

90 In this respect, Harris's fiction chimes with current theological thinking on the incipient stages of Christianity, especially that of Albert Kalthoff whose book, *The Rise of Christianity,* was translated into English by Joseph McCabe (London: Watts, 1907). In this work, Kalthoff cites the Pauline Epistles as evidence that 'everything turns on the community' and that it 'is in the community-life that Christ first has terrestrial existence' (p. 118).

91 For a discussion of women's roles in the Primitive Church, see Chapter Six of Elisabeth Schüssler Fiorenza's *In Memory of Her: A Feminist Theological Reconstruction of Christian Origins* (London: SCM Press, 2nd edn, 1995).

92 Harris takes the character of Tabitha from Acts 9:36–41; the biblical Tabitha comes from Joppa where, during Peter's mission, she is revived from the dead. Harris's Tabitha refers to her sister in Joppa and the reader familiar with the Bible text will assume that she is one and the same as the biblical personage and that she has undergone the same resuscitation experience. Tabitha's husband, Simon, also originates from Acts where he is mentioned as Peter's companion; the reader is no doubt expected to assume that the two met during Peter's stay in Joppa.

93 Ernest Renan, *The Apostles*, trans. unknown (London: N. Trübner, 1869), p. 69.

94 Elmer Gertz and A. I. Tobin, *Frank Harris: A Study in Black and White* (Chicago: Madelaine Mendelsohn, 1931), p. 187.

95 *Contemporary Portraits*. Second Series (New York: published by the author, 1919), p. 37.

96 *Contemporary Portraits*. Second Series, p. 37.

97 *Oscar Wilde: His Life and Confessions*, I, p. 136.

98 Augustus John, *Chiaroscuro* (London: Jonathan Cape, 1952), p. 129.

99 Frank Harris, *Undream'd of Shores* (London: Grant Richards, 1924), pp. 207–09.

100 See *The Playwright and the Pirate*, ed. Stanley Weintraub (Gerrards Cross: Colin Smythe, 1982), p. 98.

101 Harris, *Undream'd of Shores*, p. 295.

102 Weintraub, ed., *The Playwright and the Pirate*, p. 23.

103 Harris, *My Life and Loves*, IV, p. 137.

CHAPTER 6

A Peculiar Protestant:
The Gospels According to George Moore

> Paul was a cosmopolitan and Jesus was a provincial. Had they ever met in
> person, they would presumably have had little to say to each other […]
> Gerd Lüdemann, *Jesus After Two Thousand Years*

By the early twentieth century, the Gospels had undergone imaginative treatment in poetry, prose fiction and dramatic scenarios, but any
ambitions to present them on stage were held firmly at bay by the rigid
adherence of successive Examiners of Plays to the Theatres Act of
1843. Prohibiting dramas adapted from the Scriptures and placing an
outright ban on the depiction of Christ or the Deity on stage, the legislation proved a more or less insurmountable barrier to aspiring
religious dramatists – orthodox and unorthodox – and a bone of
contention for members of the artistic community.[1] Encounters with
the censor, such as Wilde's over *Salome*, prompted a variety of public
reactions, including a series of articles published in the *New Review* in
1893. Speaking for the traditionalists, F. W. Farrar insisted that:

> The events narrated in the Bible are associated with the deepest and
> most sacred of our religious feelings. They have entered into our
> religious teaching from earliest childhood […] It seems altogether
> undesirable that they should be set before us amid the inevitable
> surroundings of the stage. Their representations in plays would be
> mixed up with questions of literary taste, or journalistic criticism, of
> the dress, the appearance, the success or the failure of particular
> actors.[2]

Putting the case for the liberals, Henry Arthur Jones argued:

> I see no reason why the great human stories of the Bible should not
> be utilised on our stage. I am speaking here with the utmost rever-

ence for a Book, or rather Books, which I have clearly loved and constantly studied from my childhood [...] The English theatre could not make a worse use of the Bible than the sects have done, or misunderstand it so completely.[3]

As the nineteenth century turned into the twentieth, so the Theatres Act appeared more and more an anachronism to all but the staunchest traditionalists, prompting satirical responses such as this by the writer and civil servant Humbert Wolfe:

C is for Censor
Who keeps the stage clean
By ruling out God and the Crown as obscene.[4]

As with any law commonly regarded as otiose and outdated, various attempts were made to circumvent it. One of these was to revive the mystery and morality plays that had enjoyed great popularity from the thirteenth century to the Reformation, and that were exempt from the current legislation. However, it was not an option that held much appeal for those with radical new ideas, aspiring to create a drama for the modern age. A more artistically satisfying way round the problem was the establishment of private theatre societies, as these did not require stage licences to mount productions. Two dramatists who took advantage of this loophole in the law were Laurence Housman and Mabel Dearmer. Housman formed the Bethlehem Society for which he staged his nativity play, *Bethlehem*, in 1902, the same year that it had been denied a licence by the Examiner of Plays. Following suit in 1911, Mabel Dearmer founded The Morality Play Society which presented her own works, *The Soul of the World* (1911) and *The Dreamer* (1912), and works by others, including W. B. Yeats's *The Hour Glass* (1904) and Lady Gregory's *The Travelling Man* (1909). This means of evading the censor was not without its drawbacks. Prohibited from taking any form of financial reward from performances, such companies were commercially unattractive and, for the majority of playwrights, economically impossible.

By far the most popular way of staging religious subjects while still staying within the stage law was a dramatic sub-genre that came to be known as 'toga drama': plays set in the era of the Primitive Church. The well-known actor, dramatist and stage manager Wilson Barrett was the foremost exponent of these religious melodramas, enjoying great popular success in the late 1890s with his production of *The Sign of the Cross*. Set in Rome in the days of the Early Church, Barrett's play tells the tale of the Roman prefect, Marcus, who falls deeply in love with the Christian heroine, Mercia, and accompanies her to her death in an amphitheatre of hungry lions. Barrett's decision to set his drama in post-crucifixion days ensured that it would not upset the Examiner of Plays, at the same time capitalizing on the interest in the Primitive Church that had featured prominently in theological works of the final thirty years or so of the nineteenth century. *The Sign of the Cross* played to great acclaim in both the United States and Great Britain, gaining plaudits from clergymen and the more conservative elements of the press. Yet it was not without its detractors. G. W. Foote considered the play 'as primitive as the religion it advocates',[5] and George Bernard Shaw wrote about finding in the play 'a terrible contrast between the Romans [...] with their straightforward sensuality, and the strange, perverted voluptuousness of the Christians, with their shuddering exaltations of the longing for the whip, the rack, the stake and the lions'.[6] While the toga play would enjoy considerable popular success in the emerging world of cinema, by the second decade of the twentieth century it was clear that it had outstayed its welcome in the theatre.

In the Edwardian period, then, the restrictions placed upon the performance of religious plays were both highly inconsistent and highly frustrating for those with ambitions to stage biblical drama. On 27 October 1907, 71 authors expressed such frustration publicly by signing a letter to *The Times* as a formal protest against the 'power lodged in the hands of a single official – who judges without a public hearing, and against whose dictum there is no appeal'; its signatories included Laurence Housman, John Masefield, G. B. Shaw and W. B. Yeats, all of whom produced some form of biblical drama in the course of their writing careers.[7] Two years later, a Joint Select Committee was set up to examine the Theatres Act of 1843 and to gauge its suitability for the new century.[8] With the publication of the Committee's report, following three months' consideration and consultation, it was clear that few concessions would be afforded to the anti-censorship lobby. With regard to the dramatization of religious subjects, the Committee recommended that the strict regulations concerning the representation of scriptural characters should be relaxed, at the same time advising that dramas should not 'do violence to the sentiment of religious reverence'. It was in this prevailing climate of artistic restriction that George Moore wrote *The Apostle: A Drama in Three Acts* (1911), a work that certainly held the potential to 'do violence' to traditional notions of the Gospels.

Regarded as a minor work in the canon of Moore's writings, *The Apostle* tends to be treated only fleetingly by his critics and biographers. Yet, though the drama has never been performed, it marks the genesis of one of the twentieth century's most significant fictional representations of Jesus: *The Brook Kerith: A Syrian Story* (1916). A brief survey of Moore's *oeuvre* up to this point in his career reveals an engagement with a variety of literary movements and causes, and yet, whether in the grip of Naturalism, writing a polemic against the three-volume novel or experimenting with literary Wagnerism, his interest in the religious temperament is ever-present. In Susan Mitchell's acerbic monograph on the author, published in 1916, she recalls that

> it was once said of Mr. Moore by a member of his family that he would end his days as a monk, and it is certainly true that his later writings show the attraction of religion drawing him closer and closer. It seems, however, to be an attraction of repulsion and to consist rather in renunciations than confessions of faith.[9]

Though Mitchell was far from a reliable recorder of Moore and his work, she was, in this instance, close to the truth. Moore was indeed both attracted and repelled by religion. He devoted a significant proportion of his work to religious subjects, and never held back from criticizing what he saw as its inadequacies. Writing a heterodox fifth Gospel such as that sketched out in *The Apostle* offered Moore the opportunity to indulge his life-long fascination with the religious temperament and to satisfy his almost compulsive instinct for troublemaking.

The shaping of a Protestant identity: Moore's entry into theology

In the first twenty years or so of Moore's literary career, his interest in religion manifested itself largely by way of individual characters in his novels and short stories. *A Modern Lover* (1883), *A Mummer's Wife* (1885) and *Esther Waters* (1894) all explore the female religious temperament through the struggle of the heroines to come to terms with the conflict between their religious upbringings and their natural desires. From out of this early exploration of women's spirituality developed a more specific study of conventual life in works such as *A Drama in Muslin* (1886), *Celibates* (1895), *Evelyn Innes* (1898) and *Sister Teresa* (1901). It is not, however, until *The Lake* (1905) that we see any clear indications that Moore's religious interests had widened to include biblical criticism. A few years prior to the novel's publication, the writer and critic Edouard Dujardin, to whom *The Lake* was dedicated, had turned his attentions to biblical exegesis, his researches being published in *La Source du fleuve chrétien* (1904), a volume that served to quicken Moore's interest in theology.[10] Regarded by Moore as his 'master in exegesis', Dujardin appears in *The Lake* in fictional form as the theologian Walter Poole, and it is through this character that the author is able to debate issues such as the debt theology owes to history, the authorship of the Gospels and the relationship between the teachings of Christ and those of Paul, all of which were to preoccupy him throughout the next ten years or so.[11]

In addition to serving as one of Moore's major sources of knowledge about the Bible, Jewish and Roman history and the Higher Criticism, Dujardin introduced him to several other writers engaged in biblical studies who would influence his future fictionalizing of the Gospels. Moore encountered the work of the French modernist theologian Alfred Loisy in 1904, when he translated Dujardin's article on his influential study *Les évangiles synoptiques*.[12] While it cannot be assumed that Moore went on to read Loisy's work in its entirety, there is no doubt that he would have been drawn to a writer who strongly believed that 'the adaptation of the gospel to the changing conditions of humanity is as pressing a need to-day as it ever was and ever will be', and who had been excommunicated by the Roman Catholic Church Moore so despised.[13] It was also through Dujardin that Moore was to make the acquaintance of the freethinker Joseph McCabe, the translator of *La Source du fleuve chrétien*, as well as studies by rather more influential (and able) modernist theologians such as Albert Kalthoff and Arthur Drews.[14] In a letter to Dujardin, Moore recounts his first meeting with McCabe in May 1911, describing his new friend as 'a very pleasant fellow, very much alive, keen and a great scholar'.[15] It was perhaps this final attribute that held most attraction for Moore in a year when he had set out to apprise himself of the latest scholarly thinking on Christianity.

The first two decades of the twentieth century was an invigorating time to be considering the figure of Jesus, as Moore no doubt realized.

In *The Life of Christ in Recent Research*, William Sanday expressed his belief that 'the year 1906 may be said to mark the turning down of one page in the history of English theology and the opening of another'.[16] It was no coincidence that this was the same year that Albert Schweitzer's ground-breaking work *The Quest of the Historical Jesus* was published, an event that may well have contributed to Sanday's view that a profound shift was happening in the study of the Gospel narratives. And it was not only theology that would introduce new perspectives on the figure of Christ and Christianity. By the time *The Apostle* was a work in progress, Nietzschean philosophy was very much of the moment and works such as *The Antichrist* offered a harsh reappraisal of the principal characters in Moore's play. Anthropology held even more dramatic possibilities concerning the origins of Christianity, most especially in Sir James Frazer's highly influential study of primitive rites and belief systems, *The Golden Bough*. First published in 1890, this vast undertaking included one particularly contentious chapter entitled 'Killing the God', which drew parallels between Christ's crucifixion and pagan and Semitic rituals, and which would be developed more fully in the Second Edition of 1900.[17] In setting out on his own exploration of the figure of Jesus, then, Moore was responding to the lively intellectual climate of the early twentieth century, as well as to the interests and preoccupations of his immediate circle of friends and acquaintances.

Reading the Bible for the first time

In 1904 Moore converted to Protestantism, an event dismissed by his friend W. K. Magee as 'a piece of play-acting which impressed no one'.[18] In a similar vein, Joseph McCabe commented that Moore professed 'genially to be a "Protestant" – solely because he hates Catholicism'.[19] Certainly, there is plenty of evidence to suggest that McCabe was right in his opinion that Moore's embracing of Protestantism was little more than a means of casting off the faith of his birth. Responding to news of his brother Maurice's engagement to a Catholic, Moore wrote to his younger brother Julian: 'my hatred of Catholicism is limitless; it is the strongest fibre in my nature'.[20] It was an aversion that Moore would express time and time again with the same animus, and often very publicly. For example, when in 1910 the *Irish Times* published an obituary notice for his brother, Augustus, that stated that the deceased came from 'an old Irish and Roman Catholic family', Moore penned a furious letter in response, stating:

> I take this opportunity of telling that my family was Protestant until my great grandfather went to Spain [...] My grandfather was a man of letters [...] He was a disciple of Gibbon, and many passages in his published writings show him to be an agnostic. Of my father's beliefs I know nothing; he went to Mass on Sundays, so I suppose he was a Catholic [...] I shall have no hesitation in leaving any money I may have on the condition that my heir shall carry on the Protestant traditions of the family.[21]

Moore's understanding of these Protestant traditions was, to say the least, somewhat eccentric. He had a tendency to form his own notion of Protestant doctrine by creating a crude dichotomy whereby 'Protestants and Catholics are [...] two eternal attitudes of the human mind'.[22] Protestantism, Moore avows in *Hail and Farewell!*, 'leaves the mind free, or very nearly', and this freedom of mind is considered to stem mainly from the unrestricted reading of the Bible and the religious discussion it generates.[23] Moore claimed that his own reading of the Scriptures began when, already in middle age, he received a Bible from Mary Hunter, the dedicatee of *The Brook Kerith*, which he claimed led him 'into the society of scholars'.[24] Verging on the solipsistic, his version of Protestantism defiantly overlooked the literal-mindedness of certain evangelical readers of the Bible, such as those chronicled in his friend Edmund Gosse's autobiographical novel *Father and Son*; instead it was made to bolster his own self-image, becoming synonymous with free-thinking, scepticism and, most importantly, great literary creativity.[25] In 'Epistle to the Cymry' Moore explains how 'every Protestant invents a religion out of the Bible for himself, and that is one of the reasons why Protestants are more literary than Catholics'.[26] Maurice Moore was particularly well versed in this somewhat dubious theory, thanks to his brother's fondness for expounding it in his correspondence. In a letter of 1904, for example, George explains to his younger brother that 'Catholicism is compatible with existence, and so is alcoholism; but life, the creative energy is almost wholly with agnostics and Protestants [...] There is some life in the convert, but in the born Catholic hardly any.'[27] To support his highly questionable generalizations about the relationship between faith and creativity, Moore supplied some equally questionable statistics. In the first edition of *Salve*, the second volume of his autobiographical trilogy *Hail and Farewell!*, he relates a conversation with George Russell regarding the connection between religion and literary talent, in which he insists that 'ninety and five per cent. of the world's literature was written by Protestants and agnostics'.[28] Moore also tried out his religio-aesthetic theory on his friend Joseph McCabe, who relates the following anecdote in his memoirs:

> I was dining one night at George Moore's with the French novelist Edouard Dujardin and, the talk falling upon Newman, I confessed my literary hero-worship. Moore, whose blood-pressure rose whenever he heard this literary praise of Newman, jumped up from the table with his customary bluntness and fetched his copy of the 'Apologia', with a marked page. 'Read that,' he said truculently, 'and tell Dujardin how many mistakes there are in that one page.' I read it through. 'Eleven,' I confessed. 'Thirteen,' Moore snorted.[29]

And so, in asserting what he believed to be his innate Protestantism, Moore convinced himself that he was also taking on the spirit of great writers, and *The Apostle* was no doubt his way of paying homage to what he saw as the intellectual freedom of his newly declared faith.

The Apostle started out as a brief 'Prefatory Note', published in *The English Review* in June 1910.[30] Moore introduces what amounts to work in progress – a deposit for the published drama a year later – by explaining his main reason for putting such rudimentary writing in print; namely, to claim ownership of an idea:

> The story of 'The Apostle' is one of those striking stories that one is tempted to relate to amuse one's friends after dinner, and I have related it sufficiently often to invite collaboration [...] our friends have their friends, and a story wanders far like thistle-down, and somebody hearing it [...] might unexpectedly feel himself called upon to write it.[31]

And, true enough, the idea of fictionalizing a meeting between Jesus and his apostle was already being contemplated by fellow writer Frank Harris. Joseph Hone, Moore's authorized biographer, recalls how Moore and Harris were both 'on the trail of the same subject – a post-Crucifixion meeting between Jesus and St. Paul'.[32] It was a state of affairs that developed into what Samuel Roth described as Harris's

'famous disagreement with George Moore', and that is well docu-
mented in the writings of the two opponents and those of their friends
and enemies.[33] Harris puts on record what he believed to be the origin
of Moore's Jesus-and-Paul scenario in an article wryly entitled
'George Moore and Jesus':

> 'Please tell me before you go,' he persisted, 'where you got the idea
> that Jesus didn't die on the cross. That interests me enormously…'.
>   'Jesus is said to have died in a few hours,' I said. 'That astonished
> even Pilate and so I thought – '
>   'Oh,' cried Moore, disappointed. 'It's only a guess of yours; but
> why take him to Cæsarea? Why bring Paul there? Why…?'
>   I knew he was merely informing himself in his usual dexterous
> way, so tried to cut him short.
>   'An early tradition,' I cried; 'my dear fellow, an early tradition',
> and ever since Moore has talked about this 'early tradition', though
> it would puzzle him to say where it's to be found.[34]

Moore's version of finding inspiration for his New Testament fiction
is, as might be expected, somewhat at odds with Harris's. It is detailed
in 'A Prefatory Letter on Reading the Bible for the First Time', first
published in *The English Review* in February 1911, and later forming
the introduction to *The Apostle*.[35] In this letter Moore recalls meeting
his friend W. K. Magee, librarian of the National Library of Ireland,
and hearing from him about a work by a French medical doctor that
put forward the view that 'it was some cataleptic swoon that Christ
had suffered, and not death on the Cross' (PL 464). Adverted to again
in Moore's preface to the 1921 edition of *The Brook Kerith*, this was
evidently a memorable meeting for the author, though the actual title
of the book under discussion is not mentioned in any account of it.
One possible contender for Moore's inspiration was *Jésus de
Nazareth: Au Point de Vue Historique, Scientifique et Social* by Paul
Régla, a practising physician.[36] The main thesis of this work is that
Jesus was educated in an Essene community and that his life and
ministry were driven by Essenian ideals and religious teachings. Yet
despite affording the library incident a certain significance by
including it in the Prefatory Letter, Moore goes on to insist that the
French doctor's study had done no more than jog his memory, his
being already acquainted with the theory that Christ survived the
cross and that 'he had been supposed by many to be an Essene monk'

(PF 464). It was Moore's decision to fictionalize this Essene theory that gave his play – and the novel that grew from it – a strong claim to originality.[37]

The Prefatory Letter to *The Apostle* serves as a declaration of Moore's newly awakened interest in the Bible and modernist theology, as well as an admission of his fledgling knowledge of both. Additionally, it functions as an autobiographical frame through which the play can be read and interpreted.[38] What is immediately evident from the letter is that the playwright's response to the Gospel narratives is almost entirely literary. The New Testament authors are likened to established writers or characters from their fictions: Mark is the Maupassant of the Evangelists and Paul is Don Quixote to Peter's Sancho Panza (PL 458, 459). These allusions to literary artists recall the intertextuality of Victorian liberal Lives of Jesus, where unattributed words from Shakespeare and Milton frequently interweave with those of Christ; a likeness that sits rather oddly with Moore's avowedly heterodox intentions. But Moore's foregrounding of the literary aspects of the Gospels and his decision to 'put the man of letters in front of the Biblical critic' (PL 454) comes more from necessity than choice. Joseph Hone states emphatically in his biography that his subject was, at this time, 'without scholarship', an observation that several of his compatriots took pleasure in pointing out in their writings about the author and his work.[39] Virginia Woolf's analysis of Moore as 'at once diffident and self-assertive' seems especially perceptive when applied to his attitude to religious scholarship.[40] In the Prefatory Letter, his 'self-assertive' side is very much in evidence as he challenges the theological experts to sneer at his lack of learning:

> If this prefatory note should fall into the hands of [...] learned German critics I will ask him [*sic*] to smile indulgently at the criticism of a man of letters who reads the Bible for the first time, and who, through no fault of his own, has been committed to record his impressions. But why should the fear of writing something silly or commonplace stay my pen? (PL 458)

However, in a personal letter to his German translator and friend Max Meyerfeld, Moore reveals his more diffident side. Having made a number of rudimentary theological errors, Moore admits that he is 'quite ignorant of documentary evidence' and that he 'should have kept to literary criticism – how the Bible narrative appears to a modern story-teller'.[41] While there is no doubt that Moore's theological insights made around this time were indeed 'commonplace', gleaned, as he readily admits, from erudite friends rather than his own reading, his intellectual grasp of the Bible far outweighed that of some of the more popular writers of religious fiction.[42] Tracing his correspondence through the first two decades of the twentieth century reveals an author steadily acquiring Higher Critical knowledge, knowledge that would shape his religious drama and fiction – for better or worse.

About half of the Prefatory Letter is devoted to Paul and his writings. Moore's discussion of the apostle, like his discussion of the Evangelists, is unquestionably thin on theology and heavy on personal interpretation. In his analysis of Paul, Moore brings together three of his most abiding interests: the Protestant temperament, sexuality and literary style. The apostle is the archetypal Protestant because he holds that 'it is in ourselves that we must seek salvation and not in ritual' (PL 461), unlike Peter, who is defined as a pious Jew, dependent on religious ritual and dogma and, therefore, the pattern of the first Catholic temperament. Whereas Peter represents all that is outmoded and backward-looking, Paul 'talks to us about the very things we are debating to-day, what the newspapers call sex problems' (PL 461).[43] Borrowing rather ineptly from the final act of Shakespeare's *Othello*, Moore warms to the human frailties of the apostle who 'loved St. Eunice not wisely but too well' (PL 461), arguing that Paul's 'thorn in the flesh' lent him an invaluable insight into the human condition and, as a consequence, endowed him with the power of a great writer. In Moore's view, the Pauline Epistles are the 'most natural literature in the world' and 'in none other do we hear the voice of a man so clearly' (PL 461). He describes how the author 'flashes across his page perceptions that elude the words of every other writer' (PL 462), imagery that conjures up a picture of Paul as not so much an itinerant preacher as an inspired man of letters. In his later writings, Moore would attempt to define the power of Paul's prose: it was a quality that came from personal passion and that was 'not eloquence, nor rhetoric, nor vehemence, but heat'.[44] This 'literary heat', Moore believed, would go on to influence great writers, a theory that harmonized conveniently with his claim that only those of the Protestant spirit could produce fine literature.

It is characteristic of Moore that he interprets such a famously complex figure with absolute certainty, perceiving no grey between the black and the white. He remained unconcerned by the highly contradictory nature of the Pauline Epistles and uninterested in the theological problems that biblical exegetes had worried away at for decades, such as Paul's attitude to the Judaic law and its place in the new religious order. Instead, Moore created an apostle in his own image: an innate Protestant, a gifted writer and a man susceptible to the charms of the female. Reading the Prefatory Letter alongside *The Apostle* reveals how Moore believed his literary sensibilities gave him insights beyond the reach of biblical scholars whom, he once pronounced, were but 'children in aesthetics'.[45] While acknowledging that he is a newcomer to Pauline writings, he nevertheless has the confidence as a creative artist to go against the theological grain and pronounce that 'a very considerable portion of the Acts must have been written by Paul himself' (PL 459). Writing to Dujardin, he boasted that the Prefatory Letter had procured him 'a little renown for exegesis' and, though it is tempting to dismiss this as wishful thinking on the part of an author prone to self-aggrandisement, it appears to have had some substance.[46] In the introduction to the 1916 edition of F. W. H. Myers's popular poem *St Paul*, E. J. Watson names Moore as a Pauline expert, paraphrasing words from the author's Prefatory Letter that insist that the Epistles 'portray a human soul more vividly than ever a human soul has been portrayed in literature'.[47]

Finding a form

Moore took some considerable time in selecting the best artistic form for his Gospel story. In his article 'George Moore and Jesus', Frank Harris recalls how Moore had had trouble deciding whether to write his scenario of Paul and Jesus in the form of prose fiction or drama;[48] and it is clear from his correspondence with Max Meyerfeld that he also had ambitions for an operatic treatment. In the spring of 1910, he wrote to Meyerfeld:

> In the June number of the English Review I am publishing a scenario entitled 'The Apostle'. 'The Death of Jesus' would be a better title – Paul and Christ face to face. The scenario cannot fail to interest you, and it might provide Strauss with the subject of an opera.[49]

Some years earlier, Moore had shown an interest in Richard Wagner's scenario for an operatic life of Jesus, originally sketched out in the 1840s but never developed into full opera form. In a letter of 1895, he thanks Lena Milman for her translation of the piece, adding: 'It interested me very much. It seems to be a divine arrangement [...] It will come in useful some day.'[50] Moore may well have felt that that day had come with his composition of *The Apostle* and that, in choosing Richard Strauss as his musical collaborator, he had the opportunity of repeating the *succès de scandale* enjoyed by the composer's version of Wilde's *Salome*. Though Moore persisted with his operatic ambitions until the autumn of 1910, by November he had settled on the form of a dramatic scenario and found a publisher in Maunsel and Company; it is with evident mischievous delight that Moore writes to Meyerfeld: 'The Dublin publisher called last night beaming at the thought of publishing the little booklet. I suggested Christmas as a suitable time, and he very innocently said that he thought Easter would be a better time. I agreed with him.'[51] Not everyone was quite so pleased. James Joyce was most put out by Maunsel's decision to publish Moore's 'little booklet', making his feelings felt in a broadside addressed to Maunsel shortly after they had refused to publish *Dubliners*. In it he cites *The Apostle* as a work that managed to pass their censorship regulations thanks only to the fact that it was written by 'a genuine gent / That lives on his property's ten per cent'.[52] Whether Joyce was right in his contention is difficult to judge for sure, though it is true to say that Moore's rather slight work was very much a niche publication, unlikely to attract a wide enough readership to whip up any real controversy.

The Apostle joined a rather eccentric literary sub-genre: the biblical play, constructed with the stage in mind but, given the laws of censorship, destined solely for the private reader. While never destined for the mainstream, the genre was already represented by works such as George Barlow's verse drama *Jesus of Nazareth*, published in 1896.[53] In its ample preface, Barlow acknowledges that his play is unlikely to be performed in 1890s' England, yet he also insists that he has 'been careful to throw it into an actable form' in an attempt to counteract 'the irreparable harm [...] done to the stage and to literature by the complete divorce which has for some time existed between the plays which are written to be acted and the plays which are written to be read'.[54] Moore was certainly acquainted with Barlow when living in London in the early 1880s. In a letter of 1883, Barlow congratulates Moore on the *Spectator*'s favourable review of his novel *A Modern*

Lover, and invites him to call on his return to town.[55] It is uncertain whether Moore ever encountered Barlow's play (the author was, in fact, much better known for his poetry), though if he had, he would have realized that *The Apostle* would appear positively restrained by comparison. Barlow's drama presents a torrid mix of sexual desire and intrigue, featuring such show-stopping scenes as the Magdalene stabbing to death the chief rabbi and Judas in quick succession, before instigating a fraudulent resurrection and making off to a distant land with Jesus as her husband. Though Barlow insists in the preface that he has cast the piece in 'actable form', the chances of it ever escaping the censor's blue pencil were negligible.[56]

The Apostle does not read like a drama written in 'actable form'. Its Prefatory Letter is aimed more at the reader than a theatre director, and the slight play-script that follows consists of speeches interspersed with lengthy blocks of expository prose, hovering in a kind of theatrical limbo between dialogue and stage directions. Indeed, the play opens with just such a passage:

> It was the practice among the Essenes that an elder monk should read the Scripture and interpret obscure or difficult passages. We gather from the talk between two monks, Manahem and Sadduc, who enter, that they have left their brethren still engaged in disputation. 'May we,' asks Manahem, 'regard the passages in Scripture in which God is described with human attributes as allegorical?'[57]

Even while it contains a rudimentary stage direction indicating that the play should open *in medias res*, followed by Manahem's opening line, if removed from its context this extract could easily be mistaken for prose fiction. What is clear from this introductory passage is that Moore was exercised as to how to dramatize the rather basic theology he had at his disposal, and he continues to wrestle with this difficulty throughout the three acts of the piece. Conveying Pauline theology on stage proved particularly challenging: the apostle is burdened with speeches so prolix they would be beyond the range of even the most charismatic of players, and would leave the other actors on stage with little option but to stand still and listen. Yet however provisional the script appears, Moore seems to have worked on it with some hope of performance. His correspondence with Meyerfeld, who translated the scenario into German and transformed some of its summaries into dialogue, suggests that it was primarily intended for the stage; and likewise a letter written to Dujardin shortly before completing the scenario, in which he asks 'The play will not be produced here, on account of the Censor, but in Paris it would certainly be a success [...] Could you not find someone to undertake the translation?'[58] It is clear from this that Moore realized that his play was only likely to be staged in Continental Europe. Though the jurisdiction of the Lord Chamberlain did not extend to Ireland, the Lord Lieutenant had the power to withdraw the patent allowing performance rights should a production be deemed offensive and, given Moore's literary circle, he would have been more than usually aware of the unofficial censorship at work in his home country. As things turned out the *The Apostle* never found its way onto any stage –French or otherwise – and joined the already substantial list of Moore's stage plays never to be performed.

As an author in his sixties, with a substantial number of failed plays behind him, it must have been tempting for Moore to eschew the theatre altogether. His choice of the dramatic form for his first attempt at fictionalizing the Gospels is, then, an intriguing one. In writing *The Apostle*, Moore seems to have been picking up creative threads from the very earliest stage in his career. As a young writer in Paris, he had embarked on a quest to set the theatrical world alight with a dramatic representation of a great Protestant figure in a verse drama entitled *Martin Luther*, co-written with the French author Bernard Lopèz. Its gestation is outlined in a sequence of stilted, highly artificial letters that form its preface. Shavian in length, if not in intellect, this correspondence between co-authors reveals Moore's utter lack of dramaturgical know-how and his jejune belief that a French audience would be shocked by a theatrical depiction of a Protestant hero.[59] The finished play-script was published in 1878 but, luckily for theatregoers, never produced.[60] While its contorted blank verse and melodramatic scenes would prove profoundly embarrassing to Moore in future years, its significance for his later work should not be underestimated.[61] *Martin Luther* contains the first signs of Moore's predilection for mixing historical fact with fiction and looks forward to his treatment of major religious figures; it also exhibits the pungent anti-clericalism and fascination with the issue of celibacy that would surface in later works. There are plainly discernible links between *Martin Luther* and *The Apostle*, not least in their dramatizing of Moore's typological vision: Paul is the type of true Protestantism and Luther the antitype who would deliver Christians from the dogmatic grip of Catholicism.[62]

In the fifteenth letter of the preface to Moore's first ever theatrical piece, the author inserts a poem he has penned entitled 'The Dream', which describes how Shakespeare had appeared to him in a vision and bemoaned the parlous state of the English stage. The dream progresses in a manner reminiscent of Charles Dickens's *A Christmas Carol*, with Shakespeare taking Moore to the Adelphi Theatre to see an unconscionably dull nineteenth-century play. It concludes with Shakespeare's despairing verdict that 'the drama no longer exists in England' and the dreamer is left to ponder what might be done to breathe new life into the nation's theatre.[63] In the 1890s, as a rather more mature writer, Moore had entered into ongoing debates about the 'New Drama', penning a number of articles and essays about the future of the theatre in England. In 'On the Necessity of an English Théâtre Libre', he defined the type of plays that needed to be written and produced if the English drama were to develop:

> Plays in which the characters, although true to nature, are not what are known as 'sympathetic characters', plays in which there are no comic love-scenes – plays which contain no comic relief – plays which deal with religious and moral problems in such ways as would not command the instantaneous and unanimous approval of a large audience drawn from all classes of society – plays in which there is no love-interest, plays composed entirely of male or entirely of female characters, etc.[64]

Here, then, Moore places the responsibility for good drama squarely on the audience; it is they who determine what is written. It was an opinion to which he would hold fast, telling Meyerfeld in 1910:

> As you say the Censor is not responsible for the decadence of the English stage. We do not want to see serious plays, and as only serious plays are literature there is no dramatic literature in England, and can be none until a change comes over public taste [...] I believe, or think I believe art to be a thing of spontaneous growth, and that it is impossible either to encourage or repress art.[65]

It is clear here that, despite his earlier zeal in campaigning against the censorship of the circulating libraries, he was not to be counted among those lobbying for the liberalization of the stage and, indeed, his signature is conspicuously absent from the list of 71 who made their protest in the pages of *The Times*.

For all its artistic flaws, *The Apostle* fulfils most of the artistic criteria laid out by Moore in 'On the Necessity of an English Théâtre Libre': it deals with serious religious questions, attempts to depict biblical figures in a realistic, flesh-and-blood manner and steers clear of any romance or comedy. However, stage censorship would prevent it from ever having the opportunity to provoke the displeasure or otherwise of a large audience, and the slight critical attention it received from readers was mildly disapproving rather than outraged. The *Athenaeum*, for example, while expressing reservations about the suitability of the play's theme for dramatic presentation, and judging the depiction of Paul not to be 'in good taste', adopts a measured, even wryly amused, tone when describing Moore's 'ingenuous' contribution to biblical criticism.[66] The play written to be read was, after all, a relatively inoffensive form, and it would be several years before Moore could develop it into something rather more provocative.

The strange meeting of Jesus and St Paul

The Apostle gives us a fictional meeting of two New Testament giants, transformed through Moore's imagination into a clash of opposites. Paul's vociferousness and enormous physical energy are contrasted with Jesus's self-effacement and quiet resignation. Differing as noticeably in their vision of God and the religious life, the only belief they hold in common is that Peter was 'a parcel of ancient rudiments' (*A* 94). The contradiction of Paul's passionate preaching of the Resurrection to a community that houses the ultimate proof of its falsity gives rise to a sequence of dramatic ironies. Inevitably, given the extreme nature of Moore's revision of the New Testament story, there are several points in the play when the ironies appear all too obvious. Towards the end of the second act, for example, Paul defines his Saviour in a speech redolent of the Apostles' Creed:

> Son of the living God, that took on the beggarly raiment of human flesh at Nazareth, was baptized by John in the Jordan, thereafter preached in Galilee, went up to Jerusalem, and, that the Scriptures might be fulfilled, was crucified by order of Pilate between two thieves on Mount Calvary; the third day he rose from the dead –
> (*A* 68)

This fervent declaration of faith, so close to that intoned in Christian churches down the centuries, is cut short by Manahem's disclosure that a member of the brotherhood has lived the same life, suffered the same fate, but has survived to tell the tale. From this point in the play, Paul is confronted with material evidence that the Essenian Jesus is one and the same as his 'risen' Christ. Whereas in Frank Harris's 'The Miracle of the Stigmata', Paul is only brought into the presence of Jesus after he has died of natural causes, Moore pushes the scenario one step further by keeping Jesus alive and capable of refuting Paul's story with the evidence of his own body. The moment when the marks of the cross are exhibited to the incredulous Paul is captured in one of the play's most detailed stage directions:

> *Taking Jesus' hands he looks at them and finds the marks of the nails, and looking upon his brow he finds traces of where the crown of thorns had been placed; so he is taken by a great fear and raves incoherently and dashes about and seems to lose his senses, and would strike Christ down, but at that moment falls on to a seat overcome. (A 71)*

To conjure such a scene in the imagination is one thing, to put it on stage quite another. The unpolished nature of the play-script is nowhere more evident than at this moment of crisis, when Paul's reactions threaten to tip the drama over into melodrama, if not farce. After this steadfast refusal by the apostle to believe that his Saviour has survived the cross, the drama takes on a cruel and mocking trajectory, with Jesus forced to 'go to Jerusalem to save the world from crimes that will be committed in the name of Jesus of Nazareth' (A 99). Christ's ministry seems destined to go into reverse. Whereas once he sought to convince the people of his divine purpose, he now seeks to convince them that he is merely human. Jesus's threatening to announce his survival to those newly filled with the glorious news of the resurrection prompts Paul to violent defensive action. In an audacious final scene, he strikes Christ down with his own hand, at the same time declaring that he does so in the name of Jesus of Nazareth, Moore's ultimate touch – or hammer blow – of irony.[67] Moore insisted to Meyerfeld that Paul's killing of Jesus is a result of his temperament which 'revolts and denies the evidence of his senses'; it is not, as might be assumed, a conscious and deliberate act, carried out to protect the faith that the apostle had so successfully built up. Moore's explanation of the final scene continues:

We cling to our ideas despite evidence to the contrary. The climax as described in my manuscript is that Christ having heard Paul's doctrine of faith decides to go to Jerusalem and denounce Paul, and in the struggle which follows Paul, half-accidentally, half in passion, strikes Christ with his staff and kills him. He then says that Christianity has been saved, meaning thereby that if the man were an imposter Christianity had been saved. The further question whether the man be Christ Paul does not consider. The situation seems to me an exceedingly human one, and the more you think of it the more humanity you will perceive in it.[68]

For Moore, then, Paul takes on heroic status through his humanity and a conviction so strong it transcends all empirical reality.

Moore's choice of Paul as his eponymous hero could not have been confidently forecast from his early musings on biblical drama. In the novel *Mike Fletcher*, for example, the hero might be seen to speak for his creator in sketching out his plans for a trilogy of plays outlining the life of Christ. Following a strictly chronological sequence, Mike Fletcher explains how the first play will focus on John the Baptist, the second on Jesus and the final one on Peter. While Paul does not feature in this post-crucifixion drama, the germ of *The Apostle* can be discerned when Fletcher goes on to outline his third play, which 'ends in Peter flying from Rome to escape crucifixion; but outside the city he sees Christ carrying His cross, and Christ says He is going to be crucified a second time'.[69] By the time he embarked on *The Apostle*, Moore's personal admiration for Paul was very much in tune with the contemporary theological climate. Humbert Wolfe points out in his study of Moore and his work that 'Paul and not Jesus was the Christ of Victorianism' and this interest in the apostle endured well into the twentieth century.[70] F. W. Farrar would choose Paul as the obvious subject for a sequel to *The Life of Christ* and, moving into the twentieth century, the more controversial theologian, Albert Schweitzer, would follow his *Quest of the Historical Jesus* with a study of Paul and his interpreters.

Magee believed that 'Paul surely never had a stranger champion than Moore', an understandable view considering the author's rabid anti-clericalism and frequent vows of allegiance to paganism, and it is perhaps the passion with which Moore champions his hero that is partly responsible for the artistic shortcomings of his dramatic scenario.[71] Moore demonstrates his veneration of the Epistles by weaving quotations from them into Paul's speeches. Verses from Romans, Galatians and 1 and 2 Corinthians are paraphrased or, less frequently, rendered verbatim by the fictional apostle, a transtextuality that leaves exposed the seams between textual quotation and fictional language, and undermines the credibility of his spoken presence. Paul's speeches are verbose, contorted and unnatural, one reviewer likening them to 'the sermonizings of a Salvation Army convert'.[72] Equally unsuccessful is Moore's endeavour to bring Paul to life on stage by emphasizing his corporeality. He is conceived as 'a thick-set man, of rugged appearance, hairy in the face and with a belly' (A 51), a description to which Frank Harris took particular exception, accusing Moore of 'travestying' his own portrait of Paul in 'The Miracle of the Stigmata'.[73] It is a physicality writ large when Paul delivers the death blow to Jesus. However, the quality of immediacy derived from this emphasis on Paul's fleshiness is counteracted by the unnatural rhythms of his speech, laden as it is with cumbersome scriptural citation and pseudo-archaisms.

If Moore's personal attachment to Paul is responsible for leading him into theatrical excess, his more detached attitude to Jesus helps him to a somewhat happier outcome. In contrast to the detailed description of Paul's physical features, we are told nothing of Christ's appearance, a surprising omission considering the play's insistence on his mere humanity. Another writer might have withheld this information out of a sense of respect or reverence, but this is highly unlikely in the case of Moore, who had no qualms about shocking his public. It is possible, though, that he wanted to avoid at all cost what he described as the 'ringleted, unctuous, almost delightful' Christ of Gallic persuasion, and had not yet settled on the alternative physical image that he would present in *The Brook Kerith*.[74] Jesus's stage movements are entirely consistent with his rather shadowy physical presence: he chooses to sleep in 'an obscure corner of the room' (A 51) and his calm demeanour is highlighted by the '*doves* [which] *flutter round him, lighting on his shoulder*', in a manner reminiscent of Francis of Assisi (A 45). Yet if Moore seems to be uncharacteristically sentimental in creating this image of Jesus at peace with himself and the world around him, it is only a means to a much less sentimental end. Such a picture of tranquillity makes the impact of Paul's arrival all the more unnerving, exposing as it does the pain of the suppressed memories that lie at the core of Christ's passivity.

Moore's Jesus figure does not conform to the nineteenth-century stereotypes of the charismatic teacher, the social reformer or the great poet. Flying in the face of such conventions, he presents a traumatized, mentally complex figure, more in line with the psychiatric studies of Jesus that had emerged in the early 1900s.[75] Several of these studies attempted to prove that Christ had been of unsound mind, putting forward a variety of mental diagnoses to explain how he ended up on the cross: paranoia, megalomania and delusional psychosis being the most common. Albert Schweitzer took the authors of such works to task in *The Psychiatric Study of Jesus*, first translated into English by W. Montgomery in 1913, under the title 'The Sanity of the Eschatological Jesus'. In it, Schweitzer refutes some of the best-known psychopathological studies of Jesus, exposing their poor grasp of theology and, in particular, the historical life of Jesus. While Moore is unlikely to have encountered these, he would certainly have been aware of the emerging discipline of psychiatry. Not bound by the rules of scientific or theological method, Moore is free to explore the mind of Jesus through imaginative means, his extra-biblical story of the fate of a crucifixion survivor providing a particularly interesting psychiatric case. The assertive physicality and confidence of Paul contrast emphatically with Jesus's damaged, reclusive nature, a contrast that Humbert Wolfe expresses in terms of gender characteristics, conjecturing in his monograph on Moore that the author perceives Paul as 'the man-god of Protestantism as opposed to the woman-god of Catholicism'.[76] The more the apostle persists in his deluded notions of a resurrected Saviour, the more Jesus's mental reserves are stripped away, and traumatic memories return to him. In addition to this burden, he is faced with the fear of a second crucifixion as he sets out for Jerusalem to deny his own divinity and 'to save the world from crimes that will be committed in the name of Jesus of Nazareth' (*A* 99).

The Apostle and *The Brook Kerith*

Moore's imaginative leap from the 'swoon theory' to an actual meeting between Paul and Jesus delivered up a dramatic situation beyond his – and most dramatists' – theatrical capabilities. As a play-script, *The Apostle* is an abject failure and Moore realized this before the ink was dry on the manuscript. While he put a brave face on it in his correspondence with Dujardin, claiming that he had 'never had less trouble in writing anything', he had given a very different version of the play's gestation to Magee just a month earlier.[77] In a letter of April 1911, Moore writes to his friend:

> I am much obliged to you for looking through the proofs. But your letter leaves me perplexed and wondering if I am to interpret your silence regarding the dialogue as a condemnation [...] It would be necessary to spend three months upon it, reading the while Plotinus and the New Testament. One of these days I shall try to work up each scene, but it may be that I shall not be able to do this. In prose narrative I know I could, but to press all the subtleties with which the subject is replete into dialogue seems to me a little beyond my talent.[78]

Moore's artistic humility here suggests that his writing of a biblical scenario had been a salutary experience. Jean C. Noël's opinion that 'Le *Brook Kerith* ne doit guère à *The Apostle* que l'hypothèse du sommeil léthargique de Jésus sur la croix et l'hypothèse essénienne' [*The Brook Kerith* owes barely anything to *The Apostle* except the theories that Jesus only swooned on the cross and that he was taken in by the Essenes] underestimates the significance of the play as a foundation for the novel.[79] Drafting the drama brought Moore to realize that, if he hoped to take on the challenge of exploring the inner turmoil of a failed Messiah, he would need the narrative freedom of the novel form.

Moore's struggles with *The Apostle* also seem to have helped him decide which New Testament figures to include, which to leave out and which to make the centre of his prose version. The figure of Paul, having proven too large and dominating a presence in the play, is scaled down in the novel, leaving Jesus as the more prominent and the more psychologically interesting of the two. As John Freeman rightly points out in his 1922 study of Moore, in *The Brook Kerith* Paul is 'a secondary figure, and the reader looks at him with the eyes of Jesus, and not at Jesus through the eyes of the Apostle', a change in perspective assisted by the narrative expansiveness that comes with the novel form.[80] Writing under the strictures of a three-act play-script, Moore's presentation of Jesus's monastic life amounts to little more than dressing the members of his community in white linen and giving them otiose speeches outlining the community's belief systems and daily routines. The novel form, on the other hand, allows the daily life of the Essene brotherhood to be shown rather than told, allowing the reader to understand why this community, with its ritual and security, provides the ideal place for Jesus to recover from the horrors of the cross.

One character that is quite conspicuously struck out of the novel version of Moore's post-crucifixion story is Mary Magdalene. The figure of the Magdalene featured large in late nineteenth-century and early twentieth-century biblical poetry, prose fiction and verse drama, often as a source of erotic interest. In Alexandra von Herder's play *Jesus of Nazareth* (1913), she is the mistress of the high priest Kaiaphas;[81] in Edgar Saltus's novel *Mary of Magdala* (1891), she proves a fatal attraction for Judas who, jealous of her love for Jesus, betrays him to the authorities, hanging himself shortly afterwards as an act of repentance.[82] Even more daring are those works that present her as sexually desirous of Christ himself. Robert Buchanan's *The Ballad of Mary the Mother* (1897), for example, features a Magdalene who exclaims 'O would that I were the Queen o'the King, / Or even his concubine!';[83] and, as mentioned previously, George Barlow's Mary Magdalene ends up as the actual bride of Christ. In *The Apostle*, prevented from following the established mode of depicting the Magdalene as a *femme fatale* by a twenty-five-year time gap, Moore chooses instead to show her colourful past in a faded retrospect; she appears in just one brief scene, having been brought to the Essene monastery by Paul to bear witness to the resurrection. Mary's reunion with Jesus is surprisingly subdued in dramatic tenor. Turned away from the threshold of the monastery on account of her sex, she later encounters the master she has not seen in two decades. In stark contrast to Paul, she is unperturbed by Christ's explanation of how he was nursed back to health at the house of Joseph of Arimathea. Far from denying this new truth, she implores him to return with her to Galilee where his words are still remembered and his teaching sadly missed. Moore remains true to his conviction that 'women are natural pagans and have never been Christianized' in showing the Magdalene as more disturbed at Jesus witnessing her faded physical beauty than by the revelation that her Lord has not risen.[84] Moore presents an aged Mary Magdalene, her bodily deterioration detailed not in stage directions, but through her own description of herself as 'an old woman, withered and wan, unsightly in all eyes' (*A* 90), who has 'rags only enough to cover her deformities' (*A* 91). In this respect, Moore's stage character bears a strong resemblance to Donatello's carved wooden figure of the Magdalene, described by Lord Balcarres in the first English study of the artist and his work:

> She stands upright, a mass of tattered rags, haggard, emaciated, almost toothless. Her matted hair falls down in thick knots; all feminine softness has gone from the limbs, and nothing but the drawn muscles remain. It is a thin wasted form, piteous in expression, painful in all its ascetic excess.[85]

But if the stark realism of Donatello's Magdalene beautifully evokes the paradox of 'ascetic excess', Moore's age-ravaged creature suggests a woman entirely defined by her sexuality and devoid of any higher spirituality. Often guilty of prurience when dealing with issues of sexuality, Moore's treatment of this confrontation between an ageing Magdalene and the Christ-figure proves no exception. Mary's speech recalling the wiping of Christ's feet is an example of Moore at his most indelicate:

> Draw nearer, master, for I would touch the feet over which my hair descended like a mantle – soft and silky my hair was then. That thou shouldst remember its softness as it flowed about thy feet is a great joy that must remain in my heart […] Look not on me, master, but remember me as I was when I knelt at thy feet. (A 91–92)

Certainly, his decision to remove Mary Magdalene from *The Brook Kerith* and the two subsequent stage adaptations was a wise one. Insinuating an ageing Magdalene into an all-male environment posed artistic challenges that were likely to defeat even the most accomplished of dramatists. Moore might also have felt that the foregrounding of Mary Magdalene in fictional recastings of the Gospels had become too commonplace – as indeed they had – and that Paul should take her place as the *apostola apostolorum*.

Regardless of Moore's avowed Protestantism, *The Apostle* is an entirely secular and iconoclastic work, pushing hard against the boundaries of biblical drama, boundaries that continued to hold fast despite a period of sustained campaigning for the relaxation of stage censorship in Britain. While the process of writing *The Apostle* impressed upon Moore the difficulties that inhered in composing New Testament drama, he remained tenacious in his efforts to stage his meeting between Paul and Jesus. In 1923 Heinemann published a full-

length script of *The Apostle*, an extensively revised version of the original, adapted from *The Brook Kerith*. As with the original scenario of
1911, Moore had high hopes for the piece prior to its publication. He
boasted to Gosse that he hoped to do for London 'what somebody did
for Oberammergau';[86] and a few months later he enthused in a letter
to Nancy Cunard about how he was about to read the role of Paul
aloud to 'Leslie Faber, one of our best actors'.[87] Seven years later, the
play went through a second meticulous revision and was published
under a new title: *The Passing of the Essenes*. Lionel Barton,
frequently in Moore's company around the time of this revision, told
Joseph Hone that 'he was most meticulous as to every comma'.[88]
Finally, in 1930, just a few years before Moore's death, these efforts
were rewarded with a stage performance. What was by now a twenty-
year-old scenario played at the private Arts Theatre in London
between 1 and 5 October, with the music of the Chant of the Essenes
being supplied by Gustav Holst. Though this production was warmly
received, the *Times Literary Supplement* describing Moore's dramatic
mastery as 'Sophoclean', it failed to live up to the author's expectations.[89] Writing just a few years before his death, he complained to
Eglinton that he 'found the play infinitely tedious on the stage [...]
One man barked, thinking that barking was a good conception of
Paul, and the other reduced Jesus to the image and likeness of a
monthly nurse.'[90] Moore may finally have come to realize, then, that
the imaginative representation of Jesus was better left to prose fiction,
and that he could take consolation in knowing that his decision to
transform *The Apostle* of 1911 into *The Brook Kerith* had been exactly
the right one.

Notes

1 For details of the Office of the Lord Chamberlain and its censorship of the English
   drama, see John Johnston, *The Lord Chamberlain's Blue Pencil* (London: Hodder
   & Stoughton, 1990).
2 *New Review*, 8 (1893), pp. 183–88 (p. 185).
3 *New Review*, 8 (1893), p. 189.
4 Quoted in *The Lord Chamberlain's Blue Pencil*, p. 99.
5 G. W. Foote, *The Sign of the Cross: a candid criticism of Mr Wilson Barrett's play*
   (London: R. Forder, 1896), p. 9.
6 G. B. Shaw, 'The Sign of the Cross', *Plays of the Week*, 11 January 1896; reprinted
   in *Plays and Players: Essays on the Theatre* (London: Oxford University Press,

1952), pp. 64–65.

7 See *The Times*, 29 October 1907, p. 15.

8 For details of stage censorship in Ireland, see Christopher Morash, *A History of Irish Theatre 1601–2000* (Cambridge: Cambridge University Press, 2002), pp. 143–44.

9 Susan L. Mitchell, *George Moore* (Dublin and London: Maunsel, 1916), pp. 120–21.

10 Edouard Dujardin, *La Source du fleuve chrétien* (Paris, 1904). Dujardin also composed two religious dramas: *Marthe et Marie* (Paris: Les Cahiers Idéalistes, 1923) and *Le mystère du dieu mort et ressuscité* (Paris: Albert Messein, 1924), both performed at the Théâtre Antoine in Paris.

11 *Letters from George Moore to Ed. Dujardin, 1886–1922*, ed. John Eglinton (New York: Crosby Gaige, 1929), p. 109.

12 Edouard Dujardin, 'The Abbé Loisy', trans. George Moore, *Dana: A Magazine of Independent Thought*, 1 (May 1904), pp. 18–21.

13 Alfred Firmin Loisy, *The Gospel and the Church*, trans. Christopher Home (London: Isbister, 1903), p. 276.

14 *The Source of the Christian Tradition*, trans. Joseph McCabe (London: Watts, 1911). In his autobiography, *Eighty Years a Rebel* (Girard, KS: Haldeman-Julius Publications, 1947), McCabe claimed to have written over 200 books, more than any other living author (p. 5). These works focused on topics as diverse as the history of flagellation, existentialism and the writings of Edward Clodd.

15 *Letters from George Moore to Ed. Dujardin*, p. 89.

16 Sanday, *The Life of Christ in Recent Research*, p. 148.

17 J. G. Frazer, *The Golden Bough: A Study in Comparative Religion*, 2 vols (London: Macmillan, 1890). In the twelve-volume Third Edition of 1913, Frazer relegated to an appendix his discussion of the similarities between the scourging of Christ and the treatment of the mock king of the Saturnalia and the Sacaea, and the possibility that Christ might have been put to death in the annual ritual of the killing of Haman. In a footnote to the Note headed 'The Crucifixion of Christ', Frazer admits that the parallels drawn between Jesus and ancient scapegoat rituals are 'in a high degree speculative and uncertain' and insists that his theory 'assumes the historical reality of Jesus of Nazareth as a great religious and moral teacher, who founded Christianity'. See *The Golden Bough: The Scapegoat*, 12 vols (London: Macmillan, 3rd edn, 1913), VI, p. 412, n. 1. For a detailed discussion of Frazer's paralleling of ancient rites and the crucifixion of Jesus, see Robert Fraser, *The Making of the Golden Bough* (Basingstoke: Palgrave, 2002), pp. 136–55. In *The Historical Jesus: A Survey of Positions* (London: Watts, 1916), John M. Robertson remarks on how theories such as Frazer's reignited discussion of the historical Jesus (p. xx).

18 John Eglinton, *Irish Literary Portraits* (London: Macmillan, 1935), p. 92. 'John Eglinton' was the pseudonym of William Kirkpatrick Magee.

19 Joseph McCabe, *The Myth of the Resurrection* (London: Freethought Press, 1925; repr. New York: Prometheus Books, 1993), p. 85.

20 Undated letter to Julian Moore, National Library of Ireland, MS 4479, f. 64. Moore's spelling and punctuation were frequently inaccurate. Unless otherwise indicated, I have corrected the numerous minor errors that occur in his manuscript

and autograph letters.

21 George Moore to the *Irish Times*, 30 December 1910, National Library of Ireland, MS 2648, f. 21.

22 George Moore, *Avowals* (London: William Heinemann, 1936), p. 87.

23 George Moore, *Hail and Farewell!: Salve* (London: Heinemann, 1912), p. 266.

24 In a conversation broadcast by the BBC, Larry Morrow related the story of how Moore, while staying as an overnight guest, inquired of his hostess who the author was of the 'beautifully written book' on his bedside table, the title of which he pronounced as 'The Bibble'. It is one of several anecdotes in an extensive Moore apocrypha. See W. R. Rodgers, *Irish Literary Portraits* (London: British Broadcasting Corporation, 1972), p. 85.

25 *Father and Son* (London: Heinemann, 1907) tells of Edmund Gosse's upbringing in a Plymouth Brethren community and reveals how fundamentalists such as the author's father refused to read fiction, deeming it deceptive, corrupting and in direct opposition to the 'truth' of the Scriptures. Moore had been responsible for persuading Gosse to write what was to be his most successful work and was, presumably, well acquainted with its contents.

26 George Moore, 'Epistle to the Cymry', printed as an appendix to *Confessions of a Young Man* (London: Heinemann, 1926), p. 290.

27 George Moore to Maurice Moore, 11 April 1904, National Library of Ireland, MS 2646, f. 95.

28 Moore, *Salve*, p. 195.

29 McCabe, *Eighty Years a Rebel*, p. 13.

30 George Moore, '*The Apostle* By George Moore: Prefatory Note', *The English Review*, 5 (June 1910), pp. 564–76.

31 Moore, '*The Apostle* By George Moore: Prefatory Note', p. 564. While Moore's main concerns doubtless lay with Frank Harris at this time, he may also have in mind a disagreement he had had with W. B. Yeats over the play *Where There Is Nothing* almost a decade earlier. Yeats gives his account of the dispute in *Dramatis Personae, Autobiographies* (pp. 452–53) and refers to it in a postscript to the first published text of the play: '"Where There Is Nothing" is founded upon a subject which I suggested to George Moore [...] but this did not go beyond some rambling talks. Then the need went past, and I gradually put so much of myself into the fable that I felt I must write on it alone, and I took it back into my own hands with his consent. Should he publish a story upon it some day, I shall rejoice that the excellent old custom of two writers taking one fable has been revived in a new form.' Cited in the introduction to *Where There is Nothing/The Unicorn from the Stars*, ed. Katharine Worth (Washington, DC: Catholic University of America Press; Gerrards Cross: Colin Smythe, 1987), p. 6.

32 Joseph Hone, *The Life of George Moore* (London; Victor Gollancz, 1936), p. 293.

33 Roth, *The Private Life of Frank Harris*, p. 153.

34 Harris, *Contemporary Portraits*, Second Series, pp. 125–26.

35 George Moore, 'A Prefatory Letter on Reading the Bible for the First Time', *The English Review*, 7 (February 1911), pp. 452–65 (p. 464). Hereafter cited in the text as PL.

36 Paul Régla [P. A. Desjardin], *Jésus de Nazareth: Au Point de Vue Historique, Scientifique et Social* (Paris: Georges Carré, 1891).

37 In an article describing his first and only meeting with Moore, Robert Graves points out that Moore's thesis 'that Jesus survived the cross was not new' and that it had been 'much more plausibly argued in Samuel Butler's *Fair Haven*'. See *5 Pens in Hand* (New York: Doubleday, 1958), p. 124.

38 While the play itself received scant praise, the introductory material met with approval. One reviewer insisted that 'the Prefatory Letter [...] is so fine and so exciting that it is worth buying the book for it alone'. See the *Irish Review*, I (October 1911), pp. 415–16 (p. 416).

39 Hone, *George Moore*, p. 311.

40 Virginia Woolf, *The Death of the Moth and other Essays* (London: The Hogarth Press, 1942), p. 102.

41 George Moore to Max Meyerfeld, 8 December 1910, National Library of Ireland, MS 4460, f. 161.

42 In a radio broadcast, Richard Best, W. K. Magee's colleague at the National Library, recalled how 'Moore hadn't much of a library [...] He didn't buy books, and he never really read much.' See Rodgers, *Irish Literary Portraits*, p. 85.

43 Moore had, of course, gained himself a reputation as a writer concerned with 'sex problems'. In the 1880s and early 1890s he had covered a range of sexual issues including adultery, rape, lesbianism and the effects of celibacy on the individual.

44 George Moore, *Conversations in Ebury Street* (London: Heinemann, 1924), pp. 186–87.

45 Moore, *Conversations in Ebury Street*, p. 185.

46 *Letters from George Moore to Ed. Dujardin*, p. 88.

47 F. W. H. Myers, *St Paul*, ed. E. J. Watson (London: Simpkin, Marshall, Hamilton, Kent, 1916), p. 3.

48 Harris, *Contemporary Portraits*, Second Series, p. 124.

49 George Moore to Max Meyerfeld, 24 May 1910, National Library of Ireland, MS 4460, f. 139.

50 *George Moore in Transition: Letters to T. Fisher Unwin and Lena Milman, 1984–1910*, ed. Helmut E. Gerber (Detroit: Wayne State University Press, 1968), p. 107.

51 George Moore to Max Meyerfeld, 10 November 1910, National Library of Ireland, MS 4460, f. 153.

52 See 'Gas from a Burner', *The Critical Writings of James Joyce*, ed. Ellsworth Mason and Richard Ellmann (London: Faber & Faber, 1959), p. 243.

53 George Barlow, *Jesus of Nazareth: A Tragedy* (London: The Roxburghe Press, 1896).

54 Barlow, *Jesus of Nazareth*, p. 13.

55 George Barlow to George Moore, 23 September 1883, National Library of Ireland, MS 2648, f.2.

56 Barlow, *Jesus of Nazareth*, p. 13.

57 *The Apostle: A Drama in Three Acts* (Dublin: Maunsel, 1911), p. 39. Hereafter cited in the text as *A*.

58 *Letters from George Moore to Ed. Dujardin*, p. 89.

59 Moore's choice of Martin Luther would no doubt have gone unchallenged in France where audiences were accustomed to seeing religious subjects presented on stage. In contrast, stage and film censorship in Britain withheld such treatments from the public. As late as 1929, the British Board of Film Censors banned a film

about Martin Luther as 'likely to offend a large section of the public'. See Dorothy Knowles, *The Censor, the Drama, and the Film* (London: George Allen & Unwin, 1934), p. 238.

60 Bernard Lopèz and George Moore, *Martin Luther: A tragedy in five acts* (London: Remington, 1879).

61 In her monograph on George Moore, Susan Mitchell records the author's response to being asked about *Martin Luther*: 'He instantly sprang from his chair and clutching his flaxen locks walked frantically about his room wailing: "What have I ever done to you that you should remind me of this thing?"' See Mitchell, *George Moore*, p. 19.

62 Moore extends this typology in the historical romance *Héloïse and Abélard* (1921), the hero of which he regarded as 'a light before the dawn [...] who unlocked the dungeon in which the ecclesiastics had imprisoned humanity'. See *Moore Versus Harris*, ed. Guido Bruno (Chicago: privately printed, 1925), p. 19.

63 Lopèz and Moore, *Martin Luther*, p. 34.

64 George Moore, *Impressions and Opinions* (London: David Nutt, 1891), p. 239.

65 George Moore to Max Meyerfeld, 7 April 1911, National Library of Ireland, MS 4460, f. 169.

66 *The Athenaeum*, 22 July 1911, pp. 111–12 (p. 111).

67 Moore moderated this ending in subsequent versions of the story, with Paul and Jesus parting and going in opposite directions.

68 George Moore to Max Meyerfeld, 5 December 1910, National Library of Ireland, MS 4460, f. 158.

69 See *Mike Fletcher* (London: Ward and Downey, 1889), pp. 127–28.

70 Humbert Wolfe, *George Moore* (London: Harold Shaylor, 1931), p. 23.

71 Eglinton, *Irish Literary Portraits*, p. 110.

72 *Irish Review*, I (October 1911), pp. 415–16 (p. 415).

73 Harris, *Contemporary Portraits*, Second Series, p. 127. Paul's physical appearance seems to have been a popular subject for speculation. In an entry on Paul in *A Dictionary of the Bible, comprising its Antiquities, Biography, Geography, and Natural History*, ed. William Smith, 3 vols (London, 1860–63), John Llewelyn Davies writes: 'We have no very trustworthy sources of information as to the personal appearance of Paul. Those which we have [...] are the early pictures and mosaics described by Mrs Jamieson, and passages from Malalas, Nicephorus, and the apocryphal *Acta Pauli et Theclae*. They all agree in ascribing to the Apostle, a short stature, a long face with high forehead, an aquiline nose, close and prominent eyebrows' (II, p. 762).

74 *Letters of George Moore, With an Introduction by John Eglinton to whom they were written* (Bournemouth: Sydenham, 1942), p. 52.

75 See Albert Schweitzer, *The Psychiatric Study of Jesus*, trans. Charles R. Joy (Boston: The Beacon Press, 1958). Schweitzer's study started out as a thesis offered for the degree of Doctor of Medicine, and was subsequently published in three separate articles in *The Expositor*, Eighth Series, 6, 1913.

76 See Wolfe, *George Moore*, p. 24.

77 *Letters from George Moore to Ed. Dujardin*, p. 89.

78 *Letters of George Moore, With an Introduction by John Eglinton*, p. 18.

79 Albert J. Farmer, *Le Mouvement esthétique et 'décadent' en Angleterre 1873–1900*

(Paris: Librairie Ancienne Honoré Champion, 1931), p. 382.

80 John Freeman, *A Portrait of George Moore in a Study of his Work* (London: T. W. Laurie, 1922), p. 195.

81 Alexandra von Herder, *Jesus of Nazareth: A Poetical Drama in Seven Scenes* (London: Heinemann, 1913). Von Herder wrote eight plays in all, most of which were never performed.

82 Edgar Saltus, *Mary of Magdala* (London: Osgood & McIlvaine, 1891).

83 Robert Buchanan, *The Ballad of Mary the Mother* (London: Robert Buchanan, 1897), p. 79.

84 *George Moore on Parnassus: Letters (1900–1933) to Secretaries, Publishers, Printers, Agents, Literati, Friends, and Acquaintances*, ed. Helmut E. Gerber and O. M. Brock, Jr (Newark: University of Delaware Press, 1988), p. 130.

85 Lord Balcarres, *Donatello* (London: Duckworth, 1903), p. 144.

86 George Moore to Edmund Gosse, 20 September 1922, National Library of Ireland, MS 2134.

87 George Moore to Nancy Cunard, 25 February 1923, National Library of Ireland, MS 2648, f. 42.

88 Lionel Barton to Joseph Hone, 17 April 1935, National Library of Ireland, MS 2648, f. 29.

89 *Times Literary Supplement*, 30 October 1930, p. 802.

90 *Letters of George Moore, With an Introduction by John Eglinton*, p. 87.

CHAPTER 7

George Moore's Life of Jesus

But if there is no resurrection of the dead, then Christ has
not been raised; if Christ has not been raised, then
our preaching is in vain and your faith is in vain.
1 Corinthians 15:13–14

The Brook Kerith: A Syrian Story, the prose fiction offspring of *The
Apostle*, was published in 1916, enjoying immediate critical acclaim.
The resounding success of the novel helped convince Moore that he
had produced 'the only prose epic in the English language',[1] and
ensured that it would never end up on the author's list of books best
forgotten: the writings of 'Amico Moorini'.[2] Understandably, he liked
to attribute the popularity of his book to its literary qualities, though
he must also have been aware that much of the attention it received
stemmed from its controversial subject matter. A month or so after the
novel's publication, he wrote to W. K. Magee: 'Everybody is irritated
with me for having written *The Brook Kerith*, and the issue of all the
talk has been a large sale.'[3] Moore is referring here to the raging
controversy that the novel provoked, which filled a great number of
column inches in the letter pages of the *Westminster Gazette* and the
Daily Express.[4] What these indignant, often furious, attacks on *The
Brook Kerith* confirm is that, in the first quarter of the twentieth
century, fictionalizing the life of Christ still had the potential to shock
the reading public. It must also be said, however, that with this particular work Moore had dared to tread where other writers of biblical
fiction had not.[5] While rewritings of the Gospels had hitherto narrated
events from the altitude of an omniscient narrator, or from the first-
person perspective of an anonymous disciple, Moore relates the story
of failed Messiahship partly from Christ's own viewpoint. It is not
surprising, then, that *The Brook Kerith* outraged some of its more

devout readers, used to rather more moderate imaginative reconstructions of their Saviour. One reviewer writing in the *Manchester Guardian*, while extolling the artistic virtues of the novel, nonetheless concludes that, of all the legends circulated about Jesus, Moore's is 'the most offending',[6] and Lord Alfred Douglas tried – and failed – to bring a charge of blasphemy against the author.[7] Moore's life of Jesus had certainly lived up to his reputation for flying in the face of the *bonnes mœurs* of the British public

While the controversial nature of *The Brook Kerith* goes some way to explaining its excellent sales, the timing of its publication also played its part. The novel was offered to the public at a time when the demand for fiction was high. Two years of war had brought about a marked and rather unlooked for shift in the nation's reading habits. Two months prior to the publication of *The Brook Kerith*, a leading article in the *Times Literary Supplement* entitled 'Literature and the War' reported on The English Association's conference organized to consider the effects of the war on the reading of literature. The conclusions drawn by the Association were that, while many feared the war might deter the public from reading, the reverse seemed to be the case. The apparent increase in reading was put down to the fact that the slow and monotonous life of the soldier afforded him ample time to read; at the same time, the restrictive nature of civilian life made the book one of the most attractive forms of entertainment.[8] The First World War was also a period during which debates about Christianity were particularly urgent. In a work published in the same year as Moore's novel, John M. Robertson comments on how the conflict has been 'the pretext for endless religious discussions [...] ranging between medieval miracle-mongering and the lowest forms of journalistic charlatanism, with chronic debates on theism and on the military value of faith and prayer'.[9] In this respect, Moore's choice of subject was very much in tune with the zeitgeist.

Responses to Moore's Christ novel were inevitably heightened by the fact of its being published when the Battle of the Somme was still raging and four months after the Easter Rising in Dublin. Events such as these had provoked the recreation of Christ's image in a variety of forms, for quite diverse reasons. Throughout Europe, the suffering of the First World War soldier found a correlative in the iconography of the crucified Christ, and evocations of Jesus featured large in the work of soldier-poets such as Wilfred Owen and Siegfried Sassoon, as well as in the writings of those who remained at home. In one especially arresting instance, the figurative significance of Golgotha appeared to have been literalized when a British soldier was reported to have been discovered hanging in the manner of the crucified Christ, with bayonets serving as nails. This atrocity was said to have been witnessed in Belgium by Lance Corporal George Barrie in April 1915, and his account was widely disseminated by the press and led to a significant rise in recruitment.[10] Away from the brutality of the battlefields, newspapers and periodicals carried poetry that considered the impact of wartime experience on religious faith. In the last few months of 1915, for example, Lucy Whitmell's 'Christ in Flanders', destined to be one of the most popular and frequently anthologized poems of the day, appeared in the *Spectator*, arguing the Christian case through the voice of a soldier talking directly to Christ: 'This hideous warfare seems to make things clear [...] You are here';[11] and on Christmas Eve of the same year, *The Times* carried Thomas Hardy's 'The Oxen', a poem that draws poignantly on the story of the Nativity to articulate the agnostic's sense of loss, felt all the more acutely at this time of crisis.[12] In Ireland, too, Christ's suffering served as a fitting correlative to the sacrifice of young Irish men fighting for independence. The IRB leader Patrick Pearse was one of several Republicans who would seek out and exploit parallels between the struggle for independence and the Passion, both in the rhetoric of his speeches and in his poetry.[13] *The Brook Kerith*, then, revolving as it does around the figure of the crucified Christ, could not have appeared at a more apposite or sensitive moment.

Writing in 1956, Robert Graves, by then an author of some fine war writing and a highly original Jesus novel, published just one year after the end of the Second World War, was well placed to reflect on how:

It is in wartime that books about Jesus have most appeal, and *The Brook Kerith* first appeared some forty years ago during the Battle of the Somme, when Christ was being invoked alike by the Germans and the Allies for victory in a new sort of total war. This paradox made most of us English soldiers serving in the purgatorial trenches lose all respect for organized Pauline religion, though still feeling a sympathetic reverence for Jesus as our fellow-sufferer [...] Moore's story – at the end of which Paul dramatically disowns the real Jesus [...] and goes off to preach the transcendent Jesus Christ of his own epileptic imagining among the Italians and Spaniards – made good cynical sense to us.[14]

Graves was not alone in classifying *The Brook Kerith* as a war book: several reviewers considered it primarily in the context of world conflict. Reviewing the novel for the *Dial*, Edward Garnett judged it to have captured the shift of religious sensibility brought about by the horrors of the war:

> Mr George Moore's novel [...] could not have been published at a more appropriate time. One thing that the Great War has settled for good, though I fear many honest people are too stupid to recognize it, is that in the life of the modern world Christianity is like a best suit of clothes worn to please ourselves and impress the neighbors [...] Mr George Moore's careful study of the figure of Jesus of Nazareth [...] is therefore doubly welcome to anyone who, forced to face the atrocious facts of the most hideous war known to history, examines for himself the foundations of Christ's teachings.[15]

Some involved in the armed forces took quite the opposite view, no doubt fearful of the consequences of loss of faith for men whose lives were already profoundly damaged. One such was Major-General Hardy who, in his correspondence with Moore in the *Daily Express*, insisted that *The Brook Kerith* was a 'deadly source of infection' and that its author should be excommunicated.[16] Moore's reply to the Major-General's letter confirms that his youthful hatred of Roman Catholicism had by no means abated, nor his tendency to view Catholicism and Protestantism as binary opposites. Assuming from the Major-General's use of the term 'excommunication' that he is a Catholic, he claims that in the light of this it would be 'no use discussing any religious or moral question with him', to which provocation the Major-General responds 'I am not a Roman Catholic, nor a Protestant, nor any other "ism"'.[17]

In view of its date of composition, it might be assumed that Moore intended the spiritually disenchanted and physically broken Jesus of *The Brook Kerith* to embody the pain and disillusionment of contemporary Europe. Taking just such a view, one recent critic, Elizabeth Grübgeld, argues that Moore's disgust at the war accounts for the novel's ending with 'the assertion of a most Quakerly doctrine of the inner light'.[18] It is more likely, however, that the emphasis on Jesus's passivity at the close of the novel is motivated by artistic rather than political concerns. Christ's resignation serves as a counterweight to

Paul's manic energy and as a means of reinforcing the work's final philosophy that 'God is […] a possession of the mind'.[19] Furthermore, Moore's recorded comments on the war do not ring of political engagement; rather, they have a senescent, world-weary quality about them. In a letter to Emily Lorenz Meyer, written a few months into the conflict, Moore advises that 'In these times of stress the wise man does not rage at the thunder-bolt or curse the rain that drenches him. He creeps into a quiet cave and reads the newspapers amused that they all say the same thing.'[20] His evocation here of the heath scene from *King Lear* is in some respects meet for a man approaching old age; yet he makes clear that, in contrast to the rage of Shakespeare's hero, his response to the adversity of the day will be entirely quiescent, and it seems unlikely that his composition of *The Brook Kerith* was significantly determined by the events unfolding around him.

Learning lessons

The Brook Kerith entered the literary world alongside a well-established and extensive canon of non-fiction prose works about the life of Christ, and it is evident from the critical responses the novel received that it was often judged within this generic framework. One reviewer compared the novel to J. R. Seeley's *Ecce Homo*;[21] another accused the author of having 'relied largely on Renan' and 'his own wit';[22] and one commentator pronounced that it had outstripped 'the most daring flights of Renan'.[23] Moore seems to have been both aware of and undaunted by such forefathers, declaring in a letter to Emily Lorenz Meyer that his Jesus would be 'quite different from Renan's young man, polite and charming'.[24] Yet in criticizing Renan's portrayal of Jesus, Moore is also acknowledging its importance, if only as a model to work against. Indeed, in the early stages of preparing to write *The Brook Kerith*, Moore seemed to be adhering to a positively Renanian route, adopting, like Wilde before him, Renan's phrase 'the Fifth Gospel' to define his new writing enterprise and setting out on a research journey to Palestine.[25] The experience of composing *The Apostle* had certainly brought Moore to realize that his grasp of theology and biblical history was, at best, tenuous and he set about making good his scholarly deficiencies in some earnest. The first stage of his study was to be a two-month excursion to the Middle East where he hoped to gain first-hand knowledge, as well as inspiration, for his work. Moore's decision to embark on what proved to be a gruelling journey for a man of his years is somewhat surprising.[26] Such fieldwork was very different from his usual method of preparation, as outlined in a letter to the journalist, W. T. Stead: 'I work from word of mouth description. I can describe a scene that has been related to me better than if I had witnessed it.'[27] Yet though this second-hand approach had served Moore well throughout the 1890s, whether writing about life in a convent or a woman's experience of the labour ward, his early-twentieth-century preoccupation with the Holy Land required a first-hand witness.

As a much younger man, Moore had sneered at Holman Hunt's travels in Palestine, deeming the verisimilitude so eagerly sought by the painter to be not only inimical to art but also impossible to achieve.[28] However, according to Augustus John, Moore too was concerned with factual accuracy, being keen to establish whether the crux of his story – Joseph of Arimathea carrying the barely conscious Jesus from the tomb to his home – was physically possible. John recalls Moore telling him that 'he had got his friend, the sculptor Prince Troubetskoy, to shoulder a medium-sized man and attempt to carry him from the site of the Cross to the alleged Tomb. Troubetskoy, being a kind of giant, just managed to perform this feat.'[29] This was, of course, an experiment that (if it actually happened) could have been carried out in any part of the world, and it would seem that Moore's sojourn sprang as much from a romantic attachment to the Middle East as from the necessity of practical research. In the preface written for the 1921 edition of the novel, Moore claims his father's tales of travelling to the East ensured that 'Syria and stories became part and parcel of me at a very early age'.[30] Though clearly a retrospective reflection, it nonetheless chimes with Magee's observation that 'he seemed to himself to understand a subject like the origin of Christianity if he could see it as "story"'.[31] Palestine, then, was the site of storytelling and the journey there a creative rite of passage. Indeed, according to Moore, his story did not begin to take shape until he had 'ridden through the hills and spent a night with the monks at Kerith'.[32]

Moore's travels were supported by the rather more sedate pursuit of background reading. While he continued to assume a somewhat cynical, even superior, attitude towards theological scholarship, *The Brook Kerith* holds evidence that he was keen to show off his newly acquired knowledge of first-century Jewish beliefs and customs, as well as his awareness of contemporary revisionist readings of the Gospels. Though Moore was by no means a naturally voracious reader, he was fortunate in having the very able assistance of Magee and the resources of the National Library of Ireland, and there is no doubt that, by his own standards at least, he put his back into the job. Magee maintained that he 'took prodigious pains with the composition of *The Brook Kerith*, studying Philo Judaeus, Josephus and everything he could get hold of, becoming quite a doughty controversialist in matters of Biblical criticism'.[33] His studies were also helped along by his recently formed friendship with the philosopher and theologian Thomas Whittaker, the director of the Rationalist Press Association, whose book *The Origins of Christianity* was one of the few British works to earn a place in Schweitzer's *Quest of the Historical Jesus*. In the recorded dialogue with Whittaker that forms the introduction to *The Pastoral Loves of Daphnis and Chloë*, Moore reminisces about his writing of *The Brook Kerith* when the two men 'talked of the Gospels and the Epistles, of Josephus, Philo-Judaeus, and Apollonius of Tyana'.[34] While Moore's assertion in a letter to Frank Harris that he was 'as well informed as Renan' is clearly an exaggeration intended to provoke a literary rival, his course of study succeeded in making him at least *au fait* with a number of important theological issues.[35]

From biblical scholarship to prose fiction

One area of biblical background that Moore found both engrossing and useful for his writing was the anatomical realities of crucifixion, a topic that surfaces regularly in his correspondence with Magee. The results of Moore's research in this field are conveyed through a variety of characters in *The Brook Kerith*.[36] The novel's hardened centurion, inured to watching men expire in agony on the cross, explains how 'the first day is the worst day; afterwards the crucified sinks into unconsciousness [...] on the fourth day he dies' (*BK* 228); and the loyal servant, Esora, is charged with the task of nursing Jesus back to health, allowing her to dispense Moore's newly acquired knowledge about the physical aftermath of crucifixion. She tells Joseph that 'the nails may have pierced the feet and hands without breaking any [bones]' (*BK* 265), a detail that sees Moore satisfy the demands of fiction before those of historical accuracy. Two years before the publication of *The Brook Kerith*, he had announced to Magee that Jesus was not nailed to the cross but 'crucified in the ordinary way – just tied upon the cross and left there to die of strain of muscle and starvation [...] and remember there is no mention of nails in the three synoptic gospels'.[37] The issue of the nails was to become an *idée fixe* that Moore would worry away at to the end of his days, convinced that he had noticed what Dujardin and Whittaker had missed: the Fourth Gospel is the only account of the Passion to mention nails, a detail rendered invalid by the document's historical unreliability. Moore explains the discrepancy between the accounts of the Synoptists and that of John thus:

> It came to pass that John, whilst reading the Gospels of his prede-cessors, found a passage in Luke in which Jesus appears to his disciples. The disciples cry: A phantom! and he answers, Behold my hands and my feet, that it is I myself. Jesus could not say, Behold my neck or my ears [...] He employed the ordinary language [...] John was struck by the phrase, and taking it to mean that Jesus was nailed to the cross, he introduced it into his Gospel.[38]

And so Christ's wounded hands and feet are reduced to a figure of speech, an act of semantic chicanery unlikely to have passed muster with the biblical scholar.

In the course of *The Brook Kerith*, Moore supplies fictional answers to questions that had puzzled theologians for well over a century. The spear in Christ's side (mentioned only in John) is explained away as an invention by the centurion to convince Pilate that Jesus was indeed dead when taken down from the cross on the orders of Joseph of Arimathea, a narrative detail that helps make the notion of Jesus recovering from his crucifixion injuries more feasible.[39] And the intriguingly slight references to the life and teaching of Jesus to be found in the Pauline Epistles is accounted for by Paul himself: 'A teacher Jesus was and a great teacher, but far more important was the fact that God had raised him from the dead' (*BK* 453). While hardly an original explanation, it gains impact from being confirmed through the musings of the only man who could ever validate its truth or false-hood. Moore's mixing of theology and fiction did not convince the critics. Several reviewers drew attention to the flaws in his biblical scholarship, and though his cantankerous responses to their criticisms in the press announced that he was untroubled by them, there is plenty of evidence to the contrary. A case in point is his asking Richard Best, sub-librarian at the National Library of Ireland, to read *The Brook Kerith* through for mistakes, a textual check that resulted in a dauntingly extensive list of *errata*. While none of his slips was quite as risible as Marie Corelli's in *Barabbas*, they were noticeable enough to gratify those who were not particularly well disposed to him. Robert Graves, whose 1946 novel, *King Jesus*, was described by one reviewer as 'stiff with learning',[40] found the scholarship at work in *The Brook Kerith* very flabby indeed:

> When Moore presents Jesus as conversing freely with an unclean swineherd, throwing Heaven open to the uncircumcised, and encouraging a lustful goatherd to commit the sin of self-castration, he is displaying an absurd and wilful ignorance – as when, also, he includes Ariston (the second-century presbyter credited with the revised ending of St Mark's Gospel) among the disciples, and records Joseph of Arimathea's desire for leisure 'to ponder the texts of the Talmud' – the Talmud not having been committed to parchment or papyrus for several generations after Joseph's day.[41]

Arguably, it was not entirely fair to level such criticisms at a work of fiction whose chief concerns were to explore the religious imagination rather than provide a narrative history of first-century Judea or an updated version of liberal Lives of Jesus. Unlike those New Testament fictions that had retained the critical apparatus of their biographical forerunners, *The Brook Kerith* stands out in both looking and reading like a novel, bare of all footnotes, glossaries and chapter summaries. In this, and in his treatment of the New Testament sources, Moore is more literary artist than theologian, his selection of format and textual detail being driven primarily by aesthetic concerns. Just as earlier writers of biblical harmonies had managed to combine the disparate Gospel accounts of Christ's life into one consistent whole in order to uphold an orthodox Christian picture, so Moore pieced together fragments from the four Evangels to create his own heterodox version for the twentieth century. Believing the New Testament to be 'but a collection of odds and ends [...] compiled from different sources', Moore imitated its compositors in putting together his own work of *bricolage*.[42] Despite being convinced – as were many others – that the Fourth Gospel was 'merely an ecclesiastical work', Moore has no qualms about borrowing from it liberally to add colour to *The Brook Kerith*.[43] The character of Nicodemus, who appears only in John, is portrayed as one of Jesus's more eccentric followers. Moore develops the spare Gospel portrait of the literal-minded Pharisee into that of an exotically attired young man 'with a taste for the beauty of engraved swords' (*BK* 204), creating an amusing foil to the reserved and fastidious Joseph. And though Joseph of Arimathea makes a fleeting appearance in all four Gospel accounts, Moore chooses to base his simulacrum on Matthew's description of him as 'a rich man' (Matthew 27:57). The distinction that comes from the adjective 'rich' generates one of the chief energies of the novel: the plight of a devoted disciple excluded on account of his wealth. Disregarding contemporary theorizing about the historical reliability of individual Gospels, Moore steers an impressionistic course through the New Testament narratives. In this way, he establishes a spirit of textual openness, allowing him to adapt his source to serve his novelistic purposes: Joseph can be presented as the sole mourner at the foot of the cross (*BK* 228), Mary and Martha can be charged with preparing Christ's body for burial (*BK* 235), and the Magdalene can be all but erased from the story.

In some instances, Moore goes further than simply reconfiguring the Gospel records, adding episodes and characters entirely from his own imagination. These additions are rarely successful, frequently jarring with the prevailing tone of the novel. This is certainly the case with the sub-plot concerning two young women, Ruth and Rachel, who vie for the attention of the same young man. It is a rivalry that results in the loser, Rachel, murdering the victor: a scenario more suited to a Victorian melodrama than a retelling of the life of Jesus. The story develops even more outlandishly as, just before Ruth is to be buried, Jesus raises her from the dead. Furious at being thwarted in her revenge, Rachel dashes over to her resuscitated enemy, only to be quelled by the gaze of Jesus, and 'like one overwhelmed with a great love she cast herself at his feet' (*BK* 177). From this time forward, Rachel takes on the role of Mary Magdalene, renouncing her life of the flesh along with all her wealth and finery. Unable to resist the eroticism of the sexually promiscuous woman worshipping a celibate master, Moore offers the reader the titillating picture of Rachel weaving her own golden comb through Jesus's hair, a fictional readjustment to Luke's account of the sinful woman using her hair to wipe Christ's feet. Yet, unlike the Magdalene of the Gospels, Rachel is kept very much in the background in a novel that affords women little significance. Mary and Martha might be the first to discover the empty tomb, but they are only able to 'babble about a young man in a white raiment' (*BK* 253) in response. Here, the verb 'babble' carries the full weight of a certain male disregard for the female religious tempera- ment, and Joseph's cynical certainty that they will go out and spread the untruth of Christ's resurrection is entirely in accord with his – and his society's – entrenched misogyny. On the relatively few occasions when women appear, they conform to a narrow range of essentially Victorian stereotypes: we have the faithful domestic servant in Esora, the scold in Simon Peter's wife, Miriam, and the fallen woman in Rachel. In *The Brook Kerith*, women are situated on the periphery of an entirely homosocial world, its author's chief interest lying in the three male characters at its centre. It is the stories of Joseph, Jesus and Paul that lend structure to the novel as each in turn moves away from female influences and towards the monastic seclusion of the Essene community.

Moore's abiding fascination with religious orders and the celibate life is shown through his choice of an Essene monastery for the main setting of the novel. His early works had tended to focus on the convent, presenting it as both prison and refuge. Scenes of young women escaping from convents feature in his first volume of poems, *Flowers of Passion* (1878), his first published play, *Martin Luther* (1879), and his early novel, *Mike Fletcher* (1889), while in *A Drama in Muslin* (1886) the cloister provides a sanctuary for the embittered lesbian, Cecilia. Moore continued to explore his theme in *Evelyn Innes* (1898) and *Sister Teresa* (1901), both of which offer rather more thoughtful considerations of conventual life. From the mid-point of his writing career, his attentions turned more towards the male reli- gious temperament, moving from *The Lake*, a story of one man's renunciation of priesthood, to examine the 'single strictness' of the Essene monks of *The Apostle* and *The Brook Kerith*.[44] Several theories about the roots of Moore's interest in the Essenes have been offered, both by his contemporaries and more recent critics. Almost a decade after the publication of *The Brook Kerith*, Joseph McCabe wrote that:

> Dining one night with George Moore, and discussing Jesus, I told him how I thought that Jesus was an Essenian monk. Moore [...] was more interested in Paul. But, like the great artist he is, he saw the value of my suggestion, and a little later appeared his literary drama, *The Apostle*.[45]

A more recent opinion is that his idea of associating Christ with the Essenes came to him a good deal earlier than McCabe claims, and stemmed from his reading of an essay by Thomas de Quincey, mentioned in a letter written by Moore in 1887.[46] Bearing in mind the discovery of the Dead Sea Scrolls in the 1940s, which offered a connection between Jesus and the Essenes, today's reader of *The Brook Kerith* could be forgiven for considering Moore's New Testament vision as remarkably prescient, regardless of its inspiration.[47] However, the link between the sect and Christ was a relatively commonplace idea, having attracted keen interest throughout the nineteenth century, even featuring in religious works intended for children.[48] Karl Venturini was the first writer to fully expound the theory that Essene monks had supervised Jesus from an early age and had later rehabilitated him after the trauma of crucifixion.[49] His *Natürliche Geschichte des grossen Propheten von Nazareth* was a text that, according to Albert Schweitzer, was 'plagiarized more freely than any other Life of Jesus'.[50] Indeed, Venturini's Essenian hypothesis appears frequently in a variety of narrative forms throughout the nineteenth century. For information about Essenian beliefs and practices Moore had to look no further than the well-publicized writings of Strauss, Hennell or Renan, and his study of the works of the first-century historian Josephus would also have afforded him a detailed account of the sect.

In choosing to focus on the Essenes, Moore moves away from the Gospel narratives with their emphasis on the Pharisees and the Sadducees, the Kerith monastery offering a curious, if not entirely unique, vantage point from which to reposition the life of Christ. The more traditional perspectives of Mary Magdalene, Judas, Peter and Mary Virgin, which tended to dominate contemporary imaginative treatments of the Gospels, are abandoned in favour of that of this rather enigmatic brotherhood. Moore also breaks away from previous literary versions of a resuscitated Jesus through his choice of setting. Where the Christ of Frank Harris's story 'The Miracle of the Stigmata' is an isolated man, forced to remain silent as all around him follow the new faith preached by Paul, the Jesus of *The Brook Kerith* is part of a community that rejects outright the apostle's preaching, turning inwards to its own well-established rules and belief systems. Yet in holding fast to such beliefs they are also obliged to look outwards to the stranger in need of shelter. As the novel progresses, the monks are seen to offer comfort to all three of the novel's main characters: a celibate environment for Joseph, whose distaste for women is emphasized throughout the novel; a safe house for Jesus after his trials in Jerusalem; and physical renewal for the apostle as he takes a rest from his strenuous missionary travels. And it is through the contrasting perspectives of these three main characters that Moore chooses to present his version of the New Testament and to signal the shifts in Christian belief that had taken place in the Victorian period. Joseph's idealized vision of Christ in the novel's opening section evokes the traditional image of Jesus, undisturbed by the latest in theology and science. The second stage of the novel presents Jesus through his own eyes as he is painfully brought to acknowledge the error in his claims to divinity. Such a realization places him as the novel's sceptic and brings him into direct conflict with Paul and his indomitable faith in the Resurrection. By the close of the novel, Jesus stands as the representative of modernist theology, with Paul standing for all those who stuck fast to their belief in the divinity of Christ and the inerrancy of the Bible, in defiance of all material proof to the contrary.

The figure of Joseph of Arimathea is built up from a few Gospel verses into a complex and intriguing character.[51] Moore's Joseph is of a hieratic disposition, sharing the 'almost morbid religious idealism' of Pater's Marius, a temperament that drives him to search for a religious philosophy that can satisfy both his natural asceticism and his sense of the numinous.[52] Struggling to cope with the demands of his father, Dan, alongside the demands of a life devoted to Jesus, Joseph's experiences highlight the inevitable difficulties that occur when the life of the spirit meets the life of the flesh. His devotion to his sick father incurs the wrath of Jesus, who tells him that there is 'no place among his followers for those who could not free themselves from such ghosts as father, mother and children and wife' (*BK* 184). In exploring Jesus's pronouncements on the insignificance of the family for true followers and, most especially, his own rather distant relationship with his mother, Moore was handling a subject that had long troubled some Christians. F. W. Farrar addressed such disquiet in his *Life of Christ*, explaining to his reader that Jesus's words to his mother, 'Woman, what have I to do with thee?' were not as harsh as an English translation suggested; rather, 'the address "Woman" [...] was so respectful that it might be, and was, addressed to the queenliest'.[53] Through the finely developed relationship between Joseph and his father, Moore presses home his own conviction that such demands are unreasonable and impossible to meet, at the same time preparing the way for Jesus's own realization that his former teaching 'was not less than blasphemy against God, for God has created the world for us to live in it, and he has put love of parents into our hearts because he wishes us to love our parents' (*BK* 434).

It is also through Joseph that the author explores the temperament of the natural celibate. The young man's aversion to marriage and his evident distaste for women create a certain tension within the character, conveyed through some of Moore's most ambitious narrative:

> His father desired grandchildren, and since he had partly sacrificed his life for his father's sake, he might, it seemed to him, sacrifice himself wholly. But could he? That did not depend altogether on himself, and with the view to discovering the turn of his sex instinct he called to mind all the women he had seen, asking himself as each rose up before him if he could marry her [...] He had seen some Greek women, and been attracted in a way, for they were not too like their sex; but these Jewish women – the women of his race – seemed to him as gross in their minds as in their bodies [...] (*BK* 194–95)

In this extract, Moore experiments fleetingly with free indirect discourse, presenting Joseph's question directly in the third line and suggesting his thought-processes – perhaps even a moment of recoil – through the parenthesis in the final sentence. However, the third-person perspective is never entirely relinquished, tag phrases such as 'it seemed to him' and 'he called to mind' serving to re-establish omniscient narrative control. Moore may have considered such control the most effective method of portraying Joseph's disciplined personality or he may, in this instance, have been keeping a tight rein on a subject that he realized might fall foul of the moral majority. Though Joseph's gynophobia would not in itself have caused offence to contemporary readers, its opening up of the possibility of his homosexuality most certainly would have done. In the 1927 Revised Edition of the novel, Moore seems to suggest something even more dangerous about Joseph's sexual preferences: that he is attracted to the person of Jesus. While in the first edition of the novel Joseph reflects how 'nothing interests me except Jesus' (*BK* 192), in the later version his reflection changes to 'nothing tempts me but Jesus', the change of verb hinting at something more erotic.[54] But if there are hints of homoerotic desire here, they are confined to Joseph alone. Hardened controversialist though he was, Moore could not have failed to realize that depicting a homosexual Christ was going way beyond the pale of biblical fiction.[55]

Perhaps Joseph's most crucial role in *The Brook Kerith* is to give fictional form to the theological theories that had congregated around the question of the risen Christ. As the eminent biblical scholar Geza Vermes outlines in a recent work, there are a number of competing theories that have grown up through the centuries to account for the resurrection, some of which derive from the Gospels themselves.[56] In reconstructing the post-crucifixion narrative Moore refuses to adhere strictly to any one of the main six theories outlined by Vermes. Where he follows materialist theologians in asserting that Jesus never actually died, he does not share the common rationalist belief that the resurrection was an elaborate hoax carried out by the disciples. Rather, he presents it as the decision-making of one man. Having removed the barely conscious Jesus from the tomb and carried him home to be nursed back to health, Joseph is under no illusion that his erstwhile master has risen from the dead; yet he makes no effort to prevent Mary and Martha from spreading their mistaken belief in Christ's resurrection. When asked by the sisters if he believes that Christ has 'risen', Joseph replies with lawyer-like attention to phrasing, 'Yes, I believe that Jesus lives' (*BK* 254), the semantic shift in the language of the response allowing for the false belief to be perpetuated, and setting in motion the mythopoeic process. Here, Joseph stands at the boundary line between the historical and the unhistorical. Entirely aware that he is presiding over a legend in the making, he observes with measured understatement as he watches Mary and Martha depart: 'A fine story they'll relate, one which will not grow smaller as it passes from mouth to mouth' (*BK* 254). And it is at this point that D. F. Strauss's ideas about the creation and development of the myth of the Resurrection take fictional form.

Recasting Jesus and St Paul

Moore's recasting of the New Testament story so that Jesus and his apostle are brought face to face freed him from the restraints of historical record. Allowing twenty-five years for the story of the risen Christ to take root, *The Brook Kerith* sees Paul arrive at the Essene monastery preaching the new faith to a Jesus so unaware of the falsification of his own life story that he needs to ask: 'Christians [...] And who are they?' (*BK* 429). By this stage in the narrative, we have encountered at least three distinct images of Christ: the charismatic young preacher, the failed Messiah and the Saviour born of Paul's imagination. In presenting the reader with more than one picture of Jesus, Moore moves away from former conceptions of the Christ figure that had become embedded in the British consciousness. If for some time he had been unsure about how his Jesus would turn out, he had been quite sure of the type of characterization he wanted to avoid. Moore's comment to Magee that his Jesus was 'an independent creation, and not [...] an attempt to discover what the real man was from the Gospels' is a clear assertion that he does not want to be associated with the aims of past biographers, whose Prefaces frequently declare their determination to uncover the 'true' Jesus.[57] Moore's success in distinguishing his Christ from those of so many of his forerunners lies in his presentation of him as entirely part of the Judaic world. The novel's opening chapter places the reader firmly in the world of the Old Testament, as Joseph's grandmother tells him the story of Saul's kingship, as recorded in Chapter 9 of 1 Samuel. Here, Moore takes the opportunity to rework biblical text, at the same time establishing the rhythms of the Scriptures from the outset. Later on in the novel, a contracted version of Psalm 11 (*BK* 367) and the even more familiar opening lines of the *Benedicite* (*BK* 368) are quoted directly in the context of the worship of the Essene monks, reminding the reader of the continuities between the Judaic faith and Christianity.

In representing Jesus as a culturally rooted and conditioned figure, Moore is challenging what was, for many, axiomatic to the Christian faith: that Jesus was a figure for all time, proclaiming timeless, universal truths. He is also departing from Renan and his like, who saw Jesus as the embodiment of 'an inexhaustible principle of moral regeneration for humanity'.[58] In emphasizing Jesus's Judaism, Moore seems to be adopting the more recent views of Albert Schweitzer whose *The Quest of the Historical Jesus* was already well known by the time *The Brook Kerith* was in its early stages. In his *History of New Testament Criticism*, F. C. Conybeare opens a chapter dealing with foreign works of theology with the statement: 'No work recently published in Germany has made a greater stir in England than Albert Schweitzer's *Von Reimarus zu Wrede* [*The Quest of the Historical Jesus*] [...] during the last hundred years.'[59] Considering that Moore liked nothing better than 'a stir', it is likely that he would have taken up Schweitzer's ideas through his own reading of the 1910 translation of *The Quest*, or gleaned them second-hand from the periodical press, or from some of his well-read friends. The controversial nature of Schweitzer's ideas lay in his viewing Jesus as an apocalyptic zealot, convinced that God would interrupt world history to usher in the new kingdom, and who subsequently attempts to bring about this divine intervention by suffering on the cross. The Jesus of *The Brook Kerith* is likewise steeped in Jewish eschatology, though the licence of fiction allows Moore to present his post-crucifixion realization that there is no new kingdom to be had and to explore the psychological consequences of his failed Messiahship.

Persuading the reader to consider Jesus and his ministry as part of Judaic faith and tradition rather than as the schismatic instigator of an entirely new faith required some ingenuity. Information about Jewish apocalyptic thought and the distinctive features of the three main religious sects had to be deftly introduced if the novel were not to read like one of the many nineteenth-century Lives of Jesus that overloaded the reader with 'background knowledge'. One way in which Moore strives to achieve this is through his description of the disciples. These followers of Jesus are literal-minded, slow-witted and completely incapable of grasping their master's anti-materialist philosophy; they expect Jesus to return 'in a chariot of fire by the side of his Father' (*BK* 258), and grow fractious when, three days after the crucifixion, there is still no sign of any such happening. Peter is treated with particular ridicule, most probably because he was, for Moore, the embodiment of Catholicism. He is drawn as the village idiot with a 'great head covered with frizzly hair' (*BK* 135), who can conceive of little 'beyond his sails and the fins of a fish' (*BK* 134). In presenting the apostles in such a prosaic light, Moore was following the views of numerous commentators, Matthew Arnold among them, who regarded Jesus's followers as imperfect reporters, limited in education and insight. Yet Moore exaggerates such views to a point verging on burlesque, and readers were not convinced by his rough-and-ready representation of the disciples. One reviewer dubbed them 'turbulent zanies',[60] while another considered that 'the Apostles are made out to be stupider than there is any good reason for thinking them'.[61] Nevertheless, this portrayal of what Moore himself described as a 'scurvy lot' aided him in his task of humanizing Christ. Compared to his disciples, Jesus appears very special indeed, and it seems entirely plausible that many should follow him merely on account of his earthly superiority, rather than for an ineffable quality of divinity. Moore takes an equally realistic approach to Judas. Resisting what Strauss defined as 'an over-strained supranaturalism' in his depiction of Christ's betrayer, Moore roots him firmly in the political and religious context of first-century Palestine, insisting that his act of betrayal is motivated by a genuine conviction that Christ's belief in himself as the Messiah is profoundly blasphemous.[62] And while Moore's description of Judas's 'large bony nose hanging over a thin black moustache that barely covered his lips' (*BK* 224) conforms to a certain Semitic stereotype of the time, he at least resists the well-worn tradition of presenting him as the archetypal Jew and the other disciples as fair-headed Gentiles.

Moore also attempts to give the reader a sense of Jesus in his time by exploring a range of contemporary perspectives on his life and ministry. Joseph's father, Dan, is the staunch traditionalist; it is he who poses that most memorable of Gospel questions as to whether any prophet can come out of Nazareth (John 1:46), and who counterpoints his son's eager recounting of Christ's miracles with his own highly sceptical assessment of the new leader. Further on in the narrative, Moore avoids the mawkish sentimentality with which so many authors of Lives of Jesus handled the Passion by presenting Christ's scourging, crucifixion and presumed moment of death through the dispassionate eyes of a centurion, habituated to the sight of men's sufferings on the cross and happy to make a little money out of helping Joseph acquire his master's corpse for burial. By shifting the narrative focus from one character to another, Moore ensures that the reader's impression of Christ is fragmented and multi-perspectival, offering no definitive truth about Jesus but only a number of partial truths.

It is clear from Moore's correspondence in the two years leading up to the publication of *The Brook Kerith* that he had thought long and hard about the aesthetic challenges of creating a figure human enough to bear no traces of divinity, and yet charismatic enough to command the reader's admiration and attention. In a letter to Dujardin, Moore expresses his doubts about being able to make anything out of a character whom 'Stripped of his miracles [...] is a sorry wight'.[63] However, writing to Magee a few months later, he seems to have overcome these reservations, and outlines what would form the core of his conception of Christ: 'It seems to me that great sweetness of mind and great harshness are found in the same person; Jesus was a typical example, for we find in him constantly these two strands.'[64] This bifurcation is exploited in two different ways in the course of the novel: through the dramatic fluctuations of mood Jesus undergoes during his ministry, and through the contrast between his pre-crucifixion and post-crucifixion psychological states. Leading up to the crucifixion, the disciples grow increasingly nervous of their master's black moods and, as his behaviour grows ever more violent and unpredictable, the apostle John remarks how 'he's a changed man; a lamb as long as you're agreeing with him, but at a word of contradiction, he's all claws and teeth' (BK 215). Jesus's darker moods bear the imprint of Schweitzer's conception of a deluded Messiah, consumed by apocalyptic fervour, though even Renan's much more sentimental portrait of Jesus, written four decades earlier, had indicated a similar splitting of the personality.[65] While Renan allows that Christ's vain hopes of an apocalypse might have been the 'errors of others rather than his own', he too suggests that the power of such a vision might have made the gentle, poetic prophet 'harsh and capricious' on occasions.[66]

Writing in a letter of 1927, shortly after the publication of the Revised Edition of The Brook Kerith, Moore explained how his depiction of a disillusioned Christ was not entirely fictive, but based on biblical text. He insists to Magee that the words 'said to have been spoken by Jesus on the cross before death: "My God, my God, why hast thou forsaken me?" [...] forbid the continuation of the Jesus that left the brook Kerith to reform the world', and that the phrase 'necessitated a new Jesus, a disillusioned Jesus'.[67] Here, Moore cites a scriptural text that had long perplexed Christian sensibilities and that was frequently invoked by those who denied Jesus's divinity. Moore's interpretation of the Passion narratives confirms the suspicions of the doubters: Jesus is indeed derelict on the cross, saved not by God the Father but by Joseph of Arimathea.[68] It is left to Joseph not only to nurse Jesus back to bodily strength but also to restore his sanity. Moore's detailing of Jesus's post-traumatic mental state testifies to the rapid growth of interest in psychology in the early twentieth century. In the 1800s, liberal Lives of Jesus, such as those by Seeley and Farrar, had ventured to complete a psychological reconstruction of the subject, reading in between the lines of the Gospel accounts. In general, however, they tended to impose personality traits on their subject that conformed to a Victorian notion of the perfect human being, and authors maintained a respectful distance between themselves and Christ. With the liberty that comes with prose narrative, Moore was able to present the thoughts and feelings of Jesus from an interior perspective, and to trace the steps in his mental recovery from a period of Messianic delusion.

The Brook Kerith explores a key concern of Freudian psychology: the repression of traumatic memories and its effects on the mind. While there is no good reason to suppose that Moore was acquainted first-hand with Freud's writings, he would doubtless have been aware of their existence through the discussions of his contemporaries, or the newspapers and journals of the day. Responding to an early review of the novel, Moore wrote: 'Jesus's reservation was part of the psychology of the anecdote, and it is with great care that I present him not only being unable to speak of his confusion and the idea that led up to it, but unable even to think of them.'[69] The Essene monastery provides Jesus with an environment that helps him cut off recollections of his painful past. The strict asceticism and self-sufficiency of the community serve to enclose and protect him from the harshness of the outside world. In this secluded society, his former image of himself as the good shepherd is realized quite literally in his tending of the monastery's flock of sheep, a labour that Moore had gathered a feeling for during his Palestinian travels:

> It was on my return that we came across the ideal monastery [...] I spent two nights there and climbed through a hole in the rock to the hills above, and lay there believing myself to be Jesus till a wild shepherd came by leading his flock exactly as in the story and then we talked together (through an interpreter it's true) and I learnt much about sheep farming on these desolate hills [...][70]

Yet however secure Jesus might seem in this pastoral, unthreatening world, Moore follows the logic of psychology in exposing the fragility of Jesus's state of denial. Fearful of being attacked by robbers, the brethren erect an immense wall to keep the community safe, an obvious symbol of the mind's defences; but its bricks and mortar are not enough to keep Jesus separate from external realities and his own inner demons. Accompanying his flock one day, Jesus encounters the spectacle of three robbers hanging on crosses, one of whom implores the passing shepherd to help him escape his torturous punishment. This harrowing experience releases memories long locked away and he sees his former self rise up before him: 'a man in a garden, in an agony of doubt' (*BK* 341). At this crucial point of the narrative, Jesus recovers the past he has kept at bay for so many years:

> He had lived in the ever-fleeting present for many years – how many? The question awoke him from his reverie, and he sat wondering how it was he could think so quietly of things that he had put out of his mind instinctively, till he seemed to himself to be a man detached as much from hope as from regret. (*BK* 342)

Here, though the narrative is briefly focalized through Christ himself (the self-questioning underscoring the interior nature of the observations), the omniscient viewpoint is swiftly restored, and Moore stops short at adopting a stream-of-consciousness technique. All the same, he goes further than most of the authors of biblical fiction and Lives of Jesus who precede him in presenting Christ's inner thoughts and emotions.

Moore's insistence that his story needed two Jesus figures, one driven by a Messianic mission and another disillusioned and solitary, obliged him to undertake the onerous task of explaining two distinct sets of religious and philosophical ideas held by Jesus at two different times of his life. If, in *The Apostle*, Moore had failed to incorporate the exegesis of the monks and the theological discourse of Paul into its dramatic rhythms, the prose genre allowed him the freedom to unfold such ideas incrementally, through more naturalistic dialogue. Leading up to his crucifixion, Jesus becomes increasingly immersed in Jewish eschatological thought, citing the Book of Daniel 'so that his disciples might have no fear that the priests of Jerusalem would have power to destroy him' (*BK* 152). And while his followers are entranced by the sheer narrative force of the story, he becomes rapt in its prophetic significance and begins to consider the kingdom of God to have arrived within himself.[71] Moore continues to chart Jesus's adoption of the Messianic role, revealing how his teachings become more and more apocalyptic, reaching their apex in his declaration that he 'will become one with his Father, and from that moment there will be but one God' (*BK* 224). It is a pronouncement that prompts Judas's betrayal and illustrates Moore's own conception of Jesus as 'one of the most terrifying fanatics that ever lived in the world', one who 'out-Nietzsched Nietzsche in the awful things he says in the Gospel of Luke'.[72] The arrogant, fanatical figure who enters Jerusalem with his 'heart [...] swollen with pride' (*BK* 225) belongs entirely to the early twentieth century, by which time, as Schweitzer observed, 'The liberal Jesus had given place to the Germanic Jesus' and the influence of Nietzsche had eclipsed that of Renan.[73] However, once *The Brook Kerith* abandons biblical sources for a purely imaginative narrative, Moore's Jesus breaks free of all typifications. Christ's post-crucifixion years are spent casting off his apocalyptic delusions and defining his own philosophy of life and its creator. The initial stage of this process is generated by Joseph, who disabuses him of the notion that he has been taken from the cross by angels of God. Gradually, the patient gathers enough strength to leave his disciple's care and to seek the solace of the Essene monastery. Once there, he seems to regain his communion with the God that he 'knew in Nazareth and in the hills above Jericho, and lost sight of [...] in the Book of Daniel' (*BK* 343). He embraces a philosophy whereby the creator is immanent in the natural world and rejects the texts and rituals of Judaism; though he lives with a religious brotherhood, he settles into an entirely secular role tending the community's livestock and carrying out the practical chores of the monastery. The arrival of the evangelizing Paul, however, forces Jesus to consider his relationship with God more deeply and he comes to the third stage of his theological reasoning, concluding that: 'The pursuit of an incorruptible crown leads us to sin as much as the pursuit of a corruptible crown' (*BK* 465). Jesus's final conviction is that God is an ontological phenomenon, perceptible through the consciousness of the individual alone. Unable to convince Paul that he is living proof that the resurrection never took place, Jesus prepares to 'go to Jerusalem [...] to tell the people that [he] was not raised from the dead' (*BK* 438). In a spirit of cruel irony, the novel has Jesus repudiate his own divinity and take on the disbelief of Moore's own age. While his earlier pantheism looked back to an era before the establishment of formalized religious practice, his final rejection of all concepts of God, other than that which is perceived by the individual moral consciousness, seems to look to a more secular age.

Moore was careful, however, not to modernize Jesus's thinking to the point of unfeasibility. In the process of composition he changed his plans for the ending of the novel so that Jesus's final doctrines are likened to those 'being preached by the monks from India' (*BK* 466). In repositioning his subject in the context of Eastern philosophy, Moore was also following one of the philosophical fashions of his era. Schopenhauer, and after him Nietzsche, recognized contiguities between Christianity and Buddhism, and the philosophy of *The*

Brook Kerith derives in part from Moore's interest in these thinkers.[74]
The influence of Schopenhauer can be detected in Jesus's eventual
realization that seeking God makes men 'the dupes of illusion and
desire' (*BK* 356) and that the ideal state is one of contemplative
freedom. And Nietzsche's asseveration in *The Antichrist* that
'Buddhism is a religion for the close and the worn-out-ness of civilization' seems entirely appropriate for Moore's mature Christ.[75] One
other possible influence on Moore's decision to incline Jesus's ultimate belief system towards the East is Arthur Lillie's *The Influence of
Buddhism on Primitive Christianity*. This highly conjectural work
makes the case for an historical Jesus that brings together, if in a rather
different configuration, the major elements of *The Brook Kerith*:
'Christ was an Essene monk [...] Christianity was Essenism; and [...]
Essenism was due, as Dean Mansel contended, to the Buddhist
missionaries "who visited Egypt within two generations of the time of
Alexander the Great".'[76] However, as is often the case, Moore may
well have gained his idea for a Jesus who progresses towards a form of
Buddhism from scholarly friends. Writing to Magee a few months
before the publication of *The Brook Kerith*, he places his insecure
grasp of the tenets of Buddhism in a positive light:

> you must admit that it is reasonable to suppose that his mind must
> have progressed through Pantheism to the verge of Buddhism. You
> understand Buddhism, I don't, and that was my luck, for if I had
> understood Buddhism I might have been tempted to attribute some
> of its doctrines to Jesus, whereas I had to invent a doctrine for him
> [...][77]

Here, Moore is clearly insisting upon the wholly inventive nature of
his creation. Yet the explicit references to the philosophy of Indian
monks in the novel's closing chapter invite the reader to envisage Jesus
entering a Buddhist community, rather than his adopting an entirely
independent theology. And what Moore deemed to be his invented
doctrine, that God was 'the last uncleanliness of the mind' (*BK* 357),
though entirely consistent with his characteristic relish of the
heretical, is also redolent of nineteenth-century German pessimism.

A few months prior to the publication of *The Brook Kerith*, Moore
told Magee that he had 'done better with Jesus than with Paul'.[78]
Though one relatively recent critic has dissented from such a view,
describing the Paul section of the narrative as 'striking [...] and breath-

taking', most of its readers and reviewers have tended to concur with this self-appraisal.[79] The eponymous hero of *The Apostle* is confined to the final quarter of *The Brook Kerith* and, unlike the character of Jesus, seems to have undergone little development from the drama scenario. Moore's explanation for his relative failure with Paul is that the apostle 'painted his own portrait and did it so thoroughly that he left [...] very little to add', and there is no doubt that his attempts to integrate the Epistles into the novel are not much more successful than his efforts to do so in the play.[80] Paul's account of his Damascene conversion and his subsequent evangelizing spreads over thirty or so pages (*BK* 391–423), interrupting what has been up to this point a generally fluent and mosaic narrative. His story, while presented as fascinating for the Essene brethren who hear it, fails to fully engage the reader, being little more than a maladroit modernizing of the Epistles. In the Revised Edition of 1927, Moore attempts to remedy such failings by occasionally shifting the narrative perspective to Paul by way of free indirect speech. Take, for example, the crucial moment where Jesus offers him incontrovertible physical evidence that he has not risen from the dead: 'Jesus continued talking, showing at every moment such an intimate and personal knowledge of Galilee that Paul could not doubt he was [...] a Nazarene. But what of that? There are hundreds of Nazarenes, many of which were called Jesus.'[81] By conveying Paul's thoughts in his own mental idiom, Moore underlines the extent of the apostle's self-delusion, as well as his inexhaustible resilience in the face of adversity. Jesus's silent departure after expounding his personal conception of God to Paul is in stark contrast to the violent conclusion of their meeting in *The Apostle*. By removing Jesus physically from Paul's vicinity, he allows the evangelist to recover his equilibrium and to turn his face towards Italy. The final image of Paul in Rome speaking 'from morning to evening' (*BK* 471) seems antithetical to that of the silent, introspective Jesus making his way to India. In another sense, though, Paul's impassioned preaching echoes that of Jesus shortly before his arrest and trial and is the last in a series of mirror images of Christ. Earlier in the novel Paul had considered whether he had been led to the Essene monastery 'to find twelve disciples' (*BK* 384) in imitation of the Saviour and, like Jesus before him, had expressed his belief in the incarnation of the word. This paralleling of the two men is made explicit when Jesus observes to Paul 'I can comprehend thee, for once I was thou' (*BK* 465) and demonstrates Moore's conviction that, however secular an age may be, a strong religious temperament will continue to flourish in certain men.

If there is one aspect of Paul's portrait in *The Apostle* that Moore takes particular care to retain and develop in *The Brook Kerith*, it is that of his capacity for storytelling. Just as Renan considered Paul's revelations as 'the fruit of his own brain', so Moore demonstrates through fictional means that the apostle's idea of Christ is entirely from his imagination.[82] Reliant from the first on the disciples' story-telling for his knowledge of Jesus, and later on his own powers of narrative to capture the audiences he aims to convert, Paul arrives at the Essene monastery with his own life experiences already shaped by numerous retellings. It is evident to Mathias, one of the elders of the community, that Paul 'however crude and elementary his conceptions might be […] was a story in himself' (*BK* 383). The more he repeats the account of his conversion, the more he becomes 'rapt […] in the Jesus of his imagination' (*BK* 462), and the more strength he acquires to promote and develop the story that will form the very basis of the Christian church. Jesus's resigned acceptance that 'The world cannot be else than the world' (*BK* 463) means that he no longer feels obliged to return to Jerusalem to refute accounts of the risen Christ, and Paul's myth-making is given free rein.

In keeping with both the New Testament sources and the tendency of modernist prose works to resist narrative closure, Moore with-stands the temptation to supply a fictional resolution to the life of the apostle, the final sentence of the novel stating abruptly that 'The rest of his story is unknown' (*BK* 471). However, he could not entirely resist speculating about Paul's last moments on earth. In the preface to the 1921 edition, he outlines how Paul, sixty years old and weary from his travels, is discovered in a faint by a young shepherd. The boy, who Paul mistakes for Jesus, attempts to revive him but to no avail. After speaking his final words: 'take thy faithful servant in thine arms and bear him into thy house, made not with hands but in the eternity of the heavens', Paul dies and is given an obscure burial in a cavity among the rocks. Though the young boy knows nothing about the man he has buried, he is 'conscious that something great and noble has passed out of the world'.[83]

A quest for the perfect style

It is clear from Moore's correspondence and his autobiographical writing that he wanted *The Brook Kerith* to be received as an original and well-informed revision of the New Testament. Even more than this, though, he wanted the novel to confirm his status as a great literary stylist. Moore was always anxious about his writing technique, constantly experimenting to find a signature rhythm and diction and revising previously published work with a vigour verging on the compulsive. Moore's self-consciousness about his writing militated in every way against what he most desired: a 'natural' prose style. As W. B. Yeats shrewdly – if a little unkindly – observed 'His nature, bitter, violent, discordant, did not fit him to write the sentences men murmur again and again for years. Charm and rhythm had been denied him.'[84] In taking on a biblical subject, Moore set himself two particularly demanding tasks: to work from a source text admired for centuries for its stylistic beauty, and to combine this with contemporary ideas about the New Testament narratives.

Moore worked painstakingly to ensure that the language of *The Brook Kerith* did justice to the epic nature of its subject matter. Choosing a fitting title proved especially burdensome, not least for some of his long-suffering advisers. In April 1915 he wrote to Gosse:

> I know I shall not be able to think of anything better than *The Apostle*. I thought 'The Penitents' exhaled a fine flavour. But if you don't like it I won't use it. Anything in the line of *Lost Illusions* would be silly, and would draw attention to a side of the story that speaks for itself.[85]

A reliable correspondent and willing critic, Gosse was quick to reply, and Moore wrote to him again, just three days later:

> I am within sight of my last chapter and am still without a title. I agree with you that 'The Apostle' is very dry and 'The Penitents' no longer pleases me and I can think of nothing else unless I call the book by the name of the gorge in which the Cenoby is situated – 'The Brook of the Chariots'. I would like a more human title but it does not seem to find one. To call the book 'The Brook of the Chariots' is very much like calling 'Esther Waters' 'The Traveller's Rest'. 'Jesus of Nazareth' is hackneyed and pompous. 'At John's Door' is

a criticism and is, therefore, quite impossible.[86]

Following this, and after flirting briefly with 'Hermit and Wayfarer', Moore fixed on 'The Brook of the Chariots', which was eventually to settle into the title by which the novel is known today. The agonizing process that led to the final decision is perhaps familiar to most fiction writers anxious to send their work out into the world with a title that best announces and captures its essence, though it was perhaps inevitable that naming a heterodox novel about Jesus would be more than usually tricky. What the correspondence between Moore and Gosse reveals is that Moore wanted to separate his novel from the vast number of existing fiction and non-fiction works entitled 'Jesus of Nazareth' and by far the safest option was a non-committal place name.

Finding a prose style to capture the person and milieu of Jesus himself would prove equally taxing. In reading Lives of Jesus such as Renan's, Moore would have encountered the ideal of the poet-Jesus, and while he tended to steer clear of this romanticized image, he could not but be aware of the burden that it placed on any writer repre-senting Christ's own words in fictional form. In *The Brook Kerith*, Jesus's speech is described as 'moving on with a gentle motion like that of clouds wreathing and unwreathing' (*BK* 122), and the prose of the novel itself strives to emulate such fluency. To avoid impeding the narrative flow, Moore omits speech marks, composes paragraphs of unusual density and keeps upper-case letters to a minimum. But while this has a striking effect on the page, the desired fluency is found wanting in the act of reading. The prose is interrupted by the frequent inclusion of reporting verbs which, since the standard punctuation of direct speech has been removed, are necessary to make clear who is talking. Similarly, Moore's drawing back from the consistent use of interior monologue obliges him to include phrases such as 'Jesus said to himself' and 'as these thoughts passed through his mind', which further impede the smooth line of the writing. However, one realiza-tion that saved the prose of *The Brook Kerith* from being disrupted even more severely was that 'No one can quote except Pater without bursting up his text.'[87] Moore's re-reading of *Marius* seems to have convinced him that he could never carry off Pater's subtle intertextu-ality and that, in contrast to so many of his forerunners in New Testament fiction, he should desist from using direct quotations from the Gospels to supplement his own prose writing.

Instead, Moore employed a number of indirect methods to insinuate the text of the New Testament into *The Brook Kerith*. Keeping the pre-crucifixion figure of Jesus firmly in the background for the first half of the novel, his words are presented second-hand through the voices of a variety of observers. Moore ensures that familiar sayings of Christ are slightly altered, so that, for example, the scriptural image of the camel unable to pass through the eye of the needle becomes the rather less outlandish 'sword [...] through the eye of the needle' (*BK* 202). Attention is drawn to this linguistic adjustment when Joseph tells Nicodemus how Jesus adapts expressions to suit his audience: where the wealthy listener is offered the image of the sword, his poorer brother hears how 'it is as hard for a rich man to enter the kingdom of heaven as it would be for a cow to calve in a rook's nest' (*BK* 202). In presenting the sayings of Christ as unfixed and dependent on audience, Moore reminds the reader of the orality of these teachings, and in doing so casts doubt on the inerrancy of the Gospels. If the words of Jesus are freshly minted to suit each new listener, then those that eventually found their way into the Evangelists' testimonies can only ever form a partial representation of his ministry. Yet in rewriting familiar texts to drive home ideas about the authenticity of the Gospel record, Moore laid himself open to the charge of compromising the stylistic beauties of the source text, especially the Authorized Version. One reviewer spoke for many in observing that 'To those of us who know the gospel story in that well-nigh inspired translation of 1610 [...] Mr Moore's apocryphal conversations will not impress.'[88] His attempts to create colloquial speech rhythms for the more rustic characters of the novel were met with particular derision, the phrasing of the boatman's warning to Joseph that 'there be a bit of a walk before thee' (*BK* 88) prompting one reviewer to wonder why a Palestinian ferryman should feel compelled to 'converse in the Somerset dialect'.[89] However, if there were plenty willing to point out the bathos and inconsistencies in Moore's prose style, there were others prepared to defend it. One critic suggested that *The Brook Kerith* was 'reminiscent of Pater's "Marius the Epicurean"', a flattering comparison that Moore must have found particularly gratifying.[90] Rather more interesting was the comment by one of Moore's stenographers, Anna Kelly, that the style is 'very like his physique – soft, full of light – and boneless', suggestive of a strange form of *écriture féminine*.[91] Several other critics made direct connections between the man and his writing, detecting a strong Irish lilt to the prose. Moore staunchly denied such suggestions, declaring in the postscript of a letter to Ernest Boyd that he did 'not think that there is a single Irish idiom in the book [...] all the idiomatic turns in *The Brook Kerith* are to be found in the Bible and [...] the Elizabethan prose writers'.[92]

Moore's confidence in the success of his biblical prose style was by no means secure. A year or so after its publication, he told Richard Best that *The Brook Kerith* had been written far too quickly, and Geraint Goodwin recalled the author telling him that he had 'spent ten years picking out the daisies' in order to perfect 'a green lawn'.[93] The outcome of this decade of meticulous weeding was the 1927 Revised Edition of *The Brook Kerith*. Moore's concern to create the biblical mood that some critics felt had eluded him is clearly discernible in this later version. Throughout the text the more archaic 'thee' and 'thou' forms replace the more modern 'you', regardless of the speaker's age or status, a change that Moore claimed to be a reversion to his original choice of grammar, before W. B. Yeats had convinced him otherwise. In *Conversations in Ebury Street* Moore protests that 'Yeats, whose business it is to set people on the wrong track, warned me against the second person singular, and [...] I tried to stint myself to the miserable *you*, which is not a word but a letter of the alphabet, at least in sound; but to weed out the *yous* means something more than grammatical changes; every sentence has to be recast.'[94] Unfortunately it was a recasting too far, resulting in little more than syntactical contortion. One other immediately noticeable example of restyling is in the organization of the text. The even denser conflation of paragraphs throughout the Revised Edition suggests that Moore wanted to lend his prose a more modernist, unconventional quality; yet at the same time, his replacing of lower-case letters with upper-case to indicate more clearly where new speech begins seems a concession to the more traditional reader. Some of the author's lexical revisions focus on Jesus himself, and tend to moderate the presentation given in the original version. The description of Christ's 'lean face, lit with brilliant eyes' (*BK* 100) in the 1916 edition is altered to the gentler 'lean jaws and thoughtful eyes', dissipating the unnerving energy of the original.[95] None of these revisions, however, amounts to anything of real significance for the novel's overall vision of the Gospels. The prose of the final version shows little improvement on the original, perhaps proving Yeats's point that Moore's relentless pursuit of style 'made barren his later years'.[96]

One of the major contentions of Albert Schweitzer's *The Quest of the Historical Jesus* was that nineteenth-century authors of Lives of Jesus had been unable to break free of contemporary forms of thought. By the beginning of the twentieth century, it had become a truism that writers who took on the challenge of recreating the Gospels ended up writing about their own life and times. A number of commentators discerned autobiographical elements in *The Brook Kerith*, several likening the author to Joseph of Arimathea, a character constantly in search of a philosophy for life, and while Moore was happy to go along with the parallel so far, he was anxious that it should not extend to his feelings for women, telling Magee, somewhat defensively, that 'Joseph is very nice [...] despite his aversion from women, an aversion which his creator does not share'.[97] Others read the novel in the context of Ireland and Irish Catholicism. John Freeman recognized 'the soft, green, remembered Ireland' in Moore's evocation of Palestine,[98] and the reviewer of the *Nation* regarded it as a political *roman à clef*, with Nicodemus as 'a palpable Sinn Feiner, passionately, impetuously, vigorously identifying Jesus as the O'Connor [*sic*] of Home Rule for Judea'.[99] There are, indeed, passages in the novel more redolent of a hellfire sermon delivered from a Roman Catholic pulpit in County Mayo than of first-century Palestine, such as Jesus's exhortation to Nicodemus to follow him 'or else be for ever accursed and destroyed and burnt up like weeds that the gardener throws into heaps and fires on an autumn evening' (*BK* 222). And it is difficult to ignore the author's personality when reading the novel's ten-page digression describing the visit to the Kerith monastery of Essene monks who had split from the community in order to marry. The schismatic monks' detailing to their celibate listeners of their dismal sexual experiences with their wives is a typical example of Moore's puerile sexual imagination overriding his sense of aesthetics.

Artistic flaws and critical detractors notwithstanding, *The Brook Kerith* quickly established itself as the work to which all writers of religious fiction should look. One American critic advised readers that to appreciate its greatness, one had only to compare it to Guy Thorne's 'extravagant melodrama' *When It Was Dark*[100] and, fifteen years after its publication, the *Times Literary Supplement* employed it as a literary benchmark in its review of D. H. Lawrence's Resurrection fiction, *The Man Who Died*.[101] Seen in the context of Moore's work as a whole, it stands as his most strident declaration of his own quirky brand of Protestantism and of his conviction that 'people have to make their own religion'.[102] In defining the novel as 'simply Unitarian',[103] and insisting that its Jesus is 'as Protestant as Renan's [...] is Catholic', the author remained faithful to his belief that Protestantism and agnosticism were virtually interchangeable.[104] Too inconsistent and contradictory to be considered a thesis novel, *The Brook Kerith* is rather a testament to its author's deepening personal involvement with the Gospels and the modernist theology of his day.

Notes

1 *Letters of George Moore, With an Introduction by John Eglinton*, p. 75.
2 In the preface to the New Edition of *The Lake* (London: William Heinemann, 1921), Moore lists the works that he would like to be excised from his canon, quipping that 'all these books, if they are ever reprinted again, should be issued as the works of a disciple – Amico Moorini' (p. x).
3 *Letters of George Moore, With an introduction by John Eglinton*, p. 36. In a further letter to Magee, Moore states that 5,000 copies of *The Brook Kerith* were sold in the month following its publication. See Adrian Frazier, *George Moore 1852–1933* (New Haven and London: Yale University Press, 2000), p. 403.
4 See Robert Langenfeld, *George Moore: An Annotated Secondary Bibliography of Writings About Him* (New York: AMS Press, 1987), pp. 105–17, for details of the energetic correspondence between the author and his readers.
5 The writer of the foreword to a 1950s' edition of *The Brook Kerith* still deemed it necessary to justify the novel's treatment of a biblical subject, averring that the work is 'in no sense a perverse piece of religious controversy' and will 'neither anger nor offend those who accept the Bible story of the life and death of Christ'. See *The Brook Kerith* (London: Penguin Books, 1952).
6 *Manchester Guardian*, 29 September 1916, p. 5.
7 See '"The Brook Kerith". Process for Blasphemy Refused', *The Times*, 7 September 1916, p. 3.
8 *Times Literary Supplement*, 1 June 1916, pp. 253–54.
9 Robertson, *The Historical Jesus*, pp. xxiii–xxiv.
10 This physical re-enactment of the crucifixion was translated back into symbolic form in the Derwent sculpture, later withdrawn from exhibition when the story was dismissed as propaganda; recent evidence has, however, prompted a reconsideration of the incident. See Iain Overton, 'The crucified soldier', *The Tablet*, 19 April 2003, pp. 15–16.
11 *Spectator*, 115 (11 September 1915), p. 336.
12 *The Times*, 24 December 1915, p. 7.
13 Perhaps in response to the multiplicity of Christ images that proliferated in imaginative writings during the war years, one highly dubious publication purported to transmit Christ's own pronouncements on the conflict, among them the order forbidding 'the making of images of My Crucifixion for any purpose whatsoever'. See *Recent Words from Christ upon This War and upon Our Coming Deliverance:*

Taken down by a Scribe (London: Cecil Palmer & Hayward, 1918), p. 27.

14 Graves, *5 Pens in Hand*, pp. 123–24.

15 *Dial*, 61 (21 September 1916), pp. 191–93 (p. 191).

16 *Daily Express*, 31 August 1916, p. 3.

17 *Daily Express*, 4 September 1916, p. 2; 8 September 1916, p. 2.

18 Elizabeth Grübgeld, *George Moore and the Autogenous Self* (Syracuse, NY: Syracuse University Press, 1994), p. 241.

19 George Moore, *The Brook Kerith: A Syrian Story* (Edinburgh: T. Werner Laurie, 1916), p. 465. Hereafter cited in the text as *BK*.

20 *George Moore on Parnassus*, pp. 292–93.

21 Vernon Bartlet, 'A Personal Vindication', *Westminster Gazette*, 48 (3 October 1916), p. 2.

22 *Manchester Guardian*, 29 September 1916, p. 5.

23 'A New Christian Legend', *Saturday Review*, 122 (2 September 1916), p. 228.

24 *George Moore on Parnassus*, p. 284.

25 *Letters of George Moore, With an Introduction by John Eglinton*, p. 21.

26 In a letter to Eliza Aria, Moore wrote: 'A twelve hours ride in the desert is an experience that one would prefer to have behind one than in front of one. One generally gets it behind' (*George Moore on Parnassus*, pp. 286–87).

27 George Moore to W. T. Stead, National Library of Ireland, MS 2648, f. 5.

28 George Moore, *Modern Painting* (London: Walter Scott, 1893), p. 54.

29 John, *Chiaroscuro*, p. 226.

30 George Moore, *The Brook Kerith* (Edinburgh: T. Werner Laurie, 1921), p. ix.

31 Eglinton, *Irish Literary Portraits*, p. 108.

32 Moore, *The Brook Kerith* (1921), p. x.

33 Eglinton, *Irish Literary Portraits*, p. 109.

34 *The Pastoral Loves of Daphnis and Chloë: Done into English by George Moore* (London: William Heinemann, 1924), p. 1.

35 *Moore versus Harris*, p. 12.

36 Extensive study had been made of the anatomical details of crucifixion and the wealth of material available on the subject renders it impossible to ascertain the exact provenance of Moore's information. One text that would have afforded Moore plenty of detail about Roman crucifixion was David Smith's *The Days of His Flesh* (London: Hodder and Stoughton, 1905). A popular work, it went into new editions until 1911; see especially pp. 494–97. We can be sure that Moore consulted Roman authors such as Suetonius, whose accounts of crucifixion he mentions in a letter to Magee (*Letters of George Moore, With an Introduction by John Eglinton*, p. 22).

37 *Letters of George Moore, With an Introduction by John Eglinton*, p. 22.

38 *Letters of George Moore, With an Introduction by John Eglinton*, p. 76.

39 For a survey of the numerous theories put forward to explain this Johannine detail, see J. H. Bernard, *The International Critical Commentary: A Critical and Exegetical Commentary on the Gospel According to St John*, 2 vols (Edinburgh: T. & T. Clark, 1976), II, pp. 646–48.

40 *Times Literary Supplement*, 7 December 1946, p. 601.

41 Graves, *5 Pens in Hand*, p. 125.

42 *Letters of George Moore, With an Introduction by John Eglinton*, p. 30.

43 George Moore, 'A Prefatory Letter on Reading the Bible for the First Time', *The English Review*, 7 (February 1911), pp. 452–65 (p. 457).

44 Moore was pleased with his phrase 'single strictness'; it formed the new title of the 1922 revision of the short story volume *Celibates* (1895). In the Revised Edition of *The Brook Kerith* (London: Heinemann, 1927), the phrase replaces the 'celibates' of the first edition (see p. 296 of both editions).

45 McCabe, *The Myth of the Resurrection*, p. 85.

46 Robert Stephen Becker puts forward this theory in his article 'Private Moore, Public Moore: the Evidence of the Letters', published in *George Moore in Perspective*, ed. Janet Egleson Dunleavy (Gerrards Cross: Colin Smythe, 1983), p. 78; the letter from which he derives his evidence is published in his PhD thesis: 'Letters of George Moore, 1863–1901', University of Reading, 1980, p. 151.

47 See George J. Brooke, *The Dead Sea Scrolls and the New Testament* (London: SPCK, 2005) for a recent discussion of the relationship between Essenism and Christianity.

48 See, for example, J. Estlin Carpenter, *Life in Palestine When Jesus Lived* (London: Sunday School Association, 1889), pp. 144–47.

49 Karl Venturini, *Natürliche Geschichte des grossen Propheten von Nazareth* (Copenhagen, 1800–02).

50 Schweitzer, *The Quest of the Historical Jesus*, p. 46.

51 Of course, Moore was not original in his choice of Joseph of Arimathea as one of his leading characters. Though only a fleeting presence in the Gospels, his legendary status grew steadily from the mid-twelfth century, or so, making him an attractive figure for the creative imagination. He appears in poetic works that span the centuries, including Malory's *Le Morte D'Arthur* (1470), Spenser's *The Fairie Queen* (1590–96), Blake's *The Four Zoas* (1795–1804), and Tennyson's *The Idylls of the King* (1891).

52 Walter Pater, *Marius the Epicurean*, 2 vols (London: Macmillan, 1885), I, p. 33.

53 Farrar, *The Life of Christ*, I, p. 165. In a rather less conventional work, *The Woman's Bible*, ed. E. C. Stanton et al. (New York: European Publishing Company, 1895), an anonymous contributor asks: 'How did it happen that Christ did not visit his mother after his resurrection?' and goes on to question why Mary was treated so coldly by her son (p. 144).

54 *The Brook Kerith* (1927), p. 192.

55 According to Joseph McCabe, Moore 'loathed the very sound of the word sodomy' (*Eighty Years a Rebel*, p. 64); if this had been the case, any homosexual overtones in *The Brook Kerith* must have been unconscious on the author's part. Adrian Frazier was the first of Moore's biographers to engage with the issue of his possible homosexuality.

56 Geza Vermes, *The Resurrection* (Harmondsworth: Penguin Books, 2008), pp. 143–49.

57 *Letters of George Moore, With an Introduction by John Eglinton*, pp. 29–30.

58 Renan, *The Life of Jesus*, p. 307.

59 F. C. Conybeare, *History of New Testament Criticism* (London: Watts, 1910), p. 97.

60 *The Nation*, 19 (23 September 1916), pp. 800–02 (p. 800).

61 *Times Literary Supplement*, 14 September 1916, p. 438.

62 Strauss, *The Life of Jesus Critically Examined*, III, p. 126.

63 *Letters from George Moore to Ed. Dujardin*, p. 104.

64 *Letters of George Moore, With an Introduction by John Eglinton*, p. 24.

65 Such speculations concerning the harsher elements of Jesus's personality are, of course, supportable from the New Testament texts; see, for example, Matthew 17:17 and Luke 9:41 where Jesus castigates the assembled crowd for being 'a faithless and perverse generation'.

66 Renan, *The Life of Jesus*, pp. 204, 226.

67 *Letters of George Moore, With an Introduction by John Eglinton*, p. 77.

68 Christ's words from the cross (Matthew 27:46; Mark 15:34) echo the opening verse of Psalm 22. Some commentators have speculated that the rest of the psalm was lost amid the noise and chaos of the crucifixion scene, others that the early readers of the Gospels would have understood Christ's words in terms of a Jewish midrash, where only the first part is quoted and the rest is allowed to go unspoken. Orthodox readers have explained Christ's anguish as the climax of his abandonment by his countrymen, his disciples and the crucifixion crowd, the supreme moment of pain before God's final vindication.

69 *The Westminster Gazette*, 15 September 1916, pp. 1–2 (p. 2).

70 Letter from George Moore to Edmund Gosse, 11 March 1914, National Library of Ireland, MS 2134.

71 The Book of Daniel came under increasing scrutiny as the nineteenth century wore on. Of particular interest was the relationship of Daniel's vision of 'one like a son of man' (Daniel 7:13) to Christ himself.

72 *Letters of George Moore, With an Introduction by John Eglinton*, p. 23.

73 Schweitzer, *The Quest of the Historical Jesus*, p. 275.

74 Moore had demonstrated his interest in Schopenhauer in a number of his works, most notably *A Mere Accident* (1887) and *Mike Fletcher* (1889). For a discussion of the influence of Schopenhauer on Moore's fiction see Michael W. Brooks, 'George Moore, Schopenhauer, and the origins of *The Brook Kerith*', *English Literature in Transition 1880–1920*, 12 (November 1969), pp. 21–31.

75 *The Works of Friedrich Nietzsche*, trans. Thomas Common, p. 268.

76 Arthur Lillie, *The Influence of Buddhism on Primitive Christianity* (London: Swan Sonnenschein, 1893), p. v.

77 Quoted in Hone, *The Life of George Moore*, pp. 328–29.

78 Hone, *The Life of George Moore*, p. 329.

79 William Hamilton, *A Quest for the Post-Historical Jesus* (London: SCM Press, 1993), p. 201.

80 Hone, *The Life of George Moore*, p. 329.

81 Moore, *The Brook Kerith* (1927), p. 451.

82 Renan, *The Apostles*, p. 178.

83 Moore, *The Brook Kerith* (1921), p. xiv.

84 Yeats, *Autobiographies*, p. 438.

85 George Moore to Edmund Gosse, 28 April 1915, National Library of Ireland, MS 2134.

86 George Moore to Edmund Gosse, 3 May 1915, National Library of Ireland, MS 2134.

87 *Letters of George Moore, With an Introduction by John Eglinton*, p. 25.

88 C. K. Shorter, 'A Literary Letter: Mr George Moore's Romance of Syria', *Sphere*, 66 (9 September 1916), p. 238.

89 *The Nation*, 19 (23 September 1916), pp. 800–02 (p. 800).

90 'A New Christian Legend', *Saturday Review*, 122 (2 September 1916), p. 228.

91 Rodgers, *Irish Literary Portraits*, p. 92.

92 *George Moore on Parnassus*, pp. 330–31. Moore seems to have in mind here the traditional link between the Bible and Shakespeare, a link frequently made by writers of liberal Lives of Jesus.

93 Geraint Goodwin, *Conversations with George Moore* (London: Ernest Benn, 1929), p. 148.

94 Moore, *Conversations in Ebury Street*, p. 25.

95 Moore, *The Brook Kerith* (1927), p. 99.

96 Yeats, *Autobiographies*, p. 437.

97 *Letters of George Moore, With an Introduction by John Eglinton*, p. 27.

98 Freeman, *A Portrait of George Moore*, p. 196.

99 *The Nation*, 19 (23 September 1916), p. 800.

100 'George Moore's Story of Christ', *Boston Evening Transcript*, 30 August 1916, Part II, p. 6.

101 'The Man who Died', *Times Literary Supplement*, 2 April 1931, p. 267.

102 George Moore to Mrs Virginia M. Crawford, 19 August 1902, National Library of Ireland, MS 2645, f. 36.

103 *George Moore on Parnassus*, p. 289.

104 *Letters of George Moore, With an Introduction by John Eglinton*, p. 52. Moore persisted in his conviction that his Jesus and Paul scenario was Unitarian in sentiment, telling Granville-Barker that *The Apostle* 'may be acted in America; America is full of unitarians [*sic*]'. See *Conversations in Ebury Street*, p. 227.

Conclusion

> The ideas of Christian Theology are too
> simple for eloquence, too sacred for fiction [...]
> Samuel Johnson, *The Lives of the Poets*

One of the consequences of the nineteenth-century quest for the historical Jesus was a marked growth in biblical fiction. The more energetically European theologians sought out the Jesus of fact and history, the more he became a figure of the fictive imagination. It was a paradox that was particularly pronounced in Britain. Somewhat inclined to take up a conservative, even reactionary stance to the Higher Criticism, the British turned instead to Lives of Jesus, in many respects a pragmatic response to the ever-increasing divide between the Christ of dogmatic Christology and the Jesus of history. The majority of English Lives of Jesus were not, as any serious theologian would have wished, produced by scholars of religion. William Sanday, one of Britain's foremost biblical critics during the years covered in this study, was one of those who steadfastly resisted the lure of Gospel biography, choosing instead to publicize the work of Continental scholars to an English readership through numerous critical studies and journal articles. The most influential and popular Victorian Lives were written by non-theologians: *Ecce Homo* was the work of an historian, with successive prominent biographies coming from the pens of churchmen such as F. W. Farrar, William Hanna and Alfred Edersheim. While critical apparatus in the form of footnotes and lists of scholarly authorities gave these Lives some semblance of the academic method, there was little serious theology to be found beyond the paratexts. This absence of theological rigour and engagement was very much as D. F. Strauss had predicted in 1865:

And so the conception of a life of Christ was ominous of coming change. It anticipated the broad results of modern theological development. It lay as a snare in the path of the latter, prognosticating in its special incompatibilities the general disruption of traditional belief. It was as a pit into which theology was inevitably destined to fall and to become extinguished.[1]

The prevailing taste for Lives of Jesus was not only held responsible for casting theology into the pit: it was also arraigned for failing to take seriously the responsibilities of the biographer. As one turn-of-the-century critic pointed out: '[T]here was always a desire among these writers to display more of the artist than of the biographer. Whether conservative or liberal, they aimed more at edifying their respective audiences than at making them acquainted with the real events of the time.'[2] In looking back over a half-century or so of Lives, this observer is able to identify what Strauss could not have foreseen in the 1860s – that the main method of presenting Jesus was often closer to that of the fiction writer than the theologian. In an era of increasing religious uncertainty, investing studies of Jesus with the narrative qualities of the popular novel had become a vital means of either protecting the Scriptures from the destructive influence of theological modernism or, rather less commonly, of making modern scholarship more readable for the non-specialist. Though essentially conservative in their aims, stylistic register and religious sentiments, Lives of Jesus were nonetheless the products of modernity, moving the reader slowly but surely away from notions of divinity; after all, a part-human, part-supernatural being was not the usual stuff of biography. The sheer bulk of Lives of Jesus testifies to their essentially fictive nature: the spare narratives of the New Testament could only expand to such proportions through the addition of extra-biblical material generated by a lively imagination. As the literary marketplace became ever more competitive, and society became ever more accepting of this blend of religious biography and fiction, it was perhaps inevitable that one element of the hybrid would gain prominence. Writing in the 1880s, the poet and novelist Robert Buchanan asserted confidently that:

We have reached the vantage-ground where the story of Jesus can be taken out of the realm of Supernaturalism and viewed humanly, in the domain of sympathetic Art. To even so late an observer as Rénan [sic] such a point of view was difficult, not to say impossible.[3]

And indeed, in the last quarter of the century, orthodox and heterodox alike abandoned the speculative mood of the biographer and fought out their respective views of the Gospels through the novel or short story. In most cases, writers of biblical prose fiction paid far more attention to the demands of narrative than to those of theology. Details from the four Evangels were selected for their imaginative appeal – regardless of scholarly views on their historical credibility – and were woven into a form of narrative harmony akin to those formerly constructed by pious Christians in an attempt to erase the disturbing discrepancies of the four-fold Gospels. Similarly, theological hypotheses were selected with an eye to their inventive potential rather than their academic respectability.

The formal marriage of literature and theology was not, in its early years at least, a very happy one, often failing to gain the approval of either the serious theologian or the discerning literary author or critic. Despite the tendency of most religious fiction writers to put aesthetics before theology, the resulting novels and short stories were rarely worthy of notice. Most of the works in this study show clear signs of their authors having struggled to adapt a source text whose lexis was so deeply embedded in the national consciousness. Moreover, the growing tendency of more liberal Victorians to regard the New Testament first and foremost as a great work of literature made it an even more intractable subject for creative rewriting. Just as today's filmic adaptations of classic novels are often deemed poor imitations of the originals, so artistic treatments of the Gospels were compared to their sources and found wanting. Authors attempting fictional transfigurations of the Bible risked bathos if they translated the language of the Authorized Version into the vernacular, and stylistic infelicity if they opted instead for a mix of archaism and direct quotation. And it was not only the primary sources of the New Testament that were a cause for anxiety. The shadowy presence of secondary sources such as Ernest Renan's *Life of Jesus*, which can be felt in several imaginative depictions of Jesus of the late nineteenth century, attests to the considerable weight of influence under which their authors laboured.

Of the fictional works considered here, none could be pronounced remarkable on literary grounds alone. This is due in part to the authors' unfamiliarity with the process of transforming a sacred history (or myth) into prose fiction. While poetry and drama had a long-established tradition of recreating ancient texts to suit contemporary tastes and interests, the novel was a genre relatively new to the adaptive mode, its very quiddity residing in the novelty of its subject matter. In its early stages, New Testament fiction tended to suffer from the artistic caution discernible in *Philochristus*, which, of all the works considered in this study, is the most strongly rooted in modern theology. Moreover, the historicism of such writings demanded the subtle weaving of contextual detail into the fictional narrative, a task that frequently resulted in stylistic maladroitness or pleonasm. Of the fictional recreations of the Gospels considered here, Wilde's apologues come closest to fulfilling his own artistic dictum that the 'originality [...] which we ask from the artist, is originality of treatment, not of subject'.[4] Yet this is thanks in no small part to their purely oral existence, which allowed them to be endlessly remodelled, and which bestowed on them a certain ludic quality, conspicuously absent from the vast majority of late-1890s' religious fiction. Wilde's freewheeling narratives benefited not only from their oral status, but also from their author's insouciant disregard for biblical criticism. Free from any compulsion to demonstrate scholarly know-how or affiliation, he privileges the demands of narrative over those of theology, showing a particular flair for capturing the language of the Gospels at the same time as exploiting their fictional potential. While most adaptations of the Scriptures suffered from the burden of authorial conviction, involved scholarly theories or purple prose, Wilde's managed to raise questions germane to a variety of theological issues in a manner at once subtle and arresting. Yet, as Holbrook Jackson points out in his study of Wilde, the author's intellectual playfulness was often mistaken for lack of seriousness by a public 'still to learn that one can be as serious in one's play with ideas as in one's play with a football', and the lukewarm reception of the few biblical prose poems that made it into print suggests that he may have been just a few too many steps ahead of his time.

The increasing secularity of the twentieth century made for a more liberal reading public, affording writers of biblical fiction greater freedom to experiment. Waiting until the 1910s to develop his New Testament fiction enabled George Moore to venture into territory hitherto unexplored. *The Brook Kerith* is the first recasting of the Gospels that fully attempts to imagine the workings of the mind of Jesus in a narrative that embraces multiple viewpoints and free indirect speech, and that moves the figure of Christ out of the boundaries of the Gospel story to wander freely into an unknown future in the East. Unlike Wilde, Moore was determined to effect a merger between modern theology and prose fiction, and he must surely take the prize for creating the most up-to-the-minute figure of Christ, one much more in line with the views of contemporary continental writers such as Albert Schweitzer than the long since outmoded Ernest Renan. Yet while the contemporaneity of Moore's novel is beyond dispute, its literary value is rather less certain. Though singled out in William Hamilton's 1993 study, *The Quest for the Post-Historical Jesus*, as an exception to the rule that when novelists take on the subject of Jesus the result is 'depressingly bad', *The Brook Kerith* is by no means an ideal model.[5] Moore's attempts to capture the melodic rhythms of the Bible, at the same time as demonstrating a detailed biblical-critical knowledge, are only partially successful, and the novel is undoubtedly uneven in its quality. In some respects it confirms Wilde's oft-quoted dictum that it is only the modern who ever become old-fashioned; in striving to present a Jesus figure in line with contemporary thought, Moore guarantees that it will be quick to date. Now out of fashion and out of print, Moore's Syrian story looks unlikely ever to regain its place as one of the most popular novels of its time.

No amount of authorial daring, originality or sincerity can entirely extenuate the aesthetic shortcomings of the published New Testament fictions covered in this study. Yet that is not to say that they are without value. In *The Sense of an Ending*, Frank Kermode writes that 'Fictions are for finding things out, and they change as the needs of sense-making change.'[6] It is a definition that holds particularly true for the religious fictions of the late-nineteenth and early-twentieth centuries, which, spurred on by theological revisionism, sought to make sense of rapid and profound changes in Christian thought and feeling. Representations of Christ in both the short story and the novel attest to both an enduring attachment to, and a liberation from, his image. Those who fully accepted that Jesus was not divine still needed to account for how and why he had commanded so many followers for so many centuries. As Renan points out when discussing the work of Strauss: 'What he leaves subsisting in the Gospels is not sufficient to account for the faith of the Apostles [...] It must have been, in other words, that the person of Jesus had singularly exceeded the ordinary proportions [...]'[7] And there were many competing versions of exactly how Jesus went beyond these 'ordinary proportions'. Fiction writers of all religious persuasions could interpret the Evangelical records to mould Christ into their own image: the poet, the philanthropist, the teacher, the social reformer. Robert Graves, an author who would make his own contribution to the genre of Jesuine fiction in the 1940s, observed that:

> The Gospels remind us how many irreconcilable attitudes can be adopted towards a single confused subject. Thus, the orthodox religious attitude: 'The Gospels must be accepted as a final court of appeal in all moral cases.' The unorthodox religious attitude: 'It is the greatest story in the world, but we doubt whether Jesus rose again from the dead.' The rationalistic attitude: 'A story that begins with virgin-birth and a travelling star cannot be taken seriously.'[8]

Writers of Gospel fiction offered an important means by which such varying approaches to the 'confused subject' of Jesus could be explored. In helping modern readers find significance in early Christian texts through their literary re-shaping and re-imagining, such writers fulfilled a Midrashic role, albeit one that tended to overlook the exigencies of literary aesthetics.

As the twentieth century wore on, so those intent on upholding the divinity and sanctity of the figure of Christ had to contend with ever more powerful media. The private, individual activity of fiction-reading began to look less threatening in comparison with the public, collective activity of the cinema and radio and television broadcasting, all of which were quick to take up the challenge of depicting Jesus for a twentieth-century audience.[9] Nowadays, as notions of the sacred become less and less rigid and more and more remote, those artists hoping to create new and thought-provoking images of Christ tend to resort to shock tactics to capture the modern imagination. Such tactics often involve the sexualizing of New Testament characters: Gore Vidal's novel *Live from Golgotha* (1992) imagines an obese Jesus with hormonal problems and an erotomaniacal, homosexual Paul; *Jerry Springer: The Opera* depicts a coprophiliac, nappy-wearing Jesus; and an art exhibition at the Baltic Centre in Gateshead recently featured a statue of a priapic Christ. None of these works has passed without public comment, though as *The Guardian*'s headline to an article reporting the *Jerry Springer* controversy makes clear, such images of Christ now tend only to shock 'The Moral Minority'.[10]

In our present century, then, controversies over the artistic and literary appropriation of the Bible, though by no means a thing of the past, have certainly been pushed to the sidelines. In the nineteenth century, however, radically shifting theological perspectives, coupled with a certain mistrust of fiction itself, ensured that any such controversies would be conducted *coram populo*, with an urgency that many today would find hard to fathom. Those who engaged in such controversies – be they the most hardened secularist or the most pious of evangelicals – were, generally speaking, serious-minded, well acquainted with the detail of the Scriptures and, in some cases, with developments in religious scholarship. Nineteenth-century readers of mainstream journals were likely to encounter reviews and articles concerning issues such as the historical origins of Christianity, the authorship of the Gospels and competing theories about the resurrection. This is certainly not the case with today's common reader. When, just a few years back, academics rushed to correct the egregious errors in Dan Brown's *The Da Vinci Code*, it was clear that twenty-first-century readers were, in some respects, more vulnerable to cod-theology than their Victorian predecessors – and no less attracted by the lure of biblically based fiction. The laboured prose, hackneyed characterization and implausible plot line of Brown's blockbuster novel might make us question whether the survival of New Testament fiction is really something to be celebrated and, certainly, in the last fifteen years or so, we have witnessed both the highs and lows of the genre. *Quarantine*, the Booker-shortlisted novel by Jim Crace – a post-Dawkins atheist – has won great literary acclaim for its evocation of Jesus's forty days in the Judean desert; while Jeffrey Archer's *The Gospel According to Judas*, for all its endorsement from a professor of theology, has met with almost universal ridicule. Whatever the artistic merits of today's biblical fiction might be, there is no doubt that it springs from the rich and varied foundations laid down by Victorian and Edwardian pioneers, writers who dared to re-imagine Jesus in a climate a great deal more censorious and hostile than our own.

Notes

1   Strauss, *A New Life of Jesus*, I, p. 3.
2   S. Schechter, 'As Others Saw Him', *Studies in Judaism*, Third Series (Philadelphia: The Jewish Publication Society of America, 1924); this article was first published in the *Jewish Chronicle*, 10–17 May 1895, p. 26.
3   Robert Buchanan, 'Prose Note', in *The Ballad of Mary the Mother* (London: Robert Buchanan, 1897), p. 149.
4   '*Olivia* at the Lyceum' (dramatic review), 30 May 1885, reprinted in *Complete Works of Oscar Wilde* (Glasgow: HarperCollins Publishers, 1994), p. 955.

5 Hamilton, *The Quest for the Post-Historical Jesus*, p. 134.

6 Kermode, *The Sense of an Ending*, p. 39.

7 Renan, *Studies of Religious History*, pp. 118–19.

8 Robert Graves, *Occupation: Writer* (London: Cassell, 1951), p. 171. Graves's contribution to New Testament fiction, *King Jesus* (London: Cassell, 1946), remains one of the few works of the genre to successfully combine scholarship and imagination.

9 For a discussion of the Bible and broadcasting see Angela Tilby's article, 'The Bible and Television', and Kenneth Wolfe's 'The Bible and Broadcasting', both published in *Using the Bible Today: Contemporary Interpretations of Scripture*, ed. Dan Cohn-Sherbok (London: Bellew Publishing, 1991).

10 See *The Guardian*, 11 January 2005, p. 8.

Bibliography

Details of periodical articles and manuscripts are given in the notes and are not repeated here.

Abbott, Edwin Abbott, *The Kernel and the Husk* (London: Macmillan, 1886).
—*Philochristus: Memoirs of a Disciple of the Lord* (London: Macmillan, 1878).
—*Silanus the Christian* (London: Adam & Charles Black, 1906).
—*Through Nature to Christ* (London: Macmillan, 1877).
Aiton, John, *The Lands of the Messiah, Mahomet and the Pope* (Edinburgh: A. Fullarton, 1852).
Aldington, Richard, *Life for Life's Sake* (New York: The Viking Press, 1941).
Altick, Richard D., *The English Common Reader: A Social History of the Mass Reading Public 1800–1900* (Columbus, OH: Ohio State University Press, 1998).
Anderson, Hugh, ed., *Jesus* (Englewood Cliffs: Prentice-Hall, 1967).
Arnold, Matthew, *The Complete Prose Works of Matthew Arnold*, ed. R. H. Super, 11 vols (Ann Arbor: University of Michigan Press, 1960–77).
Austin, Mary, *The Man Jesus* (New York and London: Harper & Brothers, 1915).
Ayres, Samuel, *Jesus Christ Our Lord* (New York: A. C. Armstrong & Son, 1906).
Bagnold, Enid, *Enid Bagnold's Autobiography* (London: Heinemann, 1969).
Balcarres, Lord, *Donatello* (London: Duckworth, 1903).
Barlow, George, *Jesus of Nazareth: A Tragedy* (London: The Roxburghe Press, 1896).
Barnes, W. E., *Canonical and Uncanonical Gospels* (London: Longmans, 1893).
Becker, Robert, ed., 'Letters of George Moore, 1863–1901', unpublished PhD thesis, University of Reading, 1980.
Beckson, Karl, ed., *Oscar Wilde: The Critical Heritage* (London: Routledge and Kegan Paul, 1970).
Bernard, J. H., *The International Critical Commentary: A Critical and Exegetical Commentary on the Gospel According to St John*, 2 vols (Edinburgh: T. & T. Clark, 1976).
Bernheimer, Charles, *Decadent Subjects: The Idea of Decadence in Art, Literature, Philosophy, and Culture of the Fin De Siècle in Europe* (Baltimore and

London: Johns Hopkins University Press, 2002).

Besant, Annie, *The Myth of the Resurrection* (London: Freethought Publishing Company, 1884).

Bevan, Favell Lee, *The Night of Toil: or A familiar account of the labours of the first missionaries in the South Sea Islands* (London: J. Hatchard and Son, 1838).

Bigland, Eileen, *Marie Corelli: The Woman and the Legend* (London: Jarrolds, 1953).

Bostridge, Mark, ed., *Lives for Sale: Biographers' Tales* (London: Continuum, 2004).

Brome, Vincent, *Frank Harris* (London: Cassell, 1959).

Brooke, George J., *The Dead Sea Scrolls and the New Testament* (London: SPCK, 2005).

Buchanan, Robert, *The Ballad of Mary the Mother* (London: Robert Buchanan, 1897).

Burgon, John William, *Inspiration and Interpretation: Seven Sermons Preached before the University of Oxford* (Oxford and London: J. H. and Jas. Parker, 1861).

Burridge, Richard A., *What Are the Gospels?* (Grand Rapids, MI, and Cambridge: William B. Eerdman's Publishing Company, 2004).

Butler, George William, *'Is It True?': A Protest against the employment of fiction as a channel of Christian influence* (London: William Macintosh, 1869).

Butler, Samuel, *Erewhon Revisited* (London: Grant Richards, 1901).

—*The Evidence for the Resurrection of Jesus Christ as Given by the Four Evangelists, Critically Examined* (London, 1865).

—*The Fair Haven* (London: Watts, 1938).

—*The Fair Haven*, New Edition (London: A. C. Fifield, 1913).

—*Letters between Samuel Butler and Miss E. M. A. Savage 1871–1885*, ed. Geoffrey Keynes and Brian Hill (London: Jonathan Cape, 1935).

—*The Notebooks of Samuel Butler*, ed. Henry Festing Jones (London: The Hogarth Press, 1985).

—*The Way of All Flesh* (London: Grant Richards, 1903).

[By a clergyman of the Church of England], *Dr Farrar's "Life of Christ": A Letter to Thomas Scott* (London: Thomas Scott, 1874).

Carlyle, Thomas, *On Heroes, Hero-Worship and the Heroic in History* (London: James Fraser, 1841).

Carpenter, J. Estlin, *Life in Palestine When Jesus Lived* (London: Sunday School Association, 1889).

Chadwick, Owen, *The Victorian Church, Part Two: 1860–1901* (London: SCM Press, 1987).

Christianus [Charles Tilstone Beke], *Jesus the King of the Jews* (London: Robert Hardwicke, 1864).

Clodd, Edward, *Jesus of Nazareth: Embracing a Sketch of Jewish History to the Time of His Birth* (London: C. Kegan Paul, 1880).

—*Memories* (London: Chapman and Hall, 1916).

Coates, Thomas F. G. and Bell, Warren R. S., *Marie Corelli: The Writer and the Woman* (London: Hutchinson, 1903).

Cobbe, Frances Power, *Broken Lights: An Inquiry into the Present Condition &*

Future Prospects of Religious Faith (London: Trübner, 1864).

Cohn-Sherbok, Dan, ed., *Using the Bible Today: Contemporary Interpretations of Scripture* (London: Bellew Publishing, 1991).

Coleridge, Samuel Taylor, *Confessions of an Inquiring Spirit* (London: George Bell and Sons, 1884).

Committee of the Palestine Exploration Fund, *Our Work in Palestine* (London: Bentley & Son, 1873).

Common, Thomas, ed., *Nietzsche as Critic, Philosopher, Poet and Prophet. Choice Selections from His Works* (London: Grant Richards, 1901).

Conybeare, F. C., *History of New Testament Criticism* (London: Watts, 1910).

Coppy, A, of a LETTER Written by Our Blessed Lord and Saviour Jesus Christ (London: 1724).

Corelli, Marie, *Ardath*, 3 vols (London: Richard Bentley and Son, 2nd edn, 1889).

—*Barabbas: A Dream of the World's Tragedy*, 3 vols (London: Methuen, 1893).

—*Free Opinions* (London: Archibald Constable, 1905).

—*A Romance of Two Worlds*, 2 vols (London: Richard Bentley and Son, 1886).

—'*The Vanishing Gift': An Address on the Decay of the Imagination* (Edinburgh: The Philosophical Institution, 1901).

Cowell, Peter, 'On the Admission of Fiction in Free Public Libraries', *Transactions and Proceedings of the Conference of Librarians*, ed. Edward B. Nicholson and Henry R. Tedder (London: Chiswick Press, 1878).

Crucifixion, The, by an Eye Witness (originally published by Indo American Book Co., 1907; repr. Whitefish, MT: Kessinger Publishing Company, 2000).

Crucifixion, by an Eye Witness (Muttra: Narayan Swami, 1925).

Darmesteter, James, Madame [Mary F. Robinson], *The Life of Ernest Renan* (London: Methuen, 1897).

Dickens, Charles, *The Life of Our Lord* (London: Associated Newspapers, 1934).

Didon, Henri, *The Life of Jesus Christ*, 2 vols (London: Kegan Paul, Trench, Trübner, 1891).

Dowling, Levi H., *The Aquarian Gospel of Jesus the Christ: the philosophic and practical basis of the Religion of the Aquarian Age of the World and of the Church Universal, transcribed from the Book of God's Remembrances, Known as the Akashic Records, by Levi* (London: Cazenove, 1908).

Drews, Arthur, *The Witnesses to the Historicity of Jesus*, trans. Joseph McCabe (London: Watts, 1912).

Dunleavy, Janet Egleson, ed., *George Moore in Perspective* (Gerrards Cross: Colin Smythe, 1983).

Dunn, Henry, *Facts Not Fairy Tales. Brief Notes on Mr Matthew Arnold's "Literature and Dogma"* (London: Simpkin, Marshall, 1873).

Eagleton, Terry, *After Theory* (London: Allen Lane, 2003).

Edersheim, Alfred, *The Life and Times of Jesus the Messiah*, 2 vols (London: Longmans, Green, 1883).

—*Jesus the Messiah* (London: Longmans, 1890).

Efron, John M., *Defenders of the Race: Jewish Doctors and Race Science in Fin-de-Siècle Europe* (New Haven, CT, and London: Yale University Press, 1994).

Eglinton, John [William Kirkpatrick Magee], *Irish Literary Portraits* (London:

Macmillan, 1935).

Ellmann, Richard, *Golden Codgers: Biographical Speculations* (New York and London: Oxford University Press, 1973).

—*Oscar Wilde* (Harmondsworth: Penguin Books, 1987).

Farmer, Albert J., *Le Mouvement esthétique et 'décadent' en Angleterre 1873–1900* (Paris: Librairie Ancienne Honoré Champion, 1931).

Farrar, Frederic W., *The Bible; Its Meaning and Supremacy* (London: Longmans, Green, 1897).

—*Darkness and Dawn*, 2 vols (London: Longmans, Green, 1891).

—*The Gathering Clouds*, 2 vols (London: Longmans, 1895).

—*History of Interpretation* (London: Macmillan, 1886).

—*The Life of Christ*, 2 vols (London: Cassell, Petter and Galpin, 1874).

—*The Life of Christ as Represented in Art* (London: Adam and Charles Black, 1894).

—*The Life and Works of St Paul*, 2 vols (London: Cassell, 1879).

Farrar, Reginald, *The Life of Frederic William Farrar* (London: James Nisbet, 1904).

Federico, Annette R., *Idol of Suburbia* (Charlottesville, VA, and London: University Press of Virginia, 2000).

Finkelstein, David, and McCleery, Alistair, eds, *An Introduction to Book History* (New York and London: Routledge, 2005).

Foote, G. W., *Arrows of Freethought* (London: H. A. Kemp, 1882).

—*The Book of God in the Light of the Higher Criticism, with special reference to Dean Farrar's New Apology* (London: R. Forder, 1899).

—'The Irreligion of Shakespeare', in *The Secular Almanack* (London: Freethought Publishing Company, 1900).

—*Letters to Jesus Christ* (London: Progressive Publishing Company, 1886).

—*The Sign of the Cross: a candid criticism of Mr Wilson Barrett's play* (London: R. Forder, 1896)

—*What Was Christ? A Reply to John Stuart Mill* (London: Progressive Publishing Company, 1887).

Foote, G. W., and Ball, W. P., *The Bible Handbook* (London: Progressive Publishing Company, 1888).

Foote, G. W., and Wheeler, J. M., eds, *The Jewish Life of Christ* (London: Progressive Publishing Company, 1885).

Fraser, Robert, *The Making of the Golden Bough* (Basingtoke: Palgrave, 2002).

Frazer, J. G., *The Golden Bough: a Study in Comparative Religion*, 2 vols (London: Macmillan, 1890).

—*The Golden Bough*, 12 vols, Part VI (London: Macmillan, 3rd edn, 1913).

Frazier, Adrian, *George Moore 1852–1933* (New Haven, CT, and London: Yale University Press, 2000).

Freeman, John, *A Portrait of George Moore in a Study of his Work* (London: T. W. Laurie, 1922).

Frei, Hans W., *The Eclipse of Biblical Narrative* (New Haven, CT, and London: Yale University Press, 1974).

Fremantle, W. H., *The Gospel of the Secular Life* (London: Cassell, Petter, Galpin, 1882).

Garvie, Alfred E., *Studies in the Inner Life of Jesus* (London: Hodder & Stoughton, 1907).

Gautier, Théophile, *Charles Baudelaire*, trans. Guy Thorne (London: Greening, 1915).

Geikie, Cunningham, *Entering on Life* (London, New York and Bombay: Longmans, Green, 1896).

—*The Life and Words of Christ*, 2 vols (London: Henry S. King, 1877).

Gertz, Elmer, and Tobin, A. I., *Frank Harris: A Study in Black and White* (Chicago: Madelaine Mendelsohn, 1931).

Gide, André, *In Memoriam* (Paris: Mercure de France, 1910).

Girard, Henri, and Moncel, Henri, *Bibliographie des oeuvres de Ernest Renan* (Paris: Presses Universitaire de France, 1923).

Gissing, George, *Thyrza: A Tale*, 3 vols (London: Smith, Elder, 1887).

—*Workers in the Dawn*, 3 vols (London: Remington, 1880).

Gladstone, W. E., *'Ecce Homo' by the Right Hon. W. E. Gladstone* (London: Strahan, 1868).

Glazebrook, Jas. K., *Ecce Homo: a denial of the peculiar doctrines of Christianity; a Review by the Rev. Jas. K. Glazebrook* (Blackburn, 1866).

Glover, T. R., *The Jesus of History* (London: Student Christian Movement, 1917).

Goguel, Maurice, *The Life of Jesus*, trans. Olive Wyon (London: George Allen & Unwin, 1933.

Goodspeed, Edgar J., *Strange New Gospels* (Chicago: University of Chicago Press, 1931).

Goodwin, Geraint, *Conversations with George Moore* (London: Ernest Benn, 1929).

Gosse, Edmund, *Aspects and Impressions* (London: Cassell, 1922).

—*Father and Son: a study of two temperaments* (London: William Heinemann, 1907).

Gould, Warwick and Reeves, Marjorie, *Joachim of Fiore and the Myth of the Eternal Evangel in the Nineteenth and Twentieth Century* (Oxford: Oxford University Press, rev. edn, 2001).

Grant, R. M., *The Earliest Lives of Jesus* (London: SPCK, 1961).

Graves, Robert, *5 Pens in Hand* (New York: Doubleday, 1958).

—*King Jesus* (London: Cassell, 1946).

—*Occupation: Writer* (London: Cassell, 1951).

Grübgeld, Elizabeth, *George Moore and the Autogenous Self* (Syracuse, NY: Syracuse University Press, 1994).

Guérard, Albert L., *Art for Art's Sake* (New York: Lothrop, Lee and Shepard, 1936).

—*French Prophets of Yesterday* (London: T. Fisher Unwin, 1913).

Gull, Cyril Arthur Edward Ranger, *From the Book Beautiful: Being Some Old Lights Relit* (London: Greening, 1900).

Hamilton, William, *A Quest for the Post-Historical Jesus* (London: SCM Press, 1993).

Hanna, William, *Our Lord's Life on Earth*, 6 vols (Edinburgh: Edmonston and Douglas, 1869).

Hardy, Thomas, *Tess of the D'Urbervilles* (London: Macmillan, 1912).

Harnack, Adolf von, *What Is Christianity?*, trans. Thomas Bailey Saunders (London: Williams and Norgate, 1901).

Harris, Frank, *Contemporary Portraits*, First Series (London: Methuen, 1915).

—*Contemporary Portraits*, Second Series (New York: published by the author, 1919).

—*Frank Harris to Arnold Bennett: Fifty-Eight Letters 1908–1910* (Pennsylvania: privately printed, 1936).

—*My Life and Loves*, 4 vols (Paris: Obelisk Press, 1945).

—*Oscar Wilde: His Life and Confessions*, 2 vols (New York: printed and published by the author, 1916).

—*Undream'd of Shores* (London: Grant Richards, 1924).

—*Unpath'd Waters* (London: John Lane, The Bodley Head, 1913).

—*The Women of Shakespeare* (London: Methuen, 1911).

Harris, Horton, *David Friedrich Strauss and his Theology* (Cambridge: Cambridge University Press, 1973).

Herder, Alexandra von, *Jesus of Nazareth: A Poetical Drama in Seven Scenes* (London: Heinemann, 1913).

Hone, Joseph, *The Life of George Moore* (London: Victor Gollancz, 1936).

Housman, Laurence, *Echo de Paris* (London: Jonathan Cape, 1923).

Howell, Constance, *A Biography of Jesus Christ* (London: Freethought Publishing Company, 1883).

Hughes, Thomas, *The Manliness of Christ* (London: Macmillan, 1879).

Hunt, William Holman, *Pre-Raphaelitism and the Pre-Raphaelite Brotherhood*, 2 vols (London: Macmillan, 1905).

Huysmans, J.-K., *À Rebours* (Paris: Bibliothèque Charpentier, 1891).

—*Against Nature*, trans. Robert Baldick (London: Penguin Books, 1959).

—*Là-Bas* (Paris: Tresse & Stock, 1891).

—*Le Drageoir à épices* (Paris, 1874).

—*The Road from Decadence: Selected Letters of J.-K. Huysmans*, trans. and ed. Barbara Beaumont (London: The Athlone Press, 1989).

—*Sainte Lydwine de Schiedam* (Paris: P.-V. Stock, 1901).

Hyde, H. Montgomery, *Mr and Mrs Daventry* (London: The Richards Press, 1956).

Iconoclast [Charles Bradlaugh], *Who Was Jesus Christ?* (London, 1861).

Imbert-Gourbeyre, *La Stigmatisation, l'extase divine et les miracles de Lourdes. Réponse aux libres-penseurs*, 2 vols (Clermont-Ferrand, 1894).

Ingraham, J. H., *The Prince of the House of David* (New York: Pudney & Russell, 1856).

Jackson, Holbrook, *The 1890s* (London: Grant Richards, 1913).

Jacobs, Joseph, *As Others Saw Him: A Retrospect A. D. 54* (London: William Heinemann, 1895).

—*The Book of Job with designs by Granville Fell and an introduction by Joseph Jacobs* (London: J. M. Dent, 1896).

—*Jesus: As Others Saw Him* (New York: Bernard G. Richards, 1925).

—*Jewish Ideals and other Essays* (London: David Nutt, 1896).

—*Literary Studies* (London: David Nutt, 1895).

Jenkins, Philip, *The Hidden Gospels: How the Search for Jesus Lost Its Way*

(Oxford: Oxford University Press, 2001).

Jeremias, Joachim, *The Parables of Jesus*, trans. S. H. Hooke (London: SCM Press, 1954).

Jewish Historical Society, *Publications of the Jewish Historical Society* (Baltimore: The Lord Baltimore Press, 1917).

John, Augustus, *Chiaroscuro* (London: Jonathan Cape, 1952).

Johnston, John, *The Lord Chamberlain's Blue Pencil* (London: Hodder & Stoughton, 1990).

Jones, Henry Festing, *Samuel Butler, Author of Erewhon, 1835–1902: a memoir*, 2 vols (London: Macmillan, 1919).

Jones, Peter, ed., *Shakespeare: The Sonnets – A Casebook* (Basingstoke: Macmillan, 1977).

Jordan, John, E., ed., *De Quincey as Critic* (London: Routledge & Kegan Paul, 1973).

Joyce, James, *The Critical Writings of James Joyce*, ed. Ellsworth Mason and Richard Ellmann (London: Faber & Faber, 1959).

—*Ulysses* (Harmondsworth: Penguin, 2000).

Kalthoff, Albert, *The Rise of Christianity*, trans. Joseph McCabe (London: Watts, 1907).

Kemp, Sarah, Mitchell, Charlotte, and Trotter, David, *Edwardian Fiction: An Oxford Companion* (Oxford: Oxford University Press, 1997).

Kermode, Frank, *The Genesis of Secrecy: On the Interpretation of Narrative* (Cambridge MA: Harvard University Press, 1979).

—*The Sense of an Ending: Studies in the Theory of Fiction, with a New Epilogue* (Oxford: Oxford University Press, 2000).

Kernahan, Coulson, *Celebrities: Little Stories about Famous Folk* (London: Hutchinson, 1923).

—*The Child, the Wise Man, and the Devil* (London: James Bowden, 1896).

—*In Good Company* (London: John Lane, The Bodley Head, 1917).

—*The Man of No Sorrows* (London: Cassell, 1911).

—*Spiritualism: A Personal Experience and A Warning* (London: Religious Tract Society, 1919).

—*A World without the Christ* (London: Hodder & Stoughton, 1934).

Kingsmill, Hugh, *Frank Harris* (London: Jonathan Cape, 1932).

Kissinger, Warren S., *The Lives of Jesus* (New York and London: Garland Publishing, 1985).

Klassen, William, *Judas: Betrayer or Friend of Jesus?* (London: SCM Press, 1996).

Knowles, Dorothy, *The Censor, the Drama, and the Film* (London: George Allen & Unwin, 1934).

Lagrange, M. J., *Christ and Renan*, trans. Maisie Ward (London: Sheed and Ward, 1928).

Langenfeld, Robert, *George Moore: An Annotated Secondary Bibliography of Writings About Him* (New York: AMS Press, 1987).

Lavocat, Françoise, Kapitaniak, Pierre, and Closson, Marianne, eds, *Fictions du Diable: Démonologie et littérature de saint Augustin à Léo Taxil* (Geneva: Librairie Droz, 2007).

Lawrence, D. H., *Selected Literary Criticism*, ed. Anthony Beal (London: Heinemann, 1967).

Le Gallienne, Richard, *The Romantic '90s* (London: G. P. Putnam's Sons, 1925).

Leavis, Q. D., *Fiction and the Reading Public* (London: Chatto & Windus, 1932).

Lennox, Cuthbert, *George Douglas Brown* (London: Hodder & Stoughton, 1903).

Lillie, Arthur, *The Influence of Buddhism on Primitive Christianity* (London: Sonnenschein, 1893).

Linton, Eliza Lynn, *The True History of Joshua Davidson* (London: Strahan, 1873).

—*The Autobiography of Christopher Kirkland*, 3 vols (London: Richard Bentley and Son, 1885).

Livingston, James, C., *Matthew Arnold and Christianity* (Columbia, SC: University of South Carolina Press, 1986).

Lloyd, Walter, *The Galilean* (London: Williams and Norgate, 1892).

Loisy, Alfred Firmin, *The Gospel and the Church*, trans. Christopher Home (London: Ibsister, 1903).

Long, Lady Catharine, *Sir Roland Ashton: A Tale of the Times*, 2 vols (London: James Nisbet, 1844).

Lopèz, Bernard and Moore, George, *Martin Luther: A tragedy in five acts* (London: Remington, 1879).

Lucas, Bernard, *The Fifth Gospel: being the Pauline Interpretation of the Christ* (London: Macmillan, 1907).

Lüdemann, Gerd, *The Great Deception: And What Jesus Really Said and Did*, trans. John Bowden (London: SCM Press, 1998).

—*Jesus after Two Thousand Years* (London: SCM Press, 2000).

Ludwig, Emil, *The Son of Man*, trans. Eden and Cedar Paul (London: Ernest Benn, 1928).

Maison, Margaret, *Search Your Soul, Eustace* (London and New York: Sheed and Ward, 1961).

Marlow, Louis [Louis Umfreville Wilkinson], *Seven Friends* (London: The Richards Press, 1953).

Marx, Alexander, ed., *Essays in Jewish Biography* (Philadelphia: The Jewish Publication Society of America, 1948).

Masson, David, *British Novelists and their Styles* (Cambridge: Macmillan, 1859).

Masters, Brian, *Now Barabbas Was a Rotter* (London: Hamish Hamilton, 1978).

Matthew, H. C. G., *Gladstone 1809–1874* (Oxford: Clarendon Press, 1986).

Matthew, H. C. G., and Harrison, Brian, eds, *Oxford Dictionary of National Biography*, 61 vols (Oxford: Oxford University Press, 2004).

McCabe, Joseph, *Eighty Years a Rebel* (Girard, KS: Haldeman-Julius Publications, 1947).

—*The Myth of the Resurrection* (New York: Prometheus Books, 1993).

McCormack, Jerusha, ed., *Wilde the Irishman* (New Haven and London: Yale University Press, 1998).

Mikhail, E. H., ed., *Oscar Wilde: Interviews and Recollections*, 2 vols (London: Macmillan, 1979).

Miles, Alfred H., ed., *The Poets and the Poetry of the Nineteenth Century*, 11 vols (London: George Routledge & Sons, 1906).

Mill, J. S., *Three Essays on Religion* (London: Longmans, Green, Reader, and Dyer, 1874).

Mitchell, Susan L., *George Moore* (Dublin and London: Maunsel, 1916).

Moore, George, *The Apostle: A Drama in Three Acts* (Dublin: Maunsel, 1911).

—*Avowals* (London: William Heinemann, 1936).

—*The Brook Kerith: A Syrian Story* (London: T. Werner Laurie, 1916).

—*The Brook Kerith* (Edinburgh: T. Werner Laurie, 1921).

—*The Brook Kerith* (London: Heinemann, 1927).

—*The Brook Kerith* (London: Penguin, 1952).

—*Celibate Lives* (Leipzig: Bernhard Tauchnitz, 1927).

—*Confessions of a Young Man* (London: Heinemann, 1926).

—*Conversations in Ebury Street* (London: Heinemann, 1924).

—*George Moore in Transition: Letters to T. Fisher Unwin and Lena Milman, 1894–1910*, ed. Helmut E. Gerber (Detroit: Wayne State University Press, 1968).

—*George Moore on Parnassus: Letters (1900–1933) to Secretaries, Publishers, Printers, Agents, Literati, Friends and Acquaintances*, ed. Helmut E. Gerber and O. M. Brack Jr (Newark, DE: University of Delaware Press, 1988).

—*Hail and Farewell!: Salve* (London: William Heinemann, 1912).

—*Impressions and Opinions* (London: David Nutt, 1891).

—*The Lake*, New Edition (London: William Heinemann, 1921).

—*Letters from George Moore to Ed. Dujardin 1886–1922*, ed. John Eglinton (New York: Crosby Gaige, 1929).

—*Letters of George Moore. With an Introduction by John Eglinton to whom they were written* (Bournemouth: Sydenham, 1942).

—*Mike Fletcher* (London: Ward and Downey, 1889).

—*Modern Painting* (London: Walter Scott, 1893).

—*Moore Versus Harris*, ed. Guido Bruno (Chicago: privately printed, 1925).

—*The Passing of the Essenes* (London: Heinemann, 1930).

—*The Pastoral Loves of Daphnis and Chloë, Done into English by George Moore* (London: William Heinemann, 1924).

Morash, Christopher, *A History of Irish Theatre 1601–2000* (Cambridge: Cambridge University Press, 2002).

Murry, John Middleton, *Between Two Worlds* (London: Jonathan Cape, 1935).

—*The Life of Jesus* (London: Jonathan Cape, 1926).

Myers, Alfred Moritz, *Both One in Christ* (London: L. and G. Seeley, 1840).

—*The History of A Young Jew* (London: Wertheim and Macintosh, 1857).

Myers, F. W. H., *St Paul*, ed. E. J. Watson (London: Simpkin, Marshall, Hamilton, Kent, 1916).

Neaves, Charles, *On Fiction as a Means of Popular Teaching* (Edinburgh and London: William Blackwood and Sons, 1869).

Neill, Stephen, and Wright, Tom, eds, *The Interpretation of the New Testament 1861–1986* (Oxford: Oxford University Press, 1988).

Nelson, James G., *Publisher to the Decadents: Leonard Smithers in the Careers of Beardsley, Wilde, Dowson* (Pennsylvania: Pennsylvania State University Press, 2000).

Nietzsche, Friedrich, *The Works of Friedrich Nietzsche: The Case of Wagner,*

Nietzsche Contra Wagner, The Twilight of the Idols, The Antichrist, trans. Thomas Common (London: H. Henry, 1896).

Notovitch, Nicolas, *The Unknown Life of Christ*, trans. Violet Crispe (London: Hutchinson, 1895).

Nowell-Smith, Simon, *The House of Cassell 1848–1958* (London: Cassell, 1858).

Ong, Walter, *Orality and Literacy* (London: Routledge, 2002).

Otts, J. M. P., *The Fifth Gospel: the Land where Jesus Lived* (Edinburgh and London: Oliphant, Anderson and Ferrier, 1892).

Pals, Daniel L., *The Victorian "Lives" of Jesus* (San Antonio, TX: Trinity University Press, 1982).

Parker, J., ed., *Essays and Reviews* (London: John W. Parker and Son, 1860).

Parker, Joseph, *Ecce Deus* (Edinburgh: T. & T. Clark, 1867).

Pater, Walter H., *Studies In the History of the Renaissance* (London: Macmillan, 1873).

—*Marius the Epicurean*, 2 vols (London: Macmillan, 1885).

Paterson-Smyth, J., *A People's Life of Christ* (London: Hodder & Stoughton, 1921).

Pearson, Hesketh, *The Life of Oscar Wilde* (London: Methuen, 1946).

—*Modern Men and Mummers* (London: George Allen & Unwin, 1921).

Pemble, John, *The Mediterranean Passion* (Oxford: Oxford University Press, 1988).

Phelps, Abner, *The Crucifixion of Jesus Christ Anatomically Considered* (Boston, 1853).

Phelps, Elizabeth Stuart, *The Story of Jesus Christ* (London: Sampson Low, Marston, 1897).

Pittenger, Norman, *Christology Reconsidered* (London: SCM Press, 1970).

Pressensé, Edmond de, *The Critical School and Jesus Christ: A Reply to M. Renan's Life of Jesus*, trans. L. Corkran (London: Elliot Stock, 1865).

—*Jesus Christ: His Times, Life, and Work*, trans. Annie Harwood (London: Jackson, Walford & Hodder, 1866).

Pullar, Philippa, *Frank Harris* (London: Hamish Hamilton, 1975).

Ransome, Arthur, *Oscar Wilde* (London: Martin Secker, 1912).

Reade, Winwood, *The Martyrdom of Man* (London: Trübner, 1872).

Rein, Gustav Adolf, *Sir John Robert Seeley: A Study of the Historian*, trans. John L. Herkless (Wolfeboro, NH: Longwood Academic, 1987).

Renan, Ernest, *The Apostles*, trans. unknown (London: Trübner, 1869).

—*The Gospels*, trans. unknown (London: Mathieson, n.d.).

—*The Hibbert Lectures 1880*, trans. Charles Beard (London: Williams and Norgate, 1885).

—*Lettres inédites de Ernest Renan à ses éditeurs Michel & Calmann Lévy*, ed. Jean-Yves Mollier (Paris: Calmann-Lévy, 1986).

—*Life of Jesus*, trans. unknown (London: Trübner, 1864).

—*Renan's Life of Jesus*, trans. William G. Hutchison (London: Walter Scott, 1897).

—*Studies in Religious History* [*New Studies of Religious History*], Authorized English Edition (London: Richard Bentley and Son, 1886).

—*Studies of Religious History*, trans. Henry F. Gibbons (London: William

Heinemann, 1893).

—*Vie de Jésus* (Paris: Michel Lévy, 1863).

Richardson, Ruth, *Death, Dissection and the Destitute* (London: Phoenix Press, 2nd edn, 2001).

Robertson, John M., *Ernest Renan* (London: Watts, 1924).

—*The Historical Jesus: A Survey of Positions* (London: Watts, 1916).

Rodgers, W. R., *Irish Literary Portraits* (London: British Broadcasting Corporation, 1972).

Root, E. Merrill, *Frank Harris* (New York: The Odyssey Press, 1947).

Roth, Samuel, *The Private Life of Frank Harris* (New York: William Faro, 1931).

Rothenstein, William, *Men and Memories* (London: Faber & Faber, 1931).

Royle, Edward, *Radicals, Secularists and Republicans: popular freethought in Britain, 1866–1915* (Manchester: Manchester University Press, 1980).

Said, Edward W., *Beginnings: Intention and Method* (New York: Basic Books, 1975).

Saint-Amour, Paul K., *The Copywrights: Intellectual Property and the Literary Imagination* (Ithaca, NY, and London: Cornell University Press, 2003).

Saix, Guillot de, ed., *Le Chant du Cygne: contes parlés d'Oscar Wilde. Recueillis et rédigés par Guillot de Saix* (Paris: Mercure de France, 1942). Reprinted in Ian Fletcher and John Stokes, eds, *The Decadent Consciousness* (New York and London: Garland, 1979).

Saltus, Edgar, *The Anatomy of Negation* (London: Williams and Norgate, 1886).

—*Mary of Magdala* (London: Osgood & McIlvaine, 1891).

Saltus, Marie, *Edgar Saltus, the Man* (Chicago: Pascal Covici, 1925).

Sanday, William, *The Life of Christ in Recent Research* (Oxford: Clarendon Press, 1907).

—*Outlines of the Life of Christ* (Edinburgh: T. & T. Clark, 1905).

Schechter, S., 'As Others Saw Him', *Studies in Judaism*, 3rd Series (Philadelphia: The Jewish Publication Society of America, 1924).

Schüssler Fiorenza, Elisabeth, *In Memory of Her: A Feminist Theological Reconstruction of Christian Origins* (London: SCM Press, 2nd edn, 1995).

Schweitzer, Albert, *The Psychiatric Study of Jesus*, trans. Charles R. Joy (Boston: Beacon Press, 1958).

—*The Quest of the Historical Jesus*, trans. John Bowden and Susan Cuppitt, ed. John Bowden (London: SCM Press, 2000).

Scott, Thomas, *The English Life of Jesus* (Ramsgate: Thomas Scott, 1872).

Scott, William Stuart, *Marie Corelli: The Story of a Friendship* (London: Hutchinson, 1955).

Seeley, John Robert, *Ecce Homo: A Survey of the Life and Work of Jesus* (London and Cambridge: Macmillan, 1866).

Shaw, G. B., *Plays and Players: Essays on the Theatre* (London: Oxford University Press, 1952).

—*Saint Joan* (Harmondsworth: Penguin Books, 1946).

Sherard, Robert Harborough, *Bernard Shaw, Frank Harris and Oscar Wilde* (London: T. Werner Laurie, 1937).

—*The Life of Oscar Wilde* (London: T. Werner Laurie, 1906).

Singer, Ididore, ed., *The Jewish Encyclopaedia*, 12 vols (New York: Funk and

Wagnalls, 1904).

Small, Ian, *Oscar Wilde: Recent Research* (Gerrards Cross: Colin Smythe, 2000).

—*Oscar Wilde Revalued* (Gerrards Cross: Colin Smythe, 1993).

Smith, David, *The Days of His Flesh* (London: Hodder & Stoughton, 1905).

Smith II, Philip E., and Helfand, Michael S., eds, *Oscar Wilde's Oxford Note-books: A Portrait of a Mind in the Making* (New York: Oxford University Press, 1989).

Smith, William, ed., *A Dictionary of the Bible, comprising its Antiquities, Biography, Geography, and Natural History*, 3 vols (London, 1860–63).

Smithers, Jack, *The Early Life and Vicissitudes of Jack Smithers* (London: Martin Secker, 1939).

Stalker, James, *The Life of Jesus Christ* (Edinburgh: T. & T. Clark, 1879).

Stanton, E. C. et al., eds, *The Woman's Bible* (New York: European Publishing Company, 1895).

Steinberg, Leo, *The Sexuality of Christ in Renaissance Art and in Modern Oblivion* (London: Faber & Faber, 1983).

Stephen, Leslie, *Studies of a Biographer*, 4 vols (London: Duckworth, 1898–1902).

Stewart, D. Melville, *Ecce Vir* (London: James Clarke, 1911).

Stokes, John, *Oscar Wilde: myths, miracles and imitations* (Cambridge: Cambridge University Press, 1996).

Strauss, David Friedrich, *The Life of Jesus*, trans. unknown, 4 vols (Birmingham: Taylor, 1842).

—*The Life of Jesus Critically Examined*, trans. Mary Ann Evans, 3 vols (London: Chapman, Brothers, 1846).

—*A New Life of Jesus*, Authorized Translation, 2 vols (London: Williams and Norgate, 1865).

Stroud, William, *A Treatise on the Physical Cause of the Death of Christ* (London: Hamilton and Adams, 1847).

Sylva [pseud.], *Ecce Veritas: an Ultra-Unitarian Review of the Life and Character of Jesus* (London: Trübner, 1874).

Symonds, John Addington, *The Memoirs of John Addington Symonds*, ed. Phyllis Grosskurth (London: Hutchinson, 1984).

Taxil, Lèo, *Vie de Jésus* (Paris: Librairie Anti-cléricale, 1882).

Taylor, Isaac, *Spirit of the Hebrew Poetry* (London: Bell and Daldy, 1861).

Tennyson, Alfred, Lord, *In Memoriam*, ed. Erik Gray (New York: W. W. Norton, 2004).

Thatcher, David, *Nietzsche in England 1890–1914* (Toronto: University of Toronto Press, 1970).

Thorne, Guy [Cyril Arthur Edward Ranger Gull], *'I Believe'* (London: F. V. White, 1907).

—*When It Was Dark* (London: Greening, 1903).

—*When It Was Light: A Reply to 'When It Was Dark'*, by a Well-Known Author (London: John Long, 1906).

Toomey, Deirdre, 'The Story-Teller at Fault: Oscar Wilde and Orality', in *Wilde the Irishman*, ed. Jerusha McCormack (New Haven and London: Yale University Press, 1998), pp. 24–35.

Trollope, Anthony, *An Autobiography by Anthony Trollope* (New York: John W. Lovell Company, 1883).

Venturini, C. H. G. V., *Natürliche Geschichte des grossen Propheten von Nazareth* (Copenhagen, 1800–02).

Vermes, Geza, *The Resurrection* (Harmondsworth: Penguin Books, 2008).

Vignon, Paul, *The Shroud of Christ* (Westminster: Archibald Constable, 1902).

Vyver, Bertha, *Memoirs of Marie Corelli* (London: Alston Rivers, 1930).

Walker, Thomas, *Jewish Views of Jesus* (London: George Allen & Unwin, 1931).

Wallace, Lew, *An Autobiography*, 2 vols (New York: Harper & Brothers, 1906).

Ward, Mrs Humphry, *Robert Elsmere*, 3 vols (London: Smith, Elder, 1888).

—*A Writer's Recollections* (London: W. Collins Sons, 1918).

Wardman, H. W., *Ernest Renan: A Critical Biography* (London: The Athlone Press, 1964).

Weintraub, Stanley, ed., *The Playwright and the Pirate* (Gerrards Cross: Colin Smythe, 1982).

White, Hale, *The Autobiography of Mark Rutherford*, ed. Reuben Shapcott (London: Trübner, 1881).

Wilde, Oscar, *The Complete Letters of Oscar Wilde*, ed. Merlin Holland and Rupert Hart-Davis (London: Fourth Estate, 2000).

—*The Collected Works of Oscar Wilde*, ed. Robert Ross, 15 vols (London: Routledge/Thoemmes Press, 1993).

—*Complete Works of Oscar Wilde* (Glasgow: HarperCollins Publishers, 1994).

—*The Complete works of Oscar Wilde*, vol. iv, *Criticism*, ed. Josephine M. Guy (Oxford: Oxford University Press, 2008).

—*The Complete Works of Oscar Wilde*, vol. ii, *De Profundis*, ed. Ian Small (Oxford: Oxford University Press, 2005).

—*The Complete Works of Oscar Wilde*, vol. i, *Poems and Poems in Prose*, ed. Bobby Fong and Karl Beckson (Oxford: Oxford University Press, 2000).

Wilde, W. R., *Narrative of a Voyage*, 2 vols (Dublin: William Curry, 1840).

Winter, Paul, *On the Trial of Jesus* (Berlin: Walter de Gruyter, 2nd edn, 1974).

Wolfe, Humbert, *George Moore* (London: Harold Shaylor, 1931).

Woolf, Virginia, *The Death of the Moth and other Essays* (London: The Hogarth Press, 1942).

Wordsworth, Charles, *Shakespeare's Knowledge and Use of the Bible* (London: Smith, Elder, 1864).

Yeats, W. B., *Autobiographies* (London: Macmillan, 1955).

—*Where There Is Nothing/ The Unicorn from the Stars*, ed. Katharine Worth (Washington, DC: Catholic University of America Press; Gerrards Cross: Colin Smythe, 1987).

Ziolkowski, Theodore, *Fictional Transfigurations of Jesus* (Princeton, NJ: Princeton University Press, 1972).

Index